Also available from Continuum:

A Mirror for Our Times, Paul Weller
Religious Cohesion in Times of Conflict, Andrew Holden
Understanding Christian–Muslim Relations, Clinton Bennett

Images of Jesus Christ in Islam, 2nd ed.

Oddbjørn Leirvik

continuum

Continuum International Publishing Group
The Tower Building 80 Maiden Lane
11 York Road Suite 704
London SE1 7NX New York NY 10038

www.continuumbooks.com

British Library Cataloguing-in-Publication Dat
A catalogue record for this book is available frc

ISBN: HB: 978–1-4411–7739–1
PB: 978–1-4411–8160–2

Library of Congress Cataloging-in-Publication
Images of Jesus Christ in Islam, 2nd ed./Oddbj
p. cm.
ISBN 978–1-4411–7739–1
ISBN 978–1-4411–8160–2
1. Jesus Christ—Islamic interpretations. 2. Jesus Christ—In the Koran.
3. Christianity and other religions—Islam. I. Title. BP172.L355 1999
297.2'465–dc22

2009040851

Typeset by RefineCatch Limited, Bungay, Suffolk
Printed and bound in Great Britain by CPI Antony Rowe Ltd, Chippenham, Wiltshire

Contents

Preface

This book adds to a number of studies on the image of Jesus Christ in Islam, and related issues of dialogue. During my work with Islamic Christologies,[1] I have seen the need of *a general introduction* to the issue, and a *survey of research.*

In the present study, a general introduction to the theme has been merged with a survey of research, organized in a historically oriented presentation. My approach to this matter has not, however, been that of an Islamicist or a scholar of religious studies. As a Christian theologian committed to Christian–Muslim dialogue, it has been natural to add a third section of the study, identifying *issues of dialogue* arising from inherited polemics and apologetics on both sides, as well as from serious attempts at mutual understanding.

The background of this study is not purely academic. My involvement in Christian–Muslim dialogue is rooted in a Norwegian encounter between a well-established Christian majority and a more recent Islamic minority. The starting point was in the east end of Oslo, during my time as a Lutheran minister in a district with a substantial Muslim community. From the mid-1980s, I have had the privilege of taking part in living dialogues between Christians and Muslims in different contexts and on different levels, first as a parish minister, then at the church-related Emmaus Centre for Dialogue and Spirituality. Gradually, my involvement in the field led me to academic work with issues pertaining to interreligious studies and Christian–Muslim dialogue, in the context of the Faculty of Theology at the University of Oslo.

My presentation of *Images of Jesus Christ in Islam* was first published in 1999.[2] The book relies partly on my own work with the primary sources (classical and modern), but also to a great extent on secondary sources, i.e. compilations and studies made by others. In relation to the first edition, the current edition has been updated by references to more recent research.

It goes without saying that the presentation is not exhaustive, and some strands of the Islamic tradition and of current research have been given more weight than others. Nevertheless, I hope this book will aid others in finding their way into the subject. Its theme may reveal a typical Christian concern for the image of Christ in other religions. However, as I see it, the issue of

Christology touches upon a number of other questions of shared concern between Christians and Muslims. It relates to general questions in theology and anthropology as well as in ethics.

As for the genesis of the present book, my initial work on Islamic Christologies (a typical interest of a Christian theologian approaching Islam) evolved gradually into research on questions pertaining to ethics and the philosophy of dialogue, with the notion of 'conscience' at the focal point. My interest in images of Christ in Islam led me to the innovative contributions from the modern Egyptian authors ʿAbbās Maḥmūd al-ʿAqqād, M. Kāmil Ḥusayn and Khālid Muḥammad Khālid (cf. the section about 'Christ in Egyptian Muslim literature' in Chapter 7). Remarks made by Kenneth Cragg and Olaf Schumann in their presentation of Ḥusayn and al-ʿAqqād to an international audience, drew my attention to the apparent centrality of the notion of 'conscience' (*ḍamīr*) in their works about Christ. After having become acquainted with other works of the authors in question, not least those of Khālid Muḥammad Khālid, the importance of human conscience proved to be a recurrent theme in most of their works from the 1950s and 1960s. This finding triggered a number of questions: What is meant by *ḍamīr* in the works of these authors? How is their Islamic notion of 'conscience' construed, and what influences can be detected from Islamic and Christian tradition? Can 'conscience' have a function to fulfil in the dialogue between believers of different religions? As the question of conscience in Christian–Muslim dialogue has been dealt with more fully in a separate piece of research (Leirvik 2006), it is only touched upon in the present study.

Some technical notes on quotations, bibliography and Arabic transliteration

In the historical sections, *quotations* from primary sources are rendered in italics, to distinguish them from analyses and remarks made by modern commentators.

The *bibliography* at the end (referred to by author-date in the text) contains mainly books and articles that specifically contribute to and address the issue of Islamic Christologies, although a few more general studies about Christianity and Islam have been included. Other bibliographical references are given in the footnotes only, where they are cited in full. When two years separated by a slash are given in a bibliographical reference, the first indicates the year of publication, and the second that of the first edition.

In Arabic transliteration, the letters ḥāʾ, ṣād, ḍād, ṭāʾ and ẓāʾ are rendered with the conventional dot under. The letters thāʾ, khāʾ, dhāl, shīn and ghayn are rendered as ṯ, ḫ, ḏ, š and ġ when exact transliteration of the Arabic text is intended (in italics). But in names, these letters are rendered as th, kh, dh, sh and gh, and initial hamza is dropped. Otherwise, hamza is mostly rendered as ʾ, and ʿayn as ʿ. Long vowels are rendered with macron (ā, ū, ī).

Notes

1 Cf. Leirvik (1990, 1991, 1994, 2000), and the first edition of the present book (1999).

2 The first edition was published (with the same title as the current edition) by the Swedish Institute of Missionary Research in Uppsala, Sweden (as Studia Missionalia Upsaliensia LXXVI).

Chapter 1

Introduction

A Sensitive Question

The question of Christ's image has been a sensitive one in the history of Christian–Muslim apologetics and dialogue. One might ask whether it has ever been a real issue for dialogue. Most attempted dialogue in this field has been overruled by an apologetic or polemical bias on both sides.

On the Muslim side, the view that the messages of all prophets are essentially the same, and the perceived 'self-sufficiency'[1] of the Islamic canon (Qur'ān and Ḥadīth), has implied a reluctance to recognize an image of Christ different from that of the Islamic sources. The positions vary, however. On the one hand, we will find self-sufficient statements like 'a Muslim is quite at ease as far as the attitude of Islam towards Jesus is concerned; his mind is settled, his conscience is clear, and his belief is sound'.[2]

On the other hand, there are also genuine attempts at a dialogue with Christian images of Christ that might challenge, or add to, the inherited Muslim images of Christ.

On the Christian side, it has always been hard to recognize the prophethood of Muḥammad, and even to discuss Islam as something other than a Christian heresy. This position is, of course, just as problematic to Muslims as their unwillingness to understand Christ on Christian premises is to Christians.

Christian contributions to the issue have often implied that Islam is but a poor copy of Christianity, suggesting that Islam has transferred central features of Christ to Muḥammad, and distorted the real image of Jesus Christ to conform to another religious setting. The argument, however, goes both ways. Many Muslims would hold the view that Christians distorted their Gospel and let the emperor decide about how Christ should be portrayed, in order to fit Christianity into the Greek–Roman religious world. They argue that the Muslim image of Christ comes closer to the portrayal of Christ preserved in the biblical Gospels.

In Christian apologetics, there has always been a desire to refute Islamic teachings about Christ that are not compatible with the New Testament and the Chalcedonian Christology of the Church. As a post-Christian religion, which has included much of the Christian heritage, Islam challenges Christianity by competing in its own field.

On the Muslim side, there was from the beginning an ambiguity in the approaches to Christ. One tendency was to enrich the rather scanty references to Christ in the Qur'ān by drawing on Christian legend and Gospel material, culminating in the centrality of Jesus in mature Ṣūfism. The other tendency was to refute the specific Christian teachings about Christ, and argue against the reliability of the Christian sources, culminating in the medieval polemic of Ibn Ḥazm. Both tendencies may be said to have their origin in the Qur'ān, whose revelations vary from the non-polemical references of the Meccan period to a more polemical confrontation in the Medinan context.

In the twentieth century, both tendencies continue to prevail among Muslims. The most open-minded approaches seem to be found not in theological treatises, but in Muslim biography, novel and poetry, especially in the Egyptian context. But eirenical theological contributions – especially from the Indian and Shīʿite contexts – can also be identified. On the other hand, a polemical discourse about Christ has re-emerged with some new emphases, both in the Egyptian, Pakistani and Western contexts. Muslims have utilized Western historical critical research on the New Testament to support their prevalent theory of a distorted Gospel and a deified Christ. Along with that, Muslim polemical writers on the issue have drawn heavily upon the so-called Gospel of Barnabas, which Christians have dismissed as a historical fake. Most Muslim books on Christ in the twentieth century, many of them with a broad popular audience, have based their exposition on 'the Barnabas argument' (see Chapter 7) – pointing to a long hidden (but now found), original Gospel denying the divine sonship of Christ as well as his crucifixion.

Another aspect of Muslim polemics in the twentieth century has been the missionary efforts of the Ahmadiyya movement – preaching a 'liberation from the cross' through pamphlets aimed at Christians in the West, and based on the traditional Ahmadiyya understanding of how Christ escaped the cross alive and died in Kashmir.

From the 1980s, the popular discussion about the reliability of the Bible and the image of Christ has also been marked by a polemical resurgence as represented by the mass-produced writings and videos of the South African Muslim Ahmed Deedat (d. 2005). There is a specific context for his aggressive, highly polemical books, videos and speeches about 'Is the Bible the word of God?' and 'Is Christ the Son of God?', namely the similarly aggressive evangelism of the new fundamentalist movements on the Christian side, not least in Africa. One might ask whether the serious attempts at dialogue from both sides are totally overrun by the vociferous confrontations between Muslim and Christian fundamentalists.

As for the re-emergence of polemics over Christ, the contextual explanation offered by Seyyed Hossein Nasr is worth citing:

> Centuries of confrontation with the Christian West followed by a period of intense missionary activity, which still continues in certain regions of the Islamic world in new forms, have created among some contemporary Muslims an aversion not only to Christianity but, in the case of some of the modernised classes, even to the Islamic conception of Christ and Mary.[3]

Despite this rather unfriendly debate about Christ at both the academic and popular levels, there is also a real dialogue emerging on both sides. Many Christians have made strenuous efforts to understand Islam from within and on its own terms. On the Muslim side, there is a growing awareness in many circles that Christianity has to be taken seriously on its own terms if there is ever to be a meaningful dialogue on doctrinal issues, including the image of Christ.

For a newcomer to this area, it can be difficult to find one's way into the research that has already been done in this field. This is particularly true of the Muslim sources, which are only in part accessible in European languages. The classical literature relevant to the question of Islamic Christology is very rich, representing a multitude of approaches. In Kenneth Cragg's words: 'Exegetes, moralists, poets, historians, mystics and theologians, as well as imaginative writers, all contribute to its wealth and diversity.'[4]

Therefore, a main purpose of this survey will be to sort out the relevant sources in their context, and the various kinds of approaches and positions, with a view to further dialogue. First of all, however, some considerations should be given to the status of Christology within the general context of Christian–Muslim dialogue.

The Status of Christology in Christian–Muslim Dialogue

In the context of Christian theology, there is a growing awareness that Christology has to be dealt with in the context of a dialogue with other world religions. Christ cannot be trapped inside the walls of the Church. Images of Jesus are part of global culture, Christian as well as non-Christian, and have a multitude of facets both within Christianity and in other cultures and faith communities.[5]

As observed by many, the fact that Christ plays a distinctive role in Islam 'both builds a bridge between Christianity and Islam and creates a gulf between them'.[6] Islam has challenged the Christologies of the Church from the very beginning. It was perceived by Christian theologians as a new heresy of Christian origins. If one takes Islam seriously as a distinct religious universe, however, it has its own Christology – or rather a variety of Christologies.

In the modern context of mission and global interchange, a reflection on the religious significance of Christ (as distinct from Christianity) has also emerged in religions with a pre-Christian origin, such as Hinduism and Buddhism.[7] The tendency to integrate Christ in different religious universes is most widespread in New Age oriented spirituality, with its emphasis on 'Christ-consciousness'. A Christology of today needs to be a Christology in dialogue, and the image of Christ in world religions should be recognized as a necessary aspect of systematic theology.[8] Like in the first encounters with Islam, the challenge from Islamic Christologies will be a challenge not only to reaffirm, but also to re-examine the classical controversies and dogmatic resolutions of the Church itself.

In Christian–Muslim dialogue, the *conditio sine qua non* for an exchange worthy of the name of dialogue is to overcome the self-sufficiency of one's own religious universe. This does not imply a relativizing approach, or a detached kind of 'comparative religion'. What is called for is rather a dialogue among partners that are willing to dive into the depths of the other's well-springs, not for the rebirth of some kind of universal religion, but for the sake of deeper understanding not only of the other, but equally of oneself.

What would be the status of Christology, then, in a dialogue of mutual respect? Kenneth Cragg suggests that:

> One may study the mind of Islam inclusively in its mind about Jesus, decisive clues being everywhere implicit in how it reads and 'places' him within history, theology and faith.[9]

If we take Cragg's suggestion as at least an experimental hypothesis, two points should still be kept in mind in order to avoid a disproportional image. First, the Qur'ān pays more attention to the Old Testament precedents of Muḥammad, like those of Abraham and Moses, than to Christ. The reason might be that 'paragons of success and vindication' like the iconoclast Abraham, the flood-rider Noah, the hero of successful emigration Moses and the head of state David are more congenial to Muḥammad than the suffering servant Christ. Such an approach may also explain the exclusion of the suffering precedents of Christ (like Jeremiah) from the qur'ānic universe.[10]

The obvious observation made by Kenneth Cragg and others, that the image of the suffering servant is somewhat incompatible with the idea of God's manifest victory on earth, is confirmed by one of the main Muslim contributors to the topic, M. Ali Merad:

> . . . in the Qur'ān, everything is aimed at convincing the Believer that he will experience victory over the forces of evil [. . .] Islam refuses to accept this tragic image of the Passion. Not simply because it has no place for the dogma of the Redemption, but because the Passion would imply in its eyes that God had failed.[11]

It should be noted, however, that Shīʿite Islam, with the martyrdom of Ḥusayn as a focal point, would regard this matter differently.

Secondly, what the Qu'rān says of Christ should be read with an eye to what it says of Jews, Christians and Jewish-Christian Scriptures in general. This is true not only for the theme of 'Christ in the Qur'ān', but for all contributions pertaining to the images of Christ in classical, medieval and modern Islam. The theme has to do with 'Muslim Perceptions of Christianity' (Goddard 1996). The images of Christ have to be read in a broader historical and conceptual framework, in which Muslims and Christians have met 'face to face' (cf. Zebiri 1997) in different contexts.

Third, in spite of all the attention paid to Christ in the Qur'ān, it is Muḥammad who is 'the seal of the Prophets', and the miracle of the Qur'ān is considered to surpass all preceding miracles, including those of the life-giver Christ. Accordingly, a recurring tendency in recent Christian approaches to the qur'ānic Christ has been to show how Christ is reshaped in the Qur'ān to become a role-model for Muḥammad (e.g. Robinson 1991, Schedl 1978).

It has repeatedly been pointed out that comparing Christ with Muḥammad violates both Christian and Muslim self-understanding. Christology is decisive for Christian theology, whereas Islamic theology is definitely not constituted by its Christology. Smail Balić states:

> If theology is discourse about God, then Islamic theology makes no assertions concerning Jesus Christ. Islam rules out any incursion of the human into the sphere of the divine. One cannot speak of any experience of God in the sense of Christian theology.
>
> In Islam Christ has a thoroughly human dimension [. . .]. Because of the very nature of Muslim theology no relationship can be set up between the person of Christ and Muslim theology.[12]

Islamic orthodoxy seems to rule out any induction from human experience to theology. The basis of theology is the divine, revealed Word of the Qur'ān, considered to be un-created in the theological orthodoxy that came to be victorious in the formative period of Islam. In this orthodox perspective, then, Christ as the uncreated, living Word of God in Christian tradition is the religious equivalent not to Muḥammad, but to the divine revelation of the Qur'ān.

Islam is not, then, 'Muhammedanism'. Cragg may still be right to remind us that the miracle of the Qur'ān cannot be isolated from the *sīra*, the life-history of the Prophet.[13] The *sunna* (way) of the Prophet, as laid out in the Ḥadīth collections, has been considered as decisive for the interpretation of the Qur'ān. Even more important, the decisive events of *hijra* (the Prophet's emigration to Medina), and the establishment and defence of a Muslim *umma* in Medina, are integral points of reference for the revelation-event of the Qur'ān. Accordingly, questions arising from the different life-stories of Jesus and Muḥammad relate to the very core of what is perceived as divine revelation.

Regarding Christ, Christianity interprets the event of the cross as disclosing the very heart of the divine, whereas Islam sees Christ's rescue from the cross as the decisive divine intervention. Furthermore (in the words of Kenneth Cragg):

> Some modern, indeed also medieval, Muslim writers see in this 'rescue' a symbol of Christ's lesser status, in that, given the Roman imperial power, it was not his destiny to achieve Muhammadan success in political terms. Muhammad's more 'effective' destiny is further seen as indicating his 'finality' as the 'seal of the prophets'. Jesus' lesser – albeit highly honoured – standing is explained by his not enjoying the sanction of external vindication, making no triumphal entry into a capitulating Mecca.[14]

Thus, from the different life-stories of Jesus and Muḥammad arise fundamental questions such as the theological meaning of suffering and success, cross and miracles, redeeming love and vindicating justice – and indeed those of faith and power, as expressed through word and sword. Should Islam and Christianity be taken as two fundamentally different and mutually exclusive religious universes in their resolving of these fundamental questions? Or maybe the differences in interpretation are more significant within each tradition than between them?

Bibliographical Introduction

There are many different roads towards future dialogue about Christ between Christians and Muslims. A broad variety of approaches and studies have already been presented, in the field of Islamic Christology and its bearing on Christian–Muslim dialogue.

In the following, both scholarly and more popular contributions will be presented and examined. The scope will not only be a survey of research, but also issues of dialogue, and the intersections between dialogue, apologetics and polemics. Relevant contributions will be referred to and tentatively put in perspective under the various headings below. However, a preliminary survey of some major works might be useful as a general bibliographical introduction.

In 1977, Don Wismer published *The Islamic Jesus: An Annotated Bibliography of Sources in English and French* (Wismer 1977). The bibliography lists both classical (in translation) and modern contributions, and is very valuable if one knows what one is looking for. But since the bibliography only lists authors, and is not thematically organized, it is of limited value for a newcomer to the subject.

Contributions from the Christian Side and from Western Scholars

Early modern contributions, from the nineteenth century, include those of Gerock (1839), Manneval (1867[15]), Rösch (1876) and Sayous (1880).

At the end of the nineteenth and the beginning of the twentieth century, during the first quest for 'the historical Jesus' in the West, there was also some interest in the so-called *logia et agrapha* attributed to Jesus by Muslim writers, resulting in compilations by Margoliouth (1893–94) and Michaël Asin et Palacios (1917, 1926).

During the first half of the twentieth century, three books from the Christian side presenting the Muslim sources (Qur'ān, Ḥadīth, commentaries and legend) in some detail deserve special mention: *The Moslem Christ* by Samuel M. Zwemer (1912), *Christ in Islam* by J. Robson (1930),[16] and *Le Christ de l'Islam* (1959) by the Catholic Lebanese Michel Hayek.[17] Hayek writes in the tradition of the French scholar Louis Massignon, drawing especially on Ṣūfī sources, but presenting a wide range of Christ-related material from Islamic sources.

Although these books present interesting historical material, the compilation of sources is often uncritical.

From the beginning of the century, the journal *The Moslem/Muslim World* has presented smaller studies and apologetic treatises on the subject.[18] More recently, the Rome-based *Islamochristiana* as well as the journal *Islam and Christian–Muslim Relations* have published articles relevant to the subject.

From the mid-1950s, significant contributions to this topic have been published in the 'Mélanges de l'Institut Dominican d'Etudes Orientales' (*MIDEO*), in Cairo. The magazine *Al-Mushir* of the Christian Study Centre in Rawalpindi, Pakistan, also deserves special mention.

Furthermore, Roman Catholic newsletters like *Encounter* ('Documents for Muslim–Christian Understanding', published by the Pontificio Istituto di Studi Arabi, Rome) and *Encuentro Islamo-Christiano* (Madrid) have been publishing shorter presentations and studies pertaining to the subject of Christ in Islam.

From the 1960s onwards, a series of dialogically oriented presentations from the Christian point of view have been published. In 1960, Henri Michaud published the short study *Jésus selon le Coran*. His desire is that there should be a joint veneration of Jesus in a 'community of hearts' between the adherents of two monotheistic faiths. In his thematic exposition of the qur'ānic image of Christ, he interprets the Qur'ān by the Qur'ān. What he wants is a communication that may transcend the substantial differences between Christians and Muslims in their dogmatic teachings about Christ.[19] Michaud underlines that if this goal shall ever be reached, there must be a mutual respect between Christians and Muslims for the Bible and the Qur'ān.

The work of the Franciscan missionary Guilio Basetti-Sani, *The Koran in the Light of Christ* (1977), may be said to represent a category of its own. As the subtitle suggests, the author aims at a 'Christian interpretation of the sacred book of Islam'.[20] The author explains his shift in orientation (to which Louis Massignon is said to have contributed) – moving from a rather hostile approach to Islam towards a reading of Islam as a revelation that may prepare the way for Christ. Although positive in its approach, the 'inclusivist' theological tendency of the author and his 'theology of history' leave little room for the genuine otherness of Islam, and his interpretation of the Qur'ān is clearly Christian.

An earlier book published in 1938 by the Egyptian Coptic Christian Ibrahīm Lūqā, entitled *Al-Masīḥiyya fī-l-Islām* (Christianity in Islam), may be listed as another example of the inclusivist approach. The book, which tried to argue that the Qur'ān itself affirmed the Christian message, was not allowed to be re-printed in Egypt in 1967.[21]

In the field of comparative religion, the book *Jesus in the Qur'ān* by Geoffrey Parrinder (1965) must be regarded as a modern classic. His book followed a series of major works by the same author on the history of religion and comparative religion. Parrinder's study was for a long time the main introduction to the subject in English. In his examination, he cross-references between the Qur'ān and the New Testament extensively. His attempt is not only to show 'what the Qur'ān says about Jesus', but also 'to examine in what senses the qur'ānic teaching may be taken'. Therefore, 'Parallels are given to this teaching in the Gospel, where they occur'.[22] Thus, his approach is fully within the tradition of 'comparative religion'.

In 1975, the German scholar Olaf Schumann published his dissertation *Der Christus der Muslime: Christologische Aspekte in der arabisch-islamischen Literatur* (enlarged and re-edited in 1988). He argues for including the question of Christ in the dialogue with Muslim, not because of its importance in a Muslim context, but for its centrality in Christian theology. He also argues that a serious study of the Christ of the Muslims can do away with some Christian misperceptions, and even lead to a fuller understanding of the Islamic articles of faith. At the time of its publication, no other comprehensive study had been presented of the actual image of Christ among modern Muslims (i.e. not only in the Islamic sources). His study consists of two parts. First: a background-study of the polemical treatises and Islamic Christologies of ʿAli ibn Rabbān al-Ṭabarī, al-Jāḥiẓ, Ibn Ḥazm, al-Ghazālī, Ibn al-ʿArabī and the Ṣūfīs. Secondly: a presentation and discussion of modern Egyptian writers from Muḥammad ʿAbduh onwards – focusing on the Shaltūt/al-Ghumārī controversy about the return of Christ, and the books on Christ by ʿAbbās Maḥmūd al-ʿAqqād and Fatḥi ʿUthmān (from the 1950s and 1960s). He concludes his study with a discussion of concepts of God and man at issue in Muslim–Christian controversies about Christology.

Also in German, Christine Schirrmacher (1992) has examined two specific aspects of modern Christian–Muslim controversies on the Bible and Christology. In the first part of *Mit den Waffen des Gegners* ('With the weapons of the adversary'), she deals with the Indian roots of modern polemics, with reference to the nineteenth century controversy between the Indian Muslim Raḥmatullāh al-Kairānawī and the Christian missionary Karl Gottlieb Pfander. In the second part, she analyses the twentieth century controversy over the Gospel of Barnabas.

From the 1970s onwards, a series of studies on Christ in the Qur'ān have been presented by scholars working within Western academic and Christian contexts. These include the works of Heikki Räisänen (1971), Claus Schedl (1978), Günther Risse (1989) and Neal Robinson (1991). The latter focuses on the classical exegesis of the qur'ānic passages. The works mentioned are referred to and commented on in some detail in Chapter 2.

The most prolific contemporary author on Christian–Muslim dialogue, Kenneth Cragg, also published a book on this subject in 1985, with the title *Jesus and the Muslim*, as a follow-up and sequel to his book *Muhammad and the Christian*, published in 1984. Cragg's *Jesus and the Muslim* presents not only the relevant Muslim sources for the Christian, but also the New Testament for the Muslim reader. The preceding *Muhammad and the Christian* aims at a nuanced appreciation of Muḥammad's prophethood from a Christian perspective. His main perspective is thus not historical, but mildly apologetic and with a call to genuine dialogue.

During the 1980s, two comprehensive studies on Islamic Christology have been presented by Roger Arnaldez: *Jésus fils de Marie prophète de l'Islam* (1980 – cf. 1986) and *Jésus dans la pensée musulmane* (1988). In his first work, Arnaldez focuses on Christ in the Qur'ān, as viewed by various Qur'ān-commentaries. In the latter work, Arnaldez focuses on images of Jesus in Ṣūfism. He pays special attention to the Ṣūfī commentary to the Qur'ān of al-Qushayrī, the references to Christ in the works of Abū Ṭālib al-Makkī and al-Ghazālī, the image of Christ in the esoteric Ṣūfism of Ibn al-ʿArabī and the case of al-Ḥallāj. The book also contains chapters on the images of Christ in the works of the Muʿtazilite theologian al-Jāḥiẓ (cf. Schumann) and in Shīʿite Islam.

In 1996, Maurice Borrmans published a survey of the images of Jesus among Muslims of today, entitled *Jésus et les musulmans d'aujourd'hui*. After referring to the Meccan and Medinan revelations pertaining to Jesus, Mary and the Christians, he describes the image of Jesus in some modern textbooks for Islamic education. He then proceeds to deal with four influential commentaries on the Qur'ān from the twentieth century, and the images of Jesus that can be found in some other works by modern Muslim theologians. The last part of his presentation focuses on modern Muslim literature, more specifically Jesus-biographies by Egyptian Muslims, and Muslim poetry that includes Jesus-symbolism. Borrmans concludes his book with a dialogical chapter, entitled 'Jésus, énigme ou mystère?'

In addition to the works mentioned in English, French and German, there are of course numerous works relevant to the issue in other languages, some of them in the form of general introductions relying on internationally recognized research.

Contributions from Muslim Contexts

Several attempts have been made by Christian/Western scholars to classify dominant trends in modern Muslim approaches to Christ and Christianity. Hugh Goddard, in his *Muslim Perceptions of Christianity* (1996), distinguishes between 'polemical', 'eirenical' and 'intermediate' literature. Kate Zebiri, in her *Muslims and Christians Face to Face* (1997), underlines the difference between popular, missionary and scholarly contributions on both sides. She highlights the different approaches found in Muslim popular literature on Christianity and in Protestant missionary literature on Islam on the one hand, and the study of Christianity by Muslim intellectuals and approaches to Islam by Christian Islamicists and theologians on the other.

From the Muslim side, the Egyptian context represent a variety of approaches – ranging from the apologetic approaches to Christian tradition and the polemical exegesis of the Bible developed in the school of al-Manār, to eirenical approaches to Christianity and ground-breaking ethical reinterpretations of the Gospels by prominent Muslim intellectuals. Besides the above-mentioned study of Olaf Schumann (1988/1975), Egyptian and other Arabic contributions have been presented and discussed by Hugh Goddard (1987, 1990, 1996) and others.[23] In the 1950s and 1960s, several Egyptian writers and theologians wrote 'Christ-biographies' from a Muslim viewpoint. ʿAbbās Maḥmūd al-ʿAqqād (n.d./1953), M. Kāmil Ḥusayn (1954, 1994/1959), Khālid Muḥammad Khālid (n.d./1958), Nagīb Maḥfūẓ (1981/1959) and Fatḥī ʿUthmān (1961) deserve special mention. Their works are presented and commented on in Chapter 7, and offer a wide scope for dialogue. The issue of Christ, Muḥammad and human conscience emerges as perhaps the most intriguing aspect of the contributions from modern Egyptian writers.

Hugh Goddard has also presented a study of modern Indian and Pakistani perceptions of Christ and Christianity (Goddard 1994). Recently, there has been a marked interest to examine the image of Christ as it can be found not only in the Islamic source material, but also in contemporary Muslim literature such as Persian and Urdu poetry.[24] The poetical contributions – including those from Arab poets[25] – kindle fresh reflections on the theme of miracles and the cross in Christology.

Apart from the works by poets and novelists as essayists referred to above, many of the most eirenical contributions from the Muslim side come from authors with a Shīʿite background. One is the prolific author Seyyed Hossein Nasr. In a short essay on *Jesus Through the Eyes of Islam* (Nasr 1981), he asserts that the only irreducible 'fact' separating Christianity and Islam is the question of the crucifixion, and the related issue of redemption. He emphasizes the pre-eminence given to Christ as 'the seal of sanctity' in Ṣūfism, but still insists that Muḥammad was foretold by Christ, as the final Prophet fulfilling the faith of Abraham, the law of Moses and the spiritual way of Christ. In a different context, he suggests that Christ and the Christian tradition:

> [. . .] represent the esoteric aspect of the Abrahamic tradition, the internal dimension of the primordial religion, which is a spiritual way rather than a law. Christ did not bring a new revealed law or *sharīʿah* but a way *(ṭarīqah)* based on the love of God. Islam recognized the particular function of Christ, which thus differed from that of other prophets who usually brought a law or reformed a previous one, by acknowledging his particular nature as the 'Spirit of God' *(rūḥ Allāh)* and his 'supernatural birth', connected with the virginity of Mary.[26]

Among the attempts at overcoming simplistic apologetics and establishing a real dialogue about Christ, the contributions by the Muslim scholar Mahmoud Ayoub under the heading 'Towards a Muslim Christology' deserve special mention (Ayoub 1976, 1980). In his studies, he examines the central qur'ānic passages, the classical exegesis and the Shīʿite traditions concerning the teaching, suffering and death of Christ – all the time in search of possible bridges to the Christian image of Jesus Christ. According to Ayoub, Islam:

> [. . .] denies the expiatory sacrifice of Christ on the Cross as a ransom for sinful humanity, but . . . denies neither the actual death of Christ nor his general redemptive role in human history.[27]

In more general terms, Ayoub's approach may be characterized by the following citations: 'Islam . . . denies the divinity of Christ, but without denying his special humanity.'[28] And:

> . . . like the Christ of Christian faith and hope, the Jesus of the Qur'ān and later Muslim piety is much more than a mere human being, or even simply the messenger of a Book. While the Jesus of Islam is not the Christ of Christianity, the Christ of the Gospel often speaks through the austere, human Jesus of Muslim piety. Indeed, the free spirits of Islamic mysticism found in the man Jesus not only the example of piety, love and asceticism which they sought to emulate, but also the Christ who exemplifies fulfilled humanity, a humanity illumined by the light of God.[29]

Ayoub has also published a meditation on 'the miracle of Jesus' (1993), and a study on the terms *walad* and *ibn* as used in the qur'ānic and Tafsīr discussions of the divine sonship of Christ (Ayoub 1995). He argues that the qur'ānic denial of Christ's sonship (as *walad*), should primarily be read as a rejection of the notion of divine offspring in the physical sense. As for Jesus as a miracle, Ayoub speaks of Jesus as a divine expression of the miracle of life: 'The miracle of life that is Jesus unfolds further as a lifegiving and sanctifying divine force.'[30]

This does not imply, however, that Jesus was something other than human. Ayoub reminds Christians that the humanity of Christ was in fact one of the original christological doctrines. It is as the Word of God, in the sense of the servant of God and the messenger of God that Jesus stands forth as 'the miracle of life, of love and of healing . . . [as] one who heals the sickness of the human soul; one who infuses life into dead spirits by his own life and spirit'.[31]

By his willingness to examine critically both Muslim and Christian sources and teachings, Ayoub is opening the field for a genuine dialogue about the divine word: 'The miracle of Jesus, like the miracle of the Qur'an, is not a once-only event, but an everlasting source of blessing, guidance, and salvation.'[32]

Similar approaches can be found with another Muslim of Shīʿite orientation, Asghar Ali Engineer. In a paper from 1991, he examines Indian/Pakistani and Persian interpretations of Christ as well as their use of Christian symbolism:

> These thinkers and writers view a personality like Jesus Christ in their own way which appeals to emotion rather than to intellect. The theologians have revered and discussed Christ, but they have never been deeply moved by him. It is poets, creative writers and thinkers who seem to have been deeply moved by him and his *humane* personality. Most of the Muslim writers and thinkers have seen in him a soothing humanism, love and affection.[33]

Another most noteworthy contribution comes from the Indian Shīʿite writer Hasan Askari. In an essay from 1972 on the dialogical relationship between Christianity and Islam, he cites a poem by Rūmī: *O for a friend to know the sign, And mingle all his soul with mine.*[34] In the essay, Askari approaches Christ as a common 'sign' for Christians and Muslims. In the case of Christ, the divine Word referred to by both the Qur'ān and the Bible is a Person and not a book. Accordingly, Christ reveals the deep relational character of religion: 'To me, personally, Christ as Sign of God liberates man from the dead circle of monological religion and restores unto him his genuine dialogical relation.'[35]

Askari suggests that a dialogue about Christ as seen by the Bible and the Qur'ān might help Christians and Muslims alike to overcome the monological traps of their religions, and discover the true other of divine revelation. Such a discovery implies pain and anxiety, but should not therefore be eschewed: 'It is right in the middle of this pain and anxiety that a Divine Sign is known.'[36]

M. Ali Merad, a French Muslim of Algerian origin who wrote a book about Christ in the Qur'ān in 1968 (cf. summary of his main points in Merad 1980), also deserves special mention among those writing in a more eirenical tone. Merad laments the fact that Muslim commentaries 'in speaking of Christ . . .

are more concerned to refute Christian dogmas than to see clearly what the problem of Christ is all about'.[37] He states that:

> [. . .] it would be presumptuous of a Muslim to believe that he possesses the whole truth with regard to Jesus and to refuse to take the road opened to him by the Qur'an of seeking other testimonies.[38]

Without giving up the qur'ānic denials about Christ as compared with what is narrated in the Bible, Muslims should be sensitive to the 'incomparable lesson' emerging from Christ's life, which is singled out as extraordinary by qur'ānic titles such as 'Word of God and a Spirit from Him'.

Of the more polemical kind, Ahmed Deedat's pamphlets have already been mentioned, and deserve some serious consideration not for their scientific value, but for their widespread influence especially among Muslims in the West.[39]

Many modern polemical contributions have a Pakistani background. The most widely circulated of Muslim books basing their argument on the Gospel of Barnabas is probably *Jesus – A Prophet of Islam*, by the Pakistani Muslim Muhammad 'Ata ur-Rahim.[40] Legendary material about Christ is presented on a par with the Qur'ān and Ḥadīth, without any critical discussion of the sources. Like Ahmed Deedat's pamphlets, the book has had a wide audience and must be said to reflect a major trend in contemporary Muslim polemics. In short, the book is re-reading the New Testament and Christian doctrine from a Unitarian perspective, and presents Barnabas (and the alleged Gospel of Barnabas) as the key to early Christian history as read by Muslims. As for the general polemical tone of the book, the following description of ('Pauline') Christianity may be cited: 'mathematically absurd, historically false, yet psychologically impressive'.[41]

The Gospel of Barnabas, in various editions, has had a wide readership among Muslims, especially in Pakistan and the West.[42] Although some Muslim scholars would be reluctant to put too much emphasis on the 'Barnabas argument' – considering the highly contested historical value of the text in question – efforts are still made to re-read early Christian history from the Barnabas perspective, and to relate it to recent historical findings like the Dead Sea Scrolls (cf. M. A. Yusseff 1991b).[43]

In 2001, and in a totally different vein than the apologetic works mentioned above, the Lebanese scholar Tarif Khalidi published a book entitled *The Muslim Jesus: Sayings and Stories in Islamic Literature*.[44] By its annotated edition of 303 sayings attributed to Jesus in Muslim tradition, Khalidi's book has taken historical-critical research on the Muslim Jesus a significant step forward. His chronological arrangement of the items indicates how early and in which literary and religious contexts the different sayings and stories can be attested. In addition to items known from ancient collections such as 'Stories of the Prophets' (see Chapter 3), the works of al-Ghazālī that contain more than

100 such sayings alone (see Chapter 5), and modern compilations published by Michaël Asin (Asin et Palacios 1917, 1926) and others, Khalidi adds sayings attributed to Jesus in books about ascetic discipline from the eighth and ninth centuries. This portion of the sayings includes more than 70 items found in the works of ʿAbdallāh ibn al-Mubārak (d. 797) and Aḥmad Ibn Ḥanbal (d. 855) who both wrote a *Kitāb al-zuhd* ('Book on asceticism').

Tarif Khalidi characterizes his material, taken as a whole, as a 'Muslim gospel' which must be read on its own terms but testifies also to a close interaction between two traditions:

> In its totality, this gospel is the story of a love affair between Islam and Jesus and is thus a unique record of how one world religion chose to adopt the central figure of another, coming to recognize him as constitutive of its own identity.[45]

For Khalidi, the process of popular and literary interaction attested to by the wealth of traditions about Jesus in Muslim contexts indicates 'a deeper religious or theological reality – namely, the need that Christianity and Islam have for complementarity'.[46] Coming close to the idea launched by the Finnish New Testament scholar Heikki Räisänen, who suggests that Jesus can be seen as 'standing between' Christianity and Islam,[47] Khalidi writes:

> The Islamic Jesus of the Muslim Gospel may be a fabrication . . .. Nevertheless, he remains a towering religious figure in his own right – one who easily, almost naturally, rises above two religious environments, the one that nurtured him and the other that adopted him.[48]

As for sayings and stories related to Jesus in Shīʿite tradition, a valuable collection in Arabic and English was published in 2004 under the title *Jesus through Shīʿite Narrations* (Qā'im 2004). The sayings, which are compiled by Mahdī Muntaẓir Qā'im and translated by Al-Ḥajj Muḥammad Legenhausen, have been taken from major Ḥadīth collections of sayings attributed to Muḥammad and the twelve imams such as the comprehensive *Biḥār al-Anwār*. The sayings are arranged thematically, not chronologically, and there is no effort at contextualization or historical-critical evaluations.

Some Methodological Considerations

The present study takes as its vantage point that there is no single image of Christ in Islam. In classical as well as modern contexts, Islam offers a diversity of images of Jesus Christ.[49] These images can only be meaningfully understood when due attention is paid both to different spiritual traditions in Islam and differing historical contexts.[50]

Methodologically, my historically oriented presentation of different images of Jesus Christ in Islam is informed by the perspectives of *contextual theology*. The methodological approach of contextual theology emphasizes the social and political context of theological reflection, with a special attention to the asymmetrical power relations between parties involved in any given controversy or dialogue. In the analyses of the twentieth-century tendencies and discussions in Chapter 7, insights from post-colonial theory will also be added.[51]

In the case of Islamic images of Christ, there is of course something common to these images that correspond to the basic tenets of Islam as a world religion. However, within the house of Islam there is not one but several distinct images of Christ that correspond to different strands of Muslim tradition such as (for instance) learned *tafsīr*, folk Islam and its storytelling tradition, Ṣūfism in its many varieties, Islamic apologetics and modern dialogical interpretations of Islam. What different images of Christ have meant, and how they have been re-appropriated in ever new times and places, can only be understood when the differing religious, social and political contexts are taken into consideration.

Another perspective on the material to be presented is that of *intertextuality*. In her book *Revolution in Poetic Language*, Julia Kristeva defines intertextuality as the 'transposition of one (or several) sign system(s) into another . . .'.[52] To avoid any banal restriction of the intertextual approach to the study of mutually interrelated sources, she prefers the term 'transposition'. As a result of constant, remoulding transpositions, the denoted object of any particular discourse is never single or identical to itself, but polysemic: 'always plural, shattered, capable of being tabulated'.[53]

I find Kristeva's notion of polysemic discourse and ever-transposing intertextuality fruitful for the understanding of what takes place in the literary and theological space between Christianity and Islam. When studying a particular item – in this case, the images of Jesus Christ as they occur in the sign systems of Christianity or Islam respectively – one must always be sensitive to their function in these two contexts. Superficial similarities between two sign systems (for instance in biblical and qur'ānic references to Jesus as a Word of God) may conceal profound differences in the meaning that a certain conception is attributed within different (Christian and Islamic) systems of meaning. But one should be equally aware of the capacity of concepts and ideas of stimulating conversation between closely related religious universes.

M. M. Bakhtin's ideas about 'dialogic imagination'[54] add further insights to Muslim–Christian intertextuality. Reflecting on the relation between monologism and dialogism, he claims that however monological an utterance may be:

> . . . it cannot but be, in some measure, a response to what has already been said about the given topic, on the given issue, even though this responsiveness may not have assumed a clear-cut external expression . . .. The utterance is filled with *dialogic overtones*, and they must be taken into account in order to understand fully the style of the utterance.[55]

Dialogical overtones in Bakhtin's sense may strike a note anywhere on the scale between parody, polemics and affirmation. Bakhtin emphasizes that thought itself is born and shaped in the process of interaction and struggle with others' ideas. Any utterance, when studied in greater depth and with a view to context, will reveal 'half-concealed or completely concealed words of others with varying degrees of foreignness'.[56]

If this is so, it would also apply to the intellectual and literary history of Christianity and Islam, and their interrelated though distinctively different images of Jesus Christ. As for texts, Bakhtin too speaks of the complex interaction between text and context, in which there is always interplay between situated Selves and Others. The event of the text always 'develops *on the boundary between consciousnesses, two subjects*'.[57]

In this book, I will try to present Islamic images of 'Jesus as a Muslim' in their transposed particularity. But I will also explore their capacity for dialogical imagination on the boundaries of, or rather, as Martin Buber might have said, *in the space between* Christianity and Islam.[58]

Notes

1 W. M. Watt's expression in Watt (1991: 41–44).

2 Hammudah Abdalati, *Islam in Focus*. Indianapolis: American Trust Publications (1975: 153).

3 Nasr (1981: 209).

4 Cragg (1985a: 42).

5 Cf. Anton Wessels, *Images of Jesus: How Jesus is Perceived and Portrayed in Non-European Cultures* (Grand Rapids, MI: W.B. Eerdmans, 1990); with chapters on Christ in Christianity, Judaism, Islam (Wessels 1990), Hinduism and Taoism. See also Gregory A. Barker (ed.), *Jesus in the World's Faiths: Leading Thinkers from Five Religions Reflect on His Meaning* (Maryknoll, NY: Orbis, 2005), with chapters on Islamic images of Christ by Hasan Askari, Mustansir Mir, Neal Robinson and Mona Siddiqui.

6 Mir (2005: 116).

7 See for instance Notto R. Thelle, 'Foe and Friend: The Changing Image of Christ in Japanese Buddhism', in *Japanese Religions*, 12 (1982: 19–46), and recent works on Christ by prominent Buddhist teachers such as Dalai Lama (*The Good Heart: His Holiness Dalai Lama Explores the Heart of Christianity – and of Humanity*, London: Rider, 1996) and Thich Nhat Hanh (*Living Buddha, Living Christ*, London: Rider, 1995).

8 Cf. Gavin D'Costa, 'The End of Systematic Theology', in *Theology* 95 (1992: 324–334).

9 Cragg (1985a: 42).

10 Cragg (1984: 43).

11 Merad (1980: 14f).
12 Balić (1979: 1).
13 Cragg (1984: 15 ff).
14 Ibid., p. 45.
15 A thesis based on Gerock (1839).
16 Cf. Robson (1939).
17 In Arabic: al-Hayek (1961).
18 Contributions until 1950 include: Field (1911), Zwemer (1917), Elder (1923), Jenkinson (1928), Padwick (1939), Bishop (1941), Cannon (1942), Adams (1944), Robson (1950).
19 'Notre désir le plus cher a été, en crivant ces lignes, de créer un climat de mutuelle compréhension et de tolérance entre chrétiens et musulmans.' (Michaud 1960: 9)
20 Cf. also J. Henninger (1945–46).
21 See Schumann (1988: 263, note 5).
22 Parrinder (1979: 11).
23 See al-Husayni (1960), Anawati (1982), Cragg (1985a) for Egyptian literature, and Pinault (1987) for other Arabic literature.
24 See Engineer (1991) for Urdu and Persian poetry, Wysham (1952) and Souroudi (1979) for Persian poetry, Addleton (1990) and Goddard (1994) for Pakistani literature.
25 See Wild (1984) and Pinault (1987).
26 Seyyed Hossein Nasr, *Ideals and Realities of Islam*. Cairo: The American University of Cairo (1989: 34). (First published by Allen & Unwin, London, 1966.)
27 Ayoub (1980: 94). Cf. his work *Redemptive suffering in Islam*. The Hague: Mouton, 1980.
28 Ibid.
29 Ayoub (1976: 187).
30 Ayoub (1993: 224).
31 Ibid., p. 226.
32 Ibid., p. 227.
33 Engineer (1991: 18).
34 Askari (1972: 477).
35 Ibid., p. 483.
36 Ibid., p. 486. For this perspective on interreligious dialogue, see also David Tracy, 'The Hidden God: The Divine Other of Liberation', in *CrossCurrents*, vol. 46, 1:1996, pp. 5–16.
37 Merad (1980: 3).
38 Ibid., p. 17.
39 See his booklet *Is the Bible God's word?* (1980) for his general approach, and more specifically *Christ in Islam* (Deedat 1989/83). Cf. widespread videos with corresponding titles, and pamphlets from the Islamic Propagation Centre (UK) like *Crucifixion or crucifiction?* (Deedat

1984). His pamphlets also include titles like *Who moved the stone?* and *What was the sign of Jonah?* For a critical discussion of his works, see Zebiri (1997: 46–48, 57, 89, 98).

40 New Delhi: Taj Printers, 1979, and London: MWH London Publishers, 1979. For critical discussions of this book, see Goddard (1994: 165f) and Zebiri (1997: 61f, 68, 79, 84–89). Cf. Jan Slomp's review of the book in *Theological Review of the Near East School of Theology* (Beirut), vol. III (1980: 35–39).

41 ʿAta ur-Rahim (1979: 74).

42 Edited in English by ʿAta ur-Rahim in Karachi in 1973, later also in other editions in Pakistan. A more recent edition in the West is Yusseff (1990a).

43 Cf. Yusseff (1990b).

44 Khalidi (2001), cf. the article Khalidi (2003).

45 Khalidi (2001: 5f).

46 Ibid., p. 45.

47 Räisänen (1991); Räisänen (1997: 97).

48 Khalidi (2001: 45).

49 Robinson (2005): 'Which Islam? Which Jesus?'

50 For a contextual study of modern images, see Leirvik (2010) ('. . . from anticolonial polemics to postcolonial dialogue').

51 See the section about 'The Barnabas argument' in chapter 7, particularly the subsection about 'Historical or situated truth?'

52 Julia Kristeva, *Revolution in Poetic Language*. New York/Oxford: Columbia University Press (1984: 59f).

53 Ibid., p. 60.

54 M. M. Bakhtin, *The Dialogic Imagination: Four Essays*. Austin: University of Texas Press (1996).

55 M. M. Bakhtin, *Speech Genres and Other Late Essays*. Austin: University of Texas Press (1996: 92).

56 Ibid., p. 93.

57 Ibid., p. 106.

58 For Martin Buber's notion of the sacred space that may open between people of different religions, see his book *Between Man and Man* (London/New York: Routledge, 2004).

Chapter 2

Christ in the Qur'ān and in Ḥadīth

Christ in the Qur'ān

In academic research, a diversity of approaches to the fundamental question of how the Qur'ān portrays Christ can be identified. For purposes of popular presentation, it has always been tempting to extract 'what the Qur'ān says about Mary and Jesus' without considering the qur'ānic context, or the basic Islamic setting for the sayings. For the sake of serious dialogue, however, there should be a willingness from the Christian side to read the Christ passages in their genuine Islamic context, realizing that there can be no dialogue or 'comparative religion' if the religions are not studied in their own right. In this respect, the qur'ānic image of Christ can only be rightly understood as a presentation of Jesus as a true Muslim.[1]

Most studies of Christ in the Qur'ān have been thematic in their approach. If the relevant qur'ānic passages are arranged in accordance with a biblical Gospel structure one may identify a list of 'themes' which is focused in the qur'ānic references to Christ. It should, however, be emphasized that we speak of references, and not a proper Christ-narrative. Parts of the stories of other prophets, like those of Abraham and Moses, are also found in their narrative form in the Qur'ān. They are retold, in a non-polemical way, although with other emphases than those of the Bible owing to the different internal and external context. Only the story of Joseph is retold as a complete unit in the Qur'ān, in *Sūrat Yūsuf* (Sūra 12).

The Christ-story is not retold in the Qur'ān, only referred to.[2] Furthermore, many of the references to Christ are found within a context where Mary is the dominant figure.[3] The title of Sūra 3 is 'The House of ʿImrān' (the fatherhouse of Mary according to the Qur'ān) and that of Sūra 19 is 'Maryam'. Most of the references to Christ are found in these sūras.

More recent studies emphasize the need for a contextual approach, focusing not only on the external, historical context, but above all on the internal, qur'ānic framing of the Christ-passages.

In *Muslim Perceptions of Christianity*, Hugh Goddard (1996) reads the qur'ānic statements about Christ in the light of statements about Christians and the Bible in general. In all cases, the Medinan sūras are clearly more polemical than those revealed in Mecca. The development can be studied both in view of the internal logic of the various parts of the Qur'ān, and in the light of external factors related to Muḥammad's encounters with Jews and Christians.

Another obvious contextual approach would be to compare the qur'ānic picture of Christ with the self-understanding of Muḥammad and his role in revelation as the fulfilment of prophecy and the seal of the prophets. In his study *Christ in Islam and Christianity: The Representation of Jesus in the Qur'ān and the Classical Muslim Commentaries* (1991), Neal Robinson elaborates this perspective. Claus Schedl's *Muhammad und Jesus* (1978) approaches the qur'ānic Christologies not from a dogmatic, but from a 'dramaturgical' perspective within which Muḥammad, with his prophetic self-consciousness, is the key figure, and Medina and Mecca the two different scenarios.

The contextual approach should be linked to a history of ideas inquiry, asking how the image of Christ is transformed (or in Julia Kristeva's sense, transposed) to fit into a religious system with different concepts of God, word of God and man. The question may also be asked whether this transformation is solely to be regarded as extra-Christian, or whether it may also or rather be a further development of early Christian 'heretical' teachings. In his work *Gott ist Christus, der Sohn der Maria* (1990), Günther Risse emphasises the need to approach Islam through the 'Begriffswelt' of patristic theology, focusing particularly on the traditions of the Eastern churches.

The variety of Christian investigations of the qur'ānic picture of Christ may be classified in parallel to similar approaches to the Bible. This should be no surprise, since their frame of reference is not just (not even primarily?) Islamic studies but the historical-critical approach of modern biblical sciences as well.

Thematic Summary of the Qur'ānic References to Christ[4]

Thematically, the references to 'the Jesus story' can be grouped and summarized as follows:

Mary is dedicated to God by her mother, and is protected by God in the sanctuary, Zechariah/Zakarīya being her guardian (3.33–37; 44). References are made twice to Zechariah/Zakarīya and the annunciation of John/Yaḥyā (3.38–41, 19.2–15).

The annunciation to Mary is also related twice, in the Meccan revelations of 19.16–22, and in the revelations from the Medinan period, in 3.42–47. Her chastity and purity is emphasized, and she is said to be chosen above all women everywhere. The angels announce to Mary the glad tidings of a word from him:

'His name is the Messiah Jesus, son of Mary. Eminent he will be in this world and in the age to come, and he will have his place among those who are brought near to God's throne. He will speak to men in the cradle and in his mature years, and he will be among the righteous' (3.45f.).

In this version (Sūra 3), angels make the announcement to Mary, whereas in the earlier, Meccan version (Sūra 19) God's spirit takes the form of a perfect man, coming to Mary after she has withdrawn from her family to a place eastward, 'hidden from them behind a curtain'. As to the 'how' of the virginal conception, the reply given is that God creates what he will by simply decreeing it – saying 'Be!' and it is. Two other references allude to God's breathing into Mary of his spirit (21.91, 66.12).

After the annunciation, Sūra 19 tells about the birth of Christ (19.22–25; cf. 23.50). It occurs after Mary has withdrawn to a distant place, and she suffers the pangs of childbirth under a palm tree, where God provides her with water and ripe dates.

After the birth, Mary brings the child back to her people who accuse her of having been unchaste. The child then speaks to them from the cradle in her defence, and refers to himself as a servant of God, one to whom God has given Scripture and appointed as a prophet. God has enjoined upon him prayer, almsgiving and goodness towards his mother for the duration of his life, and granted him blessing and peace from the day of his birth to the day of his death and the day of his being raised to life (19.26–33).

Little is reported by the Qur'ān about the teachings of Christ. The basic concept is that of God teaching him the Scripture, Wisdom, the Torah and the Gospel (5.110). The Gospel (*al-injīl*) is understood as a Book given to Christ, containing guidance, light and admonition, and confirming the Torah (*al-tawrāh*) and the Prophets (5.110, 5.46). Although Christ confirmed the truth of the Torah, he is also said to have made lawful some of the things that were forbidden to the Children of Israel in the times of Christ (3.50). His teaching was Wisdom, making plain to them some of the things they disagreed about, showing them the straight path, and enjoining on them fear of God and obedience to himself (43.63f.). Being a true Muslim, his basic message was about the oneness of God, 'my Lord and your Lord' (3.51, 19.36, 43.64), and he warned the Children of Israel that Paradise would be denied to those who ascribe partners to God (5.72). He cursed those who rejected faith (5.78), but those who worship in truth are compared in the Gospel with seeds that grow up strong, to the delight and wonder of the sowers (48.29). Christ is reported to have called disciples and summoned them to be 'helpers' in God's cause (3.52f, 5.111, 61.14).

Finally, he is also said to have foretold a messenger that was to come after him, whose name would be *Aḥmad*, 'the highly praised one' (61.6).

The signs or miracles of Christ have some specific emphases in the qur'ānic version. Christ is strengthened by the Holy Spirit and given signs to support his teaching (2.87, 5.110 and 43.63). A miraculous aspect of his speech was his 'clairvoyant' ability to know what people were eating and storing in their houses (3.49 – understood like this in later Muslim legend). His healing abilities are emphasized: he healed those born blind and the lepers, and raised the dead (3.49, 5.110).

His healing powers are seen in connection with his life-giving ability, not only raising the dead but also giving life to a bird made of clay by breathing into it (3.49, 5.110). The children of Israel, however, reacted to his signs and clear proofs by accusing him of sorcery and evident magic (5.110, 61.6).

As can be seen from the references above, his miracles are reported in two similar lists, in Sūras 3 and 5. Added to the latter is a report of the miracle of the table sent down from heaven spread with food, as a proof to the disciples that he had spoken the truth. The sending of the table is referred to as a 'feast/festival' and a sign of God's providence (5.112–115). It has been discussed whether the sending of the table should be understood as an allusion to the Eucharist.

The Qur'ān makes it clear that Christ was rejected by the majority of the Children of Israel, and also refers to their intention to kill him (4.157, cf. 5.70), but God protected Christ from their violence (5.110). The qur'ānic passages about how Christ's life on earth actually ended, are open to different interpretations, and also give rise to some difficult grammatical problems (see below). In the speech from the cradle, the child Jesus is actually referring to 'the day I die and the day I am raised to life (verb: *baʿṯa*) again' (19.33). The two main passages referring to the end of his life, however, seem to deny that he suffered a normal, human death, and only confirm that he was raised to heaven. In the first key passage (3.54f.), it is said that the unbelievers schemed and God schemed, but God is the best of planners. He told Christ that he would receive him/cause him to die (depending on the translation of the verb *tawaffā*), and purify him from the unbelievers by raising him (verb: *rafaʿa*) to himself (cf. 5.117). In the second key passage (4.156–159), we are told that in spite of the enemies' intention to slay Christ Jesus, they did in fact not kill him or crucify him, but it appeared so to them (*šubbiha la-hum*). However, there is not one of them that will not believe in him before his death (i.e. Christ's death or that of the former unbeliever?).

The latter passage contains several grammatical problems, and commentators vary widely in their understanding of what made it appear to them that Christ was crucified. Was Jesus substituted on the cross? How, and by whom? Was he taken down from the cross alive to die a natural death many years later (the Ahmadiyya-interpretation)? If he was saved from the cross, was he taken to heaven in body and soul (to come again at the end of time) or did his body die, so that only his soul was raised to God (as some Ṣūfīs have interpreted it)?

As to the role of Christ in the eschatological future – a theme which is dealt with in detail in the Ḥadīth literature – there are two possible references to this in the Qur'ān, and again they are open to a variety of interpretations. The first (4.159) belongs to the second key passage about the end of his life, and refers to

Christ being a witness against the People of the Scripture on the Day of Resurrection. The second is 43.61: 'He (Christ, or 'it', i.e. the Qur'ān?) is a Sign of the Hour'. The sentence is abrupt and difficult to understand in its context, and it is not clear whether the Qur'ān itself does actually refer to the return of Christ.

Finally, the Qur'ān has a number of polemical references to the Christian belief in the sonship of Christ and the Trinity. The Qur'ān asserts: Both Christ and Mary were mortals who ate food. Christ was no more than a messenger, and many messengers have passed away before him (5.75). If God had wished to destroy Christ and his mother with everyone else on earth nothing could have hindered him (5.17). Challenged by God, Christ denies that he told mankind to worship himself and his mother as additional deities to Allāh, and pleads that God knows what is in Christ's mind but Christ does not know what is in God's (5.116). Christians should not exaggerate in their religion, and they should cease to say 'three' since God is far above begetting a son (4.171, 9.30, etc.). Those who say that God is Christ the son of Mary, or that God is one out of three in a trinity are indeed blasphemers (5.72f.).

It should be noted that all of these polemical statements against sonship and trinity belong to Sūra 5, which was one of the last to be revealed in Medina, or to other late Medinan revelations such as Sūras 4 and 9. (The denials in the Meccan revelations of any 'begetting' by God are more like general statements.) It should be noted too that with one exemption, all the references to sonship use the Arabic word *walad* which means son in the physical sense.[5]

As for the names and titles of Jesus in the Qur'ān, the following list can be given.[6] Jesus is referred to 16 times with the Arabic version of this name – *ʿĪsā* – in all cases in conjunction with *ibn Maryam*, 'the son of Mary'. In 17 additional cases, he is referred to only as *ibn Maryam* or as 'son of Mary' in conjunction with another title. He is called *al-masīḥ*, Christ or the Messiah, 11 times, and in three cases he is called messenger, *rasūl*. Other titles attributed to him by the Qur'ān are *ʿabd*/servant, *nabī*/prophet, *kalima*/word and *rūḥ*/spirit.

The etymology of the appellation *ʿĪsā* is commonly held to be derived from Syriac *Yeshūʿ* (cf. Hebrew *Yeshuaʿ*). The different titles should, of course, be understood from their qur'ānic context, and not as Christian interpolations.

Jesus is the only one to be called Messiah in Muslim tradition. As to the titles *kalima* and *rūḥ*, the qur'ānic expressions in the key passage of 4.171 are *kalimatuhu* ('His word')[7] and *rūḥun minhu* ('a spirit from Him'). In later Muslim tradition we also find the more absolute expression *rūḥ-ullāh*, 'God's Spirit', cf. the title *rasūl-ullāh* ('God's Messenger') for Muḥammad. In a letter to the Christian Negus of Abyssinia, Muḥammad said (according to his biographer Ibn Isḥāq):

> *I bear witness that Jesus son of Mary is the spirit of God and His word which he cast to Mary the Virgin, the good, the pure, so that she conceived*

> *Jesus. God created him from His spirit and His breathing as He created Adam by His hand and His breathing.*[8]

It is clear also from the qur'ānic use of 'spirit' that it is connected with creation (cf. about Adam in 15.29) and life-giving ability. In the qur'ānic perspective, Christ himself is seen as a creation of the life-giving spirit, but at the same time as a privileged vehicle of the spirit, aided by the Holy Spirit in his mighty signs (2.253).

In recent approaches to Islamic Christology, and with a view to possible dialogue, much emphasis has been put upon the title *'abd*/servant and its relation to what might be termed the 'servant Christology' of the New Testament.[9]

Thematic Studies of Qur'ānic Christology[10]

As noted above, most of the Christian studies of the qur'ānic image of Christ have been thematic in their approach.

R. C. Zaehner (1977, 1st ed. 1958) combines a thematic approach with a sort of *interpretatio christiana*, minimizing the points of conflict between the qur'ānic and biblical images of Christ. He sees the qur'ānic Christology as a reflection of the Nestorian position – denying that Mary is the mother of God, but not necessarily denying the divinity of Christ. According to Zaehner, the Qur'ān sees Christ as created by the spirit of God:

> The Incarnation of Christ, then, breathed from the Spirit of God, is thus regarded as an event as momentous as the original creation or the universal resurrection at the end of time. This would seem to indicate that Muhammad must, again unconsciously, be reproducing the Christian idea of Christ as the new Adam and as the 'first fruits' of the resurrection.[11]

Zaehner also interprets 3.59 and 19.34 to imply that Christ is the 'Word of Truth':

> Christ, then, in the Qur'ān, would appear to be both the Word of God and therefore divine, and truly man; but He is not the 'son' of God for reasons that we have already explained [implying that the Qur'ān only denies the physical sonship of Christ].[12]

In line with this harmonizing interpretation, Zaehner also contends that the Qur'ān does not deny the actual crucifixion of Christ, only that the crucifixion was carried out by the Jews.

Zaehner writes within the tradition of comparative religion. The same is true for Geoffrey Parrinder's study *Jesus in the Qur'ān* (1979, 1st ed. 1965). But Parrinder's approach is far less harmonizing. He examines all the major themes indicated above, including the titles. He also lists some qur'ānic expressions that are not attributed to Jesus, but come close to classical words of Jesus according to the Christian Gospels.[13] The qur'ānic concepts of Gospel (*injīl*) and Christians (*naṣārā*) are also discussed. The relevant historical and grammatical considerations, as well as citations from Ḥadīth, Muslim legend and qur'ānic exegesis (Tafsīr), are dealt with within his overall thematic approach. Parrinder's study is still a major source of information for those looking for an introduction to 'Jesus in the Qur'ān', but because of his thematic and 'comparative' approach, he also freely refers to non-qur'ānic sources in his exposition, and draws upon both later Muslim tradition and Christian sources in his interpretation of the Qur'ān.

Another thematic study is Heikki Räisänen's *Das koranische Jesusbild: Ein Beitrag zur Theologie des Korans* (1971). His main points are summed up in an article from 1980: 'The Portrait of Jesus in the Qur'ān: Reflections from a Biblical Scholar'. Although thematic, his approach is different from that of Parrinder, and will be commented on below (in the section 'The overall qur'ānic context').

M. Ali Merad's studies on Christ according to the Qur'ān also display a thematic approach. After confirming the qur'ānic denials (that Christ was not a part of God, and that he was not killed), Merad unfolds the affirmations. He highlights the fact that Christ's creation is referred to as exceptional like that of Adam, and that his humanity is portrayed as extraordinary. The key references are the titles 'Word of God and a Spirit from Him', Christ's life-giving miracles and the fact that Christ is never referred to as an ordinary human being (*bašar*, cf. the self-reference of Muḥammad in 17.93 and other places). Merad concludes: 'An extraordinary mission, without precedence in the history of mankind'.[14]

In his above mentioned work, Neal Robinson (1991) mainly investigates the positions of classical Tafsīr authors concerning the four major themes of Christ's return, the crucifixion, his life-giving miracles and his virginal conception. But he also deals with the more basic hermeneutical questions arising from the study of Christ in Islam. In separate articles he has dealt in greater depth with the life-giving ability ascribed to Christ by the Qur'ān: 'creating birds from clay and raising the dead' (Robinson 1989), as well as questions pertaining to the commentators' view of the virginal conception (Robinson 1988), the the qur'ānic views of Christ and Mary (Robinson 1990) and points of contact between the ministry of Jesus and that of Muḥammad (Robinson 2003).

Grammatical Problems, Literary Character and Language Structure[15]

As noted above, there are some difficult grammatical problems in the Christ passages of the Qur'ān. These have been discussed at length in the classical

Muslim exegesis (see below), and they are still the subject of investigation. This is true both for the interpretation of the expression *šubbiha la-hum* and the meaning of the verb *tawaffā*[16] in the sayings about the death of Christ (4.157 and 3.55, 5.117), and the problems of syntactical reference in the possible sayings about Christ's return (4.159, 43.61).

Zaehner (1979) has suggested that *qawl al-ḥaqq* and *al-ḥaqq min rabbika* in 19.34 and 3.60 should be taken in the nominative, as appositions to Christ, and not in the accusative, as the conventional phrase 'a statement of truth' (in 19.34).

More important questions concerning the overall understanding of Christ in the Qur'ān are, however, those related to language structure and context.

The voluminous monograph of Claus Schedl, *Muhammad und Jesus: Die christologisch relevanten Texte des Koran neu übersetzt und erklärt* (Schedl 1978), is not thematic in its approach, but entirely related to the internal context of the Qur'ān and the logic of qur'ānic language. Claus Schedl applies a rather esoteric 'logotechnical' approach to the Qur'ān, analysing the arithmetic models that can be traced in the revelations, based on the symbolism and mystical significance of numbers. His approach suggests that Muḥammad had an intimate knowledge of what Schedl calls 'Logotechnik'. He also implies that the understanding of the Qur'ān as reflecting a heavenly archetype (cf. Sūra 43.3–4) conforms to, but is still intended to supersede, the ideas of a pre-existent Torah and Logos of Jewish-Christian revelation.[17] Schedl has applied the same, rather controversial science of 'logotechnique' in a short essay on the Qur'ān and the Gospel of Thomas, focusing on the Semitic symbolism of numbers (Schedl 1987).

As for the christological implications of his logotechnical analysis, Schedl emphasizes that Jesus is highly honoured by the fact that Allāh frequently addresses him in the first person as 'I', cf. 3.55 and 5.110. Notwithstanding the fact that the Qur'ān presents Muḥammad as the final prophet, the manner of divine speech in the Qur'ān implies that Jesus is regarded as a privileged individual in his own right. According to Schedl, the implication is that the 'I' of 'Īsā is in complete consonance with the 'I' of Allāh.[18] For Schedl, the way Jesus is addressed in the Qur'ān distinguishes him as the most intimate 'Servant of God'.[19]

A kind of structuralist approach to the qur'ānic discourse in general has been developed by the Muslim scholar Mohammed Arkoun.[20] According to his analysis, the dominant structure of qur'ānic revelation is the transmission of a message from an all-knowing magisterial speaker (I, We or He) to the privileged individual of Muḥammad as the vehicle of revelation (You). His analysis indicates that all the stories of the prophets in the Qur'ān, including that of Jesus, serve to authorize the ministry of the final Prophet, Muḥammad, through whom the knowledge of earlier prophetic essence is channelled (see as examples of this, 4.163f. and 3.44).[21]

A. H. Mathias Zahniser (1991) has applied a version of narrative analysis to the third sūra of the Qur'ān, the *Āl ʿImrān*, in which the annunciation to Mary as well as central features of Jesus' mission and post-mission fate are recorded (in verses 33–62). The starting point of Zahniser's analysis is that the Qur'ān is first of all 'a liturgical text for oral recitation, especially at religious ceremonial occasions'.[22] Following the German scholar Angelika Neuwirth, Zahniser sets out to conduct a colometric analysis of the sūra, in which the structural analysis closely follows 'the breath units of speech' (*cola*) in the text. His essay represents 'an attempt to account analytically for the shaping effect of qur'ānic reading and recitation upon his readers and auditors, i.e. an attempt to demonstrate the role of form in formation'.[23]

As regards the christological implications of his study, Zahniser emphasizes the centrality of the *tawḥīd* (divine unity) theme in the overall composition of the third Sūra. He concludes that:

> [. . .] inductive analysis seems to indicate that this brief narrative, comprising the whole of the apostleship of ʿĪsā from the prenatal promise to the post-mission rescue, is dominated by the sovereignty of God.[24]

Differences between narrative and discursive elements of the Qur'ān may also prove to have some consequences for the interpretation of qur'ānic images of Christ. As noted above, there is a difference in language structure in the way various biblical prophets are represented in the Qur'ān. The stories of prophets like Joseph and Moses are retold as admonitions in a narrative form, whereas the sayings about Christ are mostly references in the context of what appears to be a more dogmatic discourse. This discourse includes emphatic statements (cf. the I-passages), but is often void of narrative qualities (with the exception of the references to Jesus' conception and birth, where, however, Mary may be said to be the key figure – under the overall theme of divine sovereignty and human subordination).

What would be the significance of this difference in literary style? Could it be an expression of close and friendly relations to Christians, with no need to elaborate well-known stories? Or is the explanation rather polemical, the Christians being the main religious competitors and Christ the most controversial pre-Islamic prophet, so that the function of the qur'ānic revelation would mainly be to correct the 'false' teachings about Christ prevalent among Christians?

The Overall Qur'ānic Context[25]

Heikki Räisänen

In the studies already referred to, the Finnish New Testament scholar Heikki Räisänen (1971, 1980) underlines heavily that 'the Qur'ān is *not* to be expounded by the New Testament'.[26] The step from the old polemical to the more dialogical approach of Parrinder and others is laudable, but as Räisänen puts it:

> [. . .] the dangers inherent in the dialogical approach are those of superficiality and anachronism. One can easily read the Qur'ān with a Christian bias, more or less ignoring the historical context of the book.

Contra the pure historical approach, he also reminds the reader that 'the Qur'ān is not just the sum of its "sources"'. Because of this:

> Every detail in the Qur'ān, whatever its origin may be, must be interpreted in the light of the new qur'ānic context. The Qur'ān must be explained by the Qur'ān and not by anything else. This is the lesson to be learnt from the 'redaction-critical' studies of the Old and the New Testament.[27]

His main conclusion is that in the Qur'ān, 'like other previous messengers of God, Jesus became an example and a precursor of Muḥammad, a guarantor of Muḥammad's message who had experienced similar things'. Everything said about Jesus should be understood as a 'creative reinterpretation on the part of the Arabian prophet, triggered off by his strictly monotheistic conception of God'.[28] All seemingly 'Christian' attributes to Jesus in the Qur'ān, like the title 'Word of God', must be interpreted in this perspective.

Despite his insistence on the qur'ānic context, Räisänen still allows himself to draw some parallels between the qur'ānic picture of Christ and specific segments of the New Testament. According to Räisänen, the qur'ānic picture comes close to some central features of Lukan Christology. His suggestion is that 'On the whole, Luke gives us a Christology characterised by the emphatic subordination of Jesus to God'.[29] In all his doings and fate, Jesus is subordinated to God's permission and plan (Acts 2.22f.). He is referred to by Luke as God's Christ (Acts 3.18, Luke 9.20) and God's servant (Acts 3.13, 4.27), and no Trinitarian doctrine can be traced within the works of Luke.

As the most obvious New Testament contrast to the Lukan Christology of subordination, Räisänen points to the Gospel of John, its doctrine of a pre-existent Christ and its identification of Christ with God. Contra Räisänen, one might argue that his contrasting of Luke and John seems to imply a simplification of the New Testament counterparts to qur'ānic Christology. It should be kept in mind that also according to John, Jesus uses the subordinating expression 'my God and your God' (John 20.17), cf. the qur'ānic 'my Lord and your Lord' (3.51, 19.36, 43.64).

It may be argued that an ambivalence between subordination and identification can be traced in all the Gospels, reflecting a process in which titles designating God's agent on earth are transcended by the 'divine analogy' in the words and works of Jesus (cf. his absolute use of 'I am', his forgiving of sins, his life-giving ability, his role as a judge). All New Testament Gospels represent different interpretations of this process.

In any case, the qur'ānic Christology may be taken as a creative reinterpretation in its own right 'outside the walls', reflecting different cultural presuppositions, and breaking radically with all traces of identification of Christ with God.

Although the Logos-Christology of the Gospel of John is considered by Räisänen to be the most obvious contrast to the overall qur'ānic Christology, he identifies one feature that may be regarded as an affinity of the Qur'ān to the Gospel language of John: The use of the notion *āya* ('sign') to designate the life and works of Jesus – understood as a challenge to belief or non-belief. *Bi-iḏni llāhi*, by the permission of God, Christ performs miracles, as signs from God. Since Muḥammad is not attributed with specific miracles in the Qur'ān, it is tempting, says Räisänen, to see an implicit elevation of Christ above the level of Muḥammad in his miraculous birth and in his ability to heal the sick and raise the dead. However, miracles are not specific to Christ. Räisänen points out that the Qur'ān (like the Bible) also puts much emphasis on the miracles of Moses. All miracles performed by prophets who have this specific permission are designated as *āyāt* – together with the wonders of Allāh in Creation.[30]

The main point of Räisänen's argument is to show that the signs of Jesus acquire a new meaning in the new qur'ānic context, not as 'signs of the only-begotten Son' as in John, but as prophetic signs in line with those of Moses and other forerunners of Muḥammad.

Räisänen also discusses the notions *rūḥ* (spirit – from God) and *kalima* (word – from God), attributed to Jesus in the Qur'ān. Again, it might be tempting to see in the notion 'word' a reflection of the Johannine conception of Jesus as Logos. However, as Räisänen points out, in the Qur'ān the word of God is clearly conceived of as created by God, and not as an agent in creation.[31]

For the Christian eye in general, formal similarities tend to overshadow the specific *interpretatio coranica* of the notions in question.[32] In his conclusion, Räisänen admits that some of the features connected with Jesus – like his birth, the art of his miracles, and his elevation to heaven – can be said to be specific to him, and not general features of the life and works of Allāh's prophets. But he argues that in the Qur'ān, the uniting bond between the prophets and the decisive feature of their prophethood is not miracles, but their strict monotheistic message. And the *āya* beyond all signs is the wonder of the Qur'ān itself.[33]

If there is still a ranking of the prophets, the Qur'ān leaves no doubt that Muḥammad is the seal of them all. Thus, Jesus is first of all a predecessor of Muḥammad. According to Räisänen, Muḥammad has consistently reinterpreted the life of Jesus through his own experience, with himself (as the medium of the final *āya*) as the culmination. In a rather controversial statement, Räisänen suggests that in spite of the strict monotheistic intentions of Muḥammad, his theology implicitly turns out to be quite 'egocentric': 'The special position of Jesus lies in the fact that he is the closest predecessor of Muhammad, having also prophesied his coming. The qur'anic Jesus points at someone who is more important and greater than himself.[34]

In accordance with this conclusion, Räisänen compares what happened to Jesus in the Qur'ān with the fate of John the Baptist in the New Testament – being reduced from a prophet in his own right to a mere precursor of Christ.

Claus Schedl

The conclusions of Claus Schedl (1978) are different. Although he reads the Jesus-passages in the qur'ānic context of fulfilment of revelation through Muḥammad, he suggests that Jesus still is portrayed as a privileged individual – notably not as 'Son of God', but as his distinguished Servant. Aiming at an *interpretatio coranica*, he nevertheless suggests that the *ʿabd-allāh* of the Qur'ān can be understood in light of the fact that the earliest Christian formula of confession was not 'Jesus is Kyrios!' but 'Jesus is the Servant of God!' (Schedl refers here to Acts 3.13, 4.27, etc.[35]).

Within his contextual approach, Schedl analyses the progression in qur'ānic 'Christology' through the Meccan and Medinan revelations. His asserts that the primary Meccan revelations do not deny the sonship of Jesus specifically, but reject the pre-Islamic notions of divine begetting in general (cf. Sūra 6.100).[36]

Instead, Jesus is emphatically portrayed as *ʿabd*, Allāh's servant – already from the cradle (19.30). Like many of his predecessors, he is *nabī* (prophet) and *rasūl* (messenger). 'But his real greatness is reflected in his self-designation as the Servant of God.'[37]

In all cases except one, the Qur'ān uses the word *walad*, 'begotten son' when it denies the sonship of Jesus.[38] In the one and only Medinan revelation (9.30) that denies the sonship of Jesus by use of the word *ibn*, the context seems to be specific phenomena prevailing in Medina. Sūra 9.31f. rejects the Christian saying that Jesus is *ibn Allāh* on a par with the Jewish elevation of ʿUzayr (Ezra) as a son of God. And notably, the Christian tendency to elevate priests and monks as lords (*arbāb*, pl. of *rabb*) is taken as another example of a general tendency to extinguish the light of the one and only God (9.33). Schedl summarizes: 'In Mecca he fought against the gods, in Medina against the Christian holy ones who – in his perception – were made companions of God.'[39]

Also in the Medinan revelations, Schedl finds an emphasis on the Servant Messiah (4.172), and notably emphatic expressions of his privileged status with Allāh in Allāh's addressing him in the first person (cf. the 'I' of 3.55 and 5.110).

In a spirit of dialogue, Schedl then puts forward the question of whether the qur'ānic image of the servant of God can be reconciled with that of the suffering servant of the Bible.[40] In an attempt at reconciliation, he identifies the context ('Sitz im Leben') of the denial of crucifixion in 4.157 as being the controversy with the Jews and their assertion that they had crucified the Messiah. Furthermore, he reads *wa-lākin šubbiha la-hum* as a reflection of the Docetic Christology of the Nag Hammadi apocrypha, implying that only the bodily ʿĪsā was crucified, whereas the spiritual Messiah was out of reach of the thugs and could simply not be nailed to the cross.[41]

Schedl thus maintains that the Qur'ān need not be taken as denying crucifixion. Neither is there any need for a substitute, if the meaning of 4.157 is that the Messiah's soul was rescued by God: 'The Jews sought to annihilate Allāh's Servant on the cross, but Allāh "elevated" his Servant on the cross.' In this interpretation, Schedl suggests, the Servant Christology of the Qur'ān need not be too different from the early Christian kerygma about the elevated Kyrios.[42]

With this conclusion, Schedl reveals a 'comparative' interest that comes close to Parrinder's investigations of 'in what senses the qur'ānic teaching may be taken'. The modalities of 'dürfen' and 'may' might still be valid also in a more immanent analysis of the Qur'ān. In their attempts at reinterpretation, some Islamic modernists (notably Mohammed Arkoun) have emphasized the need to distinguish between the categories of 'unthinkable' and 'unthought' in qur'ānic exegesis.

Günther Risse

The rejected saying in the nominal sentence of Sūra 5.17/5.72 – *inna-llāha huwa l-masīḥu bnu-maryama* – is translated by Schedl as 'Der Messias, Marjams Sohn, ist Gott' ('Messiah, the son of Marjam, is God'), and taken as a rejection of the divinity of the Messiah in a historical context where not only Jesus, but also Mary tended to be deified (5.116). Günther Risse (1989), however, translates the saying 'Gott is Christus, der Sohn der Maria'.[43] He suggests that the saying should be read as a rejection of an extreme Monophysite Christology that not only attributes divine nature to Christ, but identifies God with Christ. The aim of his historically oriented study (see below) is to show how Monophysite Christology prevailed in the Christian surroundings of Muḥammad, and thus constituted the main polemical context of the qur'ānic sayings. As Risse reminds us, Chalcedonian Christology rejected the saying 'God is Christ', but affirmed that 'Christ is God'.

Thus, both Schedl and Risse are eager to state that the polemical statements of the Qur'ān are directed towards Christian distortions and excesses, be it in the doctrine of the Trinity or in Christology; cf. the qur'ānic admonition 'commit no excesses in your religion!' (4.171). Risse is in accordance with Schedl in concluding that the previous struggle against the Arab's gods and daughters of gods formed the background for his understanding of and attitude towards Christian, in particular monophysite, Christology.[44]

In his conclusion, Risse cites Räisänen with approval:

> The point of this dogmatic discussion is not to secure the position of Muhammad along with or above Jesus. The horizon of 'Christology' is 'theology' proper, the doctrine of God. From a strict monotheistic conception Muhammad demands unyieldingly that the Christians give up their tritheistic ideas and return to the pure monotheism of Jesus and the earlier messengers of God.[45]

Neal Robinson

It should be remembered, however, that Räisänen points to the paradox that the utterly theocentric theology of Muḥammad (as well as his Christology) in a certain sense is 'egocentric', and serves to legitimize his own role as the final prophet of God.[46] At this point, the conclusion of the more recent studies of the British scholar Neal Robinson (1991) is similar to that of Räisänen. First of all, Robinson eschews any *interpretatio christiana*. According to Robinson 'any attempt to translate what the Qur'ān says about Jesus into a series of propositions is likely to reduce the impact of the qur'ānic version of the story and thus to seriously misrepresent it'. Secondly, as an alternative to a christianized interpretation, he suggests that:

> In its Quranic setting there can be little doubt that the story of Jesus serves to authenticate the prophetic ministry of Muhammad and to emphasise the authority of the message of which he is the mediator.[47]

He points to the obvious similarities in the presentation of Jesus on the one hand and Muḥammad on the other, giving the impression that Muḥammad is doing what Jesus had done before him.[48] Similar parallels of Mary to the Prophet's wife ʿĀ'isha can be identified.[49]

The perspective of Jesus as role model for Muḥammad might be overemphasized by Robinson, but is further elaborated in later Muslim biographical legend about Muḥammad (see Section 'Muḥammad and Jesus in Ḥadīth and legend', this chapter).

As underlined in the introduction, it is clear that in an orthodox Islamic perspective Jesus should not be compared to Muḥammad, but to the Qur'ān as the final 'word of God'. Accordingly, the tendency in popular Islam towards modelling Muḥammad in accordance with the miracles of Jesus and his status as pre-existent has often been dismissed as an attempt to conform Muḥammad to Christian expectations. It can still be argued that structural and contextual exegesis of the Qur'ān shows that earlier prophets are remodelled not only to prepare for the wonder of the Qur'ān, but also to elevate Muḥammad as the seal of the prophets and the fulfilment of 'perfect man'.

Historical Background and External Context

Neal Robinson: History, Literature, Theology

Neal Robinson (1991) applies three different approaches in his updated summary of the Christian context of the qur'ānic sayings about Jesus.[50]

1 The first approach investigates the historical question of the penetration of Eastern Christianity into Arabia, and Muḥammad's encounters with Christianity. As to Muḥammad's contacts with Christianity, there are many traditions, but also question marks, concerning the extent and nature of his individual contacts. Muḥammad's biographer Ibn Isḥāq mentions individuals like the Christian monk Bahīrā, Waraqa Ibn Nawfal (Khadīja's cousin) and the Christian slave Jabr (suggested by the Meccans to have influenced Muḥammad). Muḥammad's Coptic co-wife Māriya, brought to Muḥammad as slave from Alexandria with her sister and brother, may also deserve consideration.[51]

The documented 'diplomatic' encounters with African Christians of Abbyssinia and Arab Christians of Najrān probably played a role in the formation of Muḥammad's concept of Christians and their Christology. Consequently, studies of the qur'ānic references to Christians (*naṣārā*), as well as historical research about pre-Islamic Syrian, Abyssinian and Arab Christianity, should be an integral part of all studies of 'Christ in Islam' – if one accepts the presupposition that qur'ānic Christology (like all Christologies) is contextual.

A more specific question, discussed in some detail by Risse (1989), is the significance of the qur'ānic version of the Christian legend of the seven sleepers, related in Sūra 18.9–27. What external references can be thought of for the inclusion of this Christian legend in the early Meccan revelations?

2 The second approach is more of a literary character: What parallels to the qur'ānic material may be found in ancient Christian writings? The canonical New Testament scriptures were probably not translated into Arabic before the rise of Islam, but links can be traced to other early Christian literature. Syriac Christian writings in particular have been presented as among the most influential sources. A large proportion of the borrowed words in the Arabic of the Qur'ān are Syriac, and similarities can be traced between the qur'ānic Jesus material and the Syriac Church's typological exegesis as well as Tatian's Gospel harmony in Syriac, the Diatessaron.

Another obvious source is the apocryphal infancy Gospel tradition.[52] Where qur'ānic features of Jesus cannot be traced back to the canonical Gospels or to the Diatessaron, similarities can often be found in the infancy Gospels. The *Protoevangelium of James* parallels much of the qur'ānic material about the selection and upbringing of Mary. The (Latin) *Gospel of Pseudo-Matthew* includes the miracle of the palm tree and the stream of water. In the Qur'ān, this miracle is linked with Jesus' birth. In Pseudo-Matthew, it is recounted in connection with the flight to Egypt, with the child Jesus also speaking miraculously in the same context. The miraculous speaking of the baby Jesus from the cradle reported in the Qur'ān might be traced back to the *Arabic Infancy Gospel*, and the miracle of bringing clay birds to life is found in *The Infancy Story of Thomas*. Among these apocrypha, Syriac translations of the *Protoevangelium of James* and *The Infancy Story of Thomas* are found in pre-Islamic sources. The later Arabic Infancy Gospel and the Gospel of Pseduo-Mattew probably draw on pre-Islamic sources, maybe also in Syriac.

If the substitutionist interpretation of 4.157 (that Christ was replaced on the cross) is taken as a valid reading of the qur'ānic text, the question arises of whether this idea is represented in Christian sources.[53] According to Irenaeus' *Adversus Haereses*, the Egyptian Gnostic Christian Basilides (of the second century) held the view that Christ (the divine *nous*, intelligence) was not crucified, but was replaced by Simon of Cyrene. However, both Clement of Alexandria and Hippolytus denied that Basilides held this view. But the substitutionist idea in a general form is quite clearly expressed in the Gnostic Nag Hammadi documents *Apocalypse of Peter* and *The Second Treatise of the Great Seth*.[54]

3 A third approach is to investigate the theological similarities between the qur'ānic Christology and the christological traditions of Nestorianism, Monophysitism and Jewish Christianity (as exemplified, e.g. by the Ebionites and the Elkesaites). Like many others, Robinson is most impressed by the similarity of the Muslim traditions to Gnostic/Docetic speculations about Jesus' death. He refers to the fact mentioned above that Docetists like Basilides (as reported by Irenaeus) and the author of the Apocalypse of Peter even elaborate on the theory of Jesus being substituted on the cross.[55]

Günther Risse: The Theological Context

In his study *'Gott is Christus, der Sohn der Maria': Eine Studie zum Christusbild im Koran* (1989), Risse is applying a historical-descriptive method, and mainly examining the historical context of the qur'ānic image of Christ. It contains the following main chapters: Arab Christianity in pre-Islamic times; The oriental image of Christ; and Muḥammad's image of Christ. His main hypothesis is that Muḥammad's image of Christ is mainly influenced by the Monophysite Christology prevailing in Abyssinia, Egypt and Syria, as well as in his immediate surroundings among the Ghassanids in the northern part of the Arabian Peninsula and among the Christians of Najrān in the southern part. More specifically, he suggests that extreme Monophysite groups like the Julianists and Gaianists might have influenced Muḥammad's image of Christ and aroused his protest. Both Abyssinia and Southern Arabia were considered as refuges for notorious Christian heretics. According to Risse, qur'ānic Christology is modelled as a polemical Christology over against the Monophysite (non-Chalcedonian!) confession 'God is Christ, the son of Mary'. Implicitly, qur'ānic Christology is also a polemical Mariology, directed against the Monophysite (Cyrillian-Ephesinian) confession of Mary as *theotókos* (God-birther). This delineation would be all the more necessary in Muḥammad's view since he obviously perceived the doctrine of Trinity as referring to the triad God the Father, Jesus the Son and Mary the mother.

As a more positive source of Muḥammad's christology, Risse points to old Syrian traditions, especially the theology of incarnation of Ephraim the Syrian (d. 374), which was channelled to Najrān by the bishop Philoxenus from Mabbug (d. after 527), and focuses on the wonder of Jesus' birth.

Risse presents a lot of valuable historical material to support his view that Muḥammad's Christian influences are not to be found primarily in Nestorianism (as a positive influence), but rather in Monophysitism (as a negative reference). Since the aim of his study is historical-descriptive, the conclusions of his exegesis of the relevant qur'ānic passages bring few substantial new insights. Interesting though is his characterizing of Muḥammad's Christology as *theologia incarnationis*, primarily meditating on the miracle of Jesus' birth, and consistently avoiding the cross. In his exegesis of the qur'ānic passages about Jesus' death, he maintains that according to the Qur'ān, Jesus died a natural death and was raised to glory after death (based on 19.33, and 3.55). The key passage of 4.156–159 (*šubbiha la-hum*) is seen as influenced by the Docetism of extreme Monophysites, denying the cross, but – as Muḥammad would have seen it – not a later natural death of Jesus.

Claus Schedl and Others: Mecca and Medina

Another important question of external context is how the sayings about Jesus correspond to the various stages of the revelation of the Qur'ān, and the formative experiences of the first Muslim community. Most of the sayings about Jesus belong to the later Medinan revelations, but references and a few more extensive sayings are also found in the revelations of the various Meccan stages.[56]

As we have seen above in the references to Claus Schedl's book *Muhammad and Jesus*, he emphasizes the difference in religious context from Mecca to Medina. In Mecca, Muḥammad is confronting pre-Islamic polytheism. In Medina, he is confronting a significant Jewish community and also a Christian presence. In both cases, according to Schedl, his portrayal of Jesus as *ʿabd-Allāh*, Servant of God, is the clue to his kerygmatic efforts – confronting the general polytheism of Mecca, and the tendencies of Jews and Christians to elevate their prophets and religious leaders 'beyond all measures', as brought to his knowledge in Medina.

In the revelations stemming from the Meccan periods, four sūras speak of Jesus. The sayings are rather 'neutral' in their form, and positive references are made to the miracles of Jesus, both his miraculous birth and the life-giving miracles performed by him. As emphasized by many, the decisive context for the sayings pertaining to Jesus from the Meccan period seems to have been the rejection of resurrection that Muḥammad's proclamation of eternal judgement was met with in Mecca (cf. *Sūrat Maryam*, 19.66ff.). In this context, the divine ability to create life out of nothing, confirmed by the virginal conception of Jesus and his leave to perform life-giving miracles, might have been brought forward by Muḥammad as a kerygmatic proof: 'What will be done by God at the end of time is done by Jesus as a miracle during his life as a messenger of God.'[57]

In the Medinan revelations (10 sūras refer to Jesus), the sayings are marked by a gradually more polemical discourse, at a stage when Islam is organized as a distinct religious community in competition with Arab Christianity and Judaism. It should be noted, however, that the confrontations with Judaism were sharper than those with Christianity. The denial of the crucifixion in 4.157 is directed not against the Christians, but against the claims of the Jews, which, according to the Qur'ān, were just as erroneous in this case as the false charges they raised against Mary (4.156).

With this kind of contextual approach, the door is also open to a hermeneutical reading of the qur'ānic passages about Christ – taking them not as absolute or timeless assertions, but as different contextual testimonies to the one, almighty God who has no partners.

Jesus in Ḥadīth

The Qur'ān itself, as the decisive *waḥy* (revelation), is not telling the story of Muḥammad, although his life-story may be said to be implicit as the context of revelation. Some passages in the Qur'ān also refer to Muḥammad as the Muslim ideal, to be emulated by the believers (cf. 6.161–163, 39.11–12).

Accordingly, there was the need to recollect the life-story, the actions and the sayings, of Muḥammad, in order to delineate the *Sunna* (path, way) to be followed in the imitation of 'the definitive Muslim'.[58] The technical term for the collections of sayings and actions is Ḥadīth (plural: *aḥādīṯ*).

The quantity of narrative material reflecting the actions and sayings of Muḥammad and his immediate companions is massive, and many would argue that the Ḥadīth collections exercised just as much influence as the Qur'ān on the shaping of the Muslim religious consciousness.

The vast number of collections originally available, however, led to an urgent need to establish criteria for the authenticity of the Ḥadīth material. This problem became acute when, in the eighth and ninth centuries, the Ḥadīth material (together with the Qur'ān) became the frame of reference for Islamic jurisprudence. From the beginning, obvious fabrications were included in the sayings of Muḥammad (e.g. aphorisms from Greek philosophy and quotations from Jewish and Christian sources). The unbroken chain of transmitters (*isnād*) was established by the Traditionists as the decisive criterion, leading to the distinction between sound/genuine (*ṣaḥiḥ*), good and weak *aḥādīṯ*. The evaluation of the various traditions with the tools of a modern critical approach is a different question.

In Sunnī Islam, six different compilations came to be recognized as Ḥadīth: those of al-Bukhārī (d. 870), Muslim ibn al-Ḥajjāj (d. 875), Abū Dawūd (d. 888), Ibn Māja (d. 886), al-Tirmidhī (d. 892) and al-Nisā'ī (d. 916). Among these, Bukhārī and Muslim (especially Bukhārī) acquired almost canonical authority. According to tradition, Bukhārī included only a half per cent of the accounts available to him.

It should be noted that the Shīʿites repudiated the six collections of the Sunni Muslims and composed their own standard work, based on the Ḥadīth material derived from the fourth caliph and cousin of the Prophet, ʿAlī, and his supporters.

Within the Ṣūfī traditions, 40 Ḥadīth Qudsī ('sacred sayings' attributed to God such as in the Qur'ān) acquired pre-eminence as the basis of their spiritual life.[59]

In the Ḥadīth collections, references are normally not to 'Christ' (*al-masīḥ*), but to 'Jesus' (*ʿĪsā*). In Bukhārī, most of the references to Jesus are found in his book *Kitāb al-anbiyā'* ('The Prophets'), but Jesus is also referred to in a number of other books in his collection. In Muslim, references to 'The merits of the Jesus Christ' can be found in *Kitāb al-faḍā'il* ('Book of the merits of the Holy Prophet and his companions'). The eschatological references can be found in *Kitāb al-īmān* ('Book of faith') and in *Kitāb al-fitan wa-ašrāt al-sāʿa* ('Book of turmoil and portents of the last hour').[60]

With a view to content, Ḥadīth sayings with relevance for the Islamic image of Jesus may be grouped in five categories:

1 Sayings clarifying the relation between Muḥammad and Jesus.
2 Descriptions of what Jesus looked like.
3 Foretelling of the descent of Jesus, in the eschatological sayings of the Prophet.
4 Mention of specific merits of Jesus.
5 Further investigation of similarities to the Christian Gospels.

The Ḥadīth sayings about Jesus have different focuses from that of the Qur'ān. Whereas it is not clear whether the Qur'ān has any message at all about the role of Jesus in the eschatological future, this is a main focus in the Ḥadīth sayings.

Sayings Clarifying the Relation between Muḥammad and Jesus

In the first sayings reported in Muslim's chapter on the merits of Jesus Christ, Muḥammad points to himself as the most akin or close to Jesus among the whole of mankind in this worldly life and in the hereafter: 'Prophets are brothers in faith, having different mothers. Their religion is, however, one and there is no Apostle between us (between me and Jesus Christ)'.[61]

Parallel utterances can be found in Bukhārī (*Kitāb al-anbiyā'*), who adds that for the one who believes in Jesus and then believes in Muḥammad, there will be a double reward.

According to Muslim legend, the Prophet instructed his Companions to reserve a tomb for Jesus next to Muḥammad between Abū Bakr and 'Umar, where he would be buried along with Muḥammad after his return to earth and be raised with him from one grave in the Resurrection. Although this saying is in concord with the Sunna emphasis on the (spiritual) closeness of Jesus to Muḥammad, it is not included in the collections of Bukhārī and Muslim. In later sources, however, it appears frequently. That Jesus will be buried by the Muslims is referred to in the commentary to the Qur'ān by al-Ṭabarī (d. 923), who states that Jesus, in his second coming, 'will tarry on the earth for as long as God will – perhaps for 40 years. Then he will die and the Muslims will pray over him and bury him'.[62]

Traditions pertaining to the death and burial of Jesus after his second coming are included in the popular Ḥadīth collection *Miškāt al-Maṣābīḥ*, which was initiated in the eleventh century by al-Baghawī and revised in the fourteenth century by al-Tibrīzī.[63] With reference to Tirmidhī, it reports that 'the description of Muhammad is written in the Torah and also that Jesus son of Mary will be buried along with him. Abū Mawdūd said that a place for a grave had remained in the house'.[64]

It also includes the following saying, which is attributed to Ibn al-Jauzī with reference to his *Kitāb al-wafā'*:

> *Jesus, son of Mary, will descend to the earth, will marry, have children, and remain forty-five years, after which he will die and be buried along with me in my grave. Then Jesus son of Mary and I shall arise from one grave between Abū Bakr and 'Umar.*[65]

According to the reports on Muḥammad's night journey and ascension to heaven, Muḥammad met Jesus in the second or third heaven, but is himself exalted above Jesus to the seventh heaven (cf. Muslim, *Kitāb al-īmān*, and Bukhārī *Kitāb al-anbiyā'* as well as his *Kitāb bida' al-ḫalq* and *Kitāb manāqib al-anṣār*[66]).

Descriptions of Jesus' Appearance

In the reports on Muḥammad's ascension, there is also a description of what Jesus looked like. The other context in which descriptions of Jesus occur is eschatological, and the description serves the purpose of distinguishing him from Anti-Christ (*al-Dajjāl*). According to a well-known Ḥadīth reported by Muslim, *al-Dajjāl* will emerge from a place between Damascus and Iraq. After a reign of 40 days, Jesus will descend on the top of the white minaret in Damascus, pursue *al-Dajjāl* and kill him.[67]

The descriptions of Jesus vary a little in Bukhārī and Muslim,[68] and with the reporting Companion. If one should attempt to harmonize the sayings, his characteristic features would be as follows: He was of a fair complexion or even red-faced 'as if he had just come out of a bath', of moderate height and with beautiful long hair 'neither too curly nor too straight', and with water trickling from it. The general emphasis seems to be on his beauty, fairness and purity, over against the more unfortunate characteristics of Anti-Christ, the one-eyed.

Outside the Islamic sources, an interest in the physical appearance of Christ can be found in the apocryphal *Acts of John*, and in the *Letter of Lentulus*.[69]

Foretelling of the Descent of Jesus in the Eschatological Sayings Attributed to Muḥammad

The most famous eschatological saying about Jesus would be the following (from Bukhāri, *Kitāb al-anbiyā'*):

> *By him in whose Hand my soul is, surely (Jesus) the son of Mary will soon descend among you as a Just Ruler; he will break the Cross and kill the pigs and there will be no Jizya (i.e. taxation taken from non-Muslims). Money will be in abundance so that nobody will accept it, and a single prostration to Allāh (in prayer) will be better than the whole world and whatever is in it.*[70]

Muslim (*Kitāb al-īmān*) adds that he:

> [. . .] *would leave the young she-camel and no one would endeavour (to collect Zakāt on it). Spite, mutual hatred and jealousy against one another will certainly disappear, and when he summons people to accept wealth, not even one would do so.*[71]

Another, though weaker, Ḥadīth even says that when the Messiah descends, he will 'add to the lawful'.[72]

The essence of this expectation is that Jesus in his second coming will confirm that he is a Muslim, and rule according to Muslim law. He will do away with specific Christian symbols, and let Islam rule among the People of the Book. However, his Islamic reign of abundance, justice and peace will only come after he has defeated Anti-Christ and the enemies of Allāh.

As in early Christianity, the eschatological scenario envisaged by Muḥammad is imminent, and is expected to take place on the battlefields of the already accomplished Muslim expansion (for the following, see especially Muslim's *Kitāb al-fitan*, on the 'turmoil and portents of the last hour'). In this scenario, one may recognize common features and figures from Jewish-Christian apocalyptic literature such as fire, beasts, eclipses and seducers, as well as the enemy powers from the north, Gog and Magog. Jesus, the Son of Mary, descends with his palms resting on two angels in Damascus. His mission is to remove *al-Dajjāl*, the Anti-Christ, who has been seducing the faithful in Syria. It is in this context that a detailed description of Jesus is given, to discern him physically from *al-Dajjāl*. According to one tradition, the enemy of Allāh will dissolve like salt in water when Jesus descends and the call to prayer is heard. However, other sayings imply more direct violent intervention by Jesus, who will chase *al-Dajjāl* and kill him. The enemy powers of Gog and Magog are defeated by the prayers of Jesus and his Companions.

In order to underline his submission to Islam, it is said that Jesus will not lead the prayers even if he is asked to, but rather join in the lines behind the *imām*.

After *al-Dajjāl* has been defeated, there will be no hatred among men for seven years, and the Muslims will make fires of their bows and arrows. After that God will send a purifying rain on earth, and nature will be reconciled and abundant. But still, the trials are not over. The wicked people will be summoned once more by Satan to take power, and a section of Muḥammad's people will not cease fighting for the truth till the Day of Resurrection.

As for the end of this second period of Jesus' life on earth, Muslim legend has tried to fill in the gaps left by Ḥadīth. The tradition mentioned above, concluding with his burial, reports Muḥammad as having said that Jesus, when he descends to earth, will marry, and children will be born to him. And he will remain on earth for a period of 45 years, before he is buried alongside Muḥammad.

In his early classical commentary to the Qur'ān, al-Ṭabarī (d. 923), cites Ḥadīth in a way which summarizes the more scattered references listed above:

> *The prophets are brothers. They are of different mothers but their religion is one. I am the closest of mankind to Jesus son of Mary because there was no prophet between us. He is going to descend so recognise him when you see him. He is a man of average build, of reddish white complexion and with lank hair. His head flows with moisture although it only sheds a drip at a time. He will be wearing two light yellow garments. He will break the crucifixes, kill the pigs and abolish the poll tax. Wealth will abound and people will fight one another because of Islam until God destroys all the religious communities in his time with the exception of Islam. In this time God will also destroy the deceitful false messiah the Antichrist. There will be such security on the earth in his time that lions will lie down with camels, leopards with cattle and wolves with sheep. Youths and boys will play with*

snakes without harming them or being harmed by them. Then he will tarry on the earth for as long as god will – perhaps for forty years. Then he will die and the Muslims will pray over him and bury him.[73]

Jesus and al-Mahdī

A different focus in Muslim eschatology is the coming of the Mahdī, 'the guided one', from the family of the Prophet.[74] The scenario for the coming of the Mahdī appears to have been somewhat different from that of *al-Dajjāl* and Jesus. In this tradition, there are references to fighting between Arabs and people from the East, maybe reflecting the experience of Muslim civil war and the struggle between Sunnī and Shīʿite Muslims. In other traditions, the Mahdī is said to come from the West (Maghrib).

Later, some Muslims have maintained the Mahdī and Jesus as two separate figures (Jesus being subordinate to the Mahdī), whereas others have claimed that there would be no Mahdī except for Jesus. Belief in the Mahdī is not an essential part of the Sunnī creed, but is integral to Shīʿite Islam, where it is connected with the doctrine of the Hidden Imām. Sunnī Islam does affirm that there will be a final restorer in the eschatological drama, but not that he will be called al-Mahdī. In the two most respected Ḥadīth collections, Muslim and Bukhārī, there is no mention of al-Mahdī, but Abū Dawūd, Tirmidhī and Ibn Māja make several references to him in their collections.[75] Many orthodox Sunnī theologians (including the historian Ibn Khaldūn) have disputed the authenticity of the references to al-Mahdī in the Ḥadīth collections. Other prominent Islamic theologians, like the great *mufassir* Ibn Kathīr (d. 1373) have combined the prophecies about *al-Dajjāl*, Jesus and al-Mahdī into elaborate apocalyptic scenarios, expounding the signs before the day of judgement.[76]

In these traditions, al-Mahdī serves as a more specific champion of Islam than Jesus, whose business is restricted to defeat/kill *al-Dajjāl*. Accordingly, it is the traditions about al-Mahdī that have inspired Muslims to popular unrest in periods of decay and oppression. Cf. the saying of the Prophet, according to Abū Dawūd: 'The Mahdī will be one of my descendants . . .. He will fill the earth with justice and fairness just as it was filled with injustice and oppression, and he will rule for seven years.'[77]

In present-day Muslim writings about the descent of Jesus, the roles of al-Mahdī and the Anti-Christ have different emphases, depending on the context. The booklet of the Moroccan Grand *muḥaddiṯ* Abdullah Ibn as-Siddiq, *Al-Mahdī, Jesus and the Anti-Christ* (1985) – dedicated to 'the Muslim warriors of Afghanistan' – reflects the traditions of Mahdī-expectation in Maghrib and Africa, and strongly maintains the Mahdī as a distinct, eschatological figure. In his generous list of 'authentic prophetic sayings concerning al-Mahdi he includes the following: 'A nation will not be destroyed when I am at their beginning, and Jesus, son of Mary is at its end, and al Mahdi is in the middle.'[78]

In Sudan, which has a very strong and Ṣūfī-related Mahdī-tradition, there has also been a modernist interpretation of the return of Christ – notably among The Republican Brothers.[79] In their interpretation, the coming Christ stands for the final reconciliation of the Christian and Muslim traditions, melting together into 'the second message of Islam'.[80]

In India/Pakistan, books like *Descension of Jesus Christ* (Alam 1990) seem to be mainly directed against the Ahmadi Muslims, refuting their beliefs in the Ahmadi Messiah by recapitulating the necessary characteristics of the coming Christ. None of these works can be said to represent critical, scientific investigations of the subject, but they nevertheless give hints of a vivid eschatological debate with polemical overtones within Islam.

Mention of Specific Merits of Jesus

In Muslim and Bukhārī's collections about the merits of the prophets, there is a saying about Jesus being born without sin. Jesus and his mother are told to be the only ones on earth that have not been touched by the devil:

> *There is none born among the off-spring of Adam, but Satan touches it. A child therefore, cries loudly at the time of birth because of the touch of Satan, except Mary and her child.*[81]
>
> *The Satan touches every son of Adam on the day when his mother gives birth to him with the exemption of Mary and her son.*[82]

But in standard Muslim interpretation, this does not necessarily imply that Jesus was without error. Muslim goes on to cite a story in which Jesus seemingly admits to have been wrong in accusing a man of theft.[83]

Other Ḥadīth references seem to relativize the position of Jesus and Mary. Mary was only the best of women of her time, comparable to Muḥammad's wives Khadīja or ʿĀʾisha. And Jesus was only one out of three who is reported to have spoken from the cradle (cf. Bukhārī, *Kitāb al-anbiyāʾ*).

In another saying, Muḥammad reiterates some of titles of Jesus known from the Qur'ān. He is called Servant/Slave and Messenger/Apostle like Muḥammad, but also 'his Word which he bestowed on Mary and a Soul from Him' (Bukhārī, *Kitāb al-anbiyāʾ*):

> *If anyone testifies that none has the right to be worshipped but Allāh alone who has no partners, and that Muḥammad is His Slave and His Apostle, and that Jesus is Allāh's Slave and His Apostle and His Word which he bestowed on Mary and a Soul from him, and that Paradise is true, and Hell is true, Allāh will admit him into Paradise with the deeds which he has done even if those deeds were few.*[84]

[. . .] Do not exaggerate in praising me as the Christians praised the Son of Mary, for I am only a slave. So, call me the slave of Allah and His Apostle.[85]

Further Similarities to the New Testament Gospels

As in the Qur'ān, similarities to the Christian Gospels can also be found outside the passages in Ḥadīth that are actually referring to Jesus.[86]

Especially interesting is the occurrence of parables attributed to Muḥammad that come very close to those of Jesus. According to Bukhārī's book on 'Hiring' (*Kitāb al-ijāra*), Muḥammad is (re)telling the parable of the labourers in the vineyard to illuminate the relation between the Muslim period and the periods of the previous nations: 'The example of Muslims, Jews and Christians is like the example of a man who employed labourers to work for him from morning till night for specific wages.'[87]

But the point in Muḥammad's version of the parable is different from that of Jesus. In the Muslim version, the parable tells us that the Muslims are offered a double payment, although they are expected to work for a shorter time than the Jews and the Christians: 'So, that wages was the example of those people (Muslim) and the example of the light of guidance they have accepted willingly.'[88]

In the Gospel of Matthew (Chapter 20), the workers are all paid the same, whereas in the version of Muḥammad, there is a special blessing on the Muslim latecomers for the work they have done. The point of the last becoming the first, however, can be said to be a shared polemical point in the Christian and Muslim versions.

Even more intriguing is the recurrence of the judgement scenario from Chapter 25 in the Gospel of Matthew, in a Ḥadīth Qudsī (i.e. saying attributed to Allāh) according to Saḥiḥ Muslim in *Kitāb al-birr* (The Book of Piety), where he is listing merits of visiting the sick:

Verily, Allāh, the Exalted and Glorious would say on the Day of Resurrection: O son of Adam, I was sick but you did not visit Me. He would say: O my Lord, how could I visit Thee whereas Thou art the Lord of the worlds? Thereupon He would say: Didn't you know that such and such servant of Mine was sick but you did not visit him and were you not aware of this that if you had visited him, you would have found Me by him? O son of Adam, I asked food from you but you did not feed Me. He would say: My Lord, how could I feed Thee whereas Thou art the Lord of the worlds? He said: Didn't you know that such and such servant of Mine asked food from you but you did not feed him, and were you not aware that if you had fed him you would have found him by My side? (The Lord would again say:) O son of Adam, I asked drink from you but you did not provide Me. He would say: My Lord,

> *how could I provide Thee whereas Thou art the Lord of the worlds? Thereupon He would say: Such and such servant of Mine asked you for a drink but you did not provide him, and had you provided him drink you would have found him near Me.*[89]

Another similarity that comes close to citing the Gospels is the occurrence of the Lord's Prayer in a Ḥadīth reported in the collection of Abū Dawūd:

> *When any one is in suffering, or his brother suffers, then let him pray this prayer: 'Our Lord God who art in heaven, hallowed be Thy name. Thy kingdom is in heaven and on earth, and even as the mercy is in heaven, so may the mercy also be upon earth. Forgive us our debts and our sins, for Thou art the Lord of the good. Send down mercy from Thy mercy and healing from Thy healing for those suffering, that they may begin to heal.*[90]

As one can see, in this version God is not addressed as 'Our Father', but as 'Lord'. Similarities and differences between the Muslim and the Christian version of the Lord's Prayer may thus give rise to a number of theological questions between Christians and Muslims.

Similarities on the level of phrases and metaphors may also be noted, such as the use of *šahīd* in the sense of martyr, and expressions like 'salt in food' and 'pearls upon swine'.[91]

Similarities like those cited above may of course be interpreted in different ways – as theft or bad copies, or as the result of a creative dialogue with the Christian tradition. Some have seen in them a reflection of the open climate for dialogue in Syria and Damascus during the period of the early Ummayyads, who promoted a free intercourse between the followers of Islam and the Christians of their capital, even allowing Christians to visit mosques with the cross openly displayed on their breasts. As Guillaume puts it:

> In such an atmosphere of freedom and tolerance theological discussions have abounded. To this unhindered intercourse of Muslim and Christians theologians is due the similarity between many of the dogmas of Islam and Christianity. This, of course, was not the only channel through which Christian thought percolated to the Islamic mind; but it was one of the earliest, and one which has left a permanent mark on the thought and literature of Islam.[92]

The question of whether the sayings that show the most remarkable similarity to the Christian Gospels can rightly be attributed to the Prophet or should be understood as a result of later intercourse between the religions, has been much disputed also among Muslims, and can hardly be resolved. The remaining question is how to elaborate the significance of this phenomenon for Christian–Muslim dialogue.

A more structural approach, comparing literary genres in the biblical Gospels and in the Ḥadīth literature, is employed by Neal Robinson in a study of 'Varieties of Pronouncement Stories in *Ṣaḥīḥ Muslim*: A Gospel Genre in the Ḥadīth Literature' (Robinson 1994). By 'pronouncement story', Robinson (in line with New Testament scholarship) means 'brief self-contained narratives in the synoptic Gospels in which the main element is a pronouncement, or word of Jesus, bearing on some aspect of life, belief or conduct'.[93]

Having examined 150 such sayings in Muslim's Ḥadīth-collection, Robinson concludes:

> The Muhammad of *Ṣaḥīḥ Muslim* and the Jesus of the Gospels both correct and commend others, they both vindicate themselves in the face of objections, they are both approached by suppliants engaged in quests and they both answer inquiries. Finally, because they are both concerned with right belief and practice, description stories – which imply a detached philosophical attitude to life – are extremely rare in both literatures.[94]

In spite of these formal similarities, Robinson identifies major differences in the way the pronouncement stories reflect the basic religious outlooks, the degree of conflict reflected in the stories, and Muḥammad's and Jesus' understanding of authority.

The Understanding of 'Gospel' (Injīl)

When studying images of Christ in Islam, it should always be remembered that the issue is intertwined with the question of Christian and Muslim understandings of the term 'Gospel'.[95]

The qur'ānic word for Gospel, *injīl*, occurs 12 times in the Qur'ān. In 10 cases, the reference is to the revelation given to Jesus – corresponding to the prevailing Muslim perception that *injīl* refers to a 'book' given to Jesus for proclamation (compare 5.46, 57.27 with 19.30). In two cases, however (5.47, 7.157), the reference seems to be to the Scripture possessed and read by the Christians. Many would contend that the exhortation to Christians ('people of the Gospel') in 5.47 to judge by what God has revealed in the Gospel can only be understood as a reference to the actual Gospels known to be possessed by Christians.

Most probably, however, there were no Arabic translations of canonical or apocryphal Gospels available at the time of Muḥammad. In the perspective of historical influences, the knowledge of Gospel material reflected in the Qur'ān thus relies on oral transmission from Christians. As for the Ḥadīth material, a more direct knowledge of written Gospel material (biblical and apocryphal) can be detected.

Both in medieval and modern Muslim polemic, the view has been expressed that the Bible and the four Gospels have been corrupted by Jews and Christians (the doctrine of *taḥrīf*.[96] Polemicists in the twentieth century pursuing this line of argument have introduced the so-called Gospel of Barnabas as the authentic Gospel (see below, Chapter 7). Other Muslim historians and theologians hold the view that the scripture itself has not been tampered with, but only misinterpreted.

The famous Qur'ān translation and commentary of A. Yūsuf ʿAlī expresses the following view:

> The *Injīl* (Greek, Evangel = Gospel) spoken of by the Qur'ān is not the New Testament. It is not the four Gospels now received as canonical. It is the single Gospel which, Islam teaches, was revealed to Jesus, and which he taught. Fragments of it survive in the received canonical Gospels and in some others, of which traces survive (e.g. the Gospel of Childhood or the Nativity, the Gospel of St. Barnabas, etc.).[97]

Notwithstanding this critical view, Yūsuf ʿAlī asserts that:

> Muslims are . . . right in respecting the present Bible (New Testament and Old Testament), though they reject the peculiar doctrines taught by orthodox Christianity or Judaism.[98]

As we shall see, more positive evaluations of the biblical Gospels are found in some of the classical Muslim historians, in classical Shīʿite writings and in Ṣūfī mysticism. In modern times, some Egyptian authors of the mid-twentieth century in particular mark a new turn in their explicit reliance upon the biblical Gospels when writing about Christ (see Chapter 7, section 'Christ-biographies and -allegories').

Apart from the divergent views on the reliability of the biblical Gospels, it should be noted that according to most interpretations of Islam and Christianity, the notions of Holy Scripture are substantially different. R. C. Zaehner puts it this way:

> In Christianity . . . the Book depends on the Church as the Church depends on Christ who is the Word Incarnate: it is therefore strictly of tertiary importance. In Islam things are very different: it is the Book that is the Word of God . . ..[99]

From another perspective, the question arises about the positive theological significance of the fact that the Bible contains four different Gospels, all in the form of narratives. The polemical view held by many Muslims, that the Bible is unreliable because of its notorious 'contradictions', would be countered by many Christians with the argument that according to a Christian understanding, the main form of revelation is narrative. Those who point to the pre-eminence of revelation narrative in the Jewish-Christian Bible would not be embarrassed by the manifold humanity of the Scriptures, but rather regard plurality as recognition of the incapacity of human language to express the divine in unambiguous, declamatory terms.

Muḥammad and Jesus in Ḥadīth and Legend

We have seen that the 'placing' of Jesus in a correct relation to Muḥammad, his acting as a true Muslim in his second coming and his burial alongside Muḥammad, constitute the substantial part of the Ḥadīth material pertaining to Jesus.

As emphasized in the Introduction, the attempt to identify an Islamic Christology must never lose sight of the fact that it is Muḥammad, and not Christ, that is the central figure and the seal of the Prophets. Muḥammad integrates and fulfils in himself the function of prophethood, and the fact that Jesus is highly evaluated and even attributed with some specific qualities is in accordance with the view that there is a gradual evolution in prophethood towards a final, perfected revelation – through Muḥammad, the seal of prophethood.

Muslims consider Muḥammad to be 'the definitive Muslim' and the prototype of human perfection in all moral, social and political spheres. In Islamic piety, the veneration of the Prophet goes far beyond the confession of his being the mere vehicle of the qur'ānic revelation.[100] As we shall see, the veneration of Muḥammad is also highly developed in esoteric Ṣūfism, where he is seen not only as an embodiment of Perfect Man (*al-insān al-kāmil*), but also as a carrier of divine light (*nūr Muḥammadī*), and expression of divine attributes. There has also been the question of whether Muḥammad was sinless (his *ʿiṣma*), a status seemingly exclusively attributed to Jesus in Ḥadīth, and to all imāms in Shīʿite Islam. The doctrine of the Prophet's absolute impeccability came to prevail in wide circles.[101]

The central part of the development of a story-telling tradition in early Islam (see Chapter 3) is the making of a Muḥammad-legend. The process is also reflected within what came to be the recognized Ḥadīth collections, as well as in the Sıra (biography) of the Prophet.

For the purpose of popular piety and Ṣūfī *ḏikr* (recitation), devotional manuals were elaborated, in which the 201 names of Muḥammad (cf. the 99 most beautiful names of God) play a central part.[102]

A central part in the legend-making, though considered to be spurious by many Muslims, is the attribution of a number of miracles to the Prophet.[103] According to orthodox critics, this process tends to overshadow the Qur'ān as the one and decisive miracle confirming Muḥammad's prophethood.[104]

A prominent miracle reported in Ḥadīth, although not really in the category of being 'performed' by Muḥammad, is the Prophet's ascension to the heavens (his *miʿrāj*), transcending the limits of time and space. The miracles performed by Muḥammad according to Ḥadīth are most often of the type of 'nature miracles' – like the splitting of the moon for the Meccan unbelievers; the weeping of a palm tree when abandoned as pulpit in the Prophet's mosque; the flowing of water from his fingers; the raising of water in a dry well; and the increasing of the amount of dates in a garden after the Prophet had given his blessings. A kind of 'cursing miracle' is reported to have fallen upon a Christian who first converted from Christianity to Islam and then back again to Christianity. Because of his vicious calumny that 'Muḥammad knows nothing but what I have written for him', the earth refused to accept his dead body and repeatedly threw it up; and the witnesses said: 'This is the deed of Muḥammad and his companions'. Again there is an ambiguity in the reported miracle: is it performed by Muḥammad, or by Allāh, in honour of Muḥammad?

A convert from Christianity, ʿAlī Ibn Rabbān al-Ṭabarī (from the ninth century) who excelled in identifying biblical prophecies about Muḥammad (see Chapter 6), also attributes a large number of miracles to the Prophet. The list presented by the convert might have been produced in response to Christian arguments like those brought forward by John of Damascus, who refused to acknowledge Muḥammad as a prophet as long as no miracles were proved to have occurred through him.[105] It is also tempting to see the making of miracle-legends as a necessary development by the logic of popular piety, given the number of miracles attributed to Jesus and extolled in the Muslim story-telling tradition.

Given the centrality of Muḥammad as medium of the final divine revelation, and the subsequent veneration of his personality, it should be of no surprise that already in the formative period of Islam, traces can be seen of the view that his immediate predecessor among the Prophets, Jesus, had in fact foretold his coming.[106]

The theory that Jesus foretold a coming prophet, namely Muḥammad, is found already in the reported discussion that took place in Baghdad between the Caliph al-Mahdī and the Nestorian Catholicos Timothy about 781 (cf. Chapter 6, section 'Christian apologetics under Muslim rule'). Timothy is prepared to acknowledge that Muḥammad 'walked in the path of a prophet' although not being a prophet in the real sense, whereas the Caliph finds Muḥammad's prophethood foretold in Deut. 18.18, in Isaiah 21.7 as well as in the promises of a coming Paraclete in John. The latter claim is firmly refuted by Timothy.[107]

The Caliph, and later Muslims, take these and other biblical references as a confirmation of the general assertion of the Qur'ān that Muḥammad was foretold in the Torah and in the Gospel (7.157), and in Jesus' prophecy of the coming messenger Aḥmad (61.6), 'the praiseworthy' fulfilled in 'the praised one', Muḥammad.

The contemporary biographer of Muḥammad, Ibn Isḥāq (d. 768), does not take the qur'ānic Aḥmad as a proper name. Instead, he bases his argument on a translation of the Johannine *paraklētos* with the Syriac *manḥamannā*, which of course comes close to 'Muḥammad'. At some point the sound-alike of the Greek *paraklētos* with the Greek *periklutos* – meaning 'famous' or maybe 'praiseworthy' – was also included in the argument of some Muslim scholars.[108]

Later, even more examples of foretelling in the Bible were identified to strengthen the argument, amounting to 130 in the works of the above-mentioned Christian convert ʿAlī Ibn Rabbān al-Ṭabarī.[109]

Notes

1 Leirvik (2000).
2 Schedl (1978: 6), counts references in 15 out of 114 sūras, and in 93 out of 6339 verses.
3 As for Mary, see the study of Jane I. Smith and Yvonne Y. Haddad (1989).
4 Cf. Robinson (1991: 4–7), who gives a summary, and Cragg (1985a:18–25), for a full text in English. Quotations in English are following Cragg's translation, with references to the Cairo edition of the Qur'ān. Cf. also Hussain (1995: 101–136, text and comments) and Khoury (1996, in Arabic). Cf. Borrmans (1996: 19–45, in French). For a summary in Norwegian, see Leirvik (1990: 85–96).
5 Cf. Ayoub (1995).
6 Cf. Anawati (1978: 81) and Parrinder (1979: 30–54).
7 As for *kalima* in the Qur'ān, cf. the study of O'Shaughnessy (1948), *The Koranic Concept of the Word of God.*
8 Quoted from A. Guillaume, *The Life of Muhammad: A Translation of Ibn Ishaq's Sirat Rasul Allah*. Karachi: Oxford University Press (1996: 657).
9 See Schedl (1978) and Schumann (1978), and Leirvik (1990: 101–108).
10 For this kind of approach, cf. the concept of a 'New Testament theology' which presupposes that some general theological themes may be extracted from their different literary contexts, and presented thematically.
11 Zaehner (1977: 206–207).
12 Ibid., p. 209.
13 Cf. detailed studies of such sayings by other authors, such as Bishop (1941).
14 Merad (1980: 12).
15 For this methological approach, cf. the concept of at 'Literary criticism of the New Testament'.
16 See Robinson (1991) and Zahniser (1989), the latter summarising recent discussion.
17 See 'Exkurs', pp. 116–119.

18 Schedl, 'Das ICH ʿĪsā's steht . . . ganz und gar im Einklang mit dem ICH Allāh's' (1978: 558).
19 Ibid., p. 559: 'Was ein Mensch ist, wissen wir doch! ʿĪsā aber ist mehr! Dieses Mehr offenbart sich darin, dass das ICH und das ER Allāhs sowie das WIR der Engel [Schedl's understanding of the qur'ānic 'We'] in ihm wirksam wurden. Er selbst beugte sich derart unter diesen Anruf, dass nur 'Knecht Allāhs' als gültige Bezeichnung für ihn übrigblieb.'
20 See his *La Pensée Arabe*, Paris, 1979 and *Lectures du Coran*, Paris, 1982.
21 Cf. Robinson (1991: 35f.).
22 Zahniser (1991: 79).
23 Ibid., p. 108.
24 Ibid.
25 Cf. the methological approach of 'Redaction criticism of the New Testament'.
26 Räisänen (1980: 123).
27 Ibid., pp. 123f.
28 Ibid., pp. 126f.
29 Ibid., p. 127.
30 Räisänen (1971: 23f.), cf. Kuitse (1992: 357f.).
31 1971, pp. 31ff.
32 Ibid., p. 32.
33 Ibid., pp. 86–89.
34 Ibid., p. 8 – in my translation from German ('Die besondere Stellung Jesu besteht darin, dass er offenbar der nächste Vorgänger Muhammads ist, der seinen Auftritt vorausgesagt hat. Der koranische Jesus weist auf einen hin, der bedeutender und grösser ist als er selbst.')
35 Schedl (1978: 565).
36 Ibid., 329: 'In den Sog des Abwehrskampfes gegen die altarabischen Götter wurde nun auch ʿĪsā hineingerissen. Muhammad hat dadurch ein echt christliches Anliegen vertreten; denn Jesus ist nicht in die Reihe der arabischen oder griechischen Götter einzuordnen.'
37 'Seine eigentliche Grösse erreicht er aber dadurch, dass er sich selbst als *ʿabd-Allāh*, als Knecht Gottes, bekennt.' (ibid., p. 333).
38 Cf. Ayoub (1995).
39 Schedl (1978: 556): '. . . in Mekkah kämpfte er gegen die Götter, in Medinah gegen die christlichen Heiligen, die man nach seiner Auffassung, Gott als 'Söhne' zugestellte.'
40 For the following, see ibid., pp. 559ff.
41 Ibid., p. 562: 'Wirklich gekreuzigt wurde nur der sarkische, der körperhaft leibliche ʿĪsā, der pneumatisch-geistige Messias/Christus dagegen war den Händen der Schergen nicht greifbar und konnte daher gar nicht an das Kreuz geschlagen werden.'
42 Ibid.: 'Die Juden wollten den Knecht Allāhs am Kreuz vernichten, Allāh

hat aber seinen Knecht am Kreuz 'erhöht'. Damit treten Aspekte einer Knecht-Gottes-Christologie in Sicht, die dem urchristlichen Kerygma vom erhöhten Kyrios nicht allzu fern sein dürften.'

43 Risse (1989: 16ff.).

44 Ibid., p. 217.

45 In my translation from German, ibid., p. 217 – citing Räisänen (1971: 85): 'In dieser dogmatischen Auseinandersetzung geht es nicht etwa um die Sicherung der eigenen Stellung Mohammeds neben oder über Jesus. Der Horizont der 'Christologie' ist die 'Theologie' im engeren Sinne, die Lehre von Gott. Von einer strengen theozentrischen Konzeption aus fordert Mohammed unerbittlich, dass die Christen ihre tritheistischen Vorstellungen aufgeben und zum reinen Monotheismus Jesu und der früheren Gott-gesandten zurückkehren sollen.'

46 Cf. Räisänen (1971: 89). For a Muslim objection to this view, see Balić (1979: 3f.).

47 Robinson (1991: 40).

48 Robinson (1991: ch. 5).

49 Robinson (1991: ch. 15).

50 Robinson (1991: 15 ff.).

51 See Risse (1989: 183f.).

52 For an overview, see J. K. Elliot, *The Apocryphal Jesus: Legends of the Early Church*. Oxford: Oxford University Press (1996: 9–50).

53 See Risse (1989: 138–143), Parrinder (1979: 110) and Robinson (1991: 111).

54 The references are Apocalypse of Peter 81.15–24 and Great Seth 55.25–56.19. See James M. Robinson (ed.), *The Nag Hammadi Library*. San Francisco: HarperCollins (1990: 377 and 365).

55 See Robinson (1991: 110f. and 141).

56 See the chronological listing in Robinson (1991: 26–34) as well as the summaries in Borrmans (1996: 21–54) and in Schedl (1978: 325ff. and 556ff.).

57 Kuitse (1992: 358); cf. J. Bouman, *Gott und Mensch im Koran*. Darmstadt (1977: 42–44).

58 Cragg's expression; as the title of Chapter 5 in Cragg (1984).

59 The collection known as 'Forty Ḥadīth Qudsī' is attributed to al-Nawāwī (d. 1277).

60 For references, see also A. J. Wensinck, *A Handbook of Early Muhammadan Tradition*. Leiden: E. J. Brill (1960; keyword *ʿĪsā*).

61 Muslim, *Kitāb al-Faḍā'il*. Quoted from *Sahih Muslim*, transl. Mahmoud Matraji. Beyrouth: Dar el Fiker (1993: vol. IVa, p. 57, no. 2365R1).

62 Quoted from Robinson (1991: 81). A similar ḥadīth is found in the *Sunan* of Abū Dawūd, in his *Kitāb al-malāḥim*.

63 English translation by James Robson, *Miskat Al-Masabih: English*

translation with explanatory notes. Lahore: Sh. Muhammad Ashraf (1981/70).

64 Quoted from Robson, p. 1237.

65 Quoted from Robson, pp. 1159–60.

66 'Beginning of creation' and 'Merits of the helpers in Madinah'.

67 See Muslim, *Kitāb al-fitan* , cf. Saritoprak (2003: 293f.).

68 See Bukhārī, *Kitāb al-anbiyā*ʾ, and Muslim, *Kitāb al-īmān* and *Kitāb al-fitan*.

69 See J. K. Elliot, *The Apocryphal Jesus: Legends of the Early Church*. Oxford (1996: 57–59).

70 Quoted from *Sahih al-Boukhari*, transl. Mahmoud Matraji, Dar el Fiker, Beyrouth (1993: vol. IV, p. 279, no. 3448).

71 Quoted from *Sahih Muslim*, transl. Mahmoud Matraji. Beyrouth: Dar el Fiker (1993: vol. I, p. 105, no. 155R1).

72 See discussion in Alfred Guillaume, *The Traditions of Islam: An Introduction to the study of the Hadith Literature*. Oxford (1924: 72f.).

73 Quoted from Robinson (1991: 81).

74 As to the Mahdī in Sunnī and Shīʿite thought, see Ignaz Goldziher, *Introduction to Islamic Theology and Law*. Princeton (1981: 196–203).

75 See Ibn Kathīr, *The Signs Before the Day of Judgement*. Translated by Huda Khattab. London: Dar Al Taqwa Ltd. (1991: 20–24). (Selected and translated from Ibn Kathır's *Al-Bidāya wa-l-nihāya* ('The beginning and the end').

76 Ibn Kathīr, op. cit.

77 Ibid., p. 21.

78 Ibn as-Siddiq (1985: 20).

79 See the Republican Brothers 1981 (pamphlet).

80 Cf. M. M. Taha, *The second Message of Islam*. New York: Syracuse University Press (1987).

81 Bukhārī, *Kitāb al-anbiyā*ʾ. Quoted from *Sahih al-Boukhari*, transl. Mahmoud Matraji. Beyrouth: Dar el Fiker (1993: vol. IV, p. 272/541, no. 3431).

82 Muslim, *Kitāb al-faḍaʾil*. Quoted from *Sahih Muslim*, transl. Mahmoud Matraji. Beyrouth: Dar el Fiker (1993: vol. IVa, p. 58, no. 2366R2).

83 See ibid., no. 2368 and Note 1 of the translator: 'They have implied refererence to the fact that Jesus was a human being, though an eminent Prophet, and he was fully conscious of his being a member of the human race and on the basis of this awareness of his ownself he could not consider himself to be infallible'.

84 Quoted from *Sahih al-Boukhari*, transl. Mahmoud Matraji. Beyrouth: Dar el Fiker (1993: vol. IV, p. 274/545, no. 3435).

85 Quoted from ibid., p. 278/553 (no. 3445).

86 See Goldziher (1971) and Alfred Guillaume, *The Traditions of Islam* (1924), chapter VI: 'Borrowing from Christian documents and tradition', and the (polemical) listing of similarities in Zwemer (1912).

87 Quoted from *Sahih al-Boukhari*, transl. Mahmoud Matraji. Beyrouth: Dar el Fiker (1993: vol. III, p. 171/339, no. 2271, cf. no. 2268 and 2269).
88 Quoted from ibid.
89 Quoted from *Sahih Muslim*, transl. Mahmoud Matraji. Beyrouth: Dar el Fiker (1993: vol. IVa, p. 176, no. 2569).
90 Quoted from Zwemer (1912: 150).
91 Cf. Goldziher (1971: 350–356).
92 Alfred Guillaume, *The Traditions of Islam* (1924: 133).
93 Robinson (1994: 123).
94 Ibid., p. 143.
95 For the following, see de Vaux (1978), Parrinder (1979: 142–151) and Leirvik (1990: 80ff.).
96 Cf. Chapter 4 below, in the section 'Muslim polemical refutations and sympathetic reinterpretations in the medieval era'.
97 A. Yūsuf ʿAlı, *The Holy Qur'ān: Text, Translation and Commentary*. New Revised Edition, Amana Corporation, Brentwood Maryland (1989: 292).
98 Ibid.
99 Zaehner (1977: 199).
100 Cf. Annemarie Schimmel, *And Muhammad is his Messenger: The Veneration of the Prophet in Islamic Piety*. Chapel Hill, NC: University of North Carolina Press (1985) – and Michael Nazir-Ali, 'A Christian Assessment of the Cult of Prophet-Veneration', pp. 130–138 in Nazir-Ali (1987). Cf. Phipps (1996: 191–200).
101 See Schimmel, ibid. pp. 56ff.
102 Cf. Nazir-Ali (1987: 133–135). As for the names/appellations of Muḥammad, see R. Y. Ebied and M. B. J. Young, 'A List of the Appellations of the Prophet Muḥammad', *The Muslim World* (1976: 259–262), and Arne Rudvin, 'A Supplementary Note to "A List of the Appellations of the Prophet Muḥammad"', *The Muslim World* (1978: 57–60).
103 See Schimmel, ibid. ch. 4: 'Legends and miracles'.
104 Although al-Ghazālī, in his *Iḥyā' ʿulūm al-dīn*, at the end of ch. XXI about 'The character and conduct of the Prophet', states that he will only narrate a few of Muḥammad's miracles without prolonging it, he lists no less than 26 miracles, the far greatest, however, being the living miracle of the Qur'ān.
105 Cf. Watt (1991: 70).
106 Cf. Smith (1922) and Watt (1953).
107 English translation published by A. Mingana, *Woodbrooke studies*. Cambridge: Heffer (1928). See Newman (ed.) (1993: 190–196) and Gaudeul (1990: vol. I, pp. 236–238). Cf. Watt (1991: 33–34).
108 Guillaume (1996: 104, see note 8 above) cf. Watt (1991: 34f.).
109 See discussion of the various theories in Watt (1991: 33–37) and Parrinder (1979: 96–100).

Chapter 3

Jesus in Muslim Legend and Qur'ānic Exegesis

Jesus in Muslim Legend and Storytelling

By 'Muslim legend', we mean the early storytelling tradition from Wahb and onwards, and the widespread 'Stories of the Prophets' by Thaʿlabī and Tirmidhī (drawing on Wahb and others, as well as Christian sources). The historical as well as religious value of this story-telling tradition is disputed. Some would see the stories as 'designed to while away the evening hours, and at the same time serve a basis for discussion with other revealed religions'.[1] Stories of Jewish and Christian origin have, however, been told among Muslims from the beginnings of the Muslim community, and their impact on popular Islam has been considerable.

In contrast to the rich lore in classical collections of prophet stories, modern books on pre-Islamic prophets often rely solely on qur'ānic and sound Ḥadīth material.[2]

The classical Tafsīr exegesis of the Qur'ān draws on and discusses not only Ḥadīth material, but also Muslim legend and Christian sources.

Tarif Khalidi (1994) underlines the fact that Muslim lore about Jesus in many cases pre-dates the canonical Ḥadīth-material pertaining to Jesus.

> The popular Muslim Jesus . . . was the Jesus whose stories and sayings were enshrined in numerous works of *adab* [cultured manners], piety, *zuhd* [asceticism], *qiṣaṣ al-anbiyā'* [stories of the prophets] and Sufism.[3]

In the introduction to his critical edition of Jesus sayings in Islamic literature, he writes:

> The Jesus of the eschaton was enshrined in authoritative Hadīth collections, becoming a somewhat distant figure of no immediate or pragmatic moral relevance to Muslim piety. But another Jesus continued to prosper – the Jesus encountered in works of piety and asceticism and in a genre of religious literature called 'Tales of the Prophets' (*Qisas al-Anbiya*), where he

was not only a living moral force but also a figure who played a role in intra-Muslim polemics.[4]

Muslim lore about Jesus (amounting to around 500 pieces, according to Khalidi) has been collected and published by many scholars in the twentieth century.[5] But until Khalidi published his historical-critical edition of 303 sayings and stories related to Jesus in Islamic-Arabic literature, little had been done to investigate the historical origins of the various parts of this material, and their *isnād* (chain of transmitters).

Agrapha (Sayings), in Context

Among the vast amount of sayings ascribed to Jesus in Muslim tradition, many are known in similar forms from the New Testament or from non-canonical Christian sources. But quite a few are unknown from other sources. Could it be that some of these reflect an oral transmission of the sayings of Jesus in the eastern churches?

At the beginning of the twentieth century, during the first quest for 'the historical Jesus' in the West, there was considerable interest in the so-called *logia et agrapha* attributed to Jesus by Muslim writers, Margoliouth's collection from 1893–1894 being the first to be published.[6] In the most scientific study from this period, Michaël Asin y Palacios, Professor of Arabic at Madrid University, examined 103 sayings attributed to Jesus in al-Ghazālī's famous work *Iḥyāʾ ʿulūm al-dīn* ('The Revival of the Religious Sciences'), and 122 passages in Arabic and Latin from other Muslims writers (Asin et Palacios 1917, 1926). He defines *agrapha* as sayings attributed to Jesus, further qualified as sayings that with reasonable probability may be deemed to be pre-Islamic. He holds the view that some genuine fragments may have survived, and gives some criteria for identifying the more reliable.

Then in 2001, the Lebanese scholar Tarif Khalidi published a critical edition of 303 sayings and stories attributed to Jesus by Muslim collectors, from the early ascetic works of ʿAbdallāh ibn al-Mubārak (d. 797) and Aḥmad Ibn Ḥanbal (d. 855) who both wrote a book on asceticism (*Kitāb al-zuhd*), through the *adab* books on ethical behaviour and good manners of Abū ʿUthmān al-Jāḥiẓ (d. 868), ʿAbdallāh ibn Qutayba (d. 884) and Abū Bakr ibn Abī al-Dunya (d. 894), to well-known writers with Ṣūfī or Shīʿite inclination from the tenth to the twelfth century and the towering figure of al-Ghazālī (d. 1111).

In his historical-critical investigation of these sayings, Khalidi finds a marked difference between the early ascetic references, the *adab*-style sayings, and sayings that bear the mark of Ṣūfī tradition – indicating thus some important contexts for these sayings. Across different contexts, Khalidi finds that Jesus – by virtue of sayings attributed to him – played 'a role of considerable importance in formulating or fortifying certain Muslim definitions of piety, religious responsibility, and attitudes to government'.[7]

Many of the sayings are known only from Muslim tradition. But a good number of them reveal also familiarity with the biblical gospels. In particular, one finds many features from the Sermon on the Mount and other parts of the Gospel of Matthew (for instance, Jesus' warnings against the Scribes and the Pharisees in Matthew 23).

In the earliest references, Jesus stands out as 'a patron saint of Muslim asceticism', with an uncompromising renunciation of the world, strong identification with the poor and recurrent admonitions to poverty, humility, silence and patience:[8]

> *Jesus said, 'There are four [qualities] which are not found in one person without causing wonder: silence, which is the beginning of worship; humility before God; an ascetic attitude toward the world; and poverty'.*[9]

Many of the other sayings have a similar ascetic flavour, warning against the dangers of riches and worldly desire (cf. several examples cited below, in the section about al-Ghazālī in Chapter 5). In some sayings, one can also find features that might seem to be at variance with the dominant Muslim ethos, for instance markedly anti-marriage sentiments against taking a wife, begetting children and building a house.[10] In several cases, Khalidi find parallel motifs in Christian monasticism, for instance in the writings of the Egyptian desert fathers.

If one moves on to the layer which Khalidi characterizes as more tempered *adab* literature (from the ninth century), Khalidi finds that Jesus becomes here 'more like a Muslim Adib (a gentleman scholar, a sage), and loses some of his fierce asceticism. An example of this genre, cited by the *adab* pioneer al-Jāḥiẓ (d. 868), illustrates the preoccupation with inner disposition and refinement:

> *Christ passed by a group of Israelites who insulted him. Every time they spoke a word of evil, Christ answered with good. Simon the pure said to him, 'Will you answer them with good each time they speak evil?' Christ said, 'Each person spends of what he owns'.*[11]

Jesus' critical distance to the world, however, is maintained also in more tempered types of literature. An example is the well-known saying about life as a bridge, which can be found in the collections of Ibn Qutayba (d. 884) and is cited twice by al-Ghazālī. The saying was also found in 1849 on the gateway of the sixteenth century mosque of Futtehpore-Sikri, near Agra in India:

> *The world is a bridge. Cross this bridge but do not build upon it.*[12]

Another peculiar feature of the Muslim Jesus sayings is his care for the animals, and his ability to communicate with them. Perhaps the most well-known example of this genre is the story of Jesus and the dead dog. When Jesus passed by the carcass of a dog, 'The disciples said: How foul is this stench. Jesus said: 'How white are his teeth!'[13]

In the same vein, one finds also Muslim traditions about Jesus showing mercy to a cow which was calving in great distress, and saying 'pass in peace' to a pig.[14] In the cases of the dog and the pig, Jesus breaks also Muslim taboos of distasteful or unclean animals. Such stories are paralleled by Christian apocryphal stories revealing Jesus' care and respect for animals.

Khalidi summarizes the central themes of the Jesus sayings and stories from different layers in this way: 'First we have the ascetic saint; then comes the lord of nature, the miracle worker, the healer, the social and ethical model.'[15] Khalidi also notes that Jesus is increasingly referred to by Ṣūfī writers as Muslim knowledge about Christian sources increases (see Chapter 5):

> The Jesus of Islamic Sufism became a figure not easily distinguished from the Jesus of the Gospels, and one reason must undoubtedly have been the growing familiarity with the Gospels among Muslim scholars.[16]

In general, it is impossible to reach a definite conclusion as to the origin and authenticity of the ascetic, *adab*-type and mystical sayings attributed to Jesus. The most rewarding approach would probably be to study their function in the development of Muslim theology, and their place in early Christian–Muslim dialogue. As in biblical scholarship, a reductionist 'form criticism' is of limited value, over against the actual function of Jesus-logia in the writings of Islamic theologians and in the popular piety of Islam.

In later chapters, we will return to a number of these sayings and stories – in the different contexts of the storytelling tradition, Ṣūfism, Shīʿite Islam and al-Ghazālī's works.

The Storytelling Tradition, from Wahb to the 'Stories of the Prophets'

The most prominent storyteller known from the early years in Arabia is Wahb b. Munabbih (b. 696), who has always been celebrated by later writers as an authority on the traditions of the People of the Book. His knowledge must have come from extensive intellectual exchange with learned Jews and Christians. In the later 'Stories of the Prophets', as well as in the classical exegesis and in the biographies of Muḥammad, he is often referred to. Another source of Muslim lore attributed to Jesus – of the more ascetic kind – is *Kitāb al-zuhd* by Aḥmad Ibn Ḥanbal (d. 865) and similar books on asceticism and piety from the ninth century.[17]

Qiṣaṣ al-anbiyā', 'Stories of the Prophets', is the title of widespread books relating to the lives of pre-Islamic prophets and heroes, and emerging in the eleventh century. There are well-known and much used collections of such stories in Arabic, Persian, Turkish, Urdu and Malay. The most famous is that of Abū Isḥāq Aḥmad ibn Muḥammad al-Thaʿlabī (d. 1036). The section on Jesus in Thalabī's *Qiṣaṣ* is easily accessible through Arthur Jeffery's translation in *A Reader in Islam*.[18] Another famous collection is the tales of the Prophets of Muḥammad ibn ʿAbd Allāh al-Kisā'ī.[19] David Pinault (1987) has noted that 'al-Kisā'ī tended to be sensationalistic and anecdotal, and portrayed Jesus especially as a wonder-worker; whereas al-Thaʿlabī gives more of a moral tone to his stories about Christ . . .'.[20]

Both of the narrators, however, focus mainly and broadly on miracle stories. They borrow extensively from Christian sources, and the qur'ānic material is dramatized for maximum effect.

The *Qiṣaṣ* have played an important role in shaping the Jesus image among ordinary Muslims. According to those acquainted with the Persian tradition, prophet stories have been told by pious mothers to their children all the way up to the twentieth century, in an independent chain of transmission paralleling the religious education of the mullahs. The enormous emphasis on the miracles of Jesus in the *Qiṣaṣ* may also be reflected in the widespread image of Jesus as healer in Indo-Pakistani Islam. It would be a theme for further investigation to what extent the Muslim legendary material about Jesus (based mostly on Christian legends!) is really alive in the minds of ordinary Muslims of today, and in which parts of the Muslim world.

From a historical perspective, the question would be whether Muslim legend reflects legendary material about Christ originated in the Christian tradition. The loans in *Qiṣaṣ* from infancy Gospels and other Christian apocrypha are obvious. To what extent were these legends alive in early medieval Christianity (Eastern and Western)? Should medieval Muslim lore be regarded as reflections of contemporary Christian legend, or would it rather have been based on mainly literary loans from older Christian sources?

The section regarding Jesus in Thaʿlabī's *Qiṣaṣ* will be summarized in some detail below. Thaʿlabī's *Qiṣaṣ* probably give a representative picture of the Muslim image of Jesus as it developed after the formative years of Islam and was reflected in Muslim Tafsīr and theology, in Muslim polemics against Christians and in popular piety. However, it should be noted that the amount of Muslim legendary material is overwhelming, and the *Qiṣaṣ* of Thaʿlabī constitute a relatively sober example of the stories of Jesus and Mary in Muslim tradition. In other *qiṣaṣ* like that of al-Kisā'ī and in more fairy tale-like collections, the imagination seems to have no limits.[21]

Summary of the Jesus Material in Thaʿlabī's Qiṣaṣ

The main focuses in the *Qiṣaṣ*-genre as regards Jesus are as follows:

1. Mary's pregnancy, the birth of Jesus and the flight to Egypt.
2. The infancy miracles of Jesus.
3. The disciples of Jesus.
4. The virtues of the adult Jesus, again with an emphasis on his miracles.
5. The end of his life, and his descent from heaven seven days after he had been raised up.
6. The death of Mary, and 'the king of Rome'.
7. The second descent of Jesus, in the last days.

In Thaʿlabī's *Qiṣaṣ*, Joseph plays a role as Mary's cousin. Together they are responsible for keeping the sanctuary clean. The appearance of Gabriel to Mary, and the 'how' of the announced conception, is dealt with at length. There is a mention of how Gabriel breathed into the neck of her chemise, which she had put off from her. Joseph is convinced of her chastity only after a lengthy theological discussion about Allāh's power of creation. But her people were not convinced, and Mary and Joseph had to flee towards the land of Egypt before Mary could give birth to Jesus. A story is included about how Iblīs (Satan) was alarmed by his devils who told him that all the idols of the earth were turned upside down at the hour of Jesus' birth. Iblīs sets out to destroy him, for 'never was there a Prophet more dangerous to you and to me than this one who is just born'. But Iblīs is obstructed by the angels, and he is not able to touch Jesus (cf. Ḥadīth). The visit of the three men guided by a star is then reported, and their gifts are explained. When Mary returns to her people, she is in danger of being stoned for adultery, but when the child speaks from the cradle (cf. the Qur'ān) they all leave her. 'It is said that he did not speak again after that until he was of the age of other children. But Allāh knows best'. Then the flight from Herod to Egypt is related, as well as the stay in Egypt for 12 years.

During the stay in Egypt, a series of infancy miracles are reported (cf. the apocryphal infancy Gospels of the Christian tradition). Nine-month old Jesus explains the fundamentals of the Muslim creed to a school-master. An insertion follows with a summary of Jesus' exterior qualities (cf. Ḥadīth), his miracles and his ascetic way of life. Then more infancy miracles are reported, 'from his childhood to his becoming a prophet':

- The revealing of some beggar thieves for a wealthy chief.
- The making of drink in empty jars, for the same chief.
- The revealing of what the parents of some boys he was playing with were eating at home (cf. the Qur'ān), and the subsequent rather harsh miracle of turning the boys to pigs when their parents accuse Jesus of

sorcery and refuse to allow their sons to play with him (cf. similar stories in apocryphal infancy gospels).[22]

- The miraculous provision of food and wine which had to be delivered to the tyrant king by a poor client, and the subsequent raising of a dead young man to convince the king of his powers.
- The raising of a child killed accidentally while playing to confirm the innocence of Jesus, after he had been accused of the killing.
- The miracle of garments being dyed different colours in a single vat.[23]

Furthermore, the *Qiṣaṣ* of Thaʿlabī report his fabulous mastery of learning in his youth. At 30 years of age, Allāh speaks to him by revelation, summarizing his mission as follows: 'When he was thirty years of age Allah spoke to him by revelation, [telling] him that he should come forth to the people and summon them to Allah, speaking to them in parables, curing the sick and the infirm, the blind and the mad, taming the devils, rebuking them and humbling them, so that they used to die for fear of him. He did what Allah commanded him, so the people loved him and inclined towards him as they got accustomed to him, so that his followers increased and his fame grew great'.[24]

Then is reported how he used to heal the sick by prayer alone, on the condition of faith, and a prayer by which he used to heal the sick and raise to life the dead is extensively cited.

His calling of disciples is reported, and how he miraculously provided them with food and drink.

Thaʿlabī then goes on reporting the miracles performed by Jesus after his calling, introducing them with a reflection on the meaning of the qur'ānic expression 'We aided him with Holy Spirit'. The first miracle is Allāh's teaching him the *injīl* and the *tawrāh*, which he used to recite from memory.

The qur'ānic miracle of creating a bird from clay is reported and discussed. According to Thaʿlabı, it was a bat, and it only flew as long as people were looking at it, to mark the distinction between the work of a creature and that of Allāh.

Two other miracles reported by the Qur'ān – his healing of those born blind and of the lepers – are referred to and explained. According to Thaʿlabī, the reason why these two diseases were selected was because they were beyond medical help. 'Medicine was the thing in which men excelled in the days of Jesus, so he caused them to see a miracle of this kind.'

His ability to give life to the dead, also emphasized by the Qur'ān, is then illustrated at great length. Three of the miracles reported must be regarded as versions of corresponding New Testament stories: the raising of Lazarus, of the old woman's son, and of the daughter of a collector of tithes. Then follow two miracles of quite a different kind: the raising of Shem (the son of Noah) at the request of the disciples, in order to 'give life' to his narration of the Noah story, and the raising of Ezra, to testify to his opponents that Jesus is the servant of

Allāh. Underlying these miracles is the concept that 'earth does not devour the bodies of the Prophets'.

The qur'ānic reference to his clairvoyant ability is discussed, and given the deeper meaning of 'knowledge of the unseen (*al-ġayb*)'. His walking on the water is also reported. The reason why his 'short friend' was sinking when trying to imitate him was not his fear (as in Matthew 14) but his pride. A word of Muḥammad relativizing the miracle is reported: if Jesus had exercized more faith and fear he could even have walked on air.

Then the long and detailed story of Jesus and a greedy Jew, who would not share his bread with Jesus, is related. This popular story in Muslim tradition, a version of which is first found in Abū Bakr ibn Abī al-Dunya's (d. 894) large collection of Jesus stories and sayings,[25] is a narrative wonder of itself, with a lot of humour. In this story, a number of miracles are performed by Jesus, to convince the Jew that he should repent and tell the truth about the third loaf he had refused to share. The following miracles are included: the healing of a blind man and a lame man, the bringing back to life of a gazelle and a calf they had been eating, and the raising of a dead king whom the Jew had unsuccessfully tried to heal. The Jew is saved from crucifixion by Jesus' intervention, but still does not admit his deceit. He only confesses when Jesus proposes to divide three blocks of gold between the Jew and 'he who ate the third loaf'. When he confesses, ready to collect his two blocks of gold, Jesus also gives him his own block, but with the warning: 'Leave it, for verily there are people who die because of it.' In this version of the story, the Jew really leaves the gold, whereupon three men get hold of it and subsequently all kill each other. Jesus, when passing by the dead men, comments: 'There is no god but Allāh. This is what the world does to its people.' However, he raises them to life by the permission of Allāh, and they all repent. But the Jew can no longer resist the temptation, and Jesus gives him the gold with the words: 'Take it for yourself. It will be your portion in this world and in the next.' When, however, the Jew went to carry it away 'the earth sank with him', and swallowed the Jew with all his wealth.[26]

In a fascinating way this story combines two recurrent motifs in all Muslim legend about Jesus: his magic and his asceticism. The victim of this Muslim fascination for Jesus is, however, 'the greedy Jew'.

Among the miracles mentioned in the Qur'ān is also the descent of the table. When discussed in the *Qiṣaṣ*, it is connected with the multiplication of fishes and loaves known from the New Testament. In accordance with the threats in the Qur'ān, those who disbelieve in the miracle are punished – and metamorphosed into apes and pigs. In one of the expositions of the miracle, Jesus is even told to bring a fish back to life again, to be eaten anew with healing effects. The qur'ānic miracle of the table is dealt with at great length. One of the emphases is the favouring of the poor, and in a rather grotesque scene a number of rich men are also metamorphosed into pigs before dying because of their disbelief.

As can be seen from the summary above, the starting point for the miracle stories of the *Qiṣaṣ* is the kind of miracles referred to in the Qur'ān. In the *Qiṣaṣ* and in Muslim storytelling in general, the miracles are so to say revitalized as lively stories, developed from the mere mention of them in the Qur'ān. In this process, elements from the New Testament are brought in, as well as non-canonical Christian tradition, and legends of unknown origin. The general tendency seems to be emphasizing of Jesus as magician – from the cradle to his mature age. The magic emphasis in later Muslim legend also includes some crude examples of cursing alien to the New Testament, but, as noted above, these features are partly paralleled in the apocryphal infancy gospels.

Along with this magic inclination there is an emphasis on his ascetic character, and mention is made of various characteristics that contribute towards the image of Jesus as a holy man. In some contrast to the friend of sinners and tax collectors known from the New Testament Gospels, it is said in the *Qiṣaṣ* that Jesus did not follow worthless fellows, and he is depicted as a man detached from worldly joy and sorrow. He did not laugh loudly, nor busy himself with trifles. As a warning against worldly lust, a young woman who is mourned by her husband and brought back to life by Jesus, falls dead again after having left her old husband for a young prince.

Then the *Qiṣaṣ* go on to discuss Jesus' ascent to heaven and how his life was ended. Various stories are reported. In one of these, after having cursed his opponents and invoked Allāh's anger on them, Jesus is himself rescued from the anger of the Jews and taken to Allāh through a window-niche. A likeness is cast on a deceitful companion, and he is crucified instead of Jesus. With reference to Wahb, many details from the passion story of the New Testament Gospels are referred to in a somewhat altered fashion, i.e. the washing of the hands of the disciples as a symbol of humility and sacrifice, the disciples falling asleep, the denial of Simon and the betrayal of Judas. In this version, the likeness of Jesus is explicitly said to be cast upon Judas, and he is crucified in the place of Jesus. With reference to the qur'ānic expression in 3.55, it is said that Jesus himself was caused to die by Allāh for three hours, before he was raised to heaven. According to other theories of substitution reported in the *Qiṣaṣ*, the likeness of Jesus is cast either on his jailer, or on a voluntary friend of Jesus.

To explain how his followers were comforted after his appearance, traditions are related about his appearance to the mourning women 'after seven days in heaven'. He appears to his mother, and to Mary Magdalene on a mountain blazing with light. Mary Magdalene is identified with the bleeding woman known from the New Testament Gospels. Significantly, in this Muslim tradition she is depicted as a pious Israelite, 'cleansed and purified' by Jesus from her constant menstruation. Mary Magdalene gathers the disciples, who are sent out where Jesus had bidden each of them to go, enabled to speak the language of the respective countries. Interestingly enough, there is a clear emphasis on Muslim lands in the sending instructions reported.

At a later stage, the 'king of Rome, who was an idolator', is said to have saved the disciples from the persecution of the Jews. He accepts the religion of Jesus.

The report on Jesus' life is concluded by a reference to the death of his mother 'six years after his ascension'. Mary and John had to flee from the king of Rome when Simon and Andrew were ordered to be crucified upside down, and the earth swallowed their searchers. The king of Rome, recognizing that this was an affair from Allāh, then asked about Jesus, 'and he became a Muslim, as we have related'. 'So says Wahb' – 'but Allāh knows best.'

The last chapter about Jesus in Thalaʿbī's *Qiṣaṣ* deals with his descent a second time in the last days. It is not only the passage that calls him 'a sign of the Hour' that is seen as a qur'ānic reference to his descent, but also the statement that he shall speak to men 'as a grown man' (*kahlan*, 3.46), since he did not reach the age of *kahl* (considered to be 40 years) during his first appearance. The Ḥadīth material concerning his descent is summarized, with even stronger emphasis on his Muslim piety. 'He will make war on behalf of Islam, and there will be thence forward but one single prostration of obeisance.' The tradition of his being buried beside Muḥammad is mentioned, and the whole chapter is concluded by the words of Muḥammad (according to a disputed Ḥadīth, cf. Chapter 2): 'How can Allāh destroy a community at whose beginning I am, at whose end is Jesus, and in the middle of which is the Mahdī of the people of my house?'

Jesus in Muslim Perceptions of World History

According to W. M. Watt, 'by the time of the second or third generation of Muslims there were demands for fuller descriptions of the various events and incidents' in past religious history.[27] The Qur'ān, as Watt notes, only refers to the pre-Islamic times and prophets in an allusive way. Given the fact that there was little understanding of history as a process in time in pre-Islamic Arabia, it is probable that the first Muslims would have had some difficulties in relating the various prophets to each other in time. The popular storytellers referred to above met some of this demand for a fuller version of the history of prophets. Ibn Isḥāq's biography of Muḥammad also contained a fuller presentation of the history of prophets (in the lost '*Kitāb al-mubtada*', 'The Book of the Beginnings').

Ibn Isḥāq (as known from citations by the historian al-Ṭabarī and others) does not seem to have had a great deal to tell about Jesus and Mary in his 'Beginnings'. But he adds to the qur'ānic report that the birth of Jesus took place at Bethlehem, and beside the palm tree there was a manger. A man called Sergius is said to have taken the place of Jesus on the cross, and the tomb of Jesus is recorded to have been found in Medina.[28]

In the historical work of al-Yaʿqūbī (a moderate Shīʿite, d. after 891), the author reveals an extensive knowledge of New Testament material.[29] Whereas al-Ṭabarī based his description of Jesus on the Qur'ān and Christian apocryphal tradition and lore, al-Ya'qūbī seems to draw directly from an early Arabic translation of the New Testament Gospels.[30] Each of the Gospels is summarized, including a quotation of the Johannine prologue (John 1.1–18), and an almost literal summary of the Sermon on the Mount including the prohibition against retaliation as well as the duties of 'the second mile' and non-resistance. Differences between the Gospels are commented upon. The passion narrative, the crucifixion itself and the appearances of Jesus afterwards, are also referred to. Al-Ya'qūbī contrasts this with the qur'ānic account, but passes no judgement. D.S. Donaldson comments:

> If Muhammad could have learned as much about the Four Gospels and the Acts of the Apostles in the beginning of the seventh century as al-Ya'qūbī learned in the latter half of the ninth century, what a vast difference there might have been in world history.[31]

The first Muslim known to have produced a fuller 'world history', also including some political history of the Near East, is the Annales (*Aḫbār al-rusūl wa-l-mulūk*) of al-Ṭabarī (d. 923).[32] In the relatively short section about Mary and Jesus, al-Ṭabarī concentrates on Jesus' birth and his final days. In his version of the birth, he adds some further elements from the New Testament like the existence of a man called Joseph, the envoys from Persia, Herod's plot and the flight to Egypt. Al-Ṭabarī also refers to the tradition of the idols being toppled when Jesus was born and the dismay of Satan at the birth of Jesus.

The close in time work of al-Mas'ūdī (d. 956), 'The Meadows of Gold' (*Murūj al-ḏahab*), reveals a rather extensive knowledge of the biblical Gospels, as well as other Christian sources.[33] He refers to Jesus' birth on 24 December, his calling of the four evangelists as disciples, his baptism, his miracles and his passion. He refers to 'a long discourse about the Christ and Mary and Joseph the carpenter' in the (Christian) Gospel, but deliberately leaves this aside, since neither the Qur'ān nor Muḥammad have spoken of it. Most interesting is his note that the young Jesus – while studying in a synagogue – found 'traced in characters of light' the words 'You are my son and my beloved; I have chosen you for myself', with Jesus himself subsequently claiming that 'today the word of God is fulfilled in the son of Man'.[34] Al-Mas'ūdī also presents material pertaining to the Apostles and the development of Christian tradition, referring to his own research in this field.

The historian al-Bīrūnī (d. 1048), who is most famous for his writings on Indian religion, also reveals extensive knowledge of the Gospels, regarding the four Gospels as four versions which he compares to the three versions of the Bible as had by Jews, Christians and Samaritans.[35] However, he does not trust the four Gospels, and regards them as having been corrupted by the Christians.

At a later stage, Ibn al-Athīr (1160–1233), in his 'The Perfection of History' (*Al-kāmil fī-l-tārīḫ*) which became a standard work for later Muslim scholars, gives a more prominent place to Joseph than his predecessors did, but speaks of him as a relative of Mary. He refers to some of the miracle stories of the boy Jesus. As to the passion story, he holds the view that it was Judas that was substituted for Jesus on the cross.[36]

In 1996, a newly discovered biography of Jesus which is part of Ibn ʿAsākir's 'History of Damascus' (*Tārīḫ madīnat Dimašq*), was published (Mourad 1996a, 1996b). Ibn ʿAsākir lived in Damascus from 1105 to 1176, and was known as the most knowledgeable Muslim scholar in the Syria of his time. The reasons why he included a large section on Jesus in his history of Damascus were two: First, the place where Mary 'took refuge' with the child Jesus (Qur'ān 23.50), is said in one Tafsīr to have been Damascus. Secondly, according to a tradition, Jesus is to be resurrected in Damascus on the last day.[37] Ibn ʿAsākir includes material both from the Qur'ān and Ḥadīth, material derived from the Bible (but mostly altered), and material from Muslim lore and legend. Incidentally, he locates Jesus in the fourth century BC, or 933 years before the Hijra.

According to Mourad, Ibn ʿAsākir portrays Jesus in a manner completely different from that of the Gospels – as:

> . . . an ascetic (*zāhid*) who avoided all the pleasures of life, and particularly the company of women, whom he classified in the same category as the *šayātīn*, or devils, and who enjoined his followers to abandon the world and its temptations, and seek the ultimate goal of the *āḫira*, or hereafter.[38]

As Ibn ʿAsākir puts it:

> *Jesus son of Mary ate barley, walked on foot and did not ride donkeys. He did not live in a house, nor did he use lamps for light. He neither dressed in cotton, nor touched women, nor used perfume . . . He had no concern for lunch or dinner, and desired nothing of the world. He used to consort with the weak, the chronically sick and the poor . . . Of food, he ate little, saying: '[Even] this is too much for one who has to die and answer for his deeds'.*[39]

As for the relationship between Jesus and Muḥammad, Ibn ʿAsākir cites an otherwise unknown Ḥadīth. Here, the confession of Jesus is added to the *šahāda* (the basic Islamic credo), after the assertion that there is no god but God and that Muḥammad is His messenger, and before the confession that Heaven and Hell is a reality 'and that Jesus is the servant of God and His messenger and the son of His servant [Mary], and [also] His word which He gave to Mary, and a Spirit from Him . . .'.[40]

When it comes to the resurrection (*al-qiyāma*) of Jesus, ibn ʿAsākir takes this to mean the expected *qiyāma* of Jesus in Damascus. One of the principal tasks of the resurrected is said to be fighting for Islam. Mourad makes a contextual comment: 'Writing at the time of the Crusades, what Ibn ʿAsākir had in mind was an imminent *qiyāma* of Jesus in Damascus to lead the Muslim Holy War against the Crusaders.'[41]

The other contextual comment made by Mourad regards the portrayal of Jesus as a model ascetic. Mourad suggests that:

> [. . .] the Ṣūfī movement, which was rapidly gaining ascendancy in Islam by the eleventh and twelfth centuries AD, needed some prophetic authority on which to base its ascetic precepts . . .. To the Ṣūfīs, Muḥammad . . . did not seem to recommend himself as a model of *zuhd*. So the role for the ideal *zāhid* had to be transferred to some other prophet, and the one chosen – originally, perhaps, by popular Ṣūfī opinion – was Jesus.[42]

Questions of Christian Influences

As can be seen, the making of a Jesus legend within Islam relies heavily on the knowledge of Christian sources emerging from contact with the Christian heartland after the expansion of Islam. In the Qur'ān and in the sound Ḥadīth, there is obvious influence from the non-canonical ('heretical') Christianity prevailing in the Arab peninsula and in Abyssinia. At a later stage of Muslim expansion, more canonical Gospel material is included in Muslim legend. But it is reshaped not only in accordance with Muslim theology, but also with the ascetic and magic emphases known from the early stages of Christian–Muslim contact. In the Muslim reshaping, the absence of the teachings of Jesus is remarkable. What is portrayed, is the ascetic magician, aided by the Holy Spirit, whereas the Gospel (understood as a book to be preached) is only referred to.

In contrast, it is precisely the sayings and teaching of Jesus that are given pre-eminence in the Ḥadīth-collections of Shīʿite Islam, and in Ṣūfī representations of Jesus.

As we have seen, the question of Christian influences is also pressing when it comes to the subject of Islamic eschatology, and the making of a Muḥammad legend in early Islam, as noted in Chapter 2.

Classical Exegesis of the Qur'ān (Tafsīr)

In the 1980s and '90s, several studies of the representation of Jesus in Muslim exegesis (Tafsīr) were published. These include two shorter studies by Mahmoud Ayoub, writing from a Muslim perspective and focusing on Jesus' death and Jesus' contested sonship respectively (Ayoub 1980, 1995), and a more comprehensive work by Neal Robinson, focusing the four themes of the return, death, life-giving ability and virginal conception of Jesus (Robinson 1991).[43]

In his 'Study of the Death of Jesus in Tafsīr Literature', Ayoub describes the deeper meaning of Tafsīr as fulfilling the purpose of qur'ānic guidance to humankind by allowing it to 'speak to the situation of the community of its receivers at every stage of its earthly existence. This the Qur'ān has done in large measure through tafsīr, or the science of qur'ānic exegesis'.[44] He identifies three stages in the history of Tafsīr:

1. The classical tradition, represented above all by the monumental commentary of al-Ṭabarī (d. 923).[45]
2. The second stage, showing a greater interest in a historical critique as well as a greater awareness of Christian views; represented by:
   - the polemical approach of Ibn Kathīr (d. 1373),
   - the analytical approach of al-Rāzī (d. 1209), and
   - the eirenic, spiritual and universalising interpretation of the Ṣūfīs.[46]
3. The modern period, beginning in the late nineteenth century with modernist reformers like Muḥammad ʿAbduh.

Shīʿite commentators have a distinctive approach at many points, and are given special consideration both by Ayoub and by Robinson.[47]

The commentaries dealt with in length by Robinson include that of the historian al-Ṭabarī (Baghdad, d. 923, i.e. from the 'classical' period), and those of al-Zamakhsharī (d. 1144), al-Rāzī (Persia/Herat, d. 1209), al-Bayḍāwī (d. around 1300) and Ibn Kathīr (Damascus, d. 1373) from the later developments of Tafsīr. Robinson also examines the Ṣūfī commentaries of al-Qushayrī (d. 1072)[48] and al-Qāshānī (d. 1329).

Robinson reminds the reader that from al-Ṭabarī to Ibn Kathīr, a significant development in exegetical method can be identified. Al-Ṭabarī is very open in his approach, drawing on a variety of 'canonical', legendary and Christian material in his interpretation. In contrast, Ibn Kathīr establishes methodical criteria for valid interpretation. He gives primacy to the interpretation of the Qur'ān by the Qur'ān itself; secondly, the Sunna of the Prophet should be considered; third, the sayings of the Companions. These are the only sound sources according to Ibn Kathīr. Material derived from the Successors, and reports from the People of the Book can at best be given the status of supplementary attestation, assuming that they support the sound sources.[49]

The Demise of Jesus and the Substitutionist Theory

As to the expression *šubbiha la-hum* in 4.157, the commentaries reveal substantial interest in the substitutionist theory inherited from the Muslim storytelling tradition and its early Christian (Docetic) parallels. The theory is presented in different versions, the likeness of Jesus being cast either upon all the disciples resulting in an accidental substitution, or upon a willing disciple ('voluntary substitution'), or upon one of the jailers or Judas ('punishment substitution').

Ayoub presupposes that the idea of a voluntary substitution is chronologically earlier than that of the punishment substitution, the latter representing a later theological reflection. Part of this process is a gradual inclusion of Gospel material, and an increase in interest in historical accounts.

Robinson (following Louis Massignon) suggests that the idea of substitution might have been catalysed by Shīʿite speculation.[50] The idea of a voluntary substitution is said to be supported in a saying of the fifth imām.[51]

Ayoub thinks that the objection to the substitutionist idea might be found in Muʿtazilite teaching, according to which God could not possibly commit acts of injustice.

Among the later commentaries, al-Zamakhsharī discusses mainly the grammatical problems involved in the interpretation of 4.157. The question is: Who is the subject of *šubbiha la-hum* ('was made a likeness to them') – Jesus, the substitute or 'it'? Al-Rāzī is aware of the objections that can be raised on philosophical grounds to the idea of a God-willed substitution, and discusses these thoroughly. Along with the idea of a voluntary substitution, he also mentions the possibility that after God had taken Jesus to himself, the Jews might have killed a man claiming that he was Jesus.

The Qur'ān seems to affirm the death of Jesus several times, explicitly in 19.33, and by use of the verb *tawaffā* ('taking back' or 'causing to die') in 3.55 and 5.117. Thus, the Qur'ān itself could be said to resist any substitutionist idea. To avoid the problem, and being faithful to Ḥadīth material implying that Jesus will die only after his eschatological return, several metaphorical interpretations have been offered by the commentators. The sense would then be that Jesus was taken alive from this earth (maybe when asleep) and raised to God (*rafaʿa* in 3.55), thus being still alive in heaven, where he is awaiting his eschatological return to earth (cf. Ḥadīth).

Against the traditional view of Christian apologists, Robinson suggests that a metaphorical interpretation of *tawaffā* might be justified, whereas Räisänen, who generally is very much against apologetic interpretation, concludes that the use of *tawaffā* implies that according to the Qur'ān, Jesus did in fact die, although not on the cross.

The decisive argument of al-Ṭabarī and later Sunnī commentators against understanding *tawaffā* in the sense of 'causing to die' seems to be Ḥadīth material that implies that the death of Jesus will only occur after his return before the Hour. Some would argue, then, that commentators interpret the Qur'ān by Ḥadīth more than the Qur'ān by the Qur'ān. Some traditions, discussed by the commentators, avoid the problem by saying that Jesus was 'received in death' for some hours before being raised to life in heaven.

Referring to Christian ideas, al-Rāzī also discusses an alternative understanding, implying that only the body of Christ died, whereas his soul was liberated into the heavenly realms. However, he does not personally subscribe to this view, and argues that *tawaffā* must be taken metaphorically, coming close to the Ṣūfī view that Jesus was caused to die away from worldly desires and carnal soul.[52]

The various interpretations both of *šubbiha la-hum* and the verb *tawaffā* in the various commentaries are referred to in more detail by Robinson.

The Return of Jesus

As can be seen from the discussion above, the interpretation of the passages referring to the death of Jesus is intertwined with the understanding of Jesus' role in the eschatological future – his 'second coming' or 'descent'. Robinson discusses in detail the interpretation given by the commentaries to 4.159 (the People of the Book will certainly believe in him before his death, and on the Day of resurrection he will be a witness against them), and 43.61 (He – or it – is knowledge for the Hour).[53] He shows how the commentaries draw extensively on the Ḥadīth material in their interpretation, although (according to Robinson) it is not at all certain that the Qur'ān even alludes to Jesus' return. He suggests that the inclusion of Ḥadīth material in the interpretation of the Qur'ān at these points might have been prompted by a better knowledge of Christian eschatology, and even been introduced 'as an apologetic device for explaining difficult passages in the Qur'ān possibly in the face of Christian polemic'. He concludes by suggesting a possible development in stages of the Ḥadīth material concerning the descent of Jesus, and its combination with qur'ānic references.[54]

The Miracles of Jesus and his Virginal Conception

In its references to Jesus' death, and its use of titles (e.g. slave/servant over against divine Son), the qur'ānic discourse is polemical. This is not the case when it comes to the references, or rather the retelling, of his virginal conception. Also the qur'ānic references to the miracles of Jesus, from cradle to adult manhood, are non-polemical, and distinguish Jesus as a worker of life-giving miracles.

In his historical research, Robinson has given special consideration to the life-giving miracles of Jesus: his creating birds from clay and raising the dead to life.[55] He points to the fact that (according to Ibn Isḥāq) Christians from Najrān already in the lifetime of the Prophet were arguing that the Qur'ān – by its reference to the life-giving miracles – was attributing divine prerogatives to Jesus.

For his own part, Robinson lists some linguistic arguments in favour of this specific point in traditional Christian apologetic. Referring to Jesus creating birds of clay and blowing (life) into them (in 3.49 and 5.110), he maintains that all three key words in the qur'ānic reference to this miracle have some special theological connotations in the context of the Qur'ān itself:

1 the use of the verb *ḫalaqa*, which has God as its subject in 162 out of 173 occurrences;
2 the mention of clay (*ṭīn*), the substance from which man was created according to the Qur'ān; and
3 the use of the verb *nafaḫa*, which elsewhere in the Qur'ān expresses God's blowing his Spirit into man in creation, and into Mary at the moment of conception.

In spite of this, none of the commentaries see any divine analogy in the words used by the Qur'ān. Al-Zamakhsharī and al-Rāzī present various alternative understandings of *ḫalaqa* to that of creating. In his understanding of 'blowing', al-Rāzī comes close to the Ṣūfī notion of Jesus' life-giving breath, a special prerogative of Jesus according to Ṣūfism.

As to Jesus raising the dead, the commentaries do not in the least play down the importance of the miracle. On the contrary, the abounding legendary material (see above) about Jesus raising the dead is referred to and recorded. However, the miracles are given a specific qur'ānic interpretation (especially in al-Rāzī), by repeated underlining of the expression *bi-iḏni llāhi*, 'by God's leave' in the reports of Jesus' miracles. The *interpretatio coranica* of the commentaries implies that the miracles all refer to God's determining power rather than the creative power of Jesus. Against Christian apologetics, of which he appears to have personal experience in Persia, al-Rāzī refers to the fact that great miracles were also attributed to other prophets (e.g. Moses), without implying any divinity on the performer's part.[56]

Ibn Kathīr presents a theory of the meaning of miracles in human history: Moses came with magic to a people with magical expectation, Jesus came with healing in a time focusing on healing abilities and Muḥammad came with the miracle of the Arabic Qur'ān to a people skilled in eloquence and poetry. Again, the *interpretatio coranica*, aided with some philosophy of history, consistently generalizes the phenomenon of miracles, although attributing a special kind of miracles (that of healing and life-giving) to Jesus.

As regards the virginal conception, there is one specific problem identified and discussed by the commentaries. In the Meccan revelation of 19.17–22, the spirit of God (*rūḥanā*, 'our spirit') appears to Mary in the form of a well-proportioned man (*bašaran sawiyyan*). In 21.91 and 66.12, the 'how' of the conception is described as God breathing His spirit into her, and in Medinan reference to the annunciation (3.42ff.) the announcement is given by the angels (*al-malā'ikahu*).

How, then, was God's spirit blown into Mary by the man-like angel? Al-Rāzī and others discuss how the creative spirit of God could carry through its divine purpose by an angel appearing in the form of a human body.[57] The commentaries also refer to and discuss several of the speculations found in the legendary material, some of them with obvious sexual connotations.[58]

The miraculous conception of Jesus by the spirit, and his ability to perform life-giving miracles did not in themselves represent any problem for the commentators. The problem they did have to wrestle with was how to imagine the creative power of God being transmitted through human bodies, and whether the life-giving miracles indicate a unique proximity of Jesus to the divine (as many Christians would suggest), or should be relativized as being part of the divine privileges granted to prophets in general (as most Muslims would see it).

Notes

1 Balić (1979: 2).

2 Cf. Iftekar Bano Hussain, *Prophets in the Qur'ān*, vol. I–II. London: Ta-Ha Publishers (1994–1995), and the children's book by the convert Ahmad Denffer, *Islam for Children*. Leicester: The Islamic Foundation (1981; in Norwegian, *Barnas bok om islam*. Oslo: Den Islamske Informasjonsforeningen/I.I.F.S.O., 1994).

3 Khalidi (1994: 146).

4 Khalidi (2001: 26). Cf. Chapter 6 below, in the section 'The role of Christ in early intra-Muslim polemics'.

5 See Margoliouth (1893–1894), Asin et Palacios (1917/1974, 1926). Later collections include Robson (1930, 1950), Hayek/al-Hayik (1959, 1961), von Kamphoevener (1963), and Manṣūr (1976–1978).

6 See the critical review by R. Dunkerley entitled 'The Muhammadan Agrapha' (Dunkerley 1928) – referring to the early investigations of D. S. Margoliouth in 1893–1894 and the studies by Michaël Asin y Palacios published in 1917 and 1926. For the general study of Agrapha, see Joachim Jeremias, *Unbekannte Jesusworte*, Gütersloh (1951).

7 Khalidi (2001: 5).

8 Ibid., p. 34.

9 Ibid., p. 59. This saying is first attested by ibn al-Mubārak (d. 797).

10 See for instance ibid., p. 86 and Qā'im (2004: 262, 334).

11 Ibid., p. 96.

12 Quoted from Khalidi (2001: 106), cf. Dunkerley (1928: 168). As for the general motif of passing over/passing by, cf. logion 42 in the *Gospel of Thomas*.

13 Quoted from Khalidi (2001: 122), who finds the first version of this saying in the works of Abū Bakr ibn Abī al-Dunya (d. 894), in which it is connected with a moral lesson: 'He said this in order to teach them a lesson – namely, to forbid slander.' Cf. Margoliouth (1893–1894: 177) and Ṣūfī and Shīʿite versions of this story in Nurbakhsh (1982: 98–100) and Qa'im (1004: 274).

14 Khalidi (2001:108 and 123). Cf. also Jesus sayings of this genre transmitted by al-Damīrī (d. 1405), the author of a celebrated work on animals (ibid., pp. 208–210).
15 Ibid., p. 41.
16 Ibid.
17 See Khalidi (1994: 191, Note 8), cf. Mourad (1996: 44).
18 Jeffery (1962: 560–598). Also Zwemer (1912) includes translations from Thaʿlabī's *Qiṣaṣ*. In Arabic: *ʿArāʾis al-majālis: Qiṣaṣ al-anbiyā*. Cairo: Matbaʿat Ḥijāzī (AH 1371).
19 English translation by W. M. Thackston Jr., *Tales of the Prophets of al-Kisāʾī*. Boston: Twayne Publishers (1978).
20 Pinault (1987: 107, Note 3).
21 For an example, see Robson (1950).
22 It should be noted that the occurrences of 'punishment/cursing miracles' are not specific to Muslim legend, but are also found in Christian apocrypha such as *The Arabic Infancy Gospel* and *The Infancy Gospel of Thomas*, where Jesus may be said to be portrayed as 'a Wunder-kind or . . . an enfant terrible', and 'acts like an Oriental despot' (J. K. Elliot: 'The Apocryphal Gospels', *The Expository Times*, 1991, p. 11). Cf. J. K. Elliot, *The Apocryphal Jesus: Legends of the Early Church*. Oxford (1996), and Helmut Koester, *Ancient Christian Gospels*. London (1990: 311 ff.). As for the boys turned to pigs, cf. a similar miracle about boys turned to goats, but then back to boys again, in *The Arabic Infancy Gospel*, 40 (see Elliot 1996: 30).
23 Known in Christian sources from *The Arabic Infancy Gospel*, 37. See J. K. Elliot, *The Apocryphal Jesus: Legends of the Early Church*. Oxford (1996: 29–30).
24 Jeffery (1962: 575f.).
25 Khalidi (2001: 111f.).
26 The story is also well known in Shīʿite tradition, cf. Qā'im (2004: 234–236). A version of this story is also found in al-Ghazālī's *Iḥyāʾ ʿulūm al-dīn*, in chapter 27 (III.7) about the evil of wealth.
27 Watt (1991: 37).
28 Cf. ibid., p. 39.
29 About al-Yaʿqūbī, see Donaldson (1931), Ferré (1977), Goddard (1996: 19f.) and Cragg (1985a: 50f.).
30 Cf. Ferré (1977).
31 Donaldson (1931: 89). Cf. Goddard (1996: 20).
32 *Aḫbār al-rusūl wa-l-mulūk* ('Annales of Messengers and Kings'), ed. de Goeje et. al., Leiden: E. J. Brill; even being edited in English ('The History of al-Tabarı') by Ehsan Yar-Shater, Albany NY 1987/continuing. Ferré (1979), See translation of the section about Jesus in Ferré (1979). About al-Ṭabarī and Jesus, cf. Charfi (1979), and Watt (1991: 44–46).

33 For al-Masʿūdī, see de Vaux (1978: 1206), Watt (1991: 46–48) and Goddard (1996: 18f.).
34 Watt (1991: 47).
35 For al-Bīrūnī, see de Vaux (1978: 1206).
36 See Watt (1991: 48–50).
37 Cf. Ḥadīth material on Jesus' second coming, linking this with Damascus (see Chapter 2 above).
38 Mourad (1996: 40).
39 Ibid.
40 Ibid., p. 41.
41 Ibid., p. 43.
42 Ibid., pp. 43–44.
43 See also Khoury (1996, in Arabic).
44 Ayoub (1980: 91).
45 Cf. Abdelmajid Charfi: 'Christianity in the Qur'an Commentary of Ṭabarī' (Charfi 1980).
46 See Robinson (1991: 178ff and V.1f below).
47 Ibid., pp. 167–177. Cf. IV below.
48 For al-Qushayrī, cf. Arnaldez (1988), ch. 1.I: 'Jésus dans le commentaire coranique de Qushayrī'.
49 Robinson (1991: 73–77).
50 Ibid., p. 140f., cf. Ayoub (1980: 95–100).
51 Cf. Ayoub (1980: 102f.).
52 See ibid., pp. 105–109.
53 Robinson (1991: 78–105).
54 Ibid., pp. 103–105.
55 Ibid., pp. 142–155, cf. Robinson (1989).
56 Cf. Chapter 6 below, in the section about 'Muslim polemics, directed towards submitted Christians'.
57 See Robinson (1991: 156–166), and Robinson (1988) ('Fakhr al-dīn al-Rāzī and the Virginal Conception').
58 Cf. Ayoub (1995).

Chapter 4

Jesus in Shīᶜite Tradition[1]

A Shīᶜite Jesus

It has already been noted that the Shīᶜites rejected the Ḥadīth collections of the Sunnī Muslims. Believing that the imāms were infallible and inherited Muḥammad's spiritual knowledge, they composed their own standard collection of Ḥadīth derived from ᶜAlī and his supporters. In general, the Shīᶜites give pre-eminence in their teaching and piety to the sayings of the twelve imāms, and treat traditions derived from them as on a par with those from the Prophet himself.

In dealing with the Jesus passages of the Qur'ān, 'proto-Shīᶜites' and 'proto-Sunnīs' probably drew upon very similar traditions which the former traced to the imāms and the latter traced to the Companions and Successors.[2] As for the earliest Shīᶜite sources Khalidi notes that these (like many early Ṣūfī sources) originate from southern Iraq – in particular, from Kufa. The strong similarity between certain Sunnī (ascetic, mystical) and Shīᶜī traditions about Jesus is attested by the large compilation of stories and sayings related to Jesus in Shīᶜite tradition put together by Mahdi Muntaẓir Qā'im and translated by Al-Ḥajj Muḥammad Legenhausen (Qā'im 2004). The words of and about Jesus in this collection are taken from major ḥadīth collections of sayings attributed to Muḥammad and the twelve imams such as the comprehensive *Biḥār al-anwār* (which was compiled as late as in the seventeenth century) and earlier collections such as *Tuḥāf al-ᶜuqūl*, *Al-kāfī* and *Tahḏīb al-aḥkām* (compiled in the tenth and eleventh centuries).

As Khalidi notes, on the whole the Shi'ite sayings of Jesus do not differ in spirit from the Sunnī sayings and many direct parallels can be found. For instance in *Nahj ul-balāgha*, the venerated compilation of sermons, letters and sayings attributed to Imām ᶜAlī, one finds in one of the sermons a reference to the examples of Jesus which is quite in tune with the ascetic image of Jesus that persists from early (oppositional) Ṣūfism to al-Ghazālī:

If you desire I will tell you about ʿĪsā (p.b.u.h.) son of Maryam (Mary). He used a stone for his pillow, put on coarse clothes and ate rough food. His condiment was hunger. His lamp at night was the moon. His shade during the winter was just the expanse of earth eastward and westward. His fruits and flowers were only what grow from the earth for the cattle. He had no wife to allure him, nor any son to give grief, nor wealth to deviate (his attention), nor greed to disgrace him. His two feet were his conveyance and his two hands his servant.[3]

Nahj ul-balāgha contains also sayings attributed to Imām ʿAlī that come close to well-known sayings of Jesus in the New Testament Gospels, such as 'He who draws out the sword of revolt gets killed with it'.[4]

Although many similarities may be identified between Sunnī and Shīʿite images of Jesus, the Shīʿite conceptions of religious authority and divine representation imply that the image of Christ in Shīʿite Islam is put into a different theological framework. According to Mahmoud Ayoub, Shīʿite Islam:

> [. . .] has developed its own quasi-soteriological Christology in the doctrine and role of the Imāms, the spiritual heads of the community. It is noteworthy that ʿAlı, the first Imām of Shīʿite Muslims, is often compared to Jesus. In a highly interesting statement attributed to ʿAlī he had the following to say about himself and his descendants, the remaining eleven Imāms. Beginning by declaring that God is One and unique in his unity, he goes on: 'He uttered a Word which became a light. From that light He . . . created me and my progeny. Then God uttered another Word which became a spirit, and that spirit He made to dwell in the light. The light, moreover, He made to dwell in our bodies. Thus, we are the Spirit of God and His Words . . ..'
>
> The Imāms, for the Shīʿite community, are the true mediators between God and Man . . .. The twelfth and last of the Imāms will return at the end of time as the awaited Messiah (Mahdī) to establish divine rule over the earth. Jesus, Son of Mary, will also descend from heaven to aid him in this task.[5]

Tarif Khalidi too notes similarities in Shīʿite images of Jesus and Ḥusayn, 'in such things as their miraculous births and their similarity of their prophetic and spiritual genealogies, which they both inherited through their mothers'.[6]

Another peculiarity of Shīʿite traditions about Jesus is their preoccupation with the question of a spiritual successor to Jesus, reflected in several references to Peter (Shaʿmūn ibn Ḥamūn al-Ṣafā).[7] In addition, Shīʿite traditions contain also foretellings of Muḥammad by Jesus. *Biḥār al-anwār* includes a lengthy report of a dialogue between the caliph al-Maʿmūn and the Nestorian Catholicos (Patriarch) in which this issue, and the question of whether Muḥammad was foretold in the Gospel of John or not, were debated.[8] *Al-kāfi* contains a long Ḥadīth Qudsī in which God informs Jesus about Muḥammad.[9] Similarly, in a Ḥadīth Qudsī related by al-Suhrawardī (d. 1234), God informs Jesus about 'the nation of Muḥammad'.[10]

As for the general image of Jesus in Shīʿite Islam, Ayoub summarizes his characteristic features in the titles of prophet, ascetic sage and mystic. Shīʿite Islam emphasizes not only his exoteric, prophetic ministry to the people of Israel, but also the esoteric knowledge he transmitted to his disciples. According to Ayoub, the traditions about Jesus were, and still are, 'used as homiletic materials by popular preachers in services commemorating the sufferings of the Imāms . . . supposed to convey a message of suffering, wisdom, piety, and divine mercy'.[11]

Jesus in Shīʿite Ḥadīth and Tafsīr

In his exposition of 'An Image of Jesus in Early Shīʿite Muslim Literature' cited above, Ayoub (1976) presents the image of Jesus in the highly respected Ḥadīth collections *Al-kāfī* of al-Kulaynī (d. 939) and *Tuḥāf al-ʿuqūl* by al-Ḥarrānī (d. in mid-eleventh century). In both collections, a long Ḥadīth Qudsī directed to Jesus ('Colloquy of God . . . with Jesus') is included.[12] In al-Ḥarrānī's collection, it is placed at the end of the book without further explanation. Harrānī adds to this a collection of 'Sayings of Jesus . . . from the Gospel and other sources'.

In the Ḥadīth Qudsī, Jesus is instructed by God in his ministry as prophet and servant, and admonished to discipline his heart with fear of God. He is warned not to associate anything with God, and reminded of God's wrath towards the wrongdoers. Jesus is also told of the coming of Muḥammad, and commanded to announce it.

Both in the Ḥadīth Qudsī and in the Sayings of Jesus, al-Ḥarrānī alludes extensively from the Gospels, especially from the Sermon on the Mount in Matthew. For example, both *Tuḥāf al-ʿuqūl* and *Biḥār al-anwār* refer to the golden rule as well as the admonition to turn the other cheek.[13] In a large Gospel-like section of *Tuḥāf al-ʿuqūl*, one also finds an almost word-by-word rendering of the Beatitudes, as well as references to Jesus' words about forgiving the evildoer.[14] Several other features of Matthew 5–7 can also be found in this section.

Although references to the Sermon on the Mount are also well attested in Sunnī traditions about Jesus,[15] this part of Jesus' teachings seems to have been even more central to Shīʿite narrators. The fact that the Sermon on the Mount appears to have been an early and persistent feature of the Shīʿite image of Jesus is also attested by the presentation of Jesus by al-Yaʿqūbī – a historian known for his Shīʿite tendency – where the Sermon on the Mount is given pre-eminence (cf. Chapter 3, Section 'Jesus in Muslim perceptions of world history').

Al-Ḥarrānī also frequently alludes to the declarations of woe to the Pharisees and Scribes known from the Gospels (in particular, Matthew 23), although with a more general address directed to the 'slaves of iniquity' and 'slaves of this world'. For example:

O servants [slaves] of the world! Your likeness is like that of the high tombs, their exteriors cause admiration in those who look at them, and their interiors are the bones of the dead, full of misdeeds.[16]

A much later source from the seventeenth century, namely the collector of *Bihār al-anwār*, indicates that critique of false scholars has been a persistent feature of Shīʿite narrations inspired by Jesus-material:

The dinar is the illness of religion, and the scholar (al-ʿālim) *is the physician of religion. So if you see that the physician brings illness upon himself, distrust him, and know that he is not to advise others.*[17]

Another striking feature of Shīʿite traditions about Jesus (noted and commented upon by Khalidi) is his repeated warnings against excessive eating:

O Israelites, do not eat to excess, for he who eats to excess sleeps to excess, and he who sleeps to excess prays little, and he who prays little is inscribed among the negligent.[18]

In other sayings, Jesus' warnings against gluttony are moulded as dietary advices. In one case, his dietary advice aims at restoring smoothness to a woman's face, in response to his husband's complaint that 'Her face is worn out, although she is not old'.[19] In these and other health-related sayings, the image of Jesus as a healer is expanded from that of a miracle worker to an experienced advisor in issues of agriculture, hygiene and diet.[20]

As for the general image of Jesus as a healer, widespread in Shīʿite as well as in Sunnī tradition, we find in *Al-kāfī* the widespread explanation that Jesus distinguishes himself by his medical abilities, just as Moses stands out for his magic and Muḥammad for his oratory eloquence. Responding to the question, 'Why did Allah sent Moses with the miracle appearing through his staff and through his hand and means of magic, Jesus with means of medical tasks and Prophet Muḥammad (may Allah send blessings upon him, his family and all the prophets) with means of speech and sermons?', imām Abū al-Ḥasan replied:

Allah sent Jesus at a time when serious illnesses existed among the people and they needed medical treatment. Jesus brought from Allah what the people did not have. He brought from Allah the means to bring the dead back to life, cure the sick and the lepers by the permission of Allah and thus, establish the truthfulness of the message of Allah among the people.[21]

What about the Shīʿite understanding of the suffering and death of Jesus, then? All versions of the substitutionist idea are found in Shīʿite Tafsīr, such as those of al-Qummī (d. 919), al-Ṭūsī (d. 1067) and al-Ṭabarsī (d. 1153).[22] As noted above, scholars like Louis Massignon and Neal Robinson hold that the substitutionist idea itself might have originated from Shīʿite circles.[23] Thus, in Shīʿite Islam the substitutionist idea, when applied to Jesus, should probably be interpreted in a wider theological context: 'similar things could happen in the case of the Imāms or saints'.[24] However, the following saying in *Biḥār al-anwār* seems to indicate the opposite:

> *They say, 'They (the imams) were not really killed, and it was only a likeness of their affair that appeared to them'. So, they lied, may the wrath of Allah be upon them. Indeed, the affair of none of the prophets of Allah and His authorities, peace be with them, appeared doubtful to the people, except the affair of Jesus the son of Mary alone, for he was raised from the earth alive and his soul was taken between heaven and earth, then he was raised to heaven and his soul was returned to him, and that is what the saying of Allah, the Mighty and Magnificent, is about: 'When Allah said: "O Jesus! I will take you to Me, and I will raise you to Me."'*[25]

Robinson nevertheless suggests that the generalizing tendency is a salient feature of Shīʿite exegesis when it comes to Jesus: 'In comparison with the Sunnite commentators the Shīʿites tend to further reduce Jesus' uniqueness.'[26] For them, Mary is no greater than Muḥammad's daughter Fāṭima (the wife of ʿAlī and mother of Ḥasan and Ḥusayn), and when Jesus returns, his role will be subordinate to that of the Mahdī (who is regarded as identical with the obscured twelfth imām).

The Brethren of Purity

A special case in the Christology of Shīʿite Islam is the writings of 'The Brethren of Purity' (Ikhwān al-Ṣafā') who belonged to the Ismāʿılı Sevener Shīʿites.[27] In their mystic encyclopaedia *Rasā'il* ('Epistles') from the tenth century, emanationist speculations derived from Pythagorism and Neoplatonism are integrated into their esoteric version of Sevener Shīʿite theology. In the Epistles, there is also a lengthy section on Jesus, with a summary of his life (in the 44th of the 52 treatises).

Here, Christ is portrayed as a wayfaring ascetic and a 'physician of souls' as in Ṣūfism (see below), and a spiritual understanding of the miracles is conveyed. He was sent to save the souls of those who professed the religion of Moses, but only clung to the externals of the law. Instead of rebuking them severely, he approached them as a healing physician, and spoke to them in parables. The response from some was favourable:

> *They saw what Christ (peace be upon him) had told and seen with the eye of the heart and the light of certainty and sincerity of faith, and they sought the other world, abstaining from the pride and allurements of this world, and*

thus being saved from the slavery of the world and its lusts. They put on patched garments and travelled with Christ from place to place.[28]

Most noteworthy is the degree of inclusion of motifs from the passion narrative in the Gospels – introduced by the assertion that 'the time had come when God wanted Christ to die and rise again'. In the 'upper room', Jesus tells the disciples that he is 'going to my father and your father . . . I shall make a covenant with you'.

Go to the kings and the far nations and tell them all that I have taught you, and call them to the same thing to which I have called you. Do not be afraid of them, and never fear them, for when I leave my humanity, I shall stand in the air on the right hand of my Father and your Father, and I shall be with you wherever you go, and I shall strengthen you with victory by the permission of my Father. Go to them and call them with gentleness; heal them and command them to do good and shun evil. Do that until you are killed, crucified or expelled from the land.[29]

Even the crucifixion is included, with Jesus being nailed to the cross, given vinegar to drink, pierced by the lance, taken down from the cross, shrouded and laid in the tomb. However, it is only the bodily humanity (*nāsūt*) of Jesus that is crucified. Three days later he appears to the disciples, and when the news spread that he had not been killed, the Jews opened the grave but did not find his mortal remains (*nāsūt*).

Robinson concludes that the reason behind the Brethren of Purity's acceptance of the crucifixion seems to have been their inclination towards Neoplatonist metaphysics: 'The soul which constitutes the personality was liberated when the body – the prison of the soul – died on the cross.'[30]

As to the relation of Jesus to the self-understanding of the Brethren of Purity, David Pinault notes that the Brethren of Purity have made Jesus look very much like an Ismāʿīlī *dāʿī* (summoner):

Christ is said in this epistle to have known that he could not manifest himself openly to men, given their state of ignorance, imprisoned as they are in Nature and the Material. Hence he took the disguise of a physician and healer and wandered from town to town, preaching, mingling with men, and piquing their curiosity with parables. He would then initiate select listeners and offer them a Gnostic vision in which the soul is called to awaken from the sleep of ignorance and escape from the prison of the body, to ascend finally into the celestial spheres and the realms of divine majesty.[31]

The Significance of Suffering

Although there might be a generalizing tendency in some of the Shīʿite images of Jesus, some specific theological emphases in Shīʿite Islam seem (at least implicitly) to allow for a broader appreciation of the biblical images of Jesus than in Sunnī Muslim orthodoxy. In particular, one might expect that the significance of suffering in Shīʿite Islam would entail a more open approach to the passion of Christ and the issue of the cross.[32]

The *Rasāʾil* of the Brethren of Purity seem to corroborate this supposition. However, in mainstream Shīʿite traditions about Jesus (as reflected in the collection *Jesus through Shi'ite Narrations*), there seems not to be any substantial difference from the standard refutation of the crucifixion in Sunnī Islam.[33] Many contemporary Shīʿite commentaries on the Qur'ān give the same picture.[34]

A potential for mutual understanding between Christianity and Shīʿite Islam as regards the divine mystery of suffering and apparent failure might still exist. As Kenneth Cragg has underlined, the Sunnī Muslim image of Muḥammad and of prophethood in general, implies that God always grants them a 'manifest victory'.[35] Although there is much implicit suffering of Muḥammad to be traced in the initial Meccan scorn and rejection of his message, the *hijra* signifies a definitive turn of events leading to his final victory over the idolatrous unbelievers in Mecca and the deceitful among the People of the Book in Medina. After his demise, there was the rivalry among the various factions in the first *umma*, resulting in the 'manifest victory' of what became the Ummayyad caliphate over against ʿAlī, Ḥasan and Ḥusayn. Cragg comments:

> The 'manifest victory' to which initial Islam was committed, in both idea and action, by post-Hijrah success was necessarily denied to those 'unsuccessful' factions into which Muslims inevitably fragmented under the first three Caliphs and beyond . . . 'failure' was bound to be the experience of some.[36]

Consequently, a theology of suffering emerged, developing the theme of the righteous ones (the immaculate house of the Prophet) 'whose innocent suffering possessed a merit which could avail for the redemption of the unworthy and for a deep emotional release and compensation.'[37]

In devotional ritual (cf. the passion plays of Shīʿite Islam), the emotional focus passes on to the 'sufferers' of the tragedy of Karbalā, where the house of ʿAlī was defeated and Ḥusayn martyred.

Although the political and militant martyrdom of Ḥusayn is rather different from that of Jesus, the emphasis on redeeming suffering might still imply an affinity to central Christian teachings. In his book *Redemptive Suffering in Islam*[38], Mahmoud Ayoub analyses this tradition within Shīʿite Islam, and its relation to other Islamic traditions. As to the implications for an Islamic

Christology, he holds the view that although the Qur'ān denies the expiatory sacrifice of Christ on the cross once and for all, it does not necessarily deny 'his general redemptive role in human history'.[39]

Notes

1 As for the image of Jesus in classical Shıʿite Islam, see Qā'im (2004, *Jesus through Shi'ite narrations*), Ayoub (1976, 1980), Arnaldez (1988: ch. 2.II) ('Jesus dans la pensée shîʿite') and Robinson (1991: ch. 16): 'The representation of Jesus in the Shıʿite commentaries.'
2 Robinson (1991: 176).
3 Talib (1996: 324), cf. variant versions in Qā'im (2004: 222) and Khalidi (2001: 159) who notes a similar saying found in the Sūfī writer Abū Nuʿaym al-Isbaḥānī's (d. 1039) work *Hilyat al-awliyā'*.
4 Talib (1996: 653; cf. Matthew 26.52).
5 Ayoub (1976: 167f. with references).
6 Khalidi (2004: 39).
7 Qā'im (2004: 62, 68, 140ff. (a thematic section about 'His successor') 156ff., 174, 200, 240, 284).
8 Ibid., pp. 116–140.
9 Ibid., pp. 318/322.
10 Khalidi (2001: 200).
11 Qā'im (2004: 169).
12 The Ḥadīth Qudsī is also included in the collection of Shıʿite narrations about Jesus by Qā'im and Legenhausen, see Qā'im (2004: 302ff.).
13 Qā'im (2004: 318, 330, 386).
14 Ibid., 364, 360.
15 Cf. the section about Agrapha in Chapter 3 and Chapter 5 on representations of Jesus in Sufism.
16 Qā'im (2004: 364; cf. Matthew 23: 27).
17 Ibid., p. 330, cf. Khalidi (2001: 213).
18 Khalidi (2001: 198).
19 Ibid., p. 136, cf. Qā'im (2004: 276).
20 Khalidi (2001: 136–138); Qā'im (2004: 274, 276, 342f., 354).
21 *Al-Kāfī* ch. 1: 20 (quoted from http://www.al-shia.com/html/eng/books/hadith/al-kafi/)
22 See Robinson (1991: 171f.) and Ayoub (1980).
23 Robinson (1991: 140f., 176f.).
24 Ibid., p. 176, cf. Khalidi (2001: 39).
25 Ibid., p. 56.
26 Robinson (1991: 186).
27 For Ikhwān al-Ṣafā', see Levonian (1945, with translation of the section about Jesus in their *Rasā'il*), Marquet (1982), Robinson (1991: 55–57),

Goddard (1996: 20–23, citing Levonian's translation) and Khalidi (2001: 141–144).

28 Quoted from Levonian (1945: 29)/Goddard (1996: 21).

29 Quoted from Levonian (1945: 30)/Goddard (1996: 22).

30 Robinson (1991: 57).

31 Pinault (1987: 110, Note 5).

32 Hugh Goddard (1990: 259) points to an interesting book from 1971 by the Egyptian writer Muḥammad ʿĀrif Muṣṭafā Fahmī, *Yasūʿ al-Masīḥ wa-l-Imām ʿAlī* ('Jesus the Messiah and Imām ʿAlī'), in which the author compares their mystical teaching as well as their suffering. As to the end of Jesus' life, the author refers to the different Qur'ānic and Christian viewpoints, and although he concludes that Christians and Muslims can only agree that Jesus was raised to God, he compares Jesus' treatment at the hands of the Jews with ʿAlī's treatment at the hands of his enemies.

33 See the following passages in Qā'im (2004: 56, 62, 98, 188–204, 228).

34 Examining S. V. Mir Ahmed Ali's *The Holy Qur'ân (With English Translation of the Arabic Text and Commentary according to the Version of the Holy Ahl al-Bayt)*, which was published in Karachi in 1964, Michael L. Fitzgerald finds that 'The persecution of Jesus, the opposition which leads up to the verse about the crucifixion (Q. 4.157), is not in any way brought into connection with the opposition to the Third Imâm, Ḥusayn. Instead, a parallel is drawn between Ḥusayn and Yaḥyâ' (Fitzgerald 1996: 17). Instead of offering a reflection on the sufferings of Jesus, the whole burden of his exegesis of Q. 4.157f. rests on the refutation of the Christian belief in the death of Jesus on the cross (ibid., p. 14).

35 Cf. Cragg (1984, esp. ch. 2 and 3).

36 Ibid., p. 143.

37 Ibid.

38 Mouton, The Hague, 1980.

39 Ayoub (1980: 94).

Chapter 5

Jesus in Ṣūfism

Ṣūfism – as a mystical, inwardly directed movement – has often been regarded as a reaction against dry legalism and worldliness in Islam. But the roots of Ṣūfism can be traced back to the very beginnings of Islam – as the inward, mystical dimension of the Holy Book itself, and as reflection of the mystical experiences of the Prophet.

The aim of mature Ṣūfism is often described as *fanāʾ*, passing from the consciousness of the self towards *baqāʾ*, reaching a state of union with the divine – purified and transformed by God. To reach the goal, the state of *baqāʾ*, several stations have to be passed, with the aim of purifying the soul.

The first stronghold of Ṣūfism seems to have been Basra in southern Iraq, and is connected with the names of Ḥasan al-Baṣrī (d. 728) and the woman saint Rābiʿa al-ʿAdawiyya (d. 801). In the formative years of Ṣūfism, asceticism was regarded as essential for the purifying process, with Ḥasan al-Baṣrī as a typical representative. Later, more emphasis was placed on the language of love, as represented by Rābiʿa and others. Rābiʿa is credited with a famous prayer, which expresses the heartbeat of Ṣūfī devotion as yearning love for God Himself:

> *Oh, my Lord, if I worship Thee from fear of Hell, burn me in Hell,*
> *and if I worship Thee in hope of Paradise exclude me thence,*
> *but if I worship Thee for Thine own sake*
> *withhold not from me Thine Eternal beauty.*[1]

Similar sayings are attributed to Jesus by Abū Ṭālib al-Makkī (d. 996), al-Ghazālī and other Ṣūfī writers.[2] In the more controversial versions of Ṣūfism, such as with al-Bistamī (d. 875) and al-Ḥallāj (d. 922), a language marked by the search for ecstatic union with the divine became a predominant feature (see below).

Ṣūfī Reception of Jesus-Sayings and Jesus-Stories

From the beginnings of Ṣūfism, Jesus was rendered a prominent place in the spiritual teachings of Islamic mystics. Many Ṣūfī teachers speak of 'the Jesus stage' as one of the higher stations of spiritual growth. The amount of Jesus-related material in Ṣūfism is overwhelming, as can be seen from the collection of Javad Nurbakhsh: *Jesus in the Eyes of the Ṣūfīs* (1982). The collection of Nurbakhsh (head of the Khaniqahi Nimatullahi order) contains a wellspring of sayings of and stories about Jesus, derived mainly from Persian Ṣūfī poets like Rūmī, ʿAṭṭār and Hāfeẓ, but also from al-Ghazālī and from modern Ṣūfī books.

Citing of words of Jesus is widespread among Ṣūfī poets and theologians, the most famous example being al-Ghazālī's *Iḥyāʾ* (see below). In accordance with the general Ṣūfī interest in sayings attributed to God (Ḥadīth Qudsī), Islamic mystics also know a number of 'God's words to Jesus'.[3]

In addition to sayings, Ṣūfis can tell several stories about Jesus. In general, the Jesus-stories recorded in Ṣūfī works differ from the more fairy-tale like legends of the *Qiṣaṣ* (see Chapter 3) by being more 'moralist' and 'inwardly directed', often in the form of reported dialogues and parables. The stories include that of Jesus asking the disciples what they would do if they came upon a brother exposing his private parts while asleep. As a parable of listening to gossip, Jesus astonishes them in suggesting that rather than cover him up they would expose them even more.[4] Another story much appreciated by Ṣūfīs (found both in al-Qushayrī and al-Ghazālī) is that of Jesus walking with a pious worshipper whose self-righteousness is revealed and condemned when their company is sought by a notorious sinner asking for mercy.[5]

Apart from the sayings and stories, Jesus is often cited as a spiritual model in Ṣūfī poetry and meditative discourses, most notably those of Rūmī (see below).

Generally, Jesus is seen by the Ṣūfis as a model wayfaring ascetic and wisdom teacher. As a 'proto-Ṣūfī', he is reported to have worn woollen clothing.[6] Ṣūfī traditions about Jesus' self-denial abound.[7] It is told that Ḥasan al-Baṣrī, when warning the Caliph of worldly desires, attributed the following saying to Jesus:

> *My daily bread is hunger, my badge is fear, my raiment is wool, my mount is my foot, my lantern at night is the moon, my fire by day is the sun, and my fruit and fragrant herbs are such things as the earth brings forth for the wild beasts and the cattle. All the night I have nothing, yet there is none richer than I.*[8]

Also in later Ṣūfism, as with the Persian poet Farīd ud-dīn ʿAṭṭār (d. 1220), the detachment of Jesus is seen as an essential feature of his uniqueness:

> *If for only a moment you free yourself,*
> *From this prison around you,*

You will be like Jesus,
Unique in detachment.[9]

However, in later Ṣūfī poetry and theology, the name of Jesus stands not only for asceticism and detachment from the world, but also for the breath of life, and for love. In this respect too, he is a role model for Ṣūfis, as can be seen from the following words of ʿAṭṭār: 'As ʿAttar's word gives life to the soul, Clearly he is of the same breath as Jesus.'[10]

In his *Muṣībat-nāma*, Aṭṭār tells the story of Jesus and the man who desired an atom of love, with the following conclusion:

An atom even, in Love, is too much;
Conceit in Love is unbefitting.
Besides Love itself,
Whatever else subsists, is
Like an idol-temple
Within the Kaʿba.
When alien names from the heart
Are extirpated, the veils
From the Loved One's visage are raised.[11]

Various Representations of Jesus in Ṣūfism

Jesus in Ṣūfī 'Moralism'

As noted, early Ṣūfism was marked by asceticism, and a stern though non-violent critique of the masters of this world. In the writings of the ninth century moralist mystic al-Muḥāsibī (d. 857 in Baghdad), especially in his *Kitāb al-waṣāyā* ('Book of commandments'[12]), references to Jesus abound. Kenneth Cragg (1985) suggests that al-Muḥāsibī must have known the New Testament in Arabic, since he alludes extensively to motifs and sayings from the canonical Gospels. Cragg characterizes the teachings of al-Muḥāsibī as 'rigorous self-interrogation and self-discipline'. He finds that the temper of al-Muḥāsibī's teachings comes close to that of the Sermon on the Mount. An important part of the spiritual discipline recommended by al-Muḥāsibī was the motif of not repaying wrong with wrong. According to al-Muḥāsibī, one should bless, not curse the evildoer, and nourish one's soul from what he called 'the springs of compassion'. Furthermore, he wanted people to be free of care, detecting the mercy of God in the beauty of the flowers and the joy of the birds.[13]

One will find similar parallels to the Sermon on the Mount in other branches of Ṣūfism as well. Morris S. Seale (1968) has analysed the striking parallels between the 45 articles of the heterodox Malāmatiyya movement (as recorded by al-Sulamī, d.1021) and the spirituality of the Sermon on the Mount.

Transgressions of Orthodoxy in Search for Union with God

Asceticism and moral exhortation is still but one step in the mystical process. The declared goal of Ṣūfism, to attain union with God through detachment from the world and love of God, led some of the early Ṣūfīs to ecstatic expressions that orthodox Muslims deemed to transgress the borders of Islam. The ecstatic Ṣūfīs were often accused of committing the heresy of *širk* – associating with God. Al-Bistamī (d. 875) is said to have exclaimed during his ecstatic *miʿrāj* (i.e. the heavenly ascent of his soul during ecstasy): 'Glory be to me! How great is my majesty.' Several Ṣūfīs found guilty in transgression were put to death for blasphemy in Baghdad during the ninth and tenth centuries, the most famous being Manṣūr al-Ḥallāj who was executed in 922 for declaring *anā l-ḥaqq*, 'I am the Truth'.

The parallels to the transgressing God-language of Jesus (cf. John 14.6) and his subsequent fate on the accusation of blasphemy are of course obvious. Similar to the Gospel of John, where Jesus' crucifixion is seen as his ascension to God (John 12.32f.), many Ṣūfīs have regarded the execution of al-Ḥallāj as his heavenly *miʿrāj*. Also substitutionist ideas, and the view that although al-Ḥallāj was crucified, it was only his body that suffered while his soul was raised to God, can be found in Ṣūfī reflections on his fate.[14]

Similar controversial expressions of a mystical spirituality, within Shīʿite Islam, can be found in the teachings of the Ikhwān al-Ṣafā' (the Brethren of Purity) from the tenth and eleventh centuries (see Chapter 5).

Jesus in the Orthodox Ṣūfism of al-Ghazālī[15]

In the development of Sunnī Ṣūfism, the general tendency came to be its integration into orthodoxy. Ṣūfī spirituality was seen as the core of orthodox Islam, and not as an alternative to it. This tempering tendency culminated with the reconciling work of al-Ghazālī (d. 1111). In his 'Revival of the Religious Sciences' (*Iḥyā ʿulūm al-dīn*) he interprets orthodox Islamic law and theology with the typical Ṣūfī emphasis on religious experience and inner devotion.[16]

In this work, where numerous references to Jesus can be found, he is pictured as an ascetic wayfarer, a teacher of profound wisdom and a lover of God – but without any uniqueness being attributed to him. It should also be noted that although David, Moses and Jesus are repeatedly cited as supreme examples to be emulated, the tone against Jews and Christians is often critical. Like David and Moses, Jesus is appropriated for Islamic purposes, as bringing more of the same message that Muḥammad taught.

Attention is guided towards Jesus through a number of Jesus-sayings, a great part of which are derived from unknown sources.[17] The sayings are cited on a par with sayings of the Prophet, and serve general illustrative purposes as examples to be imitated:

> *He [Jesus] was asked: 'Are there any one on the earth like you?' He answered: 'Yes. Whoever has prayer for his speech, meditation for his silence and tears for his vision, he is like me.'*[18]

The sayings attributed to Jesus in the various books of al-Ghazālī's *Iḥyā'* include the agrapha about life as a bridge (cf. the section about agrapha in Chapter 3):

> *The world is a bridge. Pass over it. Do not linger on it.*[19]

The saying about the world as a bridge is quoted twice in *Iḥyā*, in book 26 (III.6) on the reproach of the world, and book 34 (IV.4) on poverty and renunciation. Both books abound with sayings attributed to Jesus, such as:

> *The seeker after the world is like one who would drink from the sea; the more he drinks the more thirsty he becomes – until it kills him in the end.*[20]
>
> *Love of the world and love of the hereafter cannot be brought together in the heart of the believer, any more than fire and water can coexist in one place.*[21]
>
> *Jesus lay down one day with his head upon a stone. Satan, passing by, said: 'O Jesus, you are fond of this world.' So Jesus took the stone and cast it from under his head, saying: 'This be yours, together with this world.'*[22]

In book 24 (III.4), on the evils of the tongue, Jesus recommends silence as the major portion of devotion:

> *Devotion is of ten parts. Nine of them consist in silence, and one in solitude.*[23]

The other side of Jesus' warnings against the world is his commitment to the poor, cited as an example in book 5 (I.5) on the secrets of *zakāt*: 'If a man sends away a beggar empty from his house, the angels will not visit that house for seven nights.'[24]

For a message to grow, it requires a soft heart:

> *Christ (peace be upon him) said: Crop grows on soft ground, and not on rock. Similarly wisdom works in the heart of the humble, and not in the heart of the haughty. Or do you not see that if a man lifts his head up to the roof it wounds him, but if he bows down his head it shelters and protects him?*[25]

Many of the sayings come close to words of Jesus known from the biblical Gospels, such as his instructions for fasting and giving in book 28 (III.8) on the evil of status and hypocrisy:

> *Jesus told his disciples: 'Whenever one of you should fast, he should smear grease on his hair and face and lips, so that no one is aware that he is fasting; and when he gives with his right hand, his left hand should not know what his right hand is doing; and when he prays, he should draw a curtain across the doorway . . . .'*[26]

A long speech of Jesus, directed against dishonest learned men, and reminiscent of his speech against the Pharisees as recorded in Matthew 23 and other places in the Gospels, is cited twice in book 27 (III.7) on the reproach of stinginess and love of wealth, and in book 28 (III.8) on the reproach of status and hypocrisy. The beatitudes are alluded to in book 29 (III.9) on the reproach of pride and vanity, where Jesus blesses those who are humble in this world and keep their minds pure. They shall gain a high rank on the day of resurrection, and they shall see God. Other parts of the Sermon on the Mount are also cited, cf. book 32 (IV.2) on patience and gratitude, in which al-Ghazālī refers to what he himself saw in the Gospel:

> *I saw in the Injīl that Jesus son of Mary said: You have been told before to take a tooth for a tooth and a nose for a nose. But I say to you: Do not fight evil with evil, but rather turn your left cheek to the one who slaps your right cheek. Give your mantle to the one who takes your loincloth. Walk two miles together with the one who makes you to walk one mile with him.*[27]

Other sayings are more in tune with the apocryphal Gospels, or they may be from other, unknown sources. A prayer attributed to Jesus is included among the selected invocations that end the section on *ḏikr* and invocations in *Iḥyāʾ ʿulūm al-dīn*. In al-Ghazālī's book on 'The beginning of guidance' (*Bidāyat al-hidāya*), which contains guidance for spiritual discipline, he recommends this prayer in connection with the dawn worship:

> *Then repeat the words of Jesus (God bless and preserve both our Prophet and him): 'O God, I here this morning am unable to repel what I loathe and to gain what I hope for; by Thy hand has this morning come, not by the hand of any other; I this morning am obliged to do my work, and no needy man is in greater need than I am of Thee, while no rich man is less in need than Thou art of me. O God, let not my enemy rejoice over me, and let not my friend think evil of me, May I not come into misfortune in my religion. May this world not be the greatest of my cares nor the sum of my knowledge. Let not him who has no mercy for me prevail over me by my sin.'*[28]

The historical appreciation of the sayings and their possible authenticity is of course difficult. More important is the observation of how they are converted to fit into a general ascetic and spiritualized perception like that of Ṣūfism, a process that begins already in the esoteric representation of Jesus in the Gnostic writings of the apocryphal Gospel tradition.

Although al-Ghazālī is critical of the traditional Christian understanding of incarnation, he teaches clearly that human beings have a God-given capacity to imitate divine qualities, in the sense of 'acquiring the character traits of God' (*taḫallaqū bi-aḫlāq Allāh*).[29] Like Muḥammad, Jesus is among those who are created with a good character.[30] But normally, the human character has to be trained through discipline. In al-Ghazālī's treatise about the 'The Highest Aim in Explanation of the Excellent Names of Allāh' (*Al-maqṣad al-asmā fī šarḥ asmā' al-ḥusna*) he explains how human beings can assume the character traits that are associated with the 99 names of God. He declares that:

> *[. . .] the perfection and happiness of man consists in conforming to the perfections of God most high, in adorning himself with the meanings of his attributes and names insofar this is conceivable for man.*[31]

The endeavour to acquire some of the character traits of God must not, however, lead to a confusion of what is human and what is divine:

> [. . .] al-Ghazālī compares those mystics who in a state of ecstasy identify themselves with God to Christians who mistakenly identify Jesus with God: in each case the individual has failed to distinguish an indwelling divine Presence from the human form It inhabits.[32]

Jesus in the Theosophical System of ibn al-ʿArabī[33]

In more heterodox representations of Ṣūfism, the uniqueness of Jesus tends to be enhanced. He is seen not only as a role model, but also as representing a cosmic principle. Born in twelfth-century Spain, the Ṣūfī Muslim Ibn al-ʿArabī (d. 1240) expressed a monistic religious view known as *waḥdat al-wujūd*, 'unity of being'. In his work *Fuṣūṣ al-ḥikam* ('Bezels of Wisdom'[34]), he dedicates one chapter to Jesus, as he does to other pre-Islamic prophets. Ibn al-ʿArabī also deals extensively with the role of Christ in his *Al-futuḥāt al-Makkiyya.*[35]

Ibn al-ʿArabī is concerned with the role of the Spirit (*rūḥ*) and the way it is imparted to matter and form. In particular, he is concerned with the role of the Spirit in the creation of Jesus, and his life-giving powers. He portrays Jesus as:

> *A Spirit from none other than God,*
> *So that he might raise the dead and bring forth birds from clay.*

And become worthy to be associated with his Lord,
By which he exerted great influence, both high and low.
God purified him in body and made him transcendent
In the Spirit, making him like Himself in creating.[36]

Ibn al-ʿArabī goes on asserting the divine origin and divine power bestowed on Jesus:

Jesus came forth raising the dead because he was a divine spirit. In this the quickening was of God, while the blowing itself came from Jesus, just as the blowing was from Gabriel, while the Word was of God.[37]

Notwithstanding Jesus' 'transcendence', Ibn al-ʿArabī underlines the humility of Jesus. He is at the same time the Spirit of God and the Slave of God:

The humility of Jesus was such that his community was commanded that they should pay the poll-tax completely, humbling themselves, that if any one of them were struck on one cheek, he should also turn the other, and that he should not hit back or seek retribution.[38]

Ibn al-ʿArabī goes on to relate the humility and the life-giving ability of Jesus to the female and male principles respectively:

This aspect [of his teaching] derives from his mother, since woman is lowly and humble, being under the man, both theoretically and physically. His powers of revival, on the other hand, derive from the blowing of Gabriel in human form, since Jesus revived the dead in human form.[39]

Ibn al-ʿArabī also pays attention to the fact that 'the various sects quarrel concerning the nature of Jesus', and refers the controversy back to the different perspectives from which Jesus can be viewed:

Considered in his [particular] mortal form, one might say that he is the son of Mary. Considered in his form of humanity, one might say that he is of Gabriel, while considered with respect to the revival of the dead, one might say that he is of God as Spirit. Thus one might call him the Spirit of God, which is to say that life is manifest into whomsoever he blows.[40]

However, by being a spirit of God, Jesus only reveals a more general aspect of the Cosmos:

Whoever wishes to know the divine Breath, then let him [first] know the Cosmos, for 'Who knows himself, knows his Lord', Who is manifest in him.[41]

Ibn al-ʿArabī's works owe much to Neoplatonism, and it is clearly the latter perspective of Jesus – that of divine spirit – that appeals most to him. Jesus is integrated in his perception of how 'the Cosmic Pole', the universal rational principle (cf. the Greek/Christian *logos*), is represented in human history through 'the Temporal Pole', or chief saint, of every period. Beneath each Temporal Pole there are seven saints deriving their power from one of the prophets of the seven heavens – of whom Jesus is one. In Ibn al-ʿArabī's system, the uniqueness of Jesus lies in his virginal conception as 'the Seal of the Saints' (*ḫātam al-awliyā*ʾ, cf. the notion of Muḥammad as 'Seal of the Prophets'), and in being a spirit from God with life-giving ability.[42]

Jesus in the Poetry and Meditative Discourses of Rūmī

A high point in Ṣūfī references to Jesus is the great poetical work *Mathnawī* of the Persian born Jalāl al-dīn Rūmī (b. 1207, d. 1273 in Konya).[43] As in the tradition of Muslim legend (cf. the section about 'Stories of the Prophets' in Chapter 3) and in Ibn al-ʿArabī's *Fuṣūṣ al-ḥikam*, a wide range of characters from the history of religions in the Middle East are called upon by Rūmī as holy examples and teachers of profound wisdom. References to Jesus can also be found in other works of Rūmī, such as his 'Discourses' (*Fīhi mā fīhi*).[44]

Through the 1980s and 1990s, several scholars have presented studies on Rūmī and Christ. John Renard (1987) has surveyed the role of Jesus and other Gospel figures in Rūmī's works. The function of Jesus and Joseph in *Mathnawī* has been examined by James Roy King (1990). Annemarie Schimmel (1995) has written a study on Jesus and Mary as poetical images in Rūmī's verse. The Konya scholar Erkan Türkmen presents a collection of sayings pertaining to Jesus in the works of Rūmī in his booklet *Rumi and Christ* (1992), and emphasizes Rūmī's historical importance for Jews, Christians and Muslims.

As for the way Rūmī approaches Christ, Renard emphasizes that in contrast to Ibn al-ʿArabī in *Fuṣūṣ al-ḥikam*, Rūmī 'never intended to elaborate a complete and "systematic" exposition of prophetic revelation'. But he was 'intensely interested in retelling the tales of the Prophets'. Although Jesus was one of his favourites, Renard notes that the space given to Jesus indicates that 'Jesus' importance for Rūmī was slightly below that of Moses, about equal to that of Abraham, and slightly greater than that of David, Solomon, and Noah'.[45]

Another biblical figure of particular interest to Rūmī is Joseph. James Roy King (1990) holds the view that prior to Rūmī, both Jesus and Joseph had acquired pre-eminence in Ṣūfī thinking as embodiments of perfect humanity.

Basically, Rūmī portrays Jesus in accordance with the main lines of Islamic Christology: as a messenger of God and conveyor of the Gospel, a miracle worker, and a sign from Allāh. He also accepts the idea that Jesus was substituted on the cross.[46] However, Rūmī goes beyond the prevailing Islamic view and portrays Jesus as an absolutely extraordinary individual, embodying perfect humanity in being absorbed in essential unity with the divine. As a spirit from the Divine Spirit, and as a fully integrated personality, Jesus stands beyond the sects and creeds. He is'unicoloured', 'as simple and one-coloured as light'.[47]

A Smiling Ascetic

Like other Ṣūfis, Rūmī portrays Jesus as the ideal ascetic. He was a homeless desert-wanderer, and by severe spiritual regime, he sought release from the body and the world. 'Jesus is the model of one who must strive to be grateful for the loving favour of being driven out by constant reminders that he is a pilgrim.'[48] But unlike many other ascetics, he was known as always smiling:

> *Jesus, upon whom be peace, laughed much; John [the Baptist] wept much. John said to Jesus: 'You have become exceedingly secure against the subtle deceits, that you laugh so much.' Jesus replied: 'You have become all too unmindful of the subtle, secret and wonderful graces and kindness of God that you weep so much.'*[49]

At this point, Rūmī seems in fact to have reworked an opposite version of the same tradition, well attested in a number of Muslim sources from the ninth century onwards, in which a smiling John reproaches Jesus for being frowning and gloomy.[50] The latter version seems to be more in tune with other well-attested traditions about Jesus, in which he is known for his sadness and also for warning against laughter.[51]

In tune with his portrait of Jesus rejoicing in God's mercy, Rūmī continues by citing a word of God given in response to 'one of God's friends who was present' who asked 'Which of them has the higher station?' God answered: 'He who thinks better of Me.'[52] In accordance with God's kindness and the example of the smiling sage, wrath should be suppressed:

> *Jesus, upon whom be peace, was asked 'Spirit of God, what is the greatest and most difficult thing in this world and the next?' He replied, 'The wrath of God'. They asked again, 'And what shall save a man from that?' He answered: 'You master your own wrath and suppress your rage.'*[53]

Healing Love, Life-Giving Breath

In Rūmī, love itself is equated with Jesus, and raises him far above this world:

> *When Jesus, Love's spirit, takes flight,*
> *Never again will he lower his wing*
> *To return to the realm of labor.*[54]

But his love is first of all a healing love for others. As Schimmel notes, for Rūmī 'The life-bestowing breath of Christ is the equivalent of a kiss':

> *When someone asks you: 'How did Christ quicken the dead?'*
> *Then give me a kiss in his presence: 'Thus!'*[55]

For Rūmī, as for Ibn al-ʿArabī, his life-giving power is symbolized by his breath (in Persian: *dam-i-masīḥ*). Jesus is the great spiritual physician:

> *Myriads were the therapeutic arts of Galen:*[56] *before Jesus and his (life-giving) breath they were a laughing stock.*[57]

His speech is like creative breath, and the speech of every spirit can become effective like the breath of Christ:

> *Spirits in their original nature have the (life-giving) breath of Jesus, (but while they remain embodied) one breath of it (the spirit) is a wound, and the other a plaster.*
> *If the (bodily) screen were removed from the spirits, the speech of every spirit would be like (the breath of) the Messiah.*[58]
> *Each one of us is the Messiah of a world (of people): in our hands is a medicine for every pain.*[59]

Although every human spirit may become like the breath of Jesus and a Messiah for his world, there is still something far beyond the ordinary human in the creative spirit of Jesus. For Rūmī, this feature of Jesus' uniqueness is related to his knowledge of the name of God, and his ability to utter it effectually. In an allegorical reading of the story about Joseph and Zalīkhā, Rūmī associates Jesus' miraculous powers with his intimate knowledge of the Name:

> *The vulgar are always pronouncing the Holy Name, (but) it does not do this work (for them) since they are not endowed with (true) love.*
> *That (miracle, i.e. bringing the dead to life) which Jesus had wrought by (pronouncing) the Name of Hú (God) was manifested to her through the name of him (Joseph).*
> *When the soul has been united with God, to speak of that (God) is to speak of this (soul), and to speak of this (soul) is to speak of that (God).*[60]

A Jesus Within, Waiting to be Born Again

At the end of his life, Jesus ascended to heaven. Ascension was possible for Jesus since he was more akin to the angels than to the 'ass' or the 'donkey' of the body. Having departed from the world of matter (the latter symbolized by

Jesus' donkey), he resides in the fourth heaven. But he can be born again in everyone, through birth pangs like those of Mary:

> *It is pain that guides a person in every enterprise . . .. It was not until the pain of labour appeared in Mary that she made for the tree . . .. Those pangs brought her to the tree, and the tree which was withered became fruitful . . .. The body is like Mary. Everyone of us has a Jesus within him, but until the pangs manifest in us our Jesus is not born. If the pangs never come, then Jesus rejoins his origin by the same secret path by which he came, leaving us bereft and without portion of him.*[61]

The Breath of Jesus, the Beauty of Joseph, the Light of Muḥammad

James Roy King (1990) has suggested that Rūmī's joyous expressions of how the divine, life-giving breath renews the surface of the world 'confirms that Islam takes a somewhat optimistic view of human nature – more optimistic, certainly than Christianity', although the life-giving wonders are set against the dark background of human folly and malice.[62] 'The breath of Jesus renews, restores and transforms human life' – but not without 'the response of the mind and heart' to the image of life-giving represented by Jesus.[63] King summarizes:

> Rūmī carries the meaning of Jesus well beyond what we would normally identify as Islamic norms, well beyond what might be required of a prophet, identifying him as one of a very rare body of individuals qualitatively different from normal human beings and endowed with a special capacity to renew and transform human lives, to render them whole and complete, but without ever going beyond the Islamic insistence that there is no god but God.[64]

Even though Jesus is highly elevated by Rūmī, it should be kept in mind that his position is relativized through the mystical assurance that all saints have a special position, before both men and God: 'All the saints are sons of God.'[65]

In his exposition, James Roy King adds some comments to the representation of Joseph in *Mathnawī*. He is recognized by the beauty of his face, as Jesus is recognized by his life-giving breath. For Rūmī, Joseph is both an archetypal figure embodying the way of a perfect man through the tribulations and temptations of human life, and a knower of the unseen, a dream-interpreter.[66] In King's summary:

> In Joseph we have a symbol of our capacity for contact with the spiritual world of which Jesus was such a master, and while the meaning of the cross for the Christians is missing from Rūmī, his emphasis on the life-giving power of Jesus suggests that he did indeed have a fundamental grasp of the darkest reaches of human experience – and the place of Jesus therein.[67]

With all the veneration of Jesus and Joseph in Rūmī's works, it should nevertheless be kept in mind that his works must be regarded above all as a climax in the Muslim veneration of Muḥammad. Rūmī gives mystical light and meaning to numerous sayings, anecdotes and legends connected with Muḥammad. And he leaves no doubt that Muḥammad is the superior prophet:

> *Certainly it is right that he should say that the Lord of Jesus, upon whom be peace, honoured Jesus and brought him nigh to Him, so that whoever serves him has served the Lord, whoever obeys him has obeyed the Lord. But inasmuch as God has sent a prophet superior to Jesus, manifesting by his hand all that He manifested by Jesus' hand and more, it behoves him to follow that Prophet, for God's sake, not for the sake of the Prophet himself.*[68]

Although Rūmī has a high appreciation for 'the way of Jesus', which meant 'wrestling with solitude and not gratifying lust', the way of Muḥammad was better, inasmuch as he endured the agonies of ordinary life as 'inflicted by men and women'. Therefore, 'The Sunnah is the safest road, and the community of the faithful your best fellow travellers'.[69]

Jesus in Ṣūfī Tafsīr

As for the image of Jesus in Ṣūfī Tafsīr, Neal Robinson has examined the commentaries of al-Qushayrī (Persia, d. 1072) and al-Qāshānī (Persia, d. 1329).[70] In general, Ṣūfī exegesis is marked by a continuous quest for the inner meaning of the text, or rather the plurality of meanings corresponding to the different spiritual stages. Al-Qushayrī is much in tune with mainstream Tafsīr, whereas the later al-Qāshānī is more esoteric in his interpretation.

Jesus' return is perceived by al-Qāshānī as a necessary step in Jesus' own spiritual development to reach the level of Muḥammad. All the outward details in the *aḥādīṯ* concerning the descent of Jesus are given a spiritual interpretation. Anti-Christ, whom Jesus (according to Ḥadīth) will defeat in his second coming, is interpreted by the Ṣūfī 'psychologist' and contemporary to Rūmī, Najm ud-dīn Rāzī (d. 1256), as the demanding ego of the one-eyed self.[71] According to Ṣūfī as well as traditional understanding, Jesus will share more fully in our human life in his second coming than he did during his first stay on earth; marrying, begetting children and being buried. But in the view of Ṣūfīs, the aim of his second coming is spiritual perfection, under similar life circumstances to those of Muḥammad.

As to the end of his first coming, the substitutionist idea is often given an esoteric interpretation by the Ṣūfīs, implying that Jesus' spirit, 'overflowing with the spirituality of the sun' was raised to God whereas his external semblance was cast upon a substitute. In the words of al-Qāshānī: 'And they did not know in their ignorance that God's spirit could not be killed.'[72]

When it comes to the miracles, we have seen that the 'orthodox' commentaries have some difficulty in deciding whether Jesus was endowed with a general life-giving ability, or only 'allowed by God' to perform specifically ordained miracles. For the Ṣūfī commentators, this is not really a problem, because Jesus is perceived as being purified from his own volition and standing entirely at God's disposal. Al-Qāshānī interprets 'by God's leave' as meaning 'My facilitating through My manifesting the attributes of My life, knowledge and power for you'.[73]

In the interpretation of the actual miracles, the focus is persistently on their inner meaning. Jesus is portrayed as healing souls from spiritual blindness and the leprosy of worldliness, bringing them to the eternal life of divine knowledge. Out of the 'clay' of our carnal soul, Jesus creates bird-like souls, by breathing divine knowledge into them. Likewise, the seclusion of Mary behind a 'curtain' (*ḥijāb*) and the virginal conception is given a metaphorical interpretation applicable to spiritual life in general. Ṣūfī commentators and thinkers ponder upon the co-operation between imagination and physical processes in the act of virginal conception. The apparition of the man-like angel is thought to arouse the passion of Mary and thus preparing her physically for conception (similarities can be found in Ibn al-ʿArabī, and possibly in Rūmī).

The affinity of al-Qāshānī to certain features of Christian tradition is noteworthy. He alludes to Johannine expressions of Jesus such as 'going to my father', and comes close to the symbolic interpretations of 'blindness' and 'death' in the Gospel of John. But he remains within the qur'ānic universe, more or less as interpreted in the theosophical system of Ibn al-ʿArabī. The aim of Jesus' return is, as we have seen, to attain the spiritual level of Muḥammad, 'the station of the spirit', which neither Jesus nor his followers can reach without Islam.

Summarizing Central Features of Ṣūfī Images of Jesus

Despite their wide influence on Ṣūfism, both al-Ḥallāj and Ibn al-ʿArabī (cf. al-Qāshānī) are regarded by mainstream Islam to be heterodox. But Jesus has persistently played a central role both in orthodox and heterodox versions of Ṣūfism. As Kenneth Cragg states:

> Nowhere is Islamic awareness of Jesus more lively or more perceptive than in the Arabic, Persian, Turkish, and Urdu poems of the mystics of Islam. Sitting loosely by doctrinal contentiousness, they are free to aspire towards that soul-affection which first kindled the theology pundits' dispute and which transcends what punditry can attain. The Jesus of Sufism kindles mutual recognition.[74]

The general mystical outlook of Ṣūfī Islam, as well as its theosophical speculation, implies a different context of interpretation from that of Sunnī Muslim orthodoxy – Jesus is perceived either as a role model for the loving ascetic, or as a cosmic agent.

Being aware of the fact that Ṣūfism has always been an undercurrent of official Islam, the image of Jesus in Ṣūfism must be given due consideration in the investigation of the actual role of Jesus in the belief of Muslims. There are different levels in this. One is the general influence of Ṣūfī teaching on the average Muslim, another esoteric transmission of a higher spiritual knowledge.

Some general points can still be made, in search for central issues for Christian–Muslim dialogue about Christ, related to Ṣūfism.

Jesus as the Perfect Man: A Generalizing Concept

The Ṣūfī concept of the Perfect Man (*al-insān al-kāmil*) is associated with Ibn al-ʿArabi,[75] and further developed in the theosophical Ṣūfism of ʿAbd al-Karīm al-Jīlī (d. after 1408), in his book *Al-insān al-kāmil*.[76] The title *al-insān al-kāmil* is linked with all the major prophets of Islam (including, of course, Muḥammad) because they reached the loftiest stages of human perfection. Following R. A. Nicholson and his commentary on Rūmī's *Mathnawī*, James Roy King summarizes the Ṣūfī view of Jesus in the light of this concept:

> 'Perfect Man' is mystical Islam's way of suggesting that Jesus (and a very few others) were individuals whose extraordinariness did not lie in any number of fine qualities they possessed but rather in the absolute uniqueness of their moral and intellectual fibre, in their particular relationship with God and man, individual and cosmos, heaven and earth, the One and the many, ultimate reality and the created word.[77]

Jesus as Theophany: A Non-Exclusive Attribute

The Perfect Man is not only perfecting humanity, but also displays to mankind the attributes of God. The Shīʿite Ṣūfī-master Javad Nurbakhsh interprets the Ṣūfī appellation of Jesus *rūḥullāh*, 'Spirit of God', as implying that 'he is that Perfect Spirit which is a theophany (*maẓhar*) of the All-Comprehensive Name: Allāh', that is to say, 'a complete mirror of the Divine Attributes'.[78]

Again, we see how Ṣūfīs come astonishingly close to a Christian image of Christ. But although Ṣūfīs may look upon 'Jesus as manifestation of the Divine Attributes of Creator and Reviver' and Mary 'as manifestation of the Attribute of Sustainer', perfected human beings like Mary and Jesus are still 'not the source but merely a mirror reflecting the Attributes'.[79]

The elevation of Jesus is relativized by attributing the capability of theophany to mankind in general:

> . . . the human being is in essence a theophany (*maẓhar*) and an object of tutelage (*marbūb*) for the All-Comprehensive Name, Allāh . . . The Rational Soul (*nafs-e nāṭeqa*) of man is unhampered by corporeal trappings and, consequently, divine and pure in nature.[80]

Sainthood and Breath

In *Mathnawī*, Rūmī retells a story of Jesus and John communicating in the wombs of their mothers.[81] In the modern context of Nurbakhsh, the story is taken in a generalizing sense 'to illustrate the telepathic nature of communication among saints'.[82] Accordingly, he points to the fact that for the Persian Ṣūfī poet ʿAṭṭār (d. 1220), the qur'ānic mention of the infant Jesus speaking from the cradle only confirms that:

> *Every Christlike saint as sweetly*
> *as Jesus spoke such secret*
> *words in his infancy.*[83]

Also the more specific attribute of Jesus in Ṣūfism, his breath, is generalized by Ṣūfī poets (as we have seen with Ibn al-ʿArabī and Rūmī above):

> *The breath of Christ*
> *That brought the dead to life*
> *Was but one breath*
> *Of My Divine Breath,*
> *The nurturer of Spirits.*
> (Fakhr ud-dīn ʿIrāqī, d. 1289)[84]

The Spiritual Meaning of the Miracles

As for the general spiritualizing interpretation of the miracles in Ṣūfism, a significant saying attributed to Jesus is found in Najm ud-dīn Rāzī's *Marmuzāt-e asadi*:

> *Jesus the prophet said: 'The Lord granted me the power to bring the dead to life and make the blind to see and the congenitally deaf to hear, but He did not give me the power to cure a fool.'*[85]

The same saying is found in Shīʿite tradition, with an additional definition of a fool being incurably self-admiring and self-righteous.[86] The point is also made in Rūmī's *Mathnawī*, in a narrative masterpiece that tells how Jesus is seen running for the hills – 'you would say that a lion wished to shed his blood'. A man is astonished by the sight of such a fear shown by the notorious miracle-maker Jesus. Jesus replies that although he has revived many a dead man, he has recited the Name in vain over the heart of a fool:

> *The disease of folly is (the result of) the wrath of God; (physical) disease and blindness are not (the result of Divine) wrath: they are (a means of) probation.*[87]

Rūmī also tells the story of how Jesus was asked by a fool to be taught the Divine Name in order to revive a pile of dead bones. Jesus complains to the Lord that the fool apparently is more concerned with reviving dead bones than putting life into his own dead self. But in the end, Jesus yields to the insisting fool, the result being, however, that the fool revives a lion that immediately strikes him dead. And the lion warns:

> *Take heed! do not wish your currish (fleshly) soul alive, for it is the enemy of your spirit since long ago.*[88]

The story about Jesus, the liar, the loaves and the gold (see the section about 'Stories of the Prophets' in Chapter 3) is retold by al-Ghazālī, as a warning against worldly desires, but with some change in the miracles performed by Jesus to convince the liar, including that of walking on water, a cherished motif in Ṣūfism.[89]

Suffering, Death, Cross

Although the purified soul will be victorious over death, meditation on death as a fearful reality is not neglected by Ṣūfism. ʿAṭṭār is sensitive to Jesus' trembling before death:

> *Though joy to Jesus was like second nature,*
> *still he trembled when he remembered death.*
> *Though endowed with warmheartedness*
> *and blessed with expansiveness,*
> *he shook in awe from head to foot,*
> *drenched in a bloody sweat,*
> *mortified by his own mortality.*[90]

In Rūmī's works, there is a significant reference to the breath of Jesus, in which his life-giving ability is contrasted with the violent fate of al-Ḥallāj:

O You! Who sometimes revive this earthen flesh
Like Jesus, with a breath,
And sometimes show up beneath the gallows
Like Hāllaj . . . Come.[91]

Does Rūmī imply a parallel both in the qualities (breath) and the fate (gallows/cross) of Jesus and Ḥallāj? Rūmī is aware that love can imply degradation and suffering, cf. his expression in *Mathnawī* – 'through love the king becomes a slave'. The world rejects life-giving breath and divine love. Does this awareness enable an acceptance of the cross as a symbol of rejection and suffering? Ṣūfism does not necessarily shun the cross, and may give it an esoteric interpretation. Kenneth Cragg points to Rukn al-dīn Awḥādī (b. 1274), who writes remarkably 'about the mystery of suffering and of Jesus as its epitome':

One day the Messiah was with his friends,
His disciples, the repositories of his secrets.
He made his exposition to them the subject of love,
Declared the matter openly and then concealed it.
In the midst of his discourse, his companions saw
He was weary, with tears streaming from his eyes.
So they asked him for a sign and proof of love.
He said: 'Tomorrow is the day of Abraham's fire.'
Upon the next day, when he proceeded to his task
And set his foot upon the plank of the gallows,
He said: 'If there be any man present here,
This surely is a sufficient proof of love.
Whoever turns his countenance to God
He must press his back against the Cross.
Until his body has been tied to the gallows
His soul cannot mount up to heaven.'[92]

The concept of the cross as a proof of love may come very close to a Christian understanding. But as Cragg also notes, al-Ḥallāj:

> . . . died more for the hiddenness of an esoteric wisdom he could not loyally divulge than for the preaching of a kingdom of grace that could not be hid. His was, we might say, a Calvary of the esoteric. For all its mysterious appeal, it belongs with a Ṣūfī view of the body, of suffering and of evil, hardly to be fitted into the history of the Gospels. So we look to Sufi poetry about Jesus for the evangelical themes of poverty, meekness and surrender, rather than for the evangelical transaction of pardon and peace.[93]

The Mystical Perfection: Muḥammad

The mystic al-Ḥallāj has often been referred to as a possible 'mirror' of Jesus in Ṣūfī tradition. To put things in proportion, it may be useful to cite some passages that show al-Ḥallāj's veneration of Muḥammad. When it comes to Muḥammad too, his ecstatic mysticism goes far beyond Muslim orthodoxy, as can be seen in later Ṣūfī veneration of the Prophet:

> *What is more manifest, more visible, greater, more famous, more luminous, more powerful or more discerning than he (Muḥammad)? He is and was, and was known before created things and existences and beings. He was and still is remembered before 'before' and after 'after', and before substances and qualities. His substance is altogether light . . ..*[94]

In Ṣūfism in general, Muḥammad is celebrated as the perfection of humanity, not merely in the sense of moral example. Far beyond Islamic orthodoxy as it may seem, Ṣūfism endows Muḥammad with a cosmic significance. He is seen as:

> . . . the animating principle of the whole creation. In him is embodied that pre-existent 'intention' that lies behind all things and is fulfilled within them . . .. What was divinely breathed into Adam at the creation, namely the 'breath' of the Creator's purpose, is incarnate in the Prophet in whom the human essence finds perfected form.[95]

He is not only the Perfect Man, in whom the divine Names and attributes are expressed (as in Christ), but a reflection of the divine Light itself. As the *nūr Muḥammadī* ('Muḥammadan light') he is venerated as the sun of creation from which all life and illumination derive.[96]

The more esoteric speculations about the pre-existent Muḥammad in Ṣūfism are paralleled by exoteric phenomena in popular Islam as the joyous celebration of his birthday (*mawlid al-nabī*), and the saying of *taṣliyah* (*ṣallā Allāhu ʿalayhi wa-sallama*, 'God celebrate and salute him' – cf. Sūra 33.56) whenever his name is mentioned. And the appellations of Muḥammad found in Ṣūfī-inspired Muslim piety, the list of names attributed to him comes astonishingly close to the '99 names of God' in Muslim tradition.[97]

Notes

1 Quoted from Margareth Smith, *Rabiʿa: The Life & Work of Rabiʿa and Other Women Mystics in Islam*. Oxford: Oneworld (1994: 50).

2 See Khalidi (2001: 140f.), two sayings in Anṣāri's *Tafsīr -e ʿerfāni*, quoted by Nurbakhsh (1982: 123f.), and several sayings cited by al-Ghazālī in *Iḥyāʾ*, in book 36/IV.6 on love.

3 See Nurbakhsh (1982: 67–69).
4 A story found both with al-Ghazālı in *Iḥyā* (in book 15/II.5 about friendship and brotherhood) and with Kāshānı (see Nurbakhsh 1982: 97f.).
5 See two classical versions in Nurbakhsh (1982: 100f.).
6 See for instance Khalidi (2001: 126f.).
7 See Robinson (1991: 53–55), with references.
8 Quoted from ibid., p. 53. Khalidi (2001: 159) finds this saying in Abu Nuʿaym al-Isbahanī's (d. 1038) work *Hilyat al-Awliyā'*.
9 Quoted from Nurbakhsh (1982: 53).
10 Quoted from ibid., p. 51.
11 Quoted from ibid., pp. 110f.
12 Translated into English by Margaret Smith, with the title *An Early Mystic of Baghdad* (London,1935).
13 Cragg (1985a: 49).
14 For the case of al-Ḥallāj, see the standard work of L. Massignon, *Le Passion de Ḥallāj*, 4 vols., 2nd ed. (Paris: Gallimard 1975); Arnaldez (1988: ch. 2.III ('Le cas de Ḥallâj')); and Robinson (1991: 54f.).
15 About al-Ghazālī and the image of Jesus, see Zwemer (1917), Asin et Palacios (1917/1974), Massignon (1932), Padwick (1939), Jomier (1987), Arnaldez (1988: ch. 1.III), Schumann (1988: ch. 4).
16 Fazul ul-Karim has made an English translation of *Iman Gazzali's Ihya Ulum-id-din*. Lahore: Sind Sagar Academy (n.d.). The translation is not, however, complete, in the sense that several passages have been omitted (cf. Preface, vol. I, p. 2).
17 See the full texts in Asin et Palacios (1917/1974, Arabic and Latin), and the selections in Margoliouth (1893–1894, English), in Nurbakhsh (1982: 71–83 and 93–101), and in Cragg (1984: 47–49). Cragg bases his quotations partly on Margoliouth (1893–1894).
18 From book 39 (IV.9) on meditative thinking (*al-tafakkur*). Quoted from Cragg (1985a: 49) – cf. Margoliouth (1893–1894: 561).
19 Nurbakhsh' translation (1982: 81).
20 This saying is first found in the writings of Abū Bakr ibn Abī al-Dunya (d. 894). It is also attested in Syriac literature (Khalidi 2001: 116f.).
21 Both sayings from are from book 26 (III.6). Quoted from Nurbakhsh (1982: 80–81).
22 From book 26 (III.6), quoted from Cragg (1985a: 48). Cf. Margoliouth (1893–1894: 107) and Khalidi (2001: 118) who finds the first occurrence of this saying in the works of Abū Bakr ibn Abī al-Dunya (d. 894). This saying is also found in al-Ghazālī's book 44 (IV.4, on poverty and renunciation of the world) and in book 31 (IV.1, on *tawba*).
23 Quoted from Margoliouth (1893–1894: 107)/Cragg (1985a: 48). Nurbakhsh (1982: 79), translates this saying differently: 'Devotion has ten degrees; the ninth is silence, and the first, flight from people.'
24 Quoted from Margoliouth (1893–1894: 59)/Cragg (1985a: 47).

25 From book 29 (III.9) on the reproach of pride and vanity. My translation, cf. Asin et Palacios (1974: 391).
26 Quoted from NurbakskSh (1982: 82). Cf. Matthew 6.3+6+17.
27 My translation, cf. Asin et Palacios (1974: 394). Cf. Matthew 5.38–41.
28 Quoted from W. Montgomery Watt, *The Faith and Practice of Al-Ghazálí*. Oxford: Oneworld (1994: 116). The prayer is found in a similar version in *Iḥyāʾ ʿulūm al-dīn*, in book 9 (I.9) on *ḏikr* and supplications, as well as in book 15 (II.5) on friendship and brotherhood.
29 Cf. T. J. Winter (ed.), *Al-Ghazālī on Disciplining the Soul ... & on Breaking the Two Desires ...* Cambridge: Islamic Texts Society (1995: xxxiv).
30 Cf. Winter (ed.), op.cit., pp. 31 and 54 (from al-Ghazālī's book 22 on disciplining the soul).
31 This is the title of the book's fourth chapter. Quoted from the translation of David B. Burrell and Nazih Daher, *Al-Ghazālī: The Ninety-Nine Beautiful Names of God*. Cambridge: Islamic Texts Society (1995/1992: 30).
32 Pinault (1987: 106, Note 2).
33 For Ibn al-ʿArabī and Jesus, see ch. XV: 'The Wisdom of Prophecy in the Word of Jesus', in Ibn al-ʿArabi, *The Bezels of Wisdom*. Transl. by R.W. J. Austin. New York: Paulist Press (1980). Cf. the studies of D'Souza (1982, 1987); Schumann (1988: ch. 5 ('Der Christus der Ṣûfîs und seine Stellung in der mystischen Kosmologie Ibn al-ʿArabīs')); Arnaldez (1988: ch. 2.I ('Les Amis de Dieu et la Sainteté dans le soufisme d'Ibn ʿArabî')); and Robinson (1991: 57f.).
34 Also translated into German by Hans Kofler (Ibn al-ʿArabī, *Fuṣūṣ al-ḥikam*, Graz 1970, 2nd ed. 1986 under the title *Die Weisheit der Propheten*).
35 See Hayek (1959) and Barr (1978) (several references).
36 Ibn al-ʿArabī, *The Bezels of Wisdom* , pp. 174–175.
37 Ibid., p. 176.
38 Ibid., p. 177.
39 Ibid.
40 Ibid., p. 178.
41 Ibid., p. 181.
42 Cf. D'Souza (1982) and Robinson (1991: 57f.).
43 See text, translation and commentary by R. A. Nicholson, *The Mathnawī of Jalaluddin Rumi*, 8 vols., London, 1925–40/3 vols., 1977 (translation only). As to Rūmī in general, see Annemarie Schimmel, *The Triumphal Sun: A study of the Works of Jalāl al-dīn Rūmī*. London/The Hague (1978).
44 English translation by Arthur J. Arberry, *Discourses of Rūmī*. London: London University Press (1961).
45 Renard (1987: 48).

46 Cf. Mathnawī VI.4367–4370.

47 See *Mathnawī* I.500–504. Cf. King (1990: 86), and Schimmel (1995: 152). Schimmel points to the fact that the idea of Jesus as unicoloured had already been expressed by the Persian mystic Sanāʿı (d. 1131), who said: *Take away this seven-coloured gown from your hand/Take a unicoloured robe like Jesus/So that you may walk on the water like Jesus/ And travel with sun and moon* (quoted from Schimmel, pp. 152f.).

48 Renard (1987: 52).

49 *Fīhi mā fīhi/Discourses* 11, quoted from Arberry, op. cit. pp. 60f., cf. Schimmel (1995: 144). The idea of Jesus as a smiling ascetic is also found with Kashf al-Mahjūb Hujwīrī (d. 1072), cf. Nurbakhsh (1982: 106) and Robinson (1991: 54). It is also attested in Shīʿite tradition (Qā'im 2004: 234).

50 See Khalidi (2001: 120).

51 See for instance Khalidi (2001: 144, 195, 200). As for Shīʿite tradition, see Qā'im (2004: 290, 304, 318). However, Shīʿite tradition knows also the opposite tradition of a laughing Jesus (Qā'im 2004: 234).

52 Ibid., Cf. *Mathnawī* V.1591, on the precedence of mercy over wrath in God's nature.

53 *Fīhi mā fīhi/Discourses* 68, quoted from Arberry, op. cit. p. 239. Cf. Türkmen (1992: 26).

54 *Diwān-e shams*, quoted from Nurbakhsh (1982: 57).

55 Quoted from Schimmel (1995: 147).

56 I.e. the famous Greek physician, d. 130 AD.

57 *Mathnawī* I.528, quoted from Nicholson, op. cit., vol. II, p. 31. Cf. Türkmen (1992: 8).

58 *Mathnawī* I.1598–1599, quoted from Nicholson, op. cit., vol. II, p. 88. Cf. Türkmen (1992: 9).

59 *Mathnawī* I.47, quoted from Nicholson, op. cit., vol. II, p. 7.

60 *Mathnawī* VI.4039–4041, quoted from Nicholson, op. cit., vol. IV, p. 481. Cf. Türkmen (1992: 18), who takes 'him' in the fifth line of the quotation as a reference to God, and not to Joseph.

61 *Fīhi mā fīhi/Discourses* 5, quoted from Arberry, op. cit., p. 33. Cf. Schimmel (1995: 155).

62 King (1990: 87).

63 Ibid., p. 88.

64 Ibid., pp. 89f.

65 Quoted from Nurbakhsh (1982: 23).

66 For the role of Joseph in Islamic spirituality, see also John Renard, *Seven Doors to Islam: Spirituality and the Religious Life of Muslims*. Berkeley/ Los Angeles: University of California Press (1996: 259–272).

67 King (1990), concluding passage, p. 105.

68 *Fīhi mā fīhi/Discourses* 29, quoted from Arberry, op. cit., p. 136. Cf. also *Mathnawī* V.274–276.

69 *Fīhi mā fīhi/Discourses* 20, quoted from Arberry, op. cit., p. 136, and *Mathnawī* VI.694.
70 See Robinson (1991: ch. 17 – 'The representation of Jesus in the Ṣūfī Commentaries').
71 See quotations from Rāzī's 'Marmuzāt-e asadi' in Nurbakhsh (1982: 61–64).
72 Quoted from Robinson (1991: 184).
73 Ibid., p. 186.
74 Cragg (1985a: 60).
75 Cf. John T. Little (1987), 'Al-Insān al-Kāmil: The Perfect Man according to Ibn al-ʿArabī', *The Muslim World*, LXXVII(1), 43–54.
76 Cf. Annemarie Schimmel, *Mystical Dimensions of Islam*. Chapel Hill: The University of North Carolina Press (1975: 280f.).
77 King (1990: 85).
78 Nurbakhsh (1982: 26).
79 Ibid., pp. 32f.
80 Ibid., pp. 26f.
81 Ibid., p. 28. Cf. Luke 1.41– 44.
82 Ibid.
83 Ibid., p. 29.
84 Ibid., p. 52.
85 Ibid., p. 86. Cf. a version of the saying in al-Abshīhī (d. 1438), Khalidi (2001: 211).
86 Qā'im (2004: 264).
87 *Mathnawī* III.2592. Quoted from Nicholson, vol. II, p. 145. Cf. Nurbakhsh (1982: 114–116).
88 *Mathnawī* II.474. Quoted from Nicholson, vol. II, p. 246. Cf. Nurbakhsh (1982: 120).
89 Cf. Nurbakhsh (1982: 107f.).
90 *Moṣibat-nāma*, quoted from ibid., pp. 108f.
91 Rūmīı, *Diwān-e shams*. Quoted from ibid., pp. 52f.
92 Quoted from Cragg (1985a: 62f.): Taken from the English translation in A. J. Arberry, *Classical Persian Literature*, London (1958: 307–308).
93 Cragg (1985a: 63).
94 Quoted from Cragg (1984: 54): Taken from *The Tawāsın of Manṣūr al-Ḥallāj*, translated by Aisha ʿAbd al-Raḥmān al-Tarjumāna, London (1974: 21).
95 Ibid., p. 60.
96 Cf. Annemarie Schimmel, *And Muhammad is His Messenger: The Veneration of the Prophet in Islamic Piety* (Chapel Hill: University of North Carolina Press, 1985) and Marcia K. Hermansen, 'The Prophet Muḥammad in Sufi Interpretations of the Light Verse (aya nur 24:35) (Part 1)', in *Islamic Quarterly*, vol. XLII(2), (1998: 144–155).

97 Cf. two articles regarding 'A List of the Appellations of the Prophet Muhammad' in *The Muslim World*, 1976, pp. 259–262 (R. Ebied/ M. Young) and 1978, pp. 57–60 (A. Rudvin).

Chapter 6

Encounters and Confrontations: Dialogue, Apologetics, Polemics[1]

The Role of Christ in Early Intra-Muslim Polemics

In a study from 1994, Tarif Khalidi suggests that the Jesus material in early Muslim lore played a specific role in intra-Muslim polemics in the first two Islamic centuries. He identifies a role conflict between the emerging class of 'state supported' *fuqahāʾ* (jurists) and *ʿulamāʾ* (religious scholars) on the one side and the story tellers (*quṣṣāṣ, qurrāʾ*) on the other. The latter groups are known to have had their strongholds in southern Iraq, in Kufa and Basra, at a critical distance from the political centres of (until 750) Damascus and (from 750) Baghdad. Khalidi suggests that Iraq, more particularly Kufa, was 'the original home of the literary Jesus', and comments:

> The *quṣṣāṣ* and *qurrāʾ* were either domesticated, i.e. taken into custody by the legitimising Establishment, where Jesus eventually became an irrelevant and circumscribed apocalyptic figure in canonical Ḥadīth; or else they turned to various forms of opposition directed against societal injustice, where Jesus became a relevant moral and political force.[2]

Khalidi suggests that the narrators in general would not favour the radical political and military opposition to the caliphate led by the Khārijites, but rather incline towards the more apolitical position of the Murjiʿite tendency. In conjunction with this general view, Khalidi presents his thesis:

> In the first place, it may be observed that a general atmosphere of *zuhd* [asceticism] tended to predispose these narrators to renunciation of the world, to leave the final computation of human sins to God and to accept a kind of division of labour whereby kings would be left to rule while the pious are left with divine wisdom. It also meant that the anger of these early *zuhhād* [ascetics], as expressed in Jesus' sayings, was vented in this period largely against their own kind, specifically those of their own number

> (*fuqahā*ʾ, ʿ*ulamā*ʾ, *quḍāt, qurrā*ʾ, *quṣṣāṣ*) who had, so to speak, 'betrayed' their mission to the community in favour of royal service. An attitude of sadness prevails towards the building of mansions and palaces which may, historically speaking, be a reference to Ummayad and Abbasid extravagance and reflect some of the sense of neglect felt in Kufa and Basra.[3]

Thus, Khalidi holds the view that most of the purveyors of the literary Jesus politically belonged to a 'middle group' – between those who made their peace with the government of the day, and those who went into active opposition.

In his more comprehensive study of sayings and stories related to Jesus in Muslim tradition, Khalidi repeats and further illustrates the role that these sayings may have played in early intra-Muslim polemics. For instance, he highlights the many examples of 'anti-scholar' sentiments in the sayings, reminiscent of Jesus' criticism of the Scribes in the biblical Gospels. In particular, many parallels can be found between the Muslim sayings and Jesus' woes against the Scribes and the Pharisees in Matthew 23: 'Nothing avails the scholar of great learning if he does not act according to it . . .. Be on your guard against false scholars . . ..'[4]

The cited saying is found in a work by a Yemeni scholar from the eighteenth century and testifies to the fact that Jesus' warnings against false scholars who do not live in accordance with their teachings, has continued to be felt as relevant by Muslim opposing hypocrisy among the ʿ*ulamā*ʾ.

Jesus's warnings against false scholars and their attachment to worldly gain are also abundantly attested in Shīʿite sources, as in the following thirteenth century source:

> *Jesus said, 'How can someone be a scholar if the afterlife is indicated to him while he remains preoccupied with this life, and if what harms him is more desirable to him than what benefits him?'*[5]

In this type of sayings, Khalidi finds also reflections of the increasing tension between Sufis and legal scholars in Islam, into which the figure of Jesus was drawn 'on the side of the Sufis because of his perceived disapproval of narrow-minded legalism'. As an example, Khalidi cites the following saying found in one of Ibn al-ʿArabī's (d. 1240) works:

> *Jesus said to the religious lawyers, 'You sit on the road to the afterlife – but you have neither walked this road to its end, nor allowed anyone else to pass by. Woe to him who is beguiled by you!'*[6]

As we shall see, Jesus' critique of legalism and worldly scholars recurs in some modern Egyptian writers of the mid-twentieth century who rallies Jesus as an ally in their efforts at modernizing Islam (Chapter 7).

Christian Apologetics under Muslim Rule

With the expansion of Islam westwards and eastwards, many Christian communities came under Muslim rule as *ḏimmīs* (protected minorities) in North Africa and Spain, in Syria and Iraq. This led to a deeper knowledge of Christianity by Muslims, and Christians were challenged to relate not only practically, but also theologically to Islam.

As for Christians in the East, there are several historical testimonies of their theological responses to Islam, during the Ummayyad and early ʿAbbasid dynasties.[7] The first Christian theologian, of whom an explicit theological evaluation of Islam is preserved, is John of Damascus (675–753), from eighth-century Syria, holding an administrative position in the Ummayyad capital of Damascus.

In the history of Christian theology, John is considered to have summarized what should become the normative christological tradition for the Greek Orthodox Church. He adds to the development of Chalcedonian Christology through his notion of *perichōrēsis*, meaning mutual penetration of Logos and human nature. In his view, the divine nature remains unchanged in *perichōrēsis*, but is perfectly represented in the *logos* becoming human, and mirrored in the icons. His evaluation of Islam is known from two versions of a 'Discussion between a Christian and a Saracen', and from his treatise about the heresies of the church, in which a chapter on the most recent of them, namely 'the heresy of the Ishmaelites', is included.[8] In this, he follows (maybe introduces) the prevailing tendency among Christians under Muslim rule to see Islam not as a different religion, but as a Christian heresy.

In general, John is arguing from a defensive position. But in his apologetic efforts, he includes attacks on what he considers to be the weak points in the teachings of Muḥammad. Muḥammad's prophethood is rejected because he did not tell the future or perform miracles, i.e. on the basis of a Christian understanding of prophethood.

In his discussion of Islamic Christology, he sees Jewish-Christian influence behind the rejection of the divinity of Christ, and maintains that Muḥammad had received his notion of *logos*/Christ as being created from the Arians, and his insistence that Jesus was not the Son of God but of Mary from the Nestorians (cf. their rejection of the Cyrillian notion *theotokos*). He is not examining the qur'ānic Christology from the viewpoint of Islamic theology, but from a Christian perspective. Accordingly, he also gives a Christian interpretation of the qur'ānic title 'Word'.

From the period of the ʿAbbāsid dynasty (750–1258), a lot of material about Christian Arab apologetics has been made available and researched.[9] As for the early ʿAbbāsid period, the Syrian theologians Theodore Abū Qurra, Ḥabīb ibn Khidam, Abū Rāʾita and Timothy deserve special mention.[10]

Theodore Abū Qurra (740–825) was a Melkite Bishop of Ḥarrān in Mesopotamia, and considered himself a disciple of John of Damascus.[11] The atmosphere of Ḥarrān was one of tolerant religious pluralism, a fact that may explain the boldness of Theodore Abū Qurra's polemics against Islam. In his works (both in Arabic and Greek), rational argument often prevails over scriptural. He sets out to refute Islam and defend the doctrines of Christ's sonship and the Trinity by the means of reason. As for Muḥammad, he speaks of him as a 'false prophet that had been taught by an Arian'.[12]

A discussion located to the ʿAbbāsid capital of Baghdad is preserved through the accounts of Timothy (727–823), who was the 'catholicos' or patriarch of the Nestorians in Iraq.[13] His discussion with Caliph al-Mahdī is said to have taken place in 781. Although the Nestorian church was in a period of expansion at this time, the Catholicos – as a resident of Baghdad – would still have to mould his argument in accordance with the limitations implicit in his *ḏimmī*-status. Thus, the Catholicos is not in a position to challenge the Caliph. It is his partner in discussion who is asking, with Timothy responding. The discussion focuses on the nature and attributes of God and the image of Christ. The Caliph presents the traditional Muslim objections to Christian teachings. He also puts forward an allegation that Jews and Christians have corrupted their scriptures, and that Muḥammad was foretold in the Bible (cf. the section about 'Muḥammad and Jesus in Ḥadīth and legend' in Chapter 2).

In his response, Timothy not only explains and defends the Christian teachings 'from within', but also refers to qur'ānic statements that could be given a Christian interpretation. He refers to the qur'ānic title 'Word of God' attributed to Jesus, and he seems to interpret the qur'ānic passages on Jesus' death as not being contrary to the Johannine insistence that the death of Christ was willed by God and consented to by Christ (John 10.17f.). In response to the Caliph's question whether God could die, Timothy refers to the classical distinction (and Nestorian separation?) between the natures of Christ, implying that it was only the human nature of Christ that died. As for the Christian estimation of Muḥammad, Timothy differs markedly from the negative evaluations of John of Damascus and Abū Qurra, with his famous statement that Muhammad is 'worthy of all praise' and 'walked in the path of the prophets' because he taught the unity of God and the way of good works:

> *Muḥammad is worthy of all praise, by all reasonable people, O my Sovereign. He walked in the path of the prophets, and trod in the track of the lovers of God. All the prophets taught the doctrine of one God, he walked, therefore, in the path of the prophets. Further, all the prophets drove men away from bad works, and brought them nearer to good works, and since Muḥammad drove his people away from bad works and brought them nearer to the good ones, he walked, therefore, in the path of the prophets. Again, all the prophets separated men from idolatry and polytheism, and attached them to God and to His cult, and since Muḥammad separated his people from idolatry and polytheism, and attached them to the cult and the knowledge of one God, beside whom there is no other God, it is obvious*

that he walked in the path of the prophets. Finally Muḥammad taught about God, His Word and His Spirit, and since all prophets had prophesied about God, His Word and His Spirit, Muḥammad walked, therefore, in the path of all the prophets.[14]

It should be noted, however, that Timothy is firm in his rejection of the argument put forward by the Caliph that the Paraclete prophesied by Jesus in the Gospel of John is Muḥammad.[15]

Another discussion in the context of Baghdad, during the ʿAbbāsid reign of caliph al-Maʿmūn (813–833), is found in letters between a Muslim al-Hāshimī and a Nestorian Christian al-Kindī – addressing a number of controversial issues including those pertaining to the doctrine of God and the life and claims of Muḥammad.[16] However, the questioning letter of al-Hāshimī is also considered to have been written by the Christian, and possibly a century or more after the alleged date of the discussion. So, the letter is probably to be counted among the apologetic treatises that abounded, especially in Arabic, after the time of John of Damascus.

Muslim Polemics, Directed towards Submitted Christians

In his exposition of Muslim perceptions of Christianity in the classical/medieval period of Islamic thought, Hugh Goddard (1996: ch. 2) points to the fact that:

> . . . the greater knowledge of Christianity available in the medieval period was used by some Muslim writers to develop a more systematic critique of Christianity. This critique never included any negative statements about Jesus himself, for whom and for whose message no disrespect ever appears; but it did develop a strong suspicion, and even explicit rejection, of what Christians said about Jesus during the course of their history. It is thus a criticism essentially of Christianity rather than of Jesus [. . .] Polemic . . . grew out of increasing Islamic assertiveness in a situation of some competition between different religious communities and of the need to preserve a separate Islamic identity.[17]

Already shortly after the death of Muḥammad, several incidents of hostility against Christians are reported – e.g. destruction of the symbol of the cross (cf. Ḥadīth sayings about Christ destroying crosses in his second coming). The conflict is, of course, not merely spiritual but also political: the cross was the ideological symbol of the Byzantine Empire.

After the Islamic conquests, there are conflicting tendencies. On the one hand, the Christians of Najrān, whom Muḥammad treated in a friendly way, were expelled from the Arabian Peninsula. On the other hand, Arab Christian churches were allowed greater freedom under Islam than they had been granted by the Byzantine Empire – although with *ḏimmī*-restrictions and the paying of a poll tax (*jizya*). After a period (culminating with Caliph al-Maʿmūn) when Christian intellectuals had been highly valued as translators of Greek and Syriac works into Arabic, the Caliph al-Mutawakkil (847–861) introduced highly restrictive and hostile measures against Christians.[18]

From the ninth century onwards, several explicitly polemical treatises against Christians have been preserved, such as the 'Letter about refutation of the Christians' (*Risāla fī-l-radd al-Naṣārā*) of the Muʿtazilite theologian ʿAmr b. Baḥr al-Jāḥiẓ (d. 869), and the *Radd ʿalā l-Naṣārā* of the Christian convert ʿAlı b. Sahl ibn Rabbān al-Ṭabarī. Polemical attacks on Christianity are also found in the manuals of theology (*kalām*) by Ashʿarite theologians such as al-Bāqillānī (d. 1013), al-Juwaynī (d. 1085) and others.

The refutation of Christianity and rather harsh polemics against Christians by the famous *adab* writer al-Jāḥiẓ may stand as a typical example of Muʿtazilite polemics against Christians.[19] Jāḥiẓ accuses the Christians of anthropomorphism in their teachings about Christ and God, and strictly rejects any attempt at isolating specific attributes of God. Hugh Goddard (1996) regards his work as 'a commissioned work of propaganda', warning ordinary Muslims against cultured, rich and efficient, but deceitful Christians.[20] Goddard comments:

> The result of these negative statements can be seen in the riots and outbreaks of anti-Christian agitation which occurred on a number of occasions in the medieval period . . .. Under certain circumstances Christians could serve as a convenient scapegoat for feelings of resentment in society. When these circumstances came about, the rather negative views of al-Jāḥiẓ, as echoed in the Ḥadīth and in other Islamic writings, undoubtedly served as a useful underpinning and foundation for such attitudes.[21]

Another polemical treatment of Christianity is found in the work of the contemporary Christian convert to Islam ʿAlı Ibn Rabbān al-Ṭabarī, *Radd ʿalā l-Naṣārā* (Refutation of the Christians); cf. his 'Book on Religion and Empire' (*Kitāb al-dīn wa-l-dawla*), which was written around 855 in the reign of al-Mutawakkil.[22] The authorship of *Kitāb al-dīn wa-l-dawla* has been disputed. In any case, Schumann (1988) argues that *Radd* was written by Ṭabarī before *Kitāb*, in which *Radd* is cited. The context of his polemical work is his conversion from Nestorian Christianity to Islam in the middle of the ninth century, and his close relationship to the court of Caliph al-Mutawakkil in Baghdad.

Islam seems to have offered ʿAlī Ibn Rabbān al-Ṭabarī a solution of the christological problem inherent in the Antiochene School and in Nestorianism: how can eternal divinity be present in a temporal being? Nestorianism was accused of separating the two natures of Christ, tending towards a Christology of 'two sons'; one eternal/divine and one temporal/human. In contrast, al-Ṭabarī underlines the unity and eternity of the human being Jesus Christ (cf. later Ṣūfī speculations of the eternal Perfect Man). His central objection to the divinity of Christ is the alleged implication that God then would be subject to change and deprived of his essential unity. As for the unique qualities of Christ documented by the Qur'ān, he generalizes them by referring to biblical parallels: Adam had neither a father nor a mother, Elijah raised people from the dead, and both Elijah and Enoch were raised to heaven alive. He also gives a generalizing and metaphorical interpretation of attributes such as Father/Son, and even refers to parallel usage where human beings can be addressed as 'Lord' or 'God', perhaps coming dangerously near to risking the accusation of *širk* (associating with God) in his argumentation.

Another prominent example of Muslim refutation of the belief in Christ's divinity is found in the book on divine unity (*Kitāb al-Tawḥīd*) written by the theologian Abū Manṣūr al-Māturīdī (from Transoxania, d. 944).[23] Like many of his fellow polemicists, al-Māturīdī reveals a good knowledge of the major Christian positions as regards the divinity of Christ, namely the Chalcedonian/Melkite, Nestorian and Monophysite doctrines. His argument is mainly directed at the notion of Christ's divine sonship, and the claim that Christ's miracle should prove his divinity. His refutation is based on rational arguments underpinned by qur'ānic assertions – not in a separate document directed against Christians as with al-Jāḥiẓ and al-Ṭabarī, but as an integral part of a systematic presentation of the Islamic faith. David Thomas (1997) suggests that his refutation may mark:

> . . . a new stage in Muslim theology, in which active involvement in live issues of debate was becoming less urgent than the need to see and understand how the elements of historical belief fitted into a continuous and comprehensible structure. If so, this attack anticipates the more elaborate but equally academic anti-Christian arguments in the great theological compendiums written a few decades later by al-Bāqillānī and ʿAbd al-Jabbār.[24]

David Thomas has also made the observation that in the works of leading Muslim thinkers from the early ʿAbbasid period who wrote on Christianity, there is hardly any reference to the cross and its implications.[25] Whereas polemicists such as al-Warrāq wrote extensively against Christian beliefs and in Trinity and Incarnation, the issue of the Cross tends simply to be ignored.[26] Ivor Mark Beaumont, on the other hand, has analysed how Christians sought to explain the cross in debates and dialogues with Muslims, in light of their counterparts' standard denial of Christ's crucifixion.[27]

A prominent example of anti-Christian polemic within the framework of Muʿtazilite theology reappears in the works of the Persian judge ʿAbd al-Jabbār (d. 1025).[28] His refutation of Christianity is preserved in a digressive section of a book in which he sets out to prove that Muḥammad was a true prophet (cf. Stern 1967, 1968). In his refutation of the claim that Jesus was crucified, al-Jabbār reproduces the substitution theory, which is inferred from a rather lengthy version of the passion narrative that differs slightly from that of the biblical Gospels. According to al-Jabbār, Christians have corrupted the teachings of Jesus, mainly by adapting to Roman customs. Against the words of Jesus, they claim that he is God, and against the practice of Jesus, they have abolished the Jewish law. Paul is singled out as the chief corrupter, and characterized as 'a cunning and roguish Jew'. The next culprit is Constantine:

> *Constantine reigned for fifty years, killing those who did not venerate the cross or accept the divinity of Christ, and thus in the end these beliefs were firmly established.*[29]

The Image of Paul in Early and Medieval Islamic Polemics

Different trajectories in classical Muslim images of Paul have been examined by P. S. van Koningsveld (1996), in connection with a recent discovery of a manuscript attributed to the early historian Sayf 'Umar al-Tamīmī (d. 796 or 797). The accounts of Sayf 'Umar al-Tamīmī are somehow different from those of al-Jabbār. Sayf depicts Paul as king of the Jews, but claims that he left his royal position and deceitfully put on the clothes of the followers of Jesus in order to prevent a major disaster for the Jews. According to Sayf 'Umar al-Tamīmī, four novelties in the subsequent teaching of Christians should be attributed to Paul: that the only correct direction for prayer was towards the east; that all food was permissible; that it was the duty of Christians to abolish any form of violence and revenge; and that God had made Himself manifest to them in the person of Jesus, but withdrew from their sight. Sayf 'Umar al-Tamīmī goes on to say that these teachings were all rebutted by an anonymous 'Believer', and that opponents to Paul's novel teachings continued to live in caves and hermitages, or wander about in the countryside. Some of them even reached the Arabian Peninsula. In the summary of van Koningsveld:

> In short, the role of Paul in the corruption of Christianity, according to this story, was twofold: he corrupted some important sacred rules of the religious law, and he spoiled the kernel of the faith itself.[30]

Among later Muslim polemicists focussing on Paul, van Koningsveld pays attention to Ibn al-Jawī (d. 1200), al-Damīrī (d. 1405) and al-Qarāfī (d. 1285). He identifies two tendencies: one depicting Paul as a cunning Jew who faked his conversion and subsequently corrupted the Christian faith; another still describing Paul as a cunning and roguish Jew, but nevertheless as a true convert, who corrupted Christianity by the introduction of pagan (Roman) customs. As we have seen, al-Jabbār belongs to this latter tendency.

In the Andalusian context, Ibn Ḥazm (d. 1064, see below in the section about *taḥrīf*) shows knowledge of this tradition, and produces his own version of the fake convert story. Ibn Ḥazm rebukes Paul for having introduced the doctrine of Jesus' divinity, and ridicules his teaching on circumcision as found in his letter to the Galatians.

The Understanding of Jesus' Miracles

A central theme in early Muslim polemics was the understanding of the miracles of Jesus. David Thomas, who has made comprehensive studies of early Muslim Polemic against Christianity (focused on the writings of Abū ʿĪsā al-Warrāq against the doctrines of Trinity and Incarnation[31]), has also paid attention to this strain in Muslim polemics (Thomas 1994). In Muslim polemical attacks on the doctrine of the incarnation, a favourite procedure was to compare the miracles performed by Jesus by those of other major prophets, in order to refute claims of his divinity based on the alleged uniqueness of his actions.[32]

Thomas examines polemical treatises from the ninth and tenth centuries, including those of ʿAlī al-Ṭabarī, al-Jāḥiẓ and al-Jabbār mentioned above. In addition, he focuses on the polemical writings of al-Māturīdī (d. 944), the convert from Christianity al-Ḥasan al-Ayyūb (mid-tenth century), the Shīʿite authors Abū ʿĪsā al-Warrāq and ʿAlī ibn Bābawayh (d. 991), and the Ashʿarite theologian al-Bāqillānī (d. 1013). The alleged letter of Caliph ʿUmar II to Basileus Leo II, probably written in the latter half of the ninth century, is also included in his discussion.[33]

A common procedure for early polemicists is to list other biblical miracles similar to those attributed to Jesus. Particular emphasis is laid upon miracles that imply command of nature, transformation of objects (like the rod of Moses) and restoration to life. Among the life-giving miracles, those performed by Elisha and Elijah are given pre-eminence, together with the prophecy of dry bones being revived in Hezekiel 37, which is taken as a miracle that actually happened. The general contention would be that of the convert al-Ḥasan (as Thomas summarizes it): if Christians take the miraculous acts of Jesus as an indication of his lordship, *rubūbiyyah*, then they must do the same with all the other persons who perform similar acts.[34]

With more discursive polemicist like al-Jabbār, there is not the same interest in listing and comparing prophetic miracles. His argument is of a more general kind:

> . . . in his system of thought all miracles originate from God and do not affect the status of the human individual upon whom they are centred. . . . God can cause miracles without being immediately present.[35]

As for the striking similarities between various lists of miracles made for polemical comparison, there are several indications that the lists may first have been compiled by those polemicists who were also converts. The lists responded to Christian claims that Jesus was God, with reference to his miracles (in particular, his raising of the dead). Such claims are reported already by Muḥammad's biographer, Ibn Isḥāq, and attributed to the Christians of Najrān.

In conclusion, Thomas notes that Christian apologetics and Muslim polemics reflected differing perspectives when dealing with miracles:

> For Christians the miracles of Jesus were significant as expressions rather than proofs of divinity, while for Muslims they were significant as signs of his human prophetic status.[36]

As demonstrated by Kate Zebiri, many elements of classical Islamic apologetics regarding Jesus' miracles persist in contemporary Muslim discourse. She also notes, however, that popular writings on Christianity from the modern period 'sometimes override classical Islamic doctrine, to the extent that miracles may even be denied'.[37] The dominant tendency in contemporary Tafsīr is nevertheless (in continuity with the classical approaches) to generalize the prophets' ability to perform miracles 'by God's permission', or to render them with a metaphorical interpretation.

Muslim Polemical Refutations and Sympathetic Reinterpretations in the Medieval Era

Two questions repeatedly arise from the polemical treatment of Christianity by medieval Muslim thinkers. First: Have the Scriptures been falsified, or only misinterpreted? Secondly: When christological dogmas are held not to be compatible with the confession of divine unity, is there any alternative interpretation of the Christian Gospels to that of Chalcedonian or Nestorian or Monophysite Christology?

The Claim of Taḥrīf (Falsification of the Scriptures)

The prevalent view among early Muslim has apparently been that Jews and Christians had only misinterpreted their Scriptures, not falsified them. Gradually, however, a theory of a conscious falsification (*taḥrīf*) of the Scriptures on the part of the Christians evolved.[38] This more polemical view – that the Scriptures themselves cannot be taken as authentic, but must somehow have been corrupted in the process of transmission – has been taken up in present-day Muslim polemics and linked with modern biblical criticism.

Among the Muslim polemicists mentioned above, al-Bāqillānī (d. 1013) gives a rationalistic interpretation of the Christian Gospels, but does not challenge the authority of the Gospels as such. More polemically, al-Juwaynī (d. 1085):

> . . . scorns the New Testament Evangelists for not being careful enough in their biographies of Jesus to omit references to events such as the Scourging at the Pillar or the Crowning with Thorns, descriptions, as Juwaynī asserts, which humiliate Jesus for the reader and diminish his claim to divinity.[39]

Applying the notion of *tabdīl* ('substitution', 'alteration'), he claims that the Jewish and Christian scriptures have in fact been altered, cf. the title of his polemical work *šifā al-ġalīl fī-bayān mā waqaʿa fī-l-tawrāt wa-l-injīl min al-tabdīl*, 'healing of the thirsty through exposing the alteration that befell the Torah and the Gospel'.[40]

The theory of falsification (*taḥrīf*) is developed by the famous polemical writer of eleventh-century Muslim Spain, Ibn Ḥazm (d. 1064), in his *Kitāb al-faṣl fī-l-milal wa-l-ahwā'wa-l-nihal* ('Book of religious communities and sects').[41] His assertion that the Jewish and Christian scriptures have been falsified should probably be read in the light of his literalist, *ẓāhirī* approach to the Qur'ān.[42] Ibn Ḥazm, a Muslim classic in this field, reveals a comprehensive knowledge of Christianity. Much of his polemic takes the form of an early biblical criticism, especially of the Gospels, in which he finds numerous contradictions and no guarantees of authenticity by means of a chain of transmitters. He holds the view that the Christian scriptures are completely corrupt. In his critique of Christians, he states that the distinctive practices of the Christians (such as observance of Sunday, their festivals, their omission of circumcision, their permission to eat pork, etc.) cannot be based on the Gospels, in which Jesus affirms that he will take nothing away from the Torah (Matthew 5.17). By this argument, he presents another typical view to be taken up in modern Muslim polemics, namely that although the Christian scriptures are generally corrupt, there is more genuine Islamic religion preserved in the Gospels than in the rest of the (mainly Pauline) New Testament.

Ibn Ḥazm is well informed about the christological disputes, and puts special effort into refuting the doctrine of divine attributes developed in the Monophysite tradition – revealing the theological contradictions of a system that implies a God-consumed humanity among the divine attributes.

W. M. Watt makes the remark that although Ibn Ḥazm lived under what was still the Islamic rule of Spain the eleventh century on the Iberian Peninsula was marked by the emerging disintegration of Muslim superiority, so that his sharpened polemic might be read as a defensive measure in an unstable political and cultural context.[43]

As for later expressions of what might have been a distinctively Iberian/Andalusian strand of polemics, van Koningsveld (1996) has identified two other voices from the thirteenth and fourteenth centuries respectively: the anonymous 'al-Imām al-Qurṭubī' and Muḥammad al-Qaysī. Both authors reveal knowledge of Sayf ʿUmar al-Tamīmī's early Muslim polemic against Paul.[44] Muḥammad al-Qaysī adds a contextual application: he identifies Sayf's 'Believer' with the Templars, who are said to have been true monotheists and crypto-Muslims, and therefore condemned by the Pope.[45]

Benign Reinterpretations

In contrast, the later work attributed to al-Ghazālī (d. 1111), *Excellent refutation of the divinity of Jesus, based on the Gospels*, at least intends to 'interpret the Gospel by the Gospel'.[46] In recent times, doubt has been raised as to whether al-Ghazālī was really the author of this work. In any case, on the authority of al-Ghazālī, the author sets out to prove that the Christians have misinterpreted the Gospel passages that appear to magnify Jesus as God, especially those in the Gospel of John, and argues that these must be taken metaphorically. The author thus accepts the authority of the Christian Gospels, but focuses on the sayings of Jesus that express his subordination to God. As a good mystic, he gives a consistently metaphorical and generalizing interpretation of the title 'Son of God'. The theophatic 'God-language' found in the self-presentation of Jesus is considered by the author to be a special dispensation granted to Jesus by God.

A main theological point in the author's argument is that the alleged divinity of Christ leads to the suffering, death and burial of God – something unthinkable in the theological framework of Islam. Therefore, a mystical/metaphorical interpretation of the God-language of Jesus is indispensable.

In the greatest work of al-Ghazālī, *Iḥyāʾ ʿulūm al-dīn* ('The Revival of the Religious Sciences'), he reveals a typical Ṣūfī interpretation of the sayings of Jesus, and an openness to the human capacity of becoming 'characterized with the characters of God' (cf. the section about al-Ghazālī in Chapter 5).

Besides al-Ghazālī, W. M. Watt singles out the Ashʿarite theologian al-Sharastānī (d. 1153) as the most sympathetic interpreter of Christianity among the tenth- and eleventh-century Muslim thinkers:

> . . . he gave prominence to points in Islamic teaching about Jesus which appear to place him above other prophets, and he avoided condemning the phrase 'son of God', instead regarding it as metaphorical . . ..[47]

Al-Sharastānī refers to Jesus as one who was granted 'manifest signs and notable evidences, such as the reviving of the dead and the curing of the blind and the leper', and concludes:

> *His very nature and innate disposition (fiṭra) are a perfect sign of his truthfulness; that is, his coming without previous seed and his speaking without prior teaching.*[48]

As for later developments, the famous Syrian-born Muslim theologian Ibn Taymiyya (1263–1328) deserves special mention.[49] Generally, Ibn Taymiyya was more concerned with the purification of the Muslim societies of his times than with polemics with Christians. His time was perceived by many as one of great outer and inner dangers for Islamic civilization (invasions and – as Ibn Taymiyya saw it – deviations from the Prophet's pure way of life). As measures of defence, Ibn Taymiyya also recommended a stricter practice of the *ḏimmī*-rules, limiting the opportunities for minorities to express their views freely and obtain influential positions in society. His recommended measures may even be seen as aiming at the total absorption of non-Muslim minorities into the Muslim *umma*.

His views about Christianity are expressed in his four volume work *Al-jawāb al-ṣaḥīḥ li-man baddala dīn al-masīḥ* ('The right answer to those who changed the religion of Christ'). The work is formulated as a response to the works of the Syrian monk Paul of Antioch, who became famous for his 'Letter to Muslim friends' from the end of the twelfth century – a document that reached Ibn Taymiyya more than a century afterwards through Cyprus.[50] In his works, Paul endeavours (in a conciliatory tone) to prove from the Qur'ān itself that Islam in fact teaches that Christianity is the true religion. His views invited, of course, a series of refutations from Muslims – among these the lengthy work of Ibn Taymiyya. Although Ibn Taymiyya thoroughly refutes the claims that the Qur'ān could be interpreted in a Christian sense, he still 'seemed to accept as authentic most of the Scriptures quoted by the Christians, apart from passages too directly contrary to the Qur'ān (i.e. the crucifixion)'.[51] According to Jean-Marie Gaudeul, 'Ibn Taymiyya's book can be seen as a Summa of all that Muslim scholars had been able to say about the claims of Christianity up to that time'.[52]

Christian Polemics against Islam in the Medieval Era: Enemy Images and Attempts at Understanding

Tracing the development of Christian apologetics, W. M. Watt states:

> While Christians living under Muslim rule like John of Damascus had to be very circumspect in their criticism of Islam, the citizens of the Byzantine Empire had no such inhibitions.[53]

Thus, in the writings of Byzantine theologians from the eighth to the thirteenth centuries, Islam is portrayed not as a heretical relative to Christianity, but as a false religion of diabolic inspiration. Their enemy image of Islam includes vicious caricatures of Muḥammad as the 'father of lies', perhaps Anti-Christ.[54]

The Byzantine polemic against Islam is clearly directed towards an enemy outside their realm, of whom they had only scarce knowledge. In contrast, the multi-religious context of the Iberian Peninsula challenged and enabled Christians to a more informed and qualified discussion with Islam. An important part of the more intimate cultural exchange between Muslim and Christian culture was the transmission in the Arabic language and Muslim context of the Hellenistic philosophical heritage through the Muslim *falāsifa* (philosophers) – of whom Ibn Sīnā/Avicenna and Ibn Rušd/Averroes were the most well-known in the West.

On the other hand, the cultural climate in the Christian West was marked by the spirit of the Crusades, from 1095 onwards. Although often regarded as a marginal episode by contemporary Muslim historians, the Crusades have had a lasting impact in that they have loaded the symbol of the cross with connotations of power and brutality on the part of the Christians, in the minds of Muslims and Jews (as well as oriental Christians).

In the context of cultural and military encounters (in the Holy Land as well as in Spain, where the Catholic *reconquista* recaptured one Muslim stronghold after the other), some Christian theologians endeavoured to reach a deeper understanding of Islam. Some of them even criticized the Crusader spirit for neglecting the primary missionary aim of the Christian church. If Muslims were to be converted, their religion must be properly known and understood.

The classic among the Spanish/French 'students of Islam' is Petrus Venerabilis, Abbot of Cluny (1094–1156).[55] After a visit to Spain, as part of his effort to understand and refute Islam, he sets out to collect a number of works about Islam, and to have them translated into Latin ('the Toledo collection', including Robert Ketton's Latin translation of the Qur'ān from 1143). He also writes his own introduction to Islam. He makes no secret of his view that the teaching of the Saracens is a heresy, and that the ultimate aim of his involvement with Islam is the conversion of Muslims. His view of Muḥammad and the Qur'ān was not particularly sympathetic:

> *Muhammad, instructed by the best Jewish and heretical doctors, produced his Quran and wove together, in that barbarian fashion of his, a diabolical scripture, put together both from the Jewish fables and the trifling songs of heretics.*[56]

In the thirteenth century, the Moghul expansion through Muslim lands also expanded the Christians' knowledge of geography, and opened their eyes to the numerous non-Christian peoples. Consequently, dealing with Islam by Christian philosophers and theologians became a part of the more general approach to non-believers. This approach is found in the writings of Roger Bacon (1214–1292). Thomas Aquinas (1225–1274) also dealt with non-

Christian beliefs (cf. his *Summa contra gentiles*) and Islam specifically (*De rationibus fidei contra Saracenos, Graecos et Armenos*) in his works.[57] For all his interest in Islam as a religion, he had no reverence for its founder Muḥammad nor for his followers:

> *The truth that he taught he mingled with many fables and with doctrine of the greatest falsity .... Those who believed in him were brutal men and desert wanderers, utterly ignorant of all divine teaching, through whose numbers Muhammad forced others to become his followers by the violence of his arms.*[58]

As for standard accusations against Islam that emerge in medieval Christian polemics, Watt summarizes his findings in four points: that Islam is a false and a deliberate perversion of truth; that Islam is a religion which spreads by violence and the sword; that Islam is a religion of self-indulgence; and that Muḥammad is the Anti-Christ.[59]

However, more eirenical voices may be identified, also in the late medieval era. A special contribution towards deeper understanding between Christians and Muslims was made by Ramon Lull of Mallorca (1235–1315), in his learned dialogue between a Gentile and a Jew, a Christian and a Muslim.[60] But also in the case of Lull, the ultimate aim is convincing the unbelievers of the Christian truth. Clashes with realities seem to have made him bitter, and what began with intellectual openness and idealism ended up in his self-provoked martyrdom in Tunisia.

On the edge of a new era – after the coming of the Ottoman empire in the East, and on the brink of the renaissance in the West – a more diplomatic voice is heard, advocating peaceful coexistence between religions: Nicolaus Cusanus (1401–1464), with his treatise *De pace fidei*.[61] The German born Cusanus was heavily involved in papal diplomacy, first towards the Byzantine emperor, and after the Muslim conquest of Constantinople in 1453, towards the Ottoman Sultan. In 1461, the Sultan was offered papal recognition as emperor of the East, on the condition that he would convert to Christianity. Albeit unsuccessfully, the pope attempted to convince the Sultan that he would lose nothing that was dear to him by conversion, since Christ only fulfilled the message of the Qur'ān. This way of reasoning was prepared by Cusanus in his *Cribatio alchorani*, finished in the same year. Before that, and as an explicit literary response to the conquest of Constantinople, Cusanus wrote his *De pace fidei* in 1453. In this remarkable work, Cusanus claims that all religions are oriented towards the same divine reality, only by means of different rites. In the heavenly dialogues exposed in his book, Cusanus addresses Islam in the clothing of an Arab and a Persian. Reference is made to the qur'ānic mention of Christ as a word from God, and Christ's ability to raise people from the dead and create birds from clay. The intention is to convince the Muslim that Christ is God not by refuting his religion, but by taking the Qur'ān 'in its best

Christian sense'. Although Cusanus pays a remarkable respect to Islam, as well as to other religions (such as the apparently polytheist teachings of the Indians), Islam is not taken seriously on its own terms, but only as a preface to Christ.

In a wider context, his attempts at an intellectual dialogue were overruled by the powerful enemy images produced to counter the Ottoman outreach for Europe (cf. the conquest of the Balkans, and siege of Vienna in 1529). In contrast to Cusanus, Martin Luther was convinced that Muslims could not be converted. In his rather belligerent writings against Islam as represented by the Turks, he refutes Islam on theological grounds, although not advocating that Islam should be combatted.[62] Trying to understanding the teaching of Islam, he finds that:

> *Turk's faith is a patchwork of Jewish, Christian and heathen beliefs. He [Muhammad] gets his praise of Christ, Mary, the apostles, and other saints from the Christians. From the Jews he gets the abstinence from wine and fasting at certain times of the year . . ..*[63]

Although he can value the monotheism of Islam, his evaluation is still basically negative: Islam contradicts evangelical faith by being a religion of good works, and by denying the divinity of Christ and hence his ability to save human beings by grace alone. In his most belligerent moments, he equates 'the Allah of the Turks' with the Devil, and 'the Koran of Muhammad' is attacked as a spirit of lies.

In politics, he held it to be incumbent on Christian authorities to defend themselves against the Turk, by the sword. But he did not advocate any unprovoked attack on Muslims. His view was rather that of *cuius regio, eius religio* (the local ruler decides about the religion of his region). As long as the Turks restricted themselves to the areas under their control, they should be allowed to live in peace:

> *Let the Turk believe and live as he will, just as one lets the papacy and other false Christians live. The emperor's sword has nothing to do with the faith; it belongs to the physical, worldy things . . ..*[64]

Again we can see how Islam is consistently seen through Christian lenses, and condemned (although respected in religio-geographical terms) on a par with 'false Christians'. The tendency to regard Islam not as a religion to be taken seriously in its otherness, but as a Christian (christological) heresy, appears as a persistent feature of Christian apologetics, all the way from John of Damascus to the Lutheran Reformation. This is also the case with the Lutheran *Confessio Augustana*, where in the first article on God and the Trinity, the 'Muhammadans' are condemned on a par with classical Christian heretics like the gnostic Valentinians and the Arians (who claimed that Christ was created in time, and not of God's essence).

Generally, the legacy from the high- and late medieval encounter with Islam is a mix of war, polemics and dialogue. Although much of Christian theology was marked by a will to approach Islam (and other religions) by word and not by sword, the image of Islam presented to Christians was still a distorted image. Many of the perceptions and misperceptions of Islam among Christian thinkers until this day can be traced back to writings on Islam from this period.

In contrast, Muslim polemic, sharp as it might be in its criticism of Christian teachings, could never discredit Jesus and the Judaeo-Christian heritage as a whole, since this heritage is recognized by the Qur'ān itself – although perceived as corrupted by Jews and Christians. Nevertheless, the medieval polemics launched from the Muslim side continue to influence modern Muslim approaches to Christianity.[65]

It should be noted that the modern controversy over the Gospel of Barnabas might shed new light on Christian–Muslim controversies, as they developed in the wake of the final expulsion of Moriscos from Spain. By the term Morisco, reference is made to those Iberian Muslims that, after having been forcefully converted to Christianity, were finally expelled from Spain in 1614–1619, and settled in North Africa as well as in more remote parts of the Ottoman Empire like Istanbul.[66] Researchers such as Bernabé Pons (1995, 1996) and Wiegers (1995) hold the view that the expulsion of the Moriscos from Spain in 1609 marked a new phase in the history of Muslim-Christian polemics, in which the Moriscos eventually were free to express themselves about the religion that had been forced upon them by the Christian authorities in Spain. As for the content of these polemical efforts, Wiegers claims that 'one of the new concepts appearing in these polemical writings is the idea that *Muḥammad is the Messiah . . .*'.[67]

This idea is found both among well known Morisco authors from the early seventeenth century, and in the Gospel of Barnabas which may have been compiled or reworked at about the same time (see the section about the Gospel of Barnabas in Chapter 7).[68]

Notes

1 For a general perspective, see Watt (1991), and the rich resource material in Gaudeul (1990: vol. I).
2 Khalidi (1994: 149).
3 Ibid., pp. 152–153.
4 Khalidi (2001: 216).
5 Ibid., 198f. and Qā'im (2004) (passim).
6 Khalidi (2001: 202).
7 For the following, see Newman (ed.) 1993, who offers English translations of documents related to this 'Early Christian–Muslim Dialogue'. See also Gaudeul (1990: vol. I, 27ff. and vol. II, 7ff.) (selected translations, with commentaries).

8 English translation with introduction and notes: see Newman (ed.) (1993: 133–162). John's writings on Islam are included in Migne *Patrologia Graeca*; in vols. 94, col. 1585ff. and 96, col. 1335–48 as for the 'Discussion' (Disceptatio), and in vol. 94, col. 764 ff. as for his treatise on Christian heretics. For discussion and (abridged) texts, see also Daniel J. Sahas, *John of Damascus on Islam*, Leiden, E. J. Brill (1972).

9 See Samir Khalil Samir and Jørgen S. Nielsen (eds.), *Christian Arabic Apologetics during the Abbasid Period (750–1258)*, Leiden, E. J. Brill (1994). For translated texts, see Newman (1993: 163ff.).

10 See Seppo Rissanen, *Theological Encounter of Oriental Christians with Islam during Early Abbasid Rule*, Åbo, Åbo Akademi University Press (1993). Rissanen discusses their views on 'Eternal God in terms of human reason' and the 'Need and threat of rationality in religion'.

11 About Abū Qurra, see Rissanen op. cit., and Gaudeul (1990: vol. I, pp. 31–33 and II, pp. 14–16).

12 Quoted from Gaudeul (1990: vol. II, p. 15).

13 English translation with introduction and notes: see Newman (ed.) (1993: 163–267) – based on the translation made from Syriac by A. Mingana in *Woodbrooke Studies*. Cambridge: Heffer (1928). As for Arabic versions, see R. Caspar, 'Les Versions arabes du dialogue entre le Catholicos Timothèe et le calife al-Mahdī', in *Islamochristiana* (1977: 107–175). See also Robinson (1991: 106–109), and Gaudeul (1990: vol. I, pp. 34–36 and vol. II, p. 17).

14 Quoted from Gaudeul (1990: vol. II p. 242) = Newman (ed.) (1993: 218).

15 See Newman (ed.) (1993: 190–196) and Gaudeul (1990: vol. II, pp. 236–238).

16 English translation with introduction and notes: see Newman (ed.) (1993: 355–545). *The Apology of al Kindy* was first published in English in London by SPCK, 2nd ed., 1885. Cf. Gaudeul (1990: vol. I, pp. 49–54 and vol. II, pp. 54–61), and Watt (1991: 64f.).

17 Goddard (1996: 26).

18 Cf. Goddard (1996: 30–32).

19 About al-Jāḥiz, see Schumann (1988), ch. 3: 'Eine Stimme aus der Muʿtazila . . . .' and Pellat (1970). As for translations with comments: see Newman (ed.) (1993: 685–717) as well as Gaudeul (1990: vol. I, pp. 45–48 and vol. II, pp. 25–33).

20 Goddard (1996: 32–33).

21 Ibid., p. 34.

22 About ʿAlı ibn Rabbān al-Ṭabarī, see Schumann (1988), ch. 2: 'Ein christlicher Gelehrter, der Muslim wurde.' Translations with comments: see Newman (ed.) (1993: 547–684) as well as Gaudeul (1990:vol. I, pp. 39–44 and vol. II, pp. 34–39).

23 See Thomas (1997).

24 Ibid., p. 49.

25 Thomas (2008: 50).
26 Ibid., p. 51, cf. Thomas (1992, 2002).
27 Beaumont (2008). Beaumont (2008: 57–59) identifies three Christian strategies: 1) to ignore the qur'ānic denial and show that Christ's death was essential to God's plan of salvation; 2) to play down the role of crucifixion in the mystery of incarnation; and 3) to reinterpret the qur'ānic apparent denial of the crucifixion.
28 About al-Jabbār and Christianity, see Stern (1967, 1968), and Goddard (1996: 26–28).
29 Quoted from Stern (1968: 145).
30 van Koningsveld (1996: 203).
31 Thomas (1992, 2002).
32 Thomas (1994: 221).
33 As for 'Umar's letter and the section about Christ, see Newman (ed.) (1993: 47–132), Gaudeul (1984: 137–149).
34 Thomas (1994: 229).
35 Ibid., p. 235.
36 Ibid., p. 240.
37 Zebiri (2000: 77).
38 As for relevant texts from various periods, see Gaudeul (1990: vol. II, pp. 272–296).
39 Pinault (1987: 103–104).
40 About al-Juwaynī, see Gaudeul (1990: vol. I, pp. 92–94 and vol. II, pp. 288–295).
41 See Schumann (1988), ch. 4: 'Spätere theologische Stellungnahmen: Ibn Ḥazm und Ghazālī', Gaudeul (1990: vol. I, pp. 87–91 and vol. II, 284–287), Watt (1991: 65–67), Goddard (1996: 35–36) and Duran (2008: 55–56).
42 The *ẓāhirī* school rejected any use of reason and speculation in reading the Qur'ān and Ḥadīth, and claimed that the Word of God must be received without any distortion by human interpretations.
43 Cf. Watt (1991: 67).
44 Cf. the section above about the image of Paul in early Muslim polemics.
45 Prior to Clement V's dissolution of the order in 1312, there were rumours in Spain (Aragon) linking the Templars with the Muslims, and after the Templars' arrest, some of them obviously entered the service of the Sultan of Granada; cf. van Koningsveld (1996: 215–216), who adds: 'Perhaps, al-Qaysı . . . was associated with the order of the Templars during his long captivity in Christian Spain.'
46 See Wilms (1966), Schumann (1988: ch. 4), Gaudeul (1990: vol. I, pp. 95–99 and vol. II, pp. 86–89) and Duran (2008: 57–62).
47 See Watt (1991: 69f.) and his translation from *Kitāb al-milal wa-n-nihal* in *Islamochristiana* (1983: 249–59) ('Ash-Sharastānī's account of Christian Doctrine').

48 Quoted from Watt (1991: 68).

49 About Ibn Taymiyya and Christianity, see Gaudeul (1991: vol. I, pp. 170–172) and the study of Thomas F. Michel, *A Muslim Theologian's Response to Christianity: Ibn Taymiyya's al-Jawab al-Sahih*. Delmar, NY: Caravan Books (1984).

50 Cf. Gaudeul (1990: vol. I, pp. 167–170).

51 Ibid.

52 Ibid., p. 172.

53 Watt (1991: 83).

54 Watt (1991: 83), referring to the work of Adel-Thèodore Khoury, *Polemique Byzantine contre l-Islam*, Leiden, E. J. Brill (1972).

55 See Gaudeul (1990: vol. I, pp. 116–121), and the standard work of James Kritzeck, *Peter the Venerable and Islam*, Princeton, Princeton University Press (1964).

56 Quoted from Kritzeck, op. cit., p. 132.

57 See James Waltz (1976), 'Muhammad and the Muslims in St. Thomas Aquinas', *The Muslim World*, LXVI, 81–95.

58 *Summa contra gentiles*, 1.6. Quoted from Phipps (1996: 5).

59 Watt (1991: 85–87).

60 In German: *Buch vom Heiden und der drei Weisen*. Freiburg/Basel/Wien: Herder (1986). Cf. Gaudeul (1990: vol. I, pp. 158–161).

61 In Norwegian, with detailed comments, see Kari Børresen, *Nicolaus Cusanus' dialog om trosfreden (De pace fidei)*. Oslo: Solum forlag (1983). Cf. Gaudeul (1990: vol. I, pp. 196–198).

62 See especially his 'On war against the Turk' (1529), in *Luther's Works*. Philadelphia: Fortress Press (1976), vol. 46 (=WA 30.2, pp. 81ff.: 'Vom Kriege wider den Tµrken 1529').

63 Quoted from *Luther's Works*, vol. 46, p. 177 ('On war against the Turk', 1529). Cf. WA 30.2:207–208 ('Libellus de ritu et moribus Turcorum').

64 *Luther's Works*, vol. 46, pp. 185–186. Jf. WA 30.2, p. 81ff.

65 Cf. Hugh Goddard (1994), 'The Persistence of Medieval Themes in Modern Christian–Muslim Discussion in Egypt', in S. K. Samir and J. S. Nielsen (eds.), *Christian Arabic apologetics during the Abbasid period*. Leiden: E. J. Brill, pp. 225–237.

66 Cf. Gaudeul (1990: vol. I, pp. 201–209).

67 Wiegers (1995: 245).

68 For other contributions to our general theme from the seventeenth century, see Karel Steenbrink's analysis of the role of Jesus and the Holy Spirit in the writings of Nūr al-dīn al-Ranīrī, from a Malay context (Steenbrink 1990).

Chapter 7

Twentieth-Century Tendencies and Discussions

Christ in Nineteenth- and Twentieth-Century Muslim Theology: Reinterpretation, Polemics and Dialogue

To give a comprehensive description of the image of Jesus in contemporary Muslim thinking is, of course, an impossible task, and the attempt might easily end up in sweeping generalizations. Similarly, Muslim writers and polemicists often fail to take into account the broad variety of theological positions and the immense diversity of academic approaches on the Christian side when they refer to 'modern Christian theology'.

Despite the difficulties in giving a representative overview of modern Muslim approaches to Christ, some Christian scholars have attempted to draw some major lines, with Egypt and India–Pakistan as main focuses.[1]

In the following, the focus will be upon contributions from the Indian-Pakistani, Egyptian/Arabic and Iranian contexts. In both Egypt and Pakistan, the discussions about Jesus will have to be read with the context in mind. They should be related both to internal trends and tensions such as those between liberal Islam and Islamism, and to the perceived cultural conflict between Islam and the West.

Some contributions reflect the controversies over the Ahmadiyya movement, the Christology of which deserves special mention. Shīʿite Islam and the Iranian tradition also deserve specific consideration.

Much space will be devoted to the controversies over the Gospel of Barnabas, because of the factual importance of this particular stumbling block in modern Christian–Muslim dialogue.

Still another level to be touched upon will be the Jesus images in modern poetry and the novel in Muslim societies – in Egypt as well as in other parts of the Muslim world. Jesus has always been a feature in Muslim, i.e. Ṣūfī, poetry. The novel is a more recent genre in Muslim societies, although it draws on the rich story-telling tradition of the Muslim world. In both types of literature, Jesus is part of the story.

Muslim books on 'Islam and Christianity' produced in the twentieth century often include chapters on the Muslim view of Christ. This is the case in books aimed at a Western audience, and also in books on Christian–Muslim dialogue published in countries with a long tradition of Christian–Muslim co-existence.[2] Needless to say, the following presentation is far from exhaustive. It mainly reflects theological exchanges about Christ appearing in Western languages, and in Arabic. The amount of literature in this field in Arabic and other Muslim languages is, of course, far more extensive than the following exposition may suggest.[3]

Nineteenth-Century Beginnings: India

After some hundred years with no significantly new contributions to the question of Christ in Islam and Muslim images of Christianity, new developments can be identified with the rise of the early modern period. Partly as a response to expanding European power in the Muslim world beginning in the nineteenth century, some new tendencies emerged with respect to Muslim approaches to Christianity. Hugh Goddard (1996) identifies three different strands: politicized religion (symbolized above all by Jamāl al-dīn al-Afghānī), modernist religion (Sayyid Aḥmad Khan in India and Muḥammad ʿAbduh in Egypt) and polemicized religion (Raḥmatullāh al-Kairānawī in India and Rashīd Riḍā in Egypt). According to Goddard, these strands correspond to three different aspects of European influence: European imperialism (provoking resistance as well as self-criticism), modern critical thinking (adopted or rejected) and Christian mission (provoking responses).[4]

Goddard emphasizes the Indian roots of positions that later came to be elaborated, particularly in Egypt. He identifies al-Kairānawī (or al-Hindī) and Sayyid Aḥmad Khan as representatives of two entirely different approaches to Christ and Christianity. The polemical innovations of al-Kairānawī have been thoroughly analysed by the German scholar Christine Schirrmacher (1992) in her study *Mit den Waffen des Gegners* ('With the weapons of the enemy'), in which the controversy between al-Kairānawī and the missionary Karl Gottlieb Pfander is presented as the most central incident in Christian–Muslim controversies in the nineteenth century.[5]

The polemical writing of Raḥmatullāh al-Kairānawī (al-Hindī, 1834–1891) emerged as a response to reinforced Christian missionary activities in the nineteenth century. More specifically, al-Kairānawī writes his polemical treatise *Iẓhār al-ḥaqq* ('Demonstration of Truth') in response to the famous missionary in Agra Karl Gottlieb Pfander and his book *Mizān al-ḥaqq* ('The Balance of Truth'). Raḥmatullāh al-Kairānawī deals with controversial issues like the invalidity of the doctrine of Trinity, and above all, the alleged corruption and abrogation of biblical scriptures. His work, which was produced at the instigation of the Ottoman Sultan ʿAbdulaziz, appeared in 1864 in both Turkish and

Arabic, and has subsequently become one of the most widely circulated Muslim works about Christianity.[6] A significant turn in modern Muslim polemic against Christianity is introduced by this book by the inclusion of insights from radical biblical criticism of Western origin (brought to India by al-Kairānawī's assistant in his debates with Pfander, Dr. Wazir Khan).

In her analysis of the al-Kairānawī/Pfander controversy, Schirrmacher notes that the central issue of nineteenth-century Muslim apologetics is clearly the claim that the Old and New Testaments have been falsified. What is new in the treatment of this old and cherished theme in Muslim polemics is the utilization of insights from historical-critical Bible interpretation in Europe ('with the weapons of the enemy'). According to Schirrmacher, the focus shifts to the question of Christology in the twentieth century, with the introduction of The Gospel of Barnabas at the turn of the century as a bridge from general biblical criticism to an apologetic or polemical focus on Christology. In *Iẓhār al-ḥaqq*, al-Kairānawī refers briefly to the Gospel of Barnabas as an early Christian document foretelling the advent of Muhammad.[7]

As for the nineteenth-century roots of later developments, India gives precedence also to more eirenical approaches from the Muslim side. The modernist Muslim reformer, Sayyid Ahmad Khan (1817–1898), was also acquainted with modern biblical criticism and wrote a book on the Bible in three volumes (published from 1862), cf. his *Tafsīr al-Qur'ān* (Agra 1903).[8] In contrast to Raḥmatullāh al-Kairānawī, Sayyid Aḥmad Khan held the view that the biblical scriptures had not been corrupted, but only misinterpreted. His rational explanation of the accounts of Jesus' miraculous birth and the miracles of Jesus was only a reflection of his general rationalizing approach to religion.[9] As for the crucifixion, he held the view that Jesus was in fact crucified, but was still alive when taken down from the cross, and subsequently treated secretly by the disciples and thus brought to life again. The ascension means that God raised his status beyond that of other human beings.

Regarding Jesus' miracles, it is interesting to note that Sayyid Ahmad Khan seeks support in the Bible when trying to explain that Jesus did not really raise people from the dead in the literal sense (as the Qur'an might seem to imply): the wording of the stories in Matthew 9: 24 and Luke 7: 11–15 might indicate that the daughter of the ruler and the widow's son were not necessarily dead: 'There are many cases where people have been thought dead and were buried, and it was later discovered that they still were alive.'[10]

The Christology of the Ahmadiyya Movement

Two specific features in Muslim approaches to Jesus in the nineteenth and twentieth centuries deserve special mention: the introduction of The Gospel of Barnabas in Muslim polemical writing (see below), and the reinterpretation of Islamic Christology by Mirza Ghulam Ahmad and the Ahmadiyya movement.

Judging by the classic *Jesus in India*, written in Urdu by Mirza Ghulam Ahmad of Qadian/India in 1899,[11] an important background for his reinterpretation of Islamic Christology was his confrontation with the popular view of *jihād* among certain Indian sects like the Ahl-i-Ḥadīth. These were accused by Mirza Ghulam Ahmad of sanctioning arbitrary killing for the cause of Islam. He accuses them of holding a totally distorted view of the coming Messiah of Muslim tradition, believing in the future coming of a violent and 'bloody' Mahdī aided by a likewise violent and 'bloody' Messiah. 'Muslims say that these two together will fill the earth with the blood of man.'[12] His very restrictive notion of *jihād* is based on the example of Muḥammad, who:

> ... *did not raise the sword against his enemies, nor did he reply to their abuse, until many of his Companions and dear friends were mercilessly murdered; and until he himself was subjected to sufferings of various kinds.*[13]

Obviously, in the background lurk the different positions taken by various Muslim groups towards the British authorities. Mirza Ghulam Ahmad himself was defended by the British magistrate when accused of promoting violence. Confronted with the popular beliefs in 'a bloody Messiah', he declares that:

> ... *the real and true Promised Messiah who is also the real Mahdi, tidings of whose appearance are to be found in the Bible and the Quran and whose coming is promised also in the Hadīth, is myself; who is, however, not provided with any sword or gun.*[14]

Whatever might have been the starting point – his conviction of fulfilling the promise of a Messiah usually identified with Jesus in his second coming, or a new reading of the Gospel narrative – his proclamation obviously required a reinterpretation of the traditional Muslim view which denied the crucifixion of Jesus, and the presupposition that he now was alive in heaven awaiting his eschatological return to earth. Accordingly, Mirza Ghulam Ahmad sets out to prove that Jesus was indeed crucified, but did not die on the cross.

In his argument, he does not begin with the Qur'ān, but by giving testimonies from the New Testament he intended to prove that Jesus only swooned, and was rescued from the cross. He takes as his starting point the sign of Jonah, implying that Jesus (like Jonah) did not die but was rescued in order to preach the message of God to those far away. In Jesus' case, 'those far away' are taken to be 'the lost tribes' of Judaism in the east that had given up their ancestral faith, adopted Buddhism and even relapsed into idolatry. Examining the biblical testimonies, he underlines the religious necessity that the holy personality of Jesus had to escape the curse of the cross; that God had to answer the prayer of his faithful prophet not to be subject to a degrading death; that Pilate staged a rescue action so that Jesus had to be taken down from the cross before death occurred; that his bones were not broken and that water and blood flowed from his body when pierced, as a sign that he was still alive; etc.

As a parenthesis in his biblical exegesis, Ahmad states that 'in the gospel of Barnabas . . . it is stated that Jesus was not crucified, nor did he die on the Cross'.[15] Apart from this reference (made in passing), Aḥmad focusses on the biblical material. Included in his biblical exegesis are some quite esoteric interpretations intended to prove that the Ahmadiyya group is the only legitimate heir to prophesies of the Gospel. Also the events after Jesus' 'resurrection' (as Aḥmad reads them) 'are conclusive that he did not die on the Cross; that his body retained its mortal character; and that it had undergone no change'. Furthermore:

> *There is no evidence in the Gospels that anyone saw Jesus ascend to heaven, and even if there had been such evidence, it would have been unworthy of credence, for making mountains out of molehills and magnifying small things into big seems to be a habit with the gospel writers.*[16]

In general, the impression of his biblical exegesis left with the reader is a mixture of rationalization and esoteric interpretation. The rationalizing points in his exegesis of the Passion narratives reoccur in the widespread Ahmadi commentary to the Qur'ān of Maulana Muhammad ʿAli.[17]

Only as a second stage in his argument, Mirza Ghulam Ahmad dedicates a few pages to references from the Qur'ān that might support his interpretation. The decisive point is, of course, that *šubbiha la-hum* is taken to mean that Jesus only seemed to be dead:

> *The Jews, seeing Jesus in a swoon, thought that he was dead. It was dark. And there was an earthquake and great excitement.*[18]

The qur'ānic assurance that Messiah, Jesus, son of Mary, shall be honoured in this world and in the hereafter (Sūra 3.45) is taken as a prophecy of his coming to the lands of Afghanistan, Punjab, Kashmir and Tibet, honouring them with his visit, and given great eminence by God when met by the lost tribes of Israel. There is also a reference to Ḥadīth material that is not commonly recognized as sound, which portrays Jesus as a 'traveller' who reached the age of 125 before he (according to Mirza Ghulam Ahmad) was buried in Kashmir.

The last part of the book contains 'evidence derived from books of medicine' and 'evidence from books of history'. He includes 'evidence from books on Buddhism', and suggests that similarities between Christianity and Buddhism originate from this journey of Jesus to Buddhist lands.

By interpreting the qur'ānic references to Jesus' death as being realized through his demise, not on the cross, but in Kashmir, Mirza Ghulam Ahmad eliminates from Islam the Christ-expectancy derived from tradition. This interpretation has caused controversy among Sunnī Muslims, since the

Ḥadīth material pertaining to this matter is not universally recognized to be sound.

As we shall see below, the prestigious al-Azhar institution in Cairo 'settled the affair' (for Sunnī Muslims) in the late 1940s. Much of the writings produced in the twentieth century about the return of Christ, especially in Indo-Pakistani Islam, has aimed at refuting Ahmadi beliefs, i.e. it is meant for internal use and not for dialogue with Christianity.

The Barnabas Argument[19]

As noted in the Introduction, during the twentieth century the Gospel of Barnabas has become a primary point of reference in Muslim polemical writings aimed at the refutation of Christianity. This new development in Muslim polemics and apologetics was triggered by the translation of the Gospel from a manuscript in Italian, first into English in 1907, then into Arabic and other languages of the Muslim world.

The alleged Gospel is regarded by many Muslims as going back to a manuscript from early Christianity, whereas Western scholars take it for granted that it was produced either in the late Middle Ages or in the early modern period. To say the least, the Barnabas controversy has not been conducive to mutual understanding and respect between Muslim and Christian scholars.

The Gospel of Barnabas: Manuscripts and Translations

The Gospel of Barnabas retells the story of Jesus in 222 chapters, in the form of a 'Gospel harmony' that contains central parts of the biblical Gospels, apocryphal Jesus-material, peculiar readings of the Old Testament and Islamic teachings. Until the beginning of the twentieth century, it was only known through an old Italian manuscript and a partial Spanish version.[20] The manuscripts have been associated by Muslim apologists and also by some Western Enlightenment writers with a 'Gospel of Barnabas' referred to in ancient Christian lists of non-canonical writings.[21]

The Spanish manuscript has been the frame of reference for the groundbreaking scientific investigations of the Spanish scholar Luis F. Bernabé Pons which were published during the 1990s.[22] Bernabé took up Mikel de Epalza's suggestion that the background of the Gospel of Barnabas should be sought in Morisco circles, i.e. among Spanish Muslims who had been forced to convert to Christianity and were later expelled from Spain.[23] The Spanish version alleges that the Aragonian Morisco Mustafá de Aranda translated the Gospel of Barnabas into Spanish while he was based in Istanbul, which was a notable Morisco refuge. But many scholars take the Spanish version to be primary. They regard the alleged primacy of the Italian text as a tactical construction, prompted by the wish to give maximum authority to the text by associating it with Rome.[24]

The Spanish manuscript, which lacks Chapters 121–200, contains also a preface attributed to the alleged detector of the manuscript, a certain monk presented as Fra Marino.[25] Here, the monk explains how he chanced upon it in the library of Pope Sixtus V (r. 1585–1590), read it and – having become convinced of its truth –converted to Islam. The preface also explains how Fra Marino, when reminded of the strife between Paul and Barnabas as reported in the Acts of the Apostles, had reached the conclusion that a number of prominent disciples of Jesus (including Barnabas) would probably have written their own version of the Gospel.

Muslim interest in the Gospel of Barnabas exploded after it had been translated into English by Lonsdale and Laura Ragg in 1907, on the initiative of a Scottish missionary.[26] Notwithstanding the Raggs' deconstruction of the text and their denial of its authenticity as a 'Gospel', the English translation was immediately expropriated by Muslims as an opportunity for intensified apologetics against Christian missionaries. In 1907, W. H. Temple Gairdner – a missionary scholar in Cairo – reported that Muslims in Egypt and India were already indulging in 'wildest talk regarding the historical value of the book'.[27]

Translations from English soon appeared in both Arabic (Egypt, 1908) and Urdu (India, 1916).[28] The initiative to an Arabic translation from English was taken by the polemical reformist Rashīd Riḍā and was subsequently published in Cairo. By a historical irony, the Arabic translation was made by a Syrian-Orthodox Christian, Khalīl Saʿāda. Perhaps not surprisingly, two separate prefaces made by Saʿāda and Riḍā respectively reveal different evaluations of the historical value of the document by the translator and the initiator.[29]

The Contents of the Gospel of Barnabas[30]

Before further analysing Muslim apologetic utilization of the alleged Gospel and subsequent Christian responses, the contents of the Gospel of Barnabas must be summarized.

In accordance with Muslim tradition, the Gospel is seen as a book given to Jesus, descending into his heart.[31] The prize argument of classical Muslim polemic, that of the falsification (*taḥrīf*) of Jewish and Christian Scriptures, is abundantly attested.[32] The Gospel of Barnabas recounts much of the biblical Gospel material, only with distinct emphases and additions. It adds a substantial amount of apocryphal material and excels in midrash-like readings of the Old Testament. The sum of it exceeds by far a normal Gospel format, and its 222 chapters amount to more than 200 pages in normal print.

Its privileged writer, Barnabas, is referred to as one of the twelve Apostles, and said to have received 'great secrets' (ch. 112). In the preamble, Barnabas presents himself as 'Apostle of Jesus the Nazarene, called Christ'. He decries those who 'being deceived of Satan, under pretence of piety, are preaching the most impious doctrine'. Their deviation consists of 'calling Jesus son of God, repudiating the circumcision ordained of God for ever, and permitting every unclean meat'. Paul is mentioned as the most prominent example of those who have been deceived. Already from the outset, then, Barnabas presents himself as a chief antagonist to Pauline Christianity, a point that is reiterated in the Gospel's last chapter: 'Others preached, and yet preach, that Jesus is the Son of God, among whom is Paul deceived' (ch. 222).

Although the Gospel of Barnabas is bent upon conforming biblical material with Islamic tradition, it is not always in consonance with the Qur'ān. For instance, against the Qur'ān, but in accordance with medieval legend, it maintains that Mary gave birth to Jesus without pain.

Guistolisi and Rizzardi have characterized the spirituality of the Gospel and its emphasis on prayer, fasting, taming the body and penitence as 'monastic'.[33] Jesus is depicted as a stern ascetic who warns against laughter (ch. 29), hates rest above all things (ch. 59) and teaches that the body is the enemy (ch. 64). He nevertheless turns water into wine (ch. 15).

A peculiar feature of the Gospel is that Jesus holds lengthy 'Greek' discourses about the four elements of nature and the three things that make up man (the soul, the sense and the flesh, ch. 105). He rebuts classical Aristotelian claims that the soul is tripartite – 'calling it the sensitive, vegetative, and intellectual soul. But verily I say to you, the soul is one' (ch. 106). Jesus seems to agree, however, with the Aristotelian notion that 'reason . . . holdeth a middle place in man' (ch. 141). Jesus' discourses on soul, senses and reason reveal the author's knowledge of similar discussions not only in Christian tradition, but also in classical Islamic philosophy and mysticism.

With groans and lengthy discourses, Jesus laments that people call him 'Son of God'.[34] As in the Qur'ān, Jesus assures his audience that he is but a mortal, subject to the judgement of God like everyone else (ch. 93). As noted, the author accuses Paul of being deceived by the idea that Jesus is God, but not really of being the source of this deception. Instead, the Gospel puts forward the idea that the origin of this belief goes back to an incident during his lifetime when the Roman soldiery 'stirred up the Hebrews, saying that Jesus was God who had come to visit them. Whereupon a great sedition arose . . .'. In the uprising, some claimed that Jesus was God who had come to visit the world, others that he was a son of God and still others that he was but a prophet of God, since God has no human similitude (ch. 91). Tranquility only returned when the Senate of Rome issued an order prohibiting people – on pain of death – from calling Jesus God or Son of God (ch. 98).

So what would be an appropriate title for Jesus, according to this Gospel? In contrast to the Qur'ān, Jesus is not presented as the Messiah (Italian: *il-Messia*, equivalent to the qur'ānic *al-masīḥ*). Instead, it is Muhammad who is honoured with this title. This is unprecedented in Islamic tradition.

Jesus is given instead the role that has traditionally been occupied by John the Baptist, as the forerunner of the Messiah.[35] A most conspicuous part of the Gospel of Barnabas is Jesus' frequent foretelling of Muhammad – either by explicit mention of his name, or by reference to 'the messenger'.[36] The Gospel of Barnabas even reflects the Muslim legend of Muhammad's pre-existence, and the notion of the eternal *nūr Muḥammadī* (light of Muhammad) is expressly referred to in one of the Arabic glosses to the Italian text.[37] Like John the Baptist in the biblical Gospels, Jesus asserts that the one to come – i.e. Muhammad, the awaited Messiah and Messenger – 'was made before me, and shall come after me' (ch. 42 and 96).

Bernabé Pons has suggested that these peculiarities should not be taken as mistakes, but rather as conscious reinterpretations of Christian and Islamic tradition. The author suggests that in the true Islamic sense, it is Muhammad – the final messenger – who is the Messiah. Christ is only the forerunner, who announces his coming.

In the version of the passion, dependence on the substitution theories of classical Muslim commentaries to the Qur'ān (*tafsīr*) is evident. The likeness of Jesus is cast upon Judas, who (after a rather crude version of the interrogations) is crucified in his place. Jesus is rescued by God through a window in a house where he has taken refuge, and installed in the third heaven until the end of time.

As a substitute for the resurrection narrative, the Gospel retells the legend of a visit from heaven by Jesus (after his ascension) to comfort Mary and the disciples, a tradition found in similar form in the popular 'Stories of the prophets' from the early Islamic era (cf. Chapter 3).

Several features characteristic of Jewish and Muslim law are reflected in the Gospel. Circumcision is said to be indispensable (ch. 22–23), and pork is prohibited (ch. 32). More specifically Muslim observances, such as ablutions before prayer (ch. 36, 61, etc.) and the celebration of Abraham's sacrifice (ch. 67), can also be identified.

The Gospel contains also a rather comprehensive 'Satanology'. Its descriptions of heaven and hell come close to medieval parallels, as in Dante. In ch. 135–127, the seven parts of hell are related to the seven deadly sins.

As for the Gospel's inserted interpretations of the Old Testament, some space is occupied by the argument that Ishmael, not Isaac, is the privileged heir of Abraham.[38] Adam is said to have seen the Muslim *šahāda* (confession) in a vision, and to have it written upon his thumbnails (ch. 39).

Apocryphal Jewish material includes the story about two hermits at the time of Elijah (ch. 148–150). These are presented as the 'true Pharisees' (cf. 144–145, 151), and associated with their alleged spiritual relatives Hosea and Haggai.

Early Western Interest in the Gospel of Barnabas

Since the early eighteenth century, Western scholars have taken some interest in the Gospel of Barnabas and its possible importance for Muslim–Christian relations.[39] Even in that period – i.e. long before the translation of the Gospel of Barnabas into English – comments by Western Orientalists triggered some interest among individual Muslims.

One of the first to draw the attention of Muslims to the manuscript known as 'The Gospel of Barnabas' appears to have been George Sale, in the 'Preliminary Discourse' to his translation of the Qur'ān in 1734. Sale refers to the claim of 'the Mohammedans' to have 'a Gospel in Arabic attributed to St. Barnabas, wherein the history of Jesus Christ is related in a manner very different from what we find in the true Gospels, and correspondent to those traditions which Mohammed has followed in his Korân'.[40] As for the historical value of the alleged Gospel, Sale dismisses it as a forgery, but with the following qualification – 'a forgery originally of some nominal Christians, but interpolated since by Mohammedans'.[41]

Before the remarks made by Sale, the rationalist Enlightenment deist John Toland hade made some references to the Italian version of the Gospel of Barnabas in his work *Nazarenus or Jewish, Gentile and Mahometan Christianity* (1718). By virtue of the Gospel's denial of Christ's divine sonship, Toland appreciated the Gospel of Barnabas for being closer to the original Jewish Christianity than the biblical Gospels.[42] In contrast to Sale, Toland argued that the Gospel of Barnabas was not a modern forgery, but rather a Muslim reworking of the apocryphal Gospel referred to in early Christian documents.[43]

Indian Origins of Modern Muslim Polemical Use of the Gospel of Barnabas

The origin of modern Muslim polemical use of the Gospel of Barnabas lies in India. This has been demonstrated by Christine Schirrmacher in her study *Mit den Waffen des Gegners* (1992), in which she analyses the Barnabas controversy in the light of the Muslim apologetics of Raḥmatullāh al-Kairānawī (1834–1891, often referred to as al-Hindī).[44] As mentioned in the section about 'twentieth-century beginnings' above, Schirrmacher sees the controversy between al-Kairānawī and the Agra missionary Karl Gottlieb Pfander as the most central incident in nineteenth-century Christian–Muslim polemics, and the Barnabas controversy as a pivotal feature of polemical clashes in the twentieth century.

By his book *Iẓhār al-ḥaqq*, al-Kairānawī introduced a significant turn in modern Muslim polemics against Christianity. The central contention in nineteenth-century Muslim apologetics was still the classical claim that the Bible has been tampered with or falsified by Jews and Christian. The new element in al-Kairānawī's treatment of this old and cherished theme in Muslim polemics was his utilization of insights from biblical criticism in Europe. As noted, in *Iẓhār al-ḥaqq*, al-Kairānawī refers also in passing to the Gospel of Barnabas – mentioned as an early Christian document foretelling the advent of Muhammad.[45]

As mentioned above, the founder of the Ahmadiyya movement, Mirza Ghulam Ahmad (cf. above), was also aware of the Gospel of Barnabas when he wrote about *Jesus in India* in 1899. Ahmad obviously believed that this was one of the Gospel manuscripts included in the collections of the British Museum: '[. . .] in the gospel of Barnabas, which must be available in the British Museum, it is stated that Jesus was not crucified, not did he die on the cross.'[46]

Polemic Use of the Gospel of Barnabas in the Twentieth Century

After its publication in English and in Arabic by Rashīd Riḍā in 1908, the Gospel of Barnabas received much attention in Egypt. For instance, Muḥammad Abū Zahra who taught at al-Azhar was much inspired by al-Kairānawī and referred to it in his influential *Muḥādarāt fī al-naṣrāniyya* ('Lectures on Christianity').[47] Through numerous translations, his book has had a considerable impact in the entire Muslim world (cf. below, in the section about 'twentieth-century Egyptian theology'). In expounding what he regards to be Christ's original message of *tawḥīd* (divine unity), Abū Zahra refers not only to the Qur'ān, but also to the Gospel of Barnabas which he holds in high esteem and cites as an authority in this respect. He quotes from the part of the Gospel that explains the substitution of Judas for Jesus on the cross and the deliverance of Jesus through divine intervention.

It is clear that Abū Zahra held the Gospel of Barnabas to be very old. He strongly affirmed its authenticity as an early Christian witness entirely in consonance with the teachings of Islam. In the part dealing with the Gospel of Barnabas, he explicitly called for a Christian response, a challenge that was eventually taken up by the comprehensive and critical study made by Jacques Jomier of the Dominican Centre for Oriental Studies in Cairo.[48]

The widespread apologetic use of the Gospel of Barnabas by Muslims includes more recent books by the Pakistani polemicist 'Ata ur-Rahim[49] and the American Muslim M. Y. Yusseff.[50] In the works of 'Ata ur-Rahim and Yusseff, the authenticity of the Gospel of Barnabas is simply taken for granted. 'Ata ur-Rahim even claims that 'The Gospel Barnabas was accepted as a Canonical Gospel in the churches of Alexandria up until 325', and that 'the Pope secured a copy of the Gospel of Barnabas in 383 AD, and kept it in his own library'. Unfortunately, he does not reveal the sources of this rather astounding information.[51]

Even in certain works of Ṣūfī inspiration, the Gospel of Barnabas may be used in an uncritical way to underpin alternative, mystic interpretations of the life and message of Jesus.[52]

Reconstructing Early Christian Controversy: Barnabas and Paul

When examining the arguments of Muslim advocates of the Gospel of Barnabas, one is struck by their efforts to construct an alleged controversy between Barnabas and Paul (which resembles the classical distinction made by liberal Christian theologians between the simple teachings of Christ and the dogmas of Paul). In the prologue of the Gospel, Barnabas presents himself as a true follower of Christ in contradistinction to Paul, who has been captured by a doctrinal deception. Modern Muslim polemicists take the argument some steps further. With reference to a rather forced interpretation of the reference in Acts 15 to a disagreement between Paul and Barnabas, Barnabas is taken as the chief opponent to Paul and his teaching of a Hellenistic Christianity. This runs rather contrary to Christian research pertaining to the role of Barnabas in the early church.[53]

'Ata ur-Rahim and Yusseff do not pay any attention to the *Epistle of Barnabas* which some Muslim authors seem to confuse with the Gospel of Barnabas.[54] Instead, Yusseff takes some interest in the much later (probably fifth century) and pseudepigraphic *Acts of Barnabas*. Yusseff cites a part of the *Acts* where it is said that Barnabas, when going to Cyprus, took with him documents that he had received from the Apostle Matthew – 'a book of the Word of God and a narrative of the miracles and doctrines'.[55] With an interesting twist, Yusseff contends that Matthew and Barnabas were in facts co-authors of the Gospel in question, which (according to Yusseff) might in fact be identical with the hypothetical Q-source known from biblical criticism.[56]

Yusseff also makes some effort to prove the spiritual affinity of Barnabas to the Essenes and the kind of Jewish spirituality reflected in the Dead Sea Scrolls. He sees the Gospel of Barnabas in the tradition of Jewish-Christian movements like the Ebionites, and above all the alleged Jewish-Christian offshoot of the Essenes, the Nazarene movement. As for the Essenes, Yusseff takes special interest in their expectation of two Messiahs.

In accordance with traditional Muslim apologetics, both 'Ata ur Rahim and Yusseff single out Paul as the main culprit of the process that led to the deification of Christ and the abandonment of circumcision in Hellenistic Christianity.[57] In contrast with the general tendency in recent biblical scholarship to focus on the Jewish/Semitic background of the Gospels, they rely on insights from the history of religions at the turn of the century. Correspondingly, they focus on the mythical language of the Gospels, the Egyptian/Hellenistic origins of ideas about death and resurrection, and the title 'Son of God'.

In Western research, the connection between ancient Muslim polemics against Paul and the more recent Barnabas controversy has been investigated by P. S. van Koningsveld (1996). Citing differing medieval Muslim images of Paul, Koningsveld searches for possible Andalusian links between the medieval traditions and the image of Paul in the Gospel of Barnabas.[58] He notes that in spite of similarities, 'one observes a radically different sentiment in the Islamic traditions and the Gospel of Barnabas'. In the latter (which may reflect indigenous Spanish tradition), Paul is 'in error', he is 'deceived', but 'he is not the ruthless and rancorous deceiver working on behalf of or against the Jews, as portrayed in the Islamic sources'.[59]

Contested History: Muslim Apologetics and Christian Responses

Notwithstanding the fact that the overwhelming majority of Muslim writing about the Gospel of Barnabas takes its authenticity for granted, dissenting voices in the Muslim community should not be overlooked. Schirrmacher mentions an article from 1977 by Muḥammad Yaḥyā al-Hāshimī in the influential organ of the World Islamic League of Mecca.[60] Al-Hāshimī refers to the famous Christian–Muslim dialogue in Tripoli (Libya) in 1976, in which some Muslims tried to put the Gospel of Barnabas at the centre of their arguments.[61] He dismisses the Gospel as a document of dubious value, comparable to the innovations of the Ahmadiyya movement who claim that Christ did not die on the cross but survived it, went to Asia and died in Kashmir. He even contends that it might have been composed by a Jew in order to instigate hatred between Christians and Muslims. A refutation of the Gospel's authenticity is also found in a newspaper article from 1959 by the Egyptian biographer of Christ ʿAbbās Maḥmūd al-ʿAqqād (cf. the section about Christ biographies below), who comes close to standard historical-critical positions taken by Western scholars.[62]

In the main, however, Muslim writers who have commented on the Gospel of Barnabas has utilized it for apologetic purpose. In their polemical project, history has been used as a weapon, in a way similar to that of the first quest for the historical Jesus in the nineteenth century. Critical hermeneutical insights in how the eye of the beholder influences the image of Jesus seem to have made little impact on Muslim apologetics.

Also in Christian apologetic responses, much emphasis has been put on historical truth. Since the publication of the English translation, Christian scholars have sought to identify historical mistakes about Palestinian antiquity and unmistakable traces of later historical events in the Gospel of Barnabas. Apologetic Christian responses, such as those by David Sox[63] and William Campbell,[64] have basically agreed with the critical evaluation that was already made by the Raggs. Launsdale and Laura Ragg pointed to the Gospel's obvious dependence on Talmudic and Islamic material. They observed that post-biblical material is interpolated 'as it were parenthetically, and mostly into discourses put into the mouth of Christ'.[65] They also noted that there seems to be a certain ignorance of the geography and circumstances of Palestine (e.g. having Jesus sailing to Nazareth in ch. 20, or locating Tiro/Tyrus close to Jordan in ch. 99), and even of Islamic tradition. Their arguments were later refined by Jacques Jomier, when he responded to Abū Zahra's challenge that Christians should state their opinion on the Gospel of Barnabas.[66]

Recent Historical Investigations in the West

Both Jan Slomp and David Sox have pointed to Fra Marino – who is referred to in the preface to the Spanish manuscript – as the most likely candidate for the authorship of the Gospel of Barnabas. Sox has sought for Fra Marino in the context of Venetian inqusition.[67] Slomp suggests that Fra Marino may in fact have been a *converso*, i.e. a Jew forcibly converted to Christianity who had eventually been forced by the inquisition to flee from Spain to Venice. In this way, Slomp stresses the repressive atmosphere that might have triggered the production of this Gospel.

Many recent Western studies have focused on a possible Spanish origin of the Gospel, but sought the author in a *morisco* (Christianized Muslim) rather than *converso* environment. This theory was launched by the Spanish scholar Mikel de Epalza in 1963 and 1982,[68] and has later been refined by the studies of Gerard A. Wiegers from 1995[69] and the works of Luis F. Bernabé Pons which have been published from 1992 onwards.[70] On the basis of his doctoral dissertation from 1992, Bernabé Pons has published studies on the content of the Gospel (1995) and a critical edition of the Spanish manuscript (1998) – proposing a sixteenth- or seventeenth-century Morisco background for the Gospel of Barnabas. His work has been considered as a major breakthrough in critical research about the alleged Gospel. In a book review of the studies by Wiegers and Bernabé Pons, Jan Slomp expresses the hope that 'this research, carried out not by missionaries but by academic scholars' may break new ground, and possibly be 'a step forward out of this unfortunate debate'.[71]

The French translation with a commentary made by Cirillo and Frémaux distinguishes itself by proposing an ancient Christian background to the present Gospel.[72] Contrary to most Western scholars, they argue that the Gospel of Barnabas is probably based on an early Judaeo-Christian document, whereas the existing version only dates as far back as the fourteenth century. They suggest the following line of tradition behind the present Gospel: an early Christian background; a medieval collector; and an Islamic reviser in the sixteenth century. Cirillo and Frémaux focus on the expression 'true Pharisees' as a possible clue to monastic, Jewish-Christian groups that may have held views similar to those reflected in the Gospel of Barnabas. These groups seem to have regarded Elijah as the main precursor of Jesus (cf. the references to 'the little book of Elijah' in ch. 145), and may have had Syria as their main base.[73]

More recently, Theodore Pulcini has taken the references to Elijah and the true Pharisees as an argument for a possible Carmelite origin to the Gospel of Barnabas.[74] He also argues in more general terms that the type of monastic practice which seems to be implied by the Gospel corresponds well to the testimony of the Carmelite rule from 1247. The end of the community on Mount Carmel came in 1291, when the last crusader strongholds on the Mediterranean coast were recaptured by the Muslims. As a possible scenario for the composition of the Gospel of Barnabas, Pulcini suggests that it may have been composed by a displaced Carmelite monk who had found a safe harbour in Cyprus and – perhaps disappointed with his monastic community and contemplating Muslim victories – may have converted to Islam. This may have happened just after the Carmelites' expulsion from the Holy Land to Cyprus, or in the sixteenth century when the Turks conquered the Venetians and the Carmelites were once more displaced, from Cyprus to Crete.

Pulcini suggests that the tradition from the ancient *Acts of Barnabas* that links the Apostle of Barnabas to Cyprus may have been another formative element in the process. If one presupposes that the monk in question was Italian by origin, this would explain the linguistic influx from Tuscan and Venetian dialects in the Italian manuscript, which were already noted by the Raggs.

External and Internal Arguments in Favour of a Spanish-Morisco Origin

The strength of Pulcini's theory lies in his concentration on internal evidence. His theory has also the advantage of confirming the stated primacy of the Italian manuscript over against the Spanish one. His construction of a possible historical scenario is more fanciful, and relies upon the constructed conversion story of a single Carmelite monk.

The contextual arguments for a much later, Morisco background are far stronger, but perhaps not the internal ones. When in 1992, Luis F. Bernabé Pons presented his thesis in Alicante, Spain, on the Morisco origin of the Gospel, he took the Spanish version as his frame of reference.[75] He argues that the Gospel of Barnabas was paralleled by a series of Morisco creations of early Christian writings, found in Granada at the end of the sixteenth century and known as 'the leaden books of Sacromonte'.[76] In the leaden books, Christian origins are presented with distinctively Islamic overtones. Bernabé Pons is careful not to speak of 'forgeries' in a derogatory way. He suggests that the Morisco literature in question should rather be taken as an expression of ideas harboured by people who participated in two religious realities, Christian and Muslim.

As for literary parallels to central features of the Gospel of Barnabas, Bernabé Pons points to the Morisco authors Ahmad al-Hayārī Bejerano (Granada/Morocco) and Ibrāhīm al-Taybilī (Toledo/Tunis, his Spanish name was Juan Peréz).[77] In a document from 1634, attributed to al-Taybilī, explicit reference is made to the Gospel of Barnabas.[78] Bernabé Pons also shows how Taybilī, in one of his poems, reproduces one of the most peculiar aspects of the Gospel of Barnabas, namely the contention that the real Messiah was not Christ but Muḥammad.[79]

In this environment, the Gospel of Barnabas may have been produced in order to demonstrate the content of the true (in the Islamic sense) Gospel of Jesus Christ. The format chosen by the author lies, according to Bernabé Pons, somewhere between the genre of Christian Gospels and that of the Hadīth collections (the sayings of the Prophet), testifying also in a formal way to the cross-influences of two distinct religious cultures. As for the outcome of the Morisco plot, Bernabé Pons suggests that the lack of any known publication of the Gospel of Barnabas may be due to the fact that after the expulsion of Moriscos from Spain, the syncretistic argument and form of this pseudepigraphic Gospel lost its force.

The hypothesis of a Morisco origin of this notion is supported by the Dutch scholar Gerard A. Wiegers, who has found the idea of Muhammad as the true Messiah expressed in the poems of the Morisco author Juan Alonso Aragonés, a convert to Islam writing between 1600 and 1620.[80] Wiegers believes that the Gospel of Barnabas may have been influenced by the ideas of this particular author. The point of departure for Wiegers' study is similar to that of Bernabé Pons, namely the hypothesis that the expulsion of the Moriscos from Spain marked a new phase in the history of Muslim–Christian polemics, in which the Moriscos were finally free to express themselves about the religion that had been forced upon them by the Christian authorities in Spain.

One of the new concepts appearing in these polemical writings is exactly the idea that Muhammad is the Messiah.[81] In a particular manuscript of Juan Alonso Aragonés, which Wiegers characterizes as an extremely interesting anti-Christian and anti-Jewish Islamic treatise, the main aspiration seems to be 'to demonstrate that Muhammad was the promised messiah of Jewish and Christian scriptures, or, *el mesias general* (the universal messiah), as the Spanish text puts it'.[82] Whereas Muhammad is depicted as the general Messiah for all peoples, Jesus' ministry – as the special Messiah of the Gospel, the *evangelico mesias* – was confined to Israel only.

As regards more conventional Muslim views, the manuscript of Alonso contends that the scriptures have been corrupted, and that Jesus was substituted on the cross (according to Alonso, the one who was crucified was in fact a king Jesus of Damascus).

Historical or Situated Truth

In his 1997 review of recent contributions to the Barnabas controversy, Jan Slomp expresses the hope that Christians and Muslims would start mutually upgrading the esteem for each other's Scriptures.[83] As he puts it, this presupposes that Muslims cease to support a culture of historical forgery and to utilize a dubious document like the Gospel of Barnabas in order to convey traditional claims that Christians have distorted their scriptures.

When approaching the question of historical truth, however, it must be kept in mind that truth claims about history are always situated in a particular context.[84] As for the Gospel of Barnabas, it is more than obvious that the protracted controversy has to do with power relations. As argued convincingly by Bernabé Pons and others, the creation of the Gospel was probably one of many examples of a strategy of resistance by Spanish Muslims who had been converted by force during the Catholic *reconquista*, and later expelled by the Inquisition. Like the leaden books of Granada, the Gospel of Barnabas may be read as Morisco literature of resistance which contested the Christian empire by claiming that Christianity rested on a historical falsification of the teachings of Jesus which were now finally corrected by the true Gospel.

Contemporary post-colonial theory shed fresh light on the dynamics of anti-imperial literature.[85] Post-colonial theory focuses on the complex interaction between the colonial language of dominance and the subtle elements of resistance reflected in language and literature emerging from the contact zone between the disparate cultures of domination and subordination. Indian Muslims' employment of Western biblical criticism against Western missionaries in the nineteenth century ('with the weapons of their adversaries') may serve as a good example.

As for the possible Morisco origin of the Gospel of Barnabas, I find James C. Scott's notion of 'hidden transcript' illuminating (as laid out in his book *Dominance and the Arts of Resistance: Hidden Transcripts*).[86] In Scott's definition, the hidden transcript is a 'privileged site for nonhegemonic, contrapuntal, dissident discourse' which is always found underneath the public transcripts of masters and subordinates, as a condition for a practical albeit mostly non-divulged resistance on the part of the dominated ones. The notion of a hidden transcript points to 'a realm of relative discursive freedom, outside the earshot of powerholders'.[87] The critical moment in any change of power relations is when the hidden transcript of the subordinates becomes public, as an act of rebellion or revenge.[88]

Behind the public performance of Conversos and Moriscos in post-reconquista Spain there was clearly – as the Inquisition suspected – a hidden transcript. When forcibly converted Jews and Muslims were eventually expelled, the time had come to reveal what had hitherto been shrouded and perhaps even to elaborate on it. Like the leaden books of Sacromonte, the Gospel of Barnabas may have been produced as an equally desperate and creative response to the loss of status and dignity. As Scott notes, 'To speak of a loss of dignity and status is necessarily to speak of a public loss. It follows, I think, that a public humiliation can be fully reciprocated only with a public revenge'.[89] As a public revenge, the production of the Gospel of Barnabas was performed with great creativity, by people who were able to draw upon elements from both Christian and Muslim tradition (granted that the Morisco theory is right).

At the time of its origin, the Gospel of Barnabas did not have the intended effect as a public performance. Failing to catch the attention of a large public, its fate resembles that of the leaden books that were buried in the ground in reconquered Granada. However, the testimony of early modern Western scholars such as Toland and Sale shows that the Gospel was not completely forgotten, and was in fact continuously invoked in certain Muslim circles.

Anyhow, it was only in the second phase of its history as literature of resistance that the Gospel of Barnabas became a success story. When rediscovered by Muslims after its translation into English in 1907, the stage had already been set for anti-colonial, anti-missionary employment of the Gospel of Barnabas. As demonstrated by Schirrmacher, a new phase of literary resistance to the Christian empire had already been introduced by eighteenth-century Muslim apologists in India who attacked the Bible and missionary teachings about Christ 'by the weapons of their enemies', i.e. by the use of modern biblical criticism.

What emerges, then (if one accepts the theory of a Morisco origin to the Gospel of Barnabas), is a double, anti-imperial context to the Barnabas controversy: in the sixteenth century, Moriscos may have struck back at the Spanish Catholic Empire by producing the Gospel of Barnabas as a sweet revenge for their forced conversion and violent expulsion. In any case, in the early twentieth century Indian and Arab Muslims found the alleged Gospel to be a useful weapon in their resistance to Christian, missionary efforts.

Twentieth-Century Egyptian Theology: al-Manār and al-Azhar

In approaching the images of Jesus in the Egyptian Muslim context, there are different levels to be analysed. One is the Jesus-images that may be identified in qur'ānic exegesis and in more general theological positioning – especially that of theologians from the al-Azhar University and Mosque. Another, but interrelated level, would be writings explicitly directed towards Christianity, polemical or attempting dialogue. Hugh Goddard (1996) identifies three modalities of such contributions, reflecting different images of and approaches to Jesus, Christianity and the Bible: 'polemical, eirenical and intermediate'.

In the following, we shall first deal with contributions from the al-Manār school and works originating from al-Azhar. We shall proceed to works about Christ from more independent writers, some of them in the genre of the novel.

Al-Manār

Olaf Schumann (1988), as well as Maurice Borrmans (1975, 1976, 1996) and Hugh Goddard (1996), have analysed the Jesus-image of the reformist thinker Muḥammad ʿAbduh (1849–1905) and his follower Rashīd Riḍā (d. 1935). Both of them are representatives of what has often been called the 'school of Manār', named after their journal *al-Manār* in which a comprehensive commentary on the Qur'ān was published. In the tradition of the reformist al-Afghānī, ʿAbduh emphasized the rationality of the Islamic creed, over against the tendency (prevailing in Christianity, as he saw it) to regard religious belief as something beyond the possibility of human comprehension. ʿAbduh seems to regard 'the blind faith' of Christianity as a parallel to obscurantist *taqlīd* among Muslims, i.e. the blind adherence to established interpretations among traditional Muslim *ʿulamā*ʾ. His theological project was to reveal the rationality of the Islamic faith in *tawḥīd* (divine unity), as reflected in the title of his main work *Risālat al-Tawḥīd* (1897).[90]

ʿAbduh's general approach to Christianity (cf. his book *Al-islām wa-l-naṣrāniyya*) is marked by his endeavour to synthesize revelation and rationality,[91] and re-establish their prophetic quality. Basically, he sees Islam as the religion of reason, whereas Christianity is more inclined towards irrationality.

His (and later Riḍā's) image of Christ is reflected in *Tafsīr al-Manār*. It first appeared in the journal *al-Manār*, and was continued and edited by Rashıd Riḍā. Riḍā was also the one who initiated the Arabic translation of the Gospel of Barnabas,[92] to which he gives numerous references in his works. As a more systematic contribution, Riḍā wrote a polemical treatise entitled *Aqīdat al-ṣalb wa-l-fidā*ʾ ('The doctrine of Cross and Redemption'). In the following, central tendencies in the works of ʿAbduh and Riḍā, as seen by Olaf Schumann (1988, ch. 6) and Yusuf Seferta (1986), will be summarized.[93]

An important part of the background for ʿAbduh and Riḍā's discussion of the Jesus passages of the Qur'ān is their knowledge of the radical biblical criticism in the West and the insights from modern religious studies in general. In Riḍā's theology, these insights are contrasted by the *a priori* view of the infallibility of the Qur'ān. In his part of *Tafsīr al-Manār*, ʿAbduh is not criticising the Christian canon, but holds the view that Christ was misinterpreted by his disciples because he spoke in parables and inclined towards metaphorical language (e.g. 'Son of God').

In Riḍā's deliberations, he reveals a general scepticism towards the canonical Gospels, although he does not explicitly maintain that they have been falsified. He is, however, advocating the view that there was an original Gospel, and without identifying the Gospel of Barnabas with the primordial *Injīl*, he refers to it as representing the correct Islamic Christology. As mentioned, Riḍā was the initiator of the Arabic edition of Barnabas which appeared in Cairo in 1908, and the one who introduced references to the Gospel of Barnabas in mainstream Muslim polemic.

As to the virginal conception, *Tafsīr al-Manār* strongly defends the qur'ānic and biblical assertions. But typically enough, rational critics are reminded that extraordinary happenings in nature are recognized by science. In the discussion of the miracles, *Tafsīr al-Manār* refers to the Ṣūfī understanding of how spiritual mastering of the body is reflected in the person of Jesus in a special way. Still, *Tafsīr al-Manār* insists that the power of Jesus to raise the dead was within the limits of resuscitating undecayed bodies, and argues that this view is held both by the Ṣūfīs and the Christians. Further, Jesus' 'creation' of birds does not imply any partnership in God's power of creation, since this miracle was not a creation out of nothing, but a mere fashioning, and only by God's special leave and power.

As for the teachings of Jesus, the Sermon on the Mount is heavily criticized by Riḍā for its naiveté towards the evils of the world, giving way to all kinds of injustice and abuses of power by its exaggerated preaching of patience and love towards enemies.

When it comes to the interpretation of Jesus' death and ascension, both ʿAbduh and Riḍā strongly reject the view that Jesus was taken up from this world without dying. Instead, they maintain that Jesus first died a natural death, and then he was taken up to heaven – though only in soul. In his rejection of the crucifixion, Riḍā puts the rational objections to the dogma of redemption and satisfaction at the centre of his argument, explaining how the Islamic way of salvation is far more sublime and logical than that of Christianity. He also attempts to find internal evidences in the Christian Gospels to support his view that Jesus did not die on the cross. Both ʿAbduh and Riḍā advocate the view that Judas was crucified instead of Jesus. As to the whereabouts of Jesus after being saved from the cross, Riḍā discusses the Ahmadi theory of Jesus' burial in Kashmir in a positive tone.

As regards Jesus' return, ʿAbduh rejects the idea for two reasons. First, because the Qur'ān says nothing about it and the Ḥadīth material concerning Jesus' descent should not be considered to be sound. Second, because Jesus had already completed his task as a reformer. His reformation was limited to the Jewish people, with the aim of bringing them back to the spirit of the Mosaic Law.

In their general discussions of Christology and Trinity, both ʿAbduh and Riḍā are specially fond of the expression in the Gospel of John 17.3: 'And this is eternal life, that they know Thee the only true God, and Jesus Christ whom Thou hast sent', an expression that in their eyes is very much in tune with Islam with its emphasis on divine unity and subordinate messengers. They claim that in the Bible, the doctrine of unity (*tawḥīd*) is more evident than that of Trinity (*taṯlīṯ*). Again, we can see how traditional Islamic approaches are combined with biblical criticism, the latter being informed by the radical criticism and the liberal approach to religion known from the West.

Generally, Riḍā is more explicitly polemical towards Christianity than ʿAbduh. An important part of Riḍā's polemic is his insistence that the departing from the true teachings of Jesus and the decay of Christianity began with Paul and his teaching of cross, redemption and Trinity. In Riḍā's view, this was the real reason for Paul's confrontation with Barnabas, who according to Riḍā faithfully defended the original Gospel. Riḍā even criticizes the alliances between Christianity and political power. He seems to hold the view that Christianity cannot survive without this alliance, although it is contrary to its self-understanding. Only with Muḥammad came the establishment of a political statesmanship that was rooted in true religion itself.

At this point, Olaf Schumann sees a difference in the approaches to Jesus of ʿAbduh and Riḍā: For Riḍā, who is 'political and Syrian' in his outlook, Christ is only a predecessor of Muḥammad in salvation history. For ʿAbduh, who is 'meditative and Egyptian', Christ's example in confronting the blindness of faith is still to be followed, and in that sense his teaching is valid for all times.[94]

ʿAbduh did not reproduce the common view (also expressed by Riḍā) that the Gospels had been corrupted. As he saw it, the problem lay rather in the way that the Christians had interpreted the words of Jesus, for instance by taking expressions like 'son of God' and 'Father' in a literal way. In this way, he may have paved the way for later Muslim biographies of Christ which take the biblical Gospel accounts as their starting point for the reconstruction of Jesus' message and mission.[95]

Influenced by Riḍā, but even more polemical and scornful towards Christianity in his writings is Muḥammad Tawfīq Ṣidqī (1891–1920).[96] His polemics finally resulted in a ban on further derisive writings, after Christian complaints to the authorities. In an almost Nietzschean spirit, he criticizes Christianity for being a religion of weakness, implying a weak God in its theology of the cross. Like other Muslim polemicists, Ṣidqī focuses on the contradictions in the Gospels, and underlines some passages in Luke that seem to imply that Jesus, in spite of his alleged non-violence, was preparing the disciples for an armed confrontation (cf. the references to swords in Luke 22.35–38). He interprets the parable of Sūra 95 as implying a value ranking of the religions, the 'strong' Mosaic religion coming closer to Islam than those of Christianity and Buddhism, both regarded as 'religions of mercy'.

Apparently, the rational objections to Christianity developed in the Manār-school, combined with a rational reinterpretation of the dogma of an infallible Qur'ān, have set the tone for much of Muslim apologetic against Christianity in the twentieth century. The development of ʿAbduh's anti-*taqlīd* reformism into the Islamist zeal for a purified Islam, cleansed not only from the obscurantism of the *ʿulamāʾ* but also from decadent Western influences (cf. the development of the Muslim Brotherhood), has been further developed by the anti-Christian polemic of preachers like the South-African Ahmed Deedat (d. 2005), who appeared to see no valuable truth in Christianity whatsoever.

Al-Azhar

Another important point in the discussion about Jesus among Muslim theologians in twentieth-century Egypt was the controversies in the 1940s over the return of Christ. Whereas the discussion about Christology of the school of al-Manār was mostly within the tradition of apologetics and polemics towards Christianity, the discussion in the 1940s was an internal, Muslim affair. It originated from a question put forward by an Indian Ahmadi Muslim and directed to a teacher (later shaykh) of al-Azhar, Maḥmūd Shaltūt: Is Jesus, according to the Qur'ān and the Sunna, alive in heaven or dead? Will he return at the end of time?[97] The fatwa (legal opinion) issued by Shaltūt in 1942 in response, and the subsequent discussion, indicate that the interpretations of the Ahmadiyya movement at this moment were not necessarily ruled out as heretical in the Egyptian context. Shaltūt's fatwa stated that according to the Qur'ān, Jesus died and was taken in soul and body to God, thus being rescued from his enemies. There is no indication in the Qur'ān, he states, that Jesus is now alive in heaven, and the Ḥadīth materials concerning his return are not secured by sufficient *isnād*. Thus, the fatwa concludes, a good Muslim does not have to believe in the return of Jesus.

As one can see, his view on this matter comes close to that of al-Manār. In defending his position, he seems to imply that those who hold the traditional, Ḥadīth-based view are captives of *taqlīd*.

With this fatwa from a teacher at the prestigious al-Azhar, barriers between the Ahmadiyya movement and Sunnī Muslim orthodoxy seemed to be falling, and of course, the Ahmadiyyas embraced the fatwa joyously. However, the fatwa immediately met with resistance and objection from other teachers at al-Azhar. Ṣiddīq al-Ghumārī issued a statement in which he carefully examines 22 Ḥadīth sayings referring to the return of Christ. He concludes that they are generally sound, and that the tradition of the living Christ returning at the end of time belongs to the fundamentals of Islam. In a later book, he elaborated the importance of this belief for the Muslim. His view implies the belief in a bodily ascension, in accordance with a literal interpretation of the Ḥadīth material, with its implication that Jesus has retained his earthly body in order to be recognized on his return.

One might ask whether this particular discussion of Jesus' return was entirely an internal affair. Obviously, the controversy was about the canonicity of Ḥadīth, as well as about the validity of the Ahmadi teachings. Could it be that the controversy also reflects the ambivalence in modern Muslim theology either to reclaim Jesus for Islam or leave him for the Christians?

From the 1940s, another work originating from al-Azhar deserves mention as an example of a polemical approach to Christianity: the 'Lectures on Christianity' (*Muḥādarāt fī-l-naṣrāniyya*, 1942) by the teacher and head of the *daʿwā* (mission) department at al-Azhar, Muḥammad Abū Zahra.[98] The book has been described as 'the basis for every other book on the subject published since'.[99] Although he presents the book as a scientific study, Abū Zahra seems to rely only on secondary Christian sources. His main references to polemic precedents are to Ibn Ḥazm and Raḥmatullāh al-Kairānawī. Abū Zahra holds the view that a faithful transmission of Jesus' message had been made impossible by the disruption of the Christian communities caused by persecution, and that Jesus' original message disappeared after the Council of Nicea.

A substantial part of his book is dedicated to a study of the ancient Christians councils. Abū Zahra takes Arius as the faithful, 'Unitarian' (*muwaḥḥid*) proponent of the true monotheism of Jesus, and traces Unitarian Christian positions in the subsequent developments of the church. Ending with modern times, Zahra refers to the emergence of biblical criticism as a reflection of the light of Islam:

> *Scientific and philosophical studies were continuing, and the light of Islam shone: we find many scholars explaining forcefully that Jesus was only an apostle, that he was no more than a man, and they quoted the Gospels themselves to that effect.*[100]

As mentioned above (in the section about 'The Barnabas argument'), when explaining what he regards to be the original *tawḥīd* message of Christ, Abū Zahra refers not only to the Qur'ān but also to the Gospel of Barnabas, which he cites as an undisputed authority.

Goddard underlines the fact that Abū Zahra's book originated from lectures given in the mission department of al-Azhar. Basically, it is an elucidation of how to undermine traditional Christian beliefs 'in order to pave the way for the Christian world's acceptance of Islam'.[101]

As noted, Goddard (1996) as well as Schirrmacher (1992) identify the Indian Raḥmatullāh al-Kairānawī/al-Hindī's *Iẓhār al-ḥaqq* as another source of inspiration also for polemical treatises in the Egyptian context. Goddard has examined two different editions of *Iẓhār al-ḥaqq* in Egypt, by Muḥammad Kamāl Farag (1978) and Aḥmad Hijāzī al-Saqqā (1977).[102] The one edited by Farag is introduced by a shaykh of al-Azhar, ʿAbd al-Hālim Maḥmūd. The second editor, Aḥmad Hijāzī al-Saqqā, was educated at al-Azhar, with a doctorate on 'The annunciation of the prophet of Islam in the Torah and the Injīl'. In his introduction to his edition of the *Iẓhār*, he argues at length in favour of the view that Muḥammad was extensively prophesied in the Bible. The author also invokes The Gospel of Barnabas in his argument. The *Iẓhār* itself is introduced with its main point being to expound the corruption of Christian scripture, especially with respect to the foretelling of Muḥammad.

Goddard (1996) also presents two other books by al-Saqqā, one on prophecy about Muḥammad in the Bible, and another on the doctrine of the Trinity. He notes that neither Zahra nor al-Saqqā knew any other language than Arabic and were thus severely restricted in their access to Christian sources and modern Christian theology. Goddard concludes:

It is therefore not surprising to note, finally, that the arguments that these authors do present bear a striking resemblance to some of the arguments put forward by the Muslim writers of the classical period, and to the work of ʿAbd al-Jabbār and ʿAli Ṭabarī in particular.[103]

Some Other Apologetic and Polemical Contributions

Among Egyptian scholars involved in Christian–Muslim dialogue and polemics, Aḥmad Shalabī deserves special mention.[104] Shalabī, a scholar in religious studies, published a famous work entitled *Muqāranat al-adyān* ('Comparison of religions'). The second volume, about Christianity, originated from lectures in Indonesia in 1959. Shalabī sees the Gospel of Barnabas as a possible link between Christianity and Islam, whereas New Testament Christianity (in its Pauline, Lukan and Johannine versions) is considered as a deviation. He traces the New Testament views of the crucifixion and the doctrine of redemption back to influences from Hellenistic and Indian spirituality.

Peter Ford (2001) has noted a more recent example of essentially the same argument as found in Shalabī. In Aḥmad ʿAbd al-Wahhāb's *Al-masīḥ fī maṣādir al-ʿaqāʾid al-masīḥiyya* (in English: 'Christ as seen in the sources of the Christian beliefs'), he cites a number of Western scholarly works in order to demonstrate how they testify to the Islamic contention that the Christian scriptures have been corrupted.[105]

Another apologetic book from the Egyptian context, with the title *Daʿwat al-ḥaqq aw al-ḥaqīqah bayn al-masīḥiyya wa-l-islām* was published by Manṣūr Ḥusayn ʿAbd al-ʿAzīz in 1963.[106] The work focuses on the themes of crucifixion and sonship. The Gospel accounts of the passion and crucifixion are referred to rather extensively, before the author sets out to refute them by way of the substitutionist theory. With reference to the Gospel account, the author suggests that God in fact answered Jesus' prayer in Gethsemane, rescuing him from the hands of his enemies, and leaving Judas in his place. The premise of his argument is that there is only one truth about this. Islam stands or falls by the denial of crucifixion and sonship, whereas Christianity, according to the author, may be meaningfully reinterpreted without these elements.

In a book published in 1966 by ʿAbd al-Karīm al-Khāṭib, *Al-masīḥ fī-l-qurʾān wa-l-tawrāh wa-l-injīl*, he points to the inconsistencies of the Bible as an indication of the errors of Christian doctrine and the supremacy of the Muslim positions.[107] In a response to a review made by Kenneth Nolin (1969), al-Khāṭib (1971) reiterates his conviction that the only authentic witness to Jesus is the Qur'ān, in its traditional interpretation.

Other examples of polemical writings against Christianity from the Egyptian context, examined by Goddard,[108] are the anti-missionary and anti-imperialist works of the mid-1970s by authors like Muḥammad al-Bahīy (writing on modern Islamic thought and its relationship to Western imperialism) and Ibrāhım

Khālid Aḥmad (a convert from Christianity who wrote on Orientalism and mission, and their relationship to world imperialism). Although these works do not deal with the issue of Christ specifically, they mark a general trend in modern Muslim polemics against Christianity: the Muslim world is presented as a victim of a plot staged by Orientalists and missionary organizations. Within this trend, dialogue-oriented scholars and institutions such as Kenneth Cragg and the journal *The Muslim World* are also considered to be part of the plot.

Twentieth-Century Indo-Pakistani Contributions

In India/Pakistan, twentieth-century discussions about Jesus have emerged within two different contexts (incidentally, similar contexts as in the case of al-Azhar): one being the apologetic and polemical efforts vis-à-vis Christianity, the other being the refutation of the beliefs of the Ahmadiyya movement, which itself originated from the Indian context. But the emergence of a Muslim modernism has also set new tones for the approaches to Jesus.

Speculative Modernism

In his review of modernism in Indo-Pakistani Islam, Malise Ruthwen has contrasted the 'intellectual modernism' of Sayyid Ahmad Khan with the 'speculative modernism' of the poet, mystic, philosopher and intellectual founder of Pakistan, Muhammad Iqbal (1875–1938).[109] Iqbal combined the mystical rationalism of Ṣūfism and the Persian tradition with modern Western thinking. But surprisingly, his poetry does not reflect the prominent place given to Jesus and the breath of Christ in Ṣūfism. Annemarie Schimmel explains:

> He had not such a relation to him [Jesus] as he had to Abraham and Moses, the powerful prophets, Jesus being regarded since the times of early Ṣūfism as a model of asceticism and renunciation of which Iqbal wanted to rid his people.[110]

In Iqbal's writings, like in those of the Egyptian writer Ṣidqī (see above), there seems to be a certain influence from Nietzsche in the perception of Christianity. Iqbal writes:

> *No religious system can ignore the moral value of suffering. The error of the builders of Christianity was that they based their religion on the factor of suffering alone, and ignored all the other factors.*[111]

Rationalist Modernism

The rationalist interpretation so characteristic for Sayyid Ahmad Khan has not been accepted in later Sunnī Islam in the Indian subcontinent. However, a similar rationalist approach is taken up and developed by Ghulam Aḥmad Parwez – the founder of the movement 'Tolu-e-Islam'.[112] Following Iqbal's desire to study Islam not as a religion in the narrow sense, but as an all-comprehensive world-view (*dīn*), he portrays Islam as a rational challenge to all religion, and holds radically different positions from those of traditional *ʿulamāʾ* in most matters.

In his commentary on the Qur'ān,[113] he gives a rational reinterpretation of the birth-passages, introduces Joseph as Jesus' father (as Sayyid Ahmad Khan did) and rejects the traditional understanding of the miracles held by the traditionalists. In his interpretation, he comes close to the spiritual meaning attributed to the miracles by Ṣūfism, with Christ giving sight and life to a dead community of blind believers. He also emphasizes the 'anti-capitalist' features of Jesus' teaching, referring to his warning against riches.

However, commenting on the Sermon on the Mount, he only accepts the commands of non-violence as a praiseworthy personal decision and not as a universal obligation. In his book *Islam – a challenge to religion*, when dealing with the verses on non-retaliation in Matthew 5.38–41, he makes it clear that:

> *To do good in return for evil is said to be the best way to fight evil. No doubt, these are noble sentiments and in the personal lives of individuals may be praiseworthy. But it is doubtful if Jesus (P) could have taught these precepts for universal behaviour, for experience do not prove their wisdom.*[114]

He cites with approval Dean Inge: 'The principle of non-resistance was laid down for a little flock in a hostile environment. But an organized society cannot abstain from the use of coercion. No one would suggest that a Christian Government must not suppress a gang of criminals within its own borders, and if this is admitted, can we doubt that it should defend itself against an invading enemy?'[115]

Although not accepted by orthodoxy, the interpretation of Parwez shows how a rationalistic and historical interpretation of the story of Jesus, as found in the Qur'ān and in the Christian Gospels, still prevails in some circles. An interesting parallel phenomenon in the writings of the intellectual nation builder Iqbal and the politically oriented philosopher Parwez is their shared critique of the emphasis on suffering and non-resistance in Christianity.

Maududi: Rational Re-Affirmation of Tradition

In the 'systematic neo-traditionalism' (Malise Ruthwen) of Sayyid Abul A'la Maududi (1904–1979), he defends orthodox teachings of Islam challenged by modernity, like life after death, by rational arguments. His general presupposition is that a man who uses his knowledge and intellect correctly will come to know God and Islam.

One of the founders of modern Islamism, Maududi combines blame of the traditional *ʿulamāʾ* for their backwardness with a strongly critical attitude towards 'the West'. His political project of Islamization, through Jamaʿat-i Islami (cf. the Muslim Brotherhood in the Arab World), was paralleled by a vision of Muḥammad as a true revolutionary and an avant-garde ideal.

In his exposition of the fundamentals of Islam,[116] he consistently diminishes the value of the pre-qur'ānic Scriptures and unfolds the theory of their general corruption, contrasted by the indisputable qualities and infallibility of the Qur'ān as the final, perfect and universal revelation. Reasons given for his rejection of the Scriptures (meaning the Bible) are their alleged contradiction of rationality and the brutal and immoral stories they contain.

His image of Jesus may be studied in his *Tafhīm al-Qur'ān*, 'Towards Understanding the Qur'ān'.[117] In accordance with a theological approach that is a rational re-affirmation of tradition rather than a rationalist reinterpretation, he affirms the literal meaning of the virginal birth and the miracles:

> *Jesus was merely a human being whom God had created in an extraordinary manner for reasons best known to Him. God had also invested Jesus with the power to perform miracles by which he could categorically establish his claim to prophethood.*[118]

As to the end of Jesus' life, he states that:

> *It seems perfectly reasonable that God should not have allowed such an extraordinary person to be crucified by unbelievers and should have raised him up to Himself.*[119]

Accordingly, he holds the view that the expression *mutawaffīka* in Sūra 3.55 'to say the least, contains the possibility of being interpreted as meaning that he had been raised into heaven alive'. But Maududi is not categorical in his interpretation at this point.[120]

After a summary of the Islamic fundamentals, and notwithstanding his general conviction that the biblical scriptures are corrupted, he asserts that 'we find scattered throughout the Gospels all the ... fundamentals mentioned above',[121] and he quotes extensively from the Gospels to support his views.

The interpretations laid out in Maududi's commentary are probably representative for mainstream neo-traditionalist theology in contemporary

Islam – re-affirming basic orthodox teachings in a non-reductionist way, and emphasizing an outwardly directed, activist interpretation of Islam over against individualistic piety, as in his commentary on the notion *ḥawārī*, 'helper/disciple', in Sūra 3.52:

> *When a man performs Prayers, keeps his fast and worships God in other ways, he is merely on the level of service and subjection to God. But when a man strives to spread God's true religion and to enthrone it in actual life, he is honoured with the status of God's ally and helper, which is the zenith of man's spiritual growth.*[122]

With his disciples, Jesus fulfils this mission in the context of a Jewish revival, whereas the universal fulfilment is left to Muḥammad, 'the greatest revolutionary'.

Apologetic and Polemical Writings of Pakistani Origin[123]

In Pakistan, several polemical writings dealing with the question of Christ in Christianity and Islam have appeared since the 1970s.

The most well known would be the book of Muhammad 'Ata ur-Rahim, *Jesus – A Prophet of Islam*, which was first published in 1977.[124] Despite the title, his book is more a study of Christianity than a book about Jesus. Much of the work for the book was done in England, with assistance of the Darqāwī Ṣūfī order and British converts to Islam. In an introduction to the British 1977-edition, the leader of the Darqāwī order shaykh ʿAbd al-Qādir asserts that the book shows:

> *. . . how the 'true' Christian teaching was diverted, one might say de-railed, by the powerful Pauline explosion [. . .]*
>
> *Why this work is so welcome is that . . . it looks at the roots of the Christian phenomenon from the only point from which it can be properly understood – I mean, the Muslim point of view.*[125]

So, no secret is made of the polemical and apologetic aim of the book, which sets out to show how Christians have not only lost, but sometimes deliberately corrupted, the true message of Jesus.

The main point of the author is to demonstrate a persistent Unitarian trend within Christianity, confessing the unity of God and denying the divinity of Christ as well as the doctrine of Trinity. According to 'Ata ur-Rahim, the Unitarian stand (which was, allegedly, that of Jesus) was first represented by the Shepherd of Hermas and the disciple Barnabas, then defended by Arius and Donatus, and subsequently by a chain of Unitarian philosophers identified by the author (among them Servetus and the Sozinis from the time of the

Reformation, and later good Englishmen like John Milton, John Locke and Isaac Newton).[126] In line with medieval polemic, Paul is listed as the main culprit for all that went in the wrong direction. With Paul's alleged opponent Barnabas as the ancient hero, a chapter of the book is dedicated to the Gospel of Barnabas.

The second last chapter of the book is dedicated to 'Jesus in the Qur'an', and the last chapter to 'Jesus in Hadith and Muslim Traditions' – in which the author cites Thaʿlabī's 'Stories of the Prophets' and other legendary material on a par with Ḥadīth.

Other polemicists seek to refute Christian teachings by a combined technique of external and internal criticism of the Bible, without putting too much emphasis on the Barnabas argument. In his book *Mirror of Trinity* (originally published in Urdu, and translated into English in 1975[127]), Kausar Niazi, then Cabinet Minister of Pakistan under Z. A. Bhutto, repeats every feature of medieval Muslim polemic towards Christianity. He focuses on the 'mutual contradictions' of the Gospels and the 'improper passages' of the Bible, explains how the last Prophet is foretold in the Bible, criticizes the notions of physical sonship and Trinity, focuses on the moral prohibitions in Jesus' teaching and argues that the miracles of Muḥammad are superior to the miracles of Christ since they brought about the establishment of a great empire. With this approach, the author's assurance in the book's preface of aiming at a peaceful coexistence between Christians and Muslims sounds rather shallow. Hugh Goddard notes, however, that despite the polemical contents, the tone of this book is friendlier than in other works in the same genre.[128]

Images of Jesus are, of course, also reflected in more general works about Christianity and Islam from the Pakistani context. Ulfat Aziz-us-Samad's book *A Comparative Study of Christianity and Islam* (al-Samad 1986 – first published in 1970) has become widespread, and deserves special mention. The author compares Muḥammad and Jesus. The former is regarded as superior, because of his greater opportunity to fulfil his mission. Basically, the author regards:

> *[. . .] the characters of Jesus and Prophet Muhammad to be equally godly, pure, noble and inspiring, yet Jesus did not get the opportunity to become a perfect model for men in all walks of life as the Prophet Muhammad did.*[129]

The author asserts that 'Jesus was faced with failure throughout his life',[130] and he 'did not live long enough to give a practical shape to his teachings and to work out the social and international implications of his message'.[131] For instance, Jesus could not enlighten the disciples 'regarding the proper occasion and right use of the sword' – the result being that Christians have always misused the sword, realizing the impracticability of pacifism, but left without instructions for the proper use of force.[132]

In other parts of the book, the author maintains well-known points in Muslim polemics and apologetics – that the Gospels are unreliable, and that Muḥammad is foretold in the Bible. In ethical matters, the teachings of the Qur'ān are favourably contrasted with those of Paul (not to mention the church fathers) – e.g. as regards the position of women.[133]

The pamphlet 'Islam and Christianity' by Muhammad Tahir ul-Qadri, head of the Pakistan-based movement Idara Minhaj ul-Qur'an, may be cited as a type of Ahmed Deedat-style polemic against Christianity.[134] The author is not satisfied with pinpointing 'contradictions in the Bible', but includes the Barnabas argument in his attacks on the authenticity of the New Testament. As regards biblical criticism, ul-Qadri seems to rely on rather superficial renderings of biblical scholarship. As for the Barnabas argument, the English translation leaves the impression that he confuses the Gospel of Barnabas (called 'Bible of Barnabas') with the Letter of Barnabas, with claims of the existence of a complete Greek version of the Gospel of Barnabas. Only material from the Gospels that supports the message of divine unity, or otherwise confirms the view that the Bible is totally unreliable, is cited. The decisive argument is left to the 'Bible of Barnabas', which is summarized as the authentic Islamic voice about Christ.

A New Gospel Harmony

Another Pakistani author, based in North America and publishing in the West, is Ahmad Shafaat. In 1979, he published the book *The Gospel According to Islam*. The ambitious aim of the book is to present the essential teachings of Islam about Jesus together with elements of the biblical Gospels in a new kind of Gospel harmony – presented as a 'new Gospel, a Muslim equivalent of, and alternative to, the existing Gospels'.[135] According to Shafaat, the need for a Gospel harmony has become even more felt in the era of biblical criticism:

> *The very fact that there are four canonical Gospels that contradict each other on almost every point (and an ever-growing recognition of this fact among the Christians of this century) demands a second coming of Gospels.*

Self-consciously enough, the author relates the idea of a second coming of Gospels to the notion of the second coming of Christ, in a maybe ironical parenthesis:

> *(Perhaps, the return of Jesus, if it has any meaning at all after its continuing and long delay, means just a second coming of Gospels and rediscovery of Jesus).*

New Testament scholarship is visited:

> *. . . we better not look for new Gospels from any schools of New Testament scholarship. The work of such schools is essentially negative in nature: they can show the inadequacy of an existing Gospel but cannot offer one of their own.*

The only remedy, then, lies in the Qur'ān:

> *A Gospel . . . is not a historical but a revelatory work and must spring from revelation. The ninety-three verses of the Qur'ān about Jesus offer a revelatory basis for a new Gospel.*[136]

Chapters 1 and 2 about the annunciation and birth of Jesus mix material from the New Testament and the Qur'ān. In ch. 3, Jesus is prophesying about Muḥammad, citing Old Testament verses usually thought to foretell the coming of Muḥammad. The point is repeated in ch. 17, as an interpretation of the transfiguration story. As for the Chapters 4–21, about Jesus life and teaching, the author relies mostly on the biblical Gospels, but much is excluded, such as the verses on non-retaliation from the Sermon on the Mount. The parables of Jesus are mostly ignored. Some extra material from the Qur'ān is included in the miracle stories.

In ch. 22, concerning the entry into Jerusalem, the author states, 'Thus ended the public ministry of this messenger of God to Israel'. His mission is summed up by the words of the Qur'ān. In a note, the author declares that Jesus' public ministry did not appear very successful. Most people rejected him. But he stirred a discontent within Judaism and the Roman Empire, enough to prepare the ground for the later coming of Islam:

> *. . . there evolved a political force that defeated the two systems that collaborated in trying to put an end to Jesus' mission. This was the planning of God, the best of planners.*[137]

A parable is then eventually included – that of the vineyard owner – but rewritten as to foretell the coming of the children of Ishmael and 'the Saviour of the nations'. Later (ch. 23–24), Jesus' foretelling of the coming Son of Man and of the Counsellor (the Paraclete) are taken as predictions of Muḥammad.

In ch. 25–26, up to the verdict of Pilate, the author relies on the Passion narrative of the biblical Gospels. At this point the author makes the following comment:

> *Up to this point, the majority of scholars are more or less willing to accept the Gospel account of the events that took place after Jesus' entry into Jerusalem. What happens afterwards is, however, a subject of fundamental difference among various first-century Christian sects and modern scholars and among Muslims and Christians.*[138]

Later in the same note, the crucifixion is tellingly misspelled for 'crucifiction', a cherished expression by modern Muslim polemicists.[139] The author then gives his version of the substitutionist theory, suggesting that 'Jesus Barabbas' was crucified instead of Jesus of Nazareth. In ch. 26–27, Jesus is said to have reached the end of his life only a few days later, as a result of flogging and fatigue. God then took him to himself. In a final note, the author explains that although Jesus was not crucified, the circumstances created such confusion as to leave the way open to resurrection stories. In that way – in the imagination of the disciples – Jesus was finally granted 'the success of his mission', and the disciples were provided 'with fresh hopes and a new source of the faith in Jesus'. The author concludes:

> *. . . the coming of the Risen Lord was not worthless, not only because man's imagination and fantasy is not worthless, but also because with the success of the risen Lord, there also survived something of Jesus, the messenger of the true living God.*[140]

Hugh Goddard comments:

> This book is thus an intriguing combination of a new approach to Muslim writings about Jesus, namely the use of a Gospel-type format, and a rather traditional line of argument.[141]

Dialogical Works from the Indian Context

Goddard (1994) and Kate Zebiri (1997) contrast the polemical tone of Pakistani writers on Christ with the more eirenical approach of the Indian Muslim philosopher Syed Vahiduddin (Hyderabad, Delhi). In a collection of articles, Vahiduddin writes about 'What Christ means to me' (Vahiduddin 1986), and speaks about 'the mystery that haunts the life of Christ from beginning to the end'. The central characteristic of Jesus is love:

> *Christ's Gospel abounds with the love that overflows itself (agape). The call to forgiveness, unlimited and without reservation, resounds throughout his teaching . . .. Christ reflects in every act of His God's jamāl [beauty] and its fullness. He is the embodiment of that tender aspect of the divine which the Quran calls raḥma, and this is what Rudolf Otto calls mysterium fascinans. . . .*[142]

As for the end of Jesus' life, Vahiduddin states that:

> *The treatment that was meted out to him makes the saddest chapter of human history. He was spat on his face, humiliated and insulted, mocked and laughed at and was condemned to be crucified, with two confirmed*

> *criminals. 'And the light shineth in the darkness and the darkness apprehendeth it not' (John 1:5). He is forsaken and betrayed. Those who stand close to him flee! But there is no complaint. It is a state of perfect surrender to God's will, of riḍa and grace, 'not what I will, but what thou wilt'.* (Mark 14:37)

Having affirmed these central elements of the New Testament understanding of the passion, Vahiduddin continues:

> *But it is here that Christ appears in all His glory, and the world and all that it stands for is exposed in all its vanity. Whether we see the end and the culmination of his earthly course in the Christian or the Muslim perspective, death is not allowed to prevail and Christ appears to be ascending to supreme heights defying death. Perhaps it is due to my Muslim background that what strikes me most, is not the suffering through which he passes but his triumph through suffering.*[143]

In other parts of this collection of articles, e.g. 'The Quranic Understanding of Inter-Religious Harmony' and 'What al-Qur'an Means to Me', Syed Vahiduddin gives a more specific Islamic underpinning of his open approach to the Christian tradition. As for the understanding of God, Vahiduddin emphasizes that Islam affirms both God's proximity and his distance:

> . . . *the Quranic consciousness has a place for both the significant moments, the intimacy possible in the framework of his proximity, and the mystery which his transcendence intimates.*[144]

Kenneth Cragg (1985b) and Kate Zebiri (1997) have highlighted the contributions to Christian–Muslim dialogue from another Indian thinker from Hyderabad, Hasan Askari (b. 1932, from a Shīʿite community).[145] Apart from Osmania University in Hyderabad, Askari has taught in universities and colleges in Beirut, Amsterdam and Birmingham. The double context of Askari's writings on dialogue is thus multi-religious India and international Christian–Muslim dialogue. As for the image of Christ, Askari holds the view that meditation on the symbol of the cross could help Muslims in crisis perception. According to Cragg, Askari reads the cross as 'an existential symbol of how tragic the relationship of man to God can be. That tragedy lies in how wilful and selfish men are in their violation of faith'.[146]

Askari also discusses the idea of incarnation. He suggests that the Qur'ān and Christ may be seen as embodiments of the divine word, and thus as essentially one. The New Testament is seen by Askari not as the word of God, but 'the address of man to God'. Still, Askari considers 'this address to be authentic, honest and true'. This view of Christ and Scripture challenges both Christians and Muslims:

> *To accept Jesus as the Word of God must imply that one accepts all revelation of God, all speech of God addressed to all men of all times . . .. The Islam of Muslims and the Scripture of Christians are then one and the same thing. Each is response to the Word of God, symbolising man speaking to God.*[147]

Askari also emphasizes that Muslims and Christians alike need to beware of idolatry – of the written Qur'ān and the Incarnation respectively.

In an essay from 1972, Askari relates his view of Christ to a more general reflection on 'The Dialogical Relationship between Christianity and Islam' (Askari 1972). Askari warns against the monological tendencies prevailing in the world of religion, and threatening humanity in new disguise in the age of cybernetics. Monological speech reduces everything to issues, and tends to annihilate the other. In the Holy Scriptures, 'Monological autonomy is instantly destroyed. A divine companionship comes to birth'.[148]

Convinced that Christianity and Islam constitute 'a dialogical whole', Askari refers to Christ as a common 'Sign' for Christians and Muslims. The Qur'ān affirms that Christ is a Sign, and in a different sense from God's signs in nature. Christ is the Word of God who 'lives as a Sign in a different realm, the realm of the deep relation between God and man'.[149] To him personally:

> *Christ as a Sign of God liberates man from the dead circle of monological religion and restores unto him his genuine dialogical existence.*[150]

According to Askari, the Word of God in Christ is not a book that might be objectivated by monological religion, but a Person: 'Here is no book as such, but the life of Christ.'[151] Still, the important thing is the Word, and not the Person. Askari sees the qur'ānic rejection of Incarnation as a correction of 'the idolatry of the Person as Word of God' – but emphasizes that 'also a Muslim has to be aware of the monological traps within his own faith'.[152]

By his investigation of the dialogical nature of the Word of God, seeing Christ as the symbol the dialogical relationship between God and man, and the Qur'ān as a warning against idolatry, Askari ventures far beyond apologetics towards a reading of the signs of God by Christians and Muslims together (see below in Chapter 8: 'Reading the signs of God').

In an article from 1985, he goes so far as to claim that Muslims 'require a Christian amidst them' to counter the danger of falling into legalism, and to give greater space to the dimensions of:

> *. . . the tragic, or suffering, of submission in silence without resistance, of confronting self-righteousness, of upholding the value of humility and poverty, of going inward, of partaking of the burdens, seen and unseen, of the other.*[153]

Another Shīʿite voice from the Indian context is that of Asghar Ali Engineer. Engineer has written extensively on Muslim liberation theology.[154]

In a paper from 1991 (Engineer 1991), he discusses some Indian/Pakistani and Persian interpretations of Christ, citing writers that 'view a personality like Jesus Christ in their own way which appeals to emotion rather than to intellect' – thinkers that 'have seen in him a soothing humanism, love and affection'.[155] He also refers positively to the works on Christ by the Egyptian authors Kāmil Ḥusayn and al-ʿAqqād (cf. the section about Christ biographies below).

He concludes his exposition about *Ḥaḍrat ʿĪsā* among Muslim writers by citing the following characteristics of Christ:

> *His emphasis was not on law but on love, not punishment but pardon, not condemnation but salvation, not contempt but affection, not violence but non-violence, not power but compassion and mercy, and it is these virtues which need to be emphasised in the conflict torn and violence prone world today.*[156]

Vahiduddin, Askari and Engineer write out of a Muslim minority and multi-religious context. All of them have an interreligious commitment. Their willingness to take Christian sources seriously when relating to Christ probably reflects both the contexts of their writings, and a personal commitment to genuine dialogue.

Jesus in Revolutionary Iran

In Iran, where creative images of Jesus have been reflected in Persian poetry both classical and modern (see below), new approaches to Christ and Christianity have emerged in the context and wake of the Islamic revolution in 1979.

In his 'sociology of Islam', the great theorist of revolutionary Islam ʿAli Shariʿati (1933–1977)[157] finds a place for Jesus in his rather 'telescoping' view of the ancient world and the Middle Ages:

> *Then came Jesus who directed society to concentrate on the hereafter, so that Rome changed its orientation from pleasure and worldliness to asceticism and contemplation of the hereafter, the ultimate result of this being the Middle Ages.*[158]

In line with his activist approach to religion, he sees some incompleteness in Jesus' focus on inwardness and eternity, as well as in his non-violent stance. For Shariʿati, 'whoever has no worldly life has no spiritual life'. In his final chapter about 'The ideal man – the viceregent of God', he writes that:

> *Ideal man . . . holds the sword of Caesar in his hand and he has the heart of Jesus in his breast . . .. Like Jesus, he bears a message of love and reconciliation, and like Moses, he is the messenger of jihad and deliverance.*[159]

Thus, according to this theorist, the religious message of Jesus is at the best incomplete, and awaits the fulfilment of Muḥammad's mission.

Shariʿati, as well as Khomeini, conceived Islam basically as a struggle for truth and justice, against falsehood and evil. They stressed not only the unity of all true Muslims beyond the limits of old confessionalism, but also the fundamental unity of all struggles for liberation in the third world. Accordingly, Khomeini addressed exponents of Christian liberation theology, and called for an interreligious alliance between advocates of a politicized, resurgent religion. The advertisement of Khomeini in *New York Times* on 12 January 1979, just before his return to Iran, has become famous for its appeal to 'freedom-loving Christians'. In this and later appeals, he reclaims Jesus for the struggle against the superpowers of the world, cf. his admonition in the magazine *Imām* (London) in 1984:

> *In contradiction to the words of the Almighty God, the superpowers act against Jesus Christ's teachings. According to the teachings of Christ and the Almighty God, the Christian clergy have a duty to wage spiritual war against the superpowers who act contrary to the way of the prophets and the way of Christ.*[160]

Another feature of the revolutionary reinterpretation of Islam in the Iranian context is the renewed veneration of Ḥusayn as a martyr of the struggle against godless tyrants. As a theology of martyrdom, but still expecting a 'manifest victory' of Islam and all the oppressed peoples of the world, Iranian liberation theology has challenged Christian theologies of liberation and reconstruction to a qualified response. Central questions would be: Can a Christ-based liberation theology accept violence in the struggle for liberation, or is Christ exclusively represented by those suffering from oppression and violence, those who carry the cross in our time?

Apologetic Writings for a Western Audience

We have seen that much of the apologetic writings of Pakistani origin about Christ in Islam are partly intended for a Western audience – both 'Muslims under Christian rule' and Christians. This seems to be particularly so for the books of 'Ata ur-Rahim (1979) and Shafaat (1979). The polemical pamphlets of Ahmed Deedat (cf. Deedat 1984, 1989) also fall into this category. Another obvious example would be the apologetic books from American Trust Publications in the USA, including those of Yusseff pertaining to the Gospel of Barnabas (Yusseff 1990a, 1990b).

M. A. Yusseff's book *The Dead Sea Scrolls, the Gospel of Barnabas and the New Testament*' (Yusseff 1990b) deserves special mention again here (cf. the section about 'The Barnabas argument' above). His contribution is marked by semi-scientific approach, a highly speculative interpretation of early Christianity and a virtual dismissal of Christianity as a serious partner in dialogue. The method of the book resembles that employed by standard Marxist writers in order to fit early Christianity into the world-view of Communism: scattered references to biblical criticism are given, but overruled by the obvious interest in finding a historical basis for one's own ideological presuppositions.

As for the image of Jesus in general presentations of Islam, one might point to Hammudah Abdalati's *Islam in Focus* – published by American Trust Publications in 1975, and 'conceived in response to certain urgent needs of both Muslim and non-Muslim readers in North America'.[161] The self-sufficient approach to Jesus of this book was cited in the Introduction above:

> *A Muslim is quite at ease as far as the attitude of Islam towards Jesus is concerned; his conscience is clear, and his belief is sound . . .. It is to be taken as the truth in which the Muslim unshakeably believes and will continue to believe.*[162]

The reader is assured that 'Islamic beliefs depict Jesus in a most respectful manner and place him as high in status as God himself has placed him'.[163] But no attempts are made at a real dialogue. The only positive references are to the Qur'ān, and the references to a Christian understanding are merely polemical. The author launches his chief attack on the notion of atonement. He claims that the mission which God entrusted to Jesus:

> *. . . was not salvation through total atonement by blood sacrifice, but salvation by virtue of right guidance and self-discipline, by quickening the stagnant minds and softening the hard souls.*[164]

The author's Christology is one of glory, rejecting the crucifixion in a traditional manner, but relativizing the how of Jesus' exaltation:

> *God crowned his mission on the earth by saving him from violent death and raising him high up to Heaven. Whether he was raised in rank by means of excellence or whether he was raised alive in soul and body or in soul only after he died a natural death has not much bearing on the Islamic beliefs.*[165]

Convert Literature

A category of its own is convert literature, in which converts from Christianity to Islam explain their reasons for leaving an old and embracing a new faith. In

The Separated Ones: Jesus, the Pharisees and Islam (1991), Ruqayyah Waris Maqsood (formerly Rosalyn Kendrick) describes her spiritual journey and explains how she came to abandon the idea of divine sacrifice and the doctrine of Trinity. For her, like for many converts, becoming a Muslim may be like:

> ... *'coming home' to something they have always known to be true in their hearts: They do not regard themselves as blasphemous renegades, turning their backs on all the Christian values they used to hold dear, nor do they feel that they are forsaking the love of their first religion for the enticement of a new one. On the contrary, what was incomprehensible in Christianity falls neatly into place* . . ..[166]

For converts, the need may arise not only to rethink christological doctrines, but also to rewrite the story of Jesus from a new perspective. In accordance with recent research about Jesus and Judaism, and the 'rehabilitation' of the Pharisees in recent scholarship, Maqsood highlights the continuity between the teaching of Jesus and that of the Pharisees. She feels that Muslims and Pharisees may have more in common with each other than with Christians.

As an ideal for contemporary Muslim, and against the blind 'Pharasaism' prevailing also in some Muslim circles, she notes that 'the true Pharisee':

> ... *did not regard any commandment as irksome requirements that had to be fulfilled, while one's real will was directed at something else. Rather, believers had to become children before their Father, not appealing to any rights or merits, but simply willing to love, and to be given a gift in return.*[167]

Maqsood also sees the Sermon on the Mount as part of a Pharisaic discourse, about the letter of the law and the rule of love.[168] In this way, she breaks new ground in Muslim approaches to Judaism and Christianity. Kate Zebiri notes that Maqsood is unusual among Muslims in expressing sympathy for the Pharisees, and remarks that 'surprisingly few Muslims explore the possibility of a *rapprochement* with Judaism in order to highlight the deviation of Christianity'. But she also points out that 'Maqsood's view . . . tends to diminish Jesus' actual prophetic contribution even in the Islamic sense, since he becomes rather less distinctive vis-à-vis other religious figures of his day'.[169]

Approaches Emerging from Christian–Muslim Dialogue

We have identified above some dialogical approaches to Christ and Christianity emerging from the pluralist, Indian context. Fresh approaches to the Bible and its witness to Christ have also emerged from organized Christian–Muslim dialogues in other contexts. A most notable example is the results from the mainly French and North African 'Muslim–Christian Research Group', as presented in

The Challenge of the Scriptures (1989). Under the heading 'Toward a Muslim Perception of the Bible', they jointly reconsider the traditional claim of *taḥrīf*, especially as regards the sensitive questions of Jesus as Son of God, the crucifixion and the proclamation of Muḥammad's prophethood.[170]

Regarding the concept of Jesus as Son of God, they believe that 'Islam could tolerate any metaphorical interpretation' that distanced itself from the literal, physical understanding of sonship, although 'it remains true that the Muslim faith categorically rejects the idea that Jesus could really be the son of God, eternally begotten of the Father in the bosom of the Trinity'.[171] As to the crucifixion, they draw attention to the verses of the Qur'ān that seem to imply that Jesus did actually die, and they discuss different interpretations. Sensitive to both converging and differing features in the Christian and Muslim accounts of Jesus' death, they conclude that Christians and Muslims not only agree on 'the historical failure of the prophet Jesus', but they also agree that 'in very different ways, on the divine intervention that followed' by raising Jesus to heaven – 'with or without a death on the cross, according to Islamic tradition, and by raising him to life after his death, according to Christian tradition'.[172]

In their general conclusion, they even suggest that Muslims can find in the Christian scripture – 'such as it is' – an emphasis on certain values that are 'insufficiently cultivated in Muslim circles, like love, forgiveness, the rejection of pharasaism, and the concern with the spirit rather than the letter of the law' (note the difference from Maqsood's approach).[173]

The challenge goes both ways, however, and this dialogical research group displays a similar openness to what Christians may learn from the Qur'ān.[174]

Jesus in Twentieth-Century Muslim Poetry

In a dialogue with Islam, there is always the question of what Islam is and who is a Muslim. 'Islam' is different from 'Muslim societies' and theological statements are something different from cultural utterances in general. Nevertheless, from the fundamental laicist perspective of Islam, it is not only the *ʿulamāʾ* or religious scholars who are capable of speaking in the name of Islam. As for the question of genre, classical Islam has been expressed not only through *tafsīr*, *kalām*, *fiqh* and fatwas, but also through moral and scientific treatises, and indeed through poetry.

In present-day Muslim societies, philosophers, novelists and poets have contributed towards the reinterpretation and contextualization of Islam. Although the question of free literary expression and fictional approaches to Islamic themes has been highly controversial in the Muslim world, many novelists and poets actively draw on the Islamic heritage in their literary production. Part of this picture is also a considerable interest in Jesus in con-temporary Muslim literature.

From Miracle to Cross: Jesus in Modern Persian Poetry

Although the Iranian revolution made some attempts to mould Jesus in its own image (cf. the section about 'Jesus in revolutionary Iran' above), Iran has traditionally been the cradle of a Persian poetry conveying a typical Ṣūfī image of Christ cf. Wysham 1952. In modern Persian poetry, other trends can also be identified.

In the year of the Iranian revolution, Sorour S. Soroudi published a survey 'On Jesus' image in Modern Persian Poetry' (Soroudi 1979). Soroudi states that of the poetic figures of Persian classical poetry, Jesus is the perhaps the most outstanding in the works of the modernist Persian poets. In classical poetry, there is an emphasis on Jesus' reviving breath and his life-giving miracles, reflecting the general Ṣūfī image of Christ but also the miracle stories from the *Qiṣaṣ al-Anbiyā'*. In contrast, 'Jesus' image as a persecuted man who bore his burden with love and who did not give up his belief even at the cost of his life which he sacrificed to save others', does not receive attention in classical Persian poetry.[175]

In modern poetry, however, this is different: In many writers, the cross emerges as a meaningful symbol. Soroudi suggest that this may reflect the fact that many contemporary poets have been engaged in social and political struggles, and suffered adversity because of their involvement.

Historically, Soroudi notes that the suffering Jesus was a major figure among the ancient Manichaeans. In the Persian Muslim context, both the Shīʿite Ḥusayn and the Ṣūfī al-Ḥallāj offer themselves as classical symbols of defending one's belief to the bitter end. Still, the framework for the passion narratives may be different:

> Hallāj acted mainly out of individual mystical daring. Jesus, on the other hand, as portrayed in the New Testament, is a spiritual shepherd who bears the burden of public responsibility. All his words and acts, including the fact that he did not oppose crucifixion, were aimed at saving others.[176]

For Soroudi, this may be the explanation of why Jesus so frequently occurs in the works of socially committed poets in Iran in the twentieth century: his suffering was in a sense political, resulting from a social commitment. He quotes the poet Aḥmad Shāmlū (A. Bāmbdād, b. 1925), who in one poem meditates on 'The Death of the Nazarene'. In another poem, from 1967, the poet openly identifies with the symbol of the cross:

> *Lo, there am I, having traversed all my bewilderments,*
> *Up to this Golgotha.*
> *There am I, standing on the inverted cross*
> *A statue as tall as a cry.*
> *There am I*
> *Having plucked the cross-nails out of the palms with my teeth.*[177]

Soroudi also cites the poet Muḥammad Riẓā Shafīʿī (M. Sirishk). In a remarkable contrasting of miracle and cross, Shafīʿī (in Soroudi's interpretation) 'employs Jesus' crucifixion and his miracles allegorically to create a false messiah who symbolizes the oppressive attitude of the Christian West towards the Islamic East as seen by the poet':

> *Lined up as beggars*
> *We reaped with the sickle of each Crescent*
> *Multiple harvests of poverty and hunger*
> *In the miracle fields of this uncrucified Jesus.*
>
> *O messiah of plunder, of hate!*
> *O artificial Messiah!*
> *Where is the rain to wash off your face*
> *The false images, the shadows of deceit.*[178]

Soroudi concludes that:

> Judging by these poems, it seems that not only Jesus' image, but also the poet's self-image and his relation with his surroundings have changed since the classical period; and it is this latter change the new image of Jesus reflects.[179]

From Miracle to Cross: Images of Jesus in the Literatures of Pakistan

The developments in Persian poetry referred to above seem to be paralleled by similar tendencies both in Arabic and Pakistani literature. In a review of images of Christ in the literary context of Pakistan, J. S. Addleton (1990) first presents the tendency in recent Arabic literature to supplant the image of the 'gentle' Jesus, symbolizing healing and life for the mystic, by one of a suffering Christ. As regards Pakistan, Addleton states:

> To a remarkable extent, the image of Jesus as portrayed in the Islamic literatures of Pakistan parallels these developments and presents many of the same themes. The references, although not numerous, are nonetheless intriguing, in particular those in which the transformation of the 'healing' Christ of classical Urdu poetry to the 'suffering' Christ is presented by more recent writers.[180]

Addleton reviews the classical tradition expressed both in the Pushtu, Punjabi, Sindhi and Urdu languages, portraying 'the familiar image of Jesus as a healer and giver of life' and developing cherished Ṣūfī motifs. Addleton notes that by a number of famous poets:

> Jesus is highly respected as a prophet, and his healing power and ability to raise the dead is given special recognition. These gifts become a symbol – at times even a metaphor – for healing experienced or described by later writers.[181]

Addleton goes on to cite some twentieth-century writers, who differently from earlier poets – but in line with their Persian contemporaries – approach the suffering of Christ and the symbol of the cross. In the poetic Jesus-biography of Mirza Qalich Beg (Sindhi; 1853–1929) entitled *Sawanih-i-umr-i Yasu Masih* ('Life of Jesus Christ'), he honours Jesus not only for his deeds and teaching but also for his sacrifice and suffering:

You know the full account of Jesus;
You know also all his deeds.
He had loved the world greatly always,
Suffered and sacrificed for the world.
He gave teaching, preached everywhere;
In every way he expressed the truth.
The ones who believe will live joyfully,
And have salvation hereafter.[182]

The Urdu writer Faiz Ahmed Faiz even touches upon the redemptive possibilities of suffering, in a jail scene poem from 1954:

In my barred window hung many a cross,
Each colored with the blood of its own Christ,
Each craving to hug tight a divine form.

On one the heaven's spring cloud is sacrificed
On one the radiant moon is crucified,
On one is torn asunder the trance-filled grove,
And on another the delicate breeze has died.

Daily these kind and beautiful godlike things,
Come weltering in their blood to my bitter cell;
And day by day before my watching eyes,
Their martyred bodies are raised up and made well.[183]

Faiz' translator, Victor Kiernan, takes Faiz to be the first Urdu poet to make an imaginative use of the idea of death on the cross.

The symbol of the cross appears also with the Urdu poet Ahmad Faraz. The symbol of the cross is used to express shared responsibility and collective blame. It is contrasted with the lack of reviving powers traditionally connected with Christ:

Come, let us mourn
the bloodied corpse of that Jesus
whom we crucified
and weep.
We have not done our duty well;
it is time to settle accounts.

Let him take the slippers
who made the cross;
the shroud belongs to the one
who nailed him;
and he deserves the crown of thorns
whose eyes had tears.

Come, let us claim now
we are all Christ;
let us alone show them
we can wake the dead!
But his word was everything:
Where is the word?[184]

Addleton concludes his review by quoting a poem of Alamgir Hashmi reflecting the deep non-violent conviction of Christ. Engineer (1991) cites some other Urdu authors. In the poems of Makdum and Sardar Jafri, both with leftist sympathies, the symbol of cross and even the theme of renewal of life after crucifixion emerges. The Indian leftist poet Muhiuddin Makhdum (d. 1969) writes:

Go on carrying our crosses towards
destination of love, destination of gallows,
Destination of beloved, carry on the cross.[185]

The tendency described in Urdu/Pakistani poetry has also been analysed by S. V. Bhajjan and A. A. Yesudas (1985). They give the following explanations for the extensive use of Christ and cross-symbolism:

> One is that the younger writers and poets are in close association with western thought and tradition. Another is the experience of pain, pressure and grief of the existential situation. It looks as though everybody is on the cross; the blood of the innocent has no value; and there seems to be no end to the misery and agony of mankind. The third factor is the Arab–Israel tension. The failure of Arab diplomacy and the plight of the Palestinian people have affected the Indo-Pakistani Urdu poets also.[186]

From Miracle to Cross: Modern Arabic Poetry (and Art)

As we have seen, commentators refer to the suffering of the Palestinian people as an impetus towards cross symbolism in Pakistani poetry. In Arabic literature too, the emergence of Christ-related cross symbolism can be identified. The same is true of Muslim-Arabic art. When in 2002, the cultural centre of the Lutheran Church in Bethlehem called for an artistic competition to paint Palestinian images of Christ, it turned out that 60% of the contributors who handed in paintings were Muslim. With one exception, all of them had chosen to paint the crucified Christ, defying thus traditional Muslim taboos in search for a symbol that might truly represent Palestinian suffering.[187]

The Christ motif can also be found in the works of modern Muslim pictorial artists, for instance in the paintings of Ala Bashir who was for a time the physician of Saddam Hussein. In an interview, he speaks of the difference between depicting Christ on the cross and trying to express what Christ saw from the cross: 'This is the only way we can cleanse ourselves from inner hatred and revenge.'[188] Another painting depicts a Christ who breaks through the surface of the cross, as if wearing the cross as a dress.

Palestinian Poetry

Many references have been made to the occurrence of Jesus and the symbol of crucifixion (e.g. as 'crucified land') in the 'poetry of resistance' of Palestinian origin, based on a shared Christian and Muslim experience of occupation and exile. Kenneth Cragg cites the poet Maḥmūd Darwīsh, who addresses 'my country' in this way: 'My love to you has brought me nothing save the wood of my cross. My country! How beautiful you are! Take my eyes, take my heart: O my love, take.'[189] Cragg remarks:

> Weighed down with the futilities and calamities of rejectionism and its anger, it is no strange thing that minds and poems should turn questioningly to the riddle of unrequited evil, yearn to unravel it and so to interrogate the Christ.[190]

Stefan Wild (1984) has examined the role of religious symbolism drawn from Judaism, Christianity and Islam in Palestinian poetry. Wild cites another poem by Maḥmūd Darwısh, in which he interrogates the representatives of three religions: Jesus, Muḥammad and the prophet Habakuk of the Jewish Bible. Addressing Jesus, he links his own people's suffering with that of the crucified one.[191]

Stefan Wild cites other Palestinian Muslim poets too (such as Maḥmūd Nadīm al- Afghānī and Fadwā Ṭūqān) who invoke passion symbols as well as parables from the Gospels when lamenting those who rule unjustly in God's name.[192] David Pinault (1987), referring to the study of Stefan Wild, notes that:

> . . . in modern Palestinian poetry questions of religion tend to be subordinated to political issues of resistance and national independence; religious motifs from both the Christian and Muslim traditions are thus incorporated into a secular nationalist literature.[193]

But, as Wild has shown, also the motif of being forgotten by God is a central one, expressing a wrestling with religious symbols and the meaning of religious language. In this, the image of the suffering Christ appears frequently.

Pinault notes that in parts of Palestinian poetry – as for Kamāl Nāṣir, in his 'Song of Hate' – Christian concepts of love and peace are regarded as worthless until Palestinian nationalist goals are realized. In a polemical poem, Nāṣir also addresses a speech to the figure of Christ directly, warning Jesus to flee Israel if He chooses to identify Himself with Western imperialist powers: 'If you belong to them, Son of Mary, then go back to their dwellings.'[194]

When the image of Christ appears in Arabic poetry, it is not always to portray the ideal of non-violence. A Christian Arab poet, Rashīd Salīm al-Khūrī (1887–1984), exclaims when advocating militancy:

> *If you would lift oppression strike*
> *With Muḥammad's sword, abandoning Jesus.*
> *O gentle lamb, who has left none but us*
> *In all mankind to be the gentle lambs,*
> *Will you not reveal a new Evangel*
> *To teach us pride and not submission?*[195]

Also on the Muslim side, the powerless Christ is sometimes invoked polemically by poets. M. M. Badawi[196] refers to the famous Egyptian neo-classical poet Aḥmad Shawqī (1868–1932). Shawqī responds critically to Western Orientalists and Christian missionaries blaming Muḥammad for excessive use of the sword. Shawqī counters the attack by asserting that evil can only be met effectively by evil. Were it not for the sword, Christianity too would have remained a religion merely for the persecuted. Presupposing the orthodox Islamic view of crucifixion, he asserts that Jesus himself would have been nailed to the cross were it not for God's intervention.

Iraqi Poetry

Both in Shawqī's neo-classical poetry, and among some modern poets, the suffering, helpless Christ is referred to as a negatively laden symbol. Totally different is the image of Christ in politically committed poetry like that of the Iraqi authors Bayyātī and Ṣayyāb, which will be presented below.

Pinault notes that in many of the modern Arabic poems treating of Christ, 'the poet does not threaten political enemies with violence; rather, he identifies with Christ in his sufferings as a victim of violence'.[197] Pinault cites the Iraqi ʿAbd al-Wahhāb al-Bayyātī's poem *Uġniya ilā shaʿbī* ('A Song to my People'):

I am here, alone, upon the cross.
They devour my flesh, the men of violence of the
highways, and the monsters, and the hyenas
O maker of flame
My beloved people
I am here, alone, upon the cross
The young assail my garden
and the elders revile
my shadow, which spreads its palms out to the stars
That it might wipe away the sorrows
from your saddened countenance
O my imprisoned people
you who lift up your brow
to the sun while it raps upon the gates
with dyed garments,
I am here, alone, driving drowsiness
from your exhausted eye
O maker of flame
My beloved people.[198]

In another poem from the same collection, Bayyātī captures the image of a Christ suddenly delivered from crucifixion, as a symbol of hope and relief for his people: 'And it was as if Jesus were with you, returning to Galilee, without a cross.'[199] But in most cases, the image of Christ is used to designate pain and despair. Pinault also cites a poem taken from Bayyātī's collection *Ashʿār fī-l-manfā* ('Poems in Exile'), in which the crucified Jesus is referred to as one who 'passed by here yesterday':

And our green earth in her birth-pangs
weakened by wounds
was dreaming of lilies in the morning,
dreaming of a thousand Jesuses who will bear
their cross in the darkness of prisons
and who will be numerous
and who will give birth
to progeny who will sow God's earth with jasmine
and make heroes and saints
and make revolutionaries.[200]

In a comment, Pinault describes Bayyātī's Christ-imagery as a 'meta-personal cosmic "Christ-mask"', designated for expressing collective suffering.[201]

As a contrast, Pinault refers to the Christian Palestinian/Lebanese poet Tawfīq Ṣāyigh (1923–1971). When Ṣāyigh borrows elements from Christ's passion and utilizes cross symbolism, the function is to express personal feelings like the agonies of an unhappy love affair. A fervent but unhappy identification with the crucified becomes the expression of existential despair and struggling with God.[202]

In other cases where the symbol of Christ and the cross is invoked by modern Arab poets, mythical overtones and more specifically allusions to the vegetation myths of Tammuz are found. A Muslim Iraqi poet cited by Pinault is Badr Shākir al-Sayyāb.[203] In his poem *Al-masīḥ baʿda l-ṣalb* ('Christ after Crucifixion'), taken from the collection *Unšūdat al-maṭar* ('Song of the Rain'), he writes:

Warmth touches my heart
My blood runs into its moist earth.
My heart is the sun, for the sun pulses with light;
My heart is the earth, pulsing with wheat, and blossoms,
and pure water.
My heart is the water, my heart is the ear of corn:
Its death is the resurrection; it gives life to him who eats.
. . .
I died by fire, darkness scorched my soil,
yet the god endured.
. . .
I died that bread might be eaten in my name,
that they might plant me in due season.
How many lives I shall live!
For in each furrow of the field
I have become a future; I have become a seedling;
I have become a generation of men:
In every man's heart is my blood,
a drop of it, or more.[204]

Also in the poem 'City of Sinbad', Sayyāb invokes the symbol of the cross, and even relates it to Muḥammad:

They have bound up Muhammad,
The prophet, on Mt. Ḥirā'
And the day was nailed down
Where they nailed him.
Tomorrow, Christ will be crucified
In Iraq, and the dogs will feast
On the blood of Burāq.[205]

In this poem, which resounds with Tammuz imagery, Sayyāb also reflects the despair of a spring without rain, and a resurrection to no avail – with Ishtar and Christ as symbols:

Then will it seem to the hungry that Ishtar,
The goddess of flowers, has brought back the captive
To mankind, and crowned his lush forehead with fruit?
Then will it seem to the hungry that the shoulder
Of Christ has rolled back the stone from the tomb
Has set out to resurrect life from the grave
And cure the leper or make the blind to see?
Who is this that let loose the wolves from their bonds?
Who is this that gave us to drink from a mirage,
And concealed the plague in the rain?
...
Women are aborting in slaughterhouses,
And the flame is dancing along the treshing floors,
And Christ will perish before Lazarus.
Let him sleep
Let him, for Christ did not call him![206]

From Miracle to Cross: Interpretations

Pinault concludes his presentation of cross and resurrection-symbolism in modern Arabic poetry with noting that:

> Contemporary Arabic poetry represents a break with the depiction of Jesus in pre-modern literature, via a process of secularisation and mythologising. The result is that Muslim and Christian Arab poets alike have felt free to use the figure of Christ as a secular symbol of political struggle and social commitment, as an image of suffering undertaken on behalf of one's people.[207]

Pinault cites both Muslim and Christian examples. Also among Christian Arab poets, the deep identification with the suffering Christ as well as the lament of a Lazarus brought back to life to no avail, are expressed.[208] Pinault thus describes a common, poetical development among Christian and Muslim Arabs. This development is linked to 1) the emergence of a non-traditional poetry, using common human symbols, 2) the later concept of a politically committed (*iltizām*) poetry,[209] and 3) the much noted tendency in modern Arabic poetry to make use of motifs of sacrifice, fertility and resurrection (cf. the Tammuz-symbolism, and the Arab reception of T. S. Eliot's Waste Land-imagery).[210]

As for poets writing out of a Muslim background, the shift of emphasis from Christ as a miracle worker in classical Ṣūfī poetry to the suffering Christ on the cross in modern poetry is remarkable. Apart from contextual interpretations, some deeper implications of the cross symbolism may also be sought. We have seen that in a poem of the Pakistani poet Faiz, the prisoners are pictured in the likeness of the crucified Christ, suspended on the barrels, as if hung on crosses in the barred cell windows. Faiz' poem recalls a crucifixion motif in the Jewish writers Chaim Potok's novel *My name is Asher Lev* (1972). The novel is a fictional reflection of the conflict between a modernist Jewish painter and the inhibitions of Jewish orthodoxy. His mother suffers from the conflict between the father, a rabbi, and his son, the artist. In a vision of his mother leaving home, the artist sees his mother crucified behind the bars of the window. Later, he is compelled to approach the tabooed image of crucifixion through painting, in order to express the depth of his mother's suffering.

In different contexts, then, the cross seems to introduce itself as a powerful expression of despair and suffering. In spite of religious inhibitions, the motif sifts into poetry as well as novel. Other significant examples will be dealt with below, when presenting Christ- and cross-symbolism in the modern literature of Egypt.

Christ in Egyptian Muslim Literature, from 1950 Onwards[211]

Several important features of the modern Egyptian context should be kept in mind when approaching images of Christ in Egyptian Muslim literature. Such features include: the diverse cultural tendencies during the twentieth century, in search of Egyptian Muslim modernity 'with or against Europe'; the contest for cultural hegemony between liberal Islam and the rising Islamism; and the strong tradition of Christian–Muslim coexistence. Egypt has a long tradition of Christian–Muslim partnership in the national project, but has also (especially since the 1970s) faced numerous tensions between Muslims and Christians.

Christian Contributions

What has been 'the role of Christ' in this context? A much discussed book from the Christian side, published in Cairo in 1938 but denied a reprint in 1967, was the Copt Ibrāhīm Lūqā's *Al-masīḥiyya fī-l-islām* ('Christianity in Islam'). His controversial approach was to make Christian teachings acceptable by referring to the Qur'ān. Concerning this kind of approach, Olaf Schumann also points to the apologetic writings of the Coptic preacher Yassa Mansūr.[212]

Of a far less apologetic kind are the books by the Coptic philosopher Naẓmī Lūqā. The books of this author, who became a controversial figure in the

Coptic Church, focus on a Christian appraisal of Muḥammad instead of on the question of Christ.[213]

The Institut Dominician d'Etudes Orientales de Caire, with Fr. Jomier and Fr. Anawati as prominent spokesmen, has contributed substantially towards a dialogue on a scholarly level. It should also be noted that the writings of Kenneth Cragg about Christ, Muḥammad and Christian–Muslim dialogue partly have dialogue with Egyptian Islam as their context.

Muslim Contributions

In his book on *Muslim Perceptions of Christianity*, Hugh Goddard (1996) makes a distinction between what he characterizes as 'polemical, eirenical and intermediate' contributions from Egyptian Muslims. Some of the polemical contributions pertaining to the question of Christ have been dealt with above.

In more 'eirenical and intermediate' works on Christ and Christianity, different focuses may be identified. In the following, we shall first deal with the question of cross-symbolism, a tendency we have seen widely represented in modern Muslim poetry in Iran, Pakistan and the Arab world. Secondly, we will focus on Jesus-biographies and Jesus-allegories by Egyptian writers. Third, the relation between Muḥammad and Jesus as seen by authors that write about Christ will be considered. Fourth, we will highlight the issue of human conscience, which appears to be a recurrent theme and focal point for those Muslim authors that pay special attention to Christ. Their focus on human conscience (*ḍamīr*) is all the more intriguing since linguistically, the use of *ḍamīr* in the sense of moral conscience is hardly found in Muslim Arabic literature until the twentieth century.

Most of the works in question are produced in the 1950s and early 1960s, a fact which invites some contextual considerations. A reason for characterizing most of the following works as 'eirenical' is the willingness shown by many authors to take the New Testament Gospels seriously as reliable sources of knowledge about Christ.

The Symbol of the Cross: Ḥusayn, ʿAbd al-Quddūs, al-Ṣabūr, al-Nowaihi

As regards the passion of Christ, Muslims who set out to write 'the life of Jesus' and who rely mostly on the biblical Gospels, are still reluctant to overstep the strictures of an orthodox Muslim reading. As for the theme of the cross, we can see both a reluctance to deal with the cross as a religiously meaningful symbol, and a relegation of the whole issue to the realm of doctrine. In Kāmil Ḥusayn's

Qarya ẓālima ('City of Wrong'), however, crucifixion of human conscience is taken as a general metaphor of human folly and crime. Also the novel by Najīb Maḥfūẓ, *Awlād ḥāratinā* ('The Children of our Quarter'), deals allegorically with the death of Christ (cf. the section about Christ biographies below).

Muḥammad Kāmil Ḥusayn

M. Kāmil Ḥusayn (1901–1977) was a surgeon by profession, but wrote extensively on Islamic philosophy, and on Arabic literature.

Ḥusayn had Christian friends, both Egyptian Copts and Western Christians, and he was deeply committed to Christian–Muslim dialogue. He was also actively involved in international peace movements. In the Western context, Kenneth Cragg has paid much attention to his works and made them known internationally through his translations of the novel *Qarya ẓālima* ('The City of Wrong') and the philosophical meditation *Al-wādī al-muqaddas* ('The Hallowed Valley'). Harold Vogelaar has examined his works in the wider perspectives of humanism and religious pluralism (Vogelaar 1978, 1995).

In his book *Al-ḏikr al-ḥākim* ('The Wise Mentor', 1972),[214] Ḥusayn presents his view on the Jewish and Christian scriptures. He holds the conventional Islamic view that the *tawrāh* and *injīl* should be understood as scriptures revealed directly to Moses and Jesus. Noting that the Jewish-Christian concept of revealed scriptures is different, rather in the sense of records made by 'inspired saints', he suggests that Muslims should still read the Bible, as 'inspired' writings although not as 'revelation' in its present form. According to Ḥusayn, the four New Testament Gospels contain portions of the original *injīl* revealed to Jesus, portions that would then have to be 'extracted' in order to identify the actual words of Jesus.[215]

In Ḥusayn's novel *Qarya ẓālima* (1954) he did not, however, set out to identify the authentic words of Jesus. Instead, he chose to write about the events of Good Friday in the form of suggestive fiction, focusing not upon Jesus himself, but upon those involved in the drama around him. The novel was rewarded with the Egyptian State Prize for literature in 1957, and had a wide readership both among the cultured public in Egypt and (through Cragg's translation) internationally.[216] The novel is a kind of moral-philosophical reflection on the trial of Christ, and the events leading towards Good Friday. Christ himself is more in the shadows of the story. The focus of the novel is on the decision of his adversaries to crucify him and – in so doing – to crucify their own conscience:

> *On that day the Jewish people conspired together to require from the Romans the crucifixion of Christ, so that they might destroy his message. Yet what was the mission of Christ save to have men governed by their conscience in all they did and thought?*[217]

In the novel, he tells the dramatic events of Good Friday as an inward drama, meditating on the deliberations and motives of those (Jews and Romans) who became part of the process against Christ and plotted to get him crucified, as well as the painful deliberations of the disciples who in the end decided not to resist the plot.

For the disciples' part, the central issue in their perplexed discussions is whether or not to use violence in an attempt to free their Lord and Master. Deciding to be true to their conscience (which bears the imprint of their Lord[218]) and not resist evil by the use of violent force, they are nevertheless overcome by grief and sadness as well as an ensuing and all-pervading self-reproach (a mood which the author believes lies at the very heart of Christian religion).

More specifically, the crucial question for the disciples is how to be true to the central, non-violent tenets of the Sermon on the Mount. For Ḥusayn as for al-ʿAqqād (cf. the section about Christ biographies below), the Sermon on the Mount represents the very centre of Christ's teachings. The story of Christ saving the woman caught in adultery from being stoned (John 8.1–11) represents the summit of his critique of a false adherence to the religious law. A Roman soldier – having been convinced by the teachings of Jesus and later being executed in the most gruesome manner for treachery against Rome – serves to underline the universality of the questions of conscientious non-violence and boundless compassion.

The first chapter of 'City of Wrong', entitled 'Friday', functions as a kind of reader's guide. Ḥusayn presents the novel as a drama of human conscience.[219] Being faithful to the qur'ānic reluctance (most often understood as a denial) as to the actual crucifixion of Christ, Ḥusayn focuses on the intention to crucify. The mission of Christ was to have people be governed by conscience in all they did and thought. Thus, the intention to crucify did in fact imply the crucifixion of conscience:

> *When they resolved to crucify him it was a decision to crucify the human conscience and extinguish its light. They considered that reason and religion alike laid upon them obligations that transcended the dictates of conscience.*[220]

According to Ḥusayn, conscience is 'a torch of the light of God'. With the loss of conscience, nothing can replace it, and there is no other guidance for humanity. Without it, every virtue collapses, and all that is good turns to evil. In this state, people resemble a darkened city (*mitla l-madinati l-muẓlimati*).[221]

Emphasizing the universal importance of the drama of conscience as unfolded on Good Friday, Ḥusayn states:

> *There is no evil afflicting humanity which does not derive from this besetting desire to ignore the dictates of conscience. The events of that day . . . are*

> *disasters renewed daily in the life of every individual. ... Men and women to the end of time will be contemporaries of that memorable day. ... The same darkness will be theirs until they are resolute not to transgress the bounds* [ḥudūd] *of conscience.*[222]

As with the Jesus-biographers al-ʿAqqād and ʿUthmān (see below), the approach of Kāmil Ḥusayn to Christ and Christianity is moral rather than metaphysical. He sees the Sermon on the Mount as the highest expression of Christian morality, and obedience to conscience as its focal point. His book is, strictly speaking, not about the passion of Christ. It neither denies nor states that Jesus was actually crucified. Although faithful to Islamic restrictions, the book still implies that the symbol of crucifixion can be dealt with constructively by a Muslim author. As a factual event, the crucifixion is shrouded in the darkness of evil intents. But for all times and places – by the intention of the evildoers – it expresses 'the greatest crime in history'.

In an Easter meditation on 'City of Wrong', teacher in Arabic literature Aisha ʿAbd al-Rahman (1961[223]) refers to a correspondence between a student of hers and Ḥusayn regarding the question of the seeming victory of evil in his novel:

> Some days passed, and we received a letter from the Doctor and man of letters. He opened it with a greeting of admiration for the attempt of critical analysis, and his sincere appreciation of the careful comment made by the critic about the story. But then he quite humbly drew her attention to the fact that what seems to be a victory for evil, in the condemnation of the Lord Christ to crucifixion, was not in historical truth or observed reality anything but a decisive end to evil and a real victory for the message of Christ. It does not degrade that victory that a prophet gave his life as the cost of his message. Rather, this is the real glory.[224]

In the annexes to Cragg's translation of *City of Wrong*, Ḥusayn confirms his open approach to the symbol of the cross and the reality of crucifixion, as well as his critical stance towards traditional Muslim explanations:

> *The idea of a substitute for Christ is a very crude way of explaining the Quranic text. They had to explain a lot to the masses. No cultured Muslim believes in this nowadays. The text is taken to mean that the Jews thought they killed Christ but God raised him unto Him in a way we can leave unexplained among the several mysteries which we have taken for granted on faith alone.*[225]

In a contextual perspective, the question arises as to what would have been the contemporary impetus for making the crucifixion of conscience a crucial theme. According to Harold Vogelaar (1995), *City of Wrong* should first of all be read in the light of the shattering experience of World War II, as 'an emotional, literary reaction to that catastrophic event', movingly depicting 'the utter failure of traditional religion to prevent it'.[226] Kenneth Cragg, on the other hand,[227] focuses on the fact that Ḥusayn relates his concept of conscience to central teachings of the Qur'ān, and to a contemporary context which is just as much Muslim as Christian. In *City of Wrong*, he names the chief lawyer among the Jews – the one responsible for issuing religious fatwas – a *mufti*. He alludes to controversial issues related to the interpretation of *šarīʿa*, such as imposing lashes for drunkenness[228] and the question of the death penalty for adultery or alleged blasphemy/apostasy.[229] Likewise, he exposes the ambiguity of the concept *ijmāʿ* (consensus of the religio-political community) when it comes to the question of the individual being true to conscience.[230] He frequently alludes to qur'ānic expressions, such as the concept of *ẓulm* ('wrong, iniquity') which underlies the title of the book. Sometimes his allusions are made in astonishing ways, displaying a profound willingness for Muslim self-criticism with regard to how qur'ānic concepts may be misused for suppression in the name of religion or society.[231]

Iḥsān ʿAbd al-Quddūs

Allusion to the death of Jesus, and a fictional use of the symbol of the cross, is also found in a short story of a leading Egyptian writer within this genre, Iḥsān ʿAbd al-Quddūs (1918–1990). His family background was marked by the conflict between his traditional Muslim grandfather and his father who was an artist (and married an actress of Christian background who had become a Muslim). In the short-story 'Martyr in Dishna',[232] the image of Christ's suffering is brought to the fore by a man returning to his village and trying to prevent further revenge killings in his family. In a symbolic act of reconciliation, he humiliates himself by carrying a coffin shroud wrapped around his head, saying to himself:

> *You are saving the blood of two families. You are bearing all this for the sake of humanity, so that love and harmony will prevail. Just like Christ you are willing to suffer for mankind's sake.*[233]

In this short story, one may see a willingness to approach suffering and possible death as a means of reconciliation – 'in the image of Christ'. The theme of suffering is not introduced as a symbol of helplessness, but of courage:

> *It obviously needed courage, great courage to bypass and disregard customs that had endured in our village for hundreds of years. It certainly needed more courage than to commit a murder.*[234]

In other writings, like the short stories 'God is love' and 'Heaven and I' from the same collection, ʿAbd al-Quddūs also shows much sensibility to difficult issues in Christian–Muslim coexistence in Egypt. The Jewish-Muslim question is touched upon in the title story 'I am Free' and in several other stories.

Salāḥ ʿAbd al-Ṣabūr

We have seen that the fate of Christ has been paralleled to the crucifixion of al-Ḥallāj by some Ṣūfī classics. In 1965, the Egyptian dramatist Salāḥ ʿAbd al-Ṣabūr (1931–1981) published a play entitled *Maʾsāt al-Ḥallāj*, 'The Tragedy of al-Ḥallāj'.[235] In the play, the trial of al-Ḥallāj is modelled in the likeness of the trial of Jesus as reported by the Gospels. The dramatic dialogue from the interrogation is transposed to the judge, al-Ḥallāj and the crowd of Baghdad. The crowd cries 'Heretic! Heretic!', 'Death! Death' and 'His blood is upon us'. Al-Ḥallāj is described as being influenced both by the Qur'ān and the example of Christ: 'My companions are the verses of the Quran and its letters, the words of him who was sad and forsaken on the Mount of Olives . . .. Come to me so that we can eat together the bread of our Lord and Master.'

In the stage directions for the play, the author carefully makes it clear that al-Ḥallāj was hung on the branch of a tree, and not on a cross. But the Christian overtones in the play seem to imply a parallelism between al-Ḥallāj and Christ – united by the cry against political oppression backed by religious sanction. As for his poetry, al-Ṣabūr describes his way of writing poetry as a kind of 'crucifixion'. He gives the title 'Meditations in a Wounded Age' to one of his collections. One of his poems is entitled *Al-ẓill wa-l-ṣalıb*, 'The Shadow and the Cross', and treats the cross as a symbol of human despair and desolation (in Cragg's translation):

I am he who lives without dimension that means,
I am he who lives without reach that attains,
I am he who lives without grandeur to gain.
I am he who lives without shade . . . without a cross.
Shade is a robber who steals happiness.
Whoever lives in his own shadow
Walks to the cross in the end.
His sorrow will crucify him.[236]

Thus, Ṣabūr joins the ranks of those poets for whom the cross may be a meaningful symbol of the cost of opposition to a repressive government, or more generally, of human despair.

Mohamed al-Nowaihi

In considering the willingness to approach the religious symbol of redemption through suffering, some writings of Professor of Arabic Language and Literature in the American University of Cairo, Mohamed al-Nowaihi (d. 1981) also deserve special mention.[237]

In a unpublished paper by al-Nowaihi from 1978 on 'Redemption: from Christianity to Islam', which has been quoted and discussed by several authors,[238] al-Nowaihi states that:

> *The God of the Qur'ān is a very personal God, intimately involved in man's innermost heart. The emphasis on the austere, forbidding image of Him was a later development, and was one that may be justly considered contrary to the ruling spirit of the Qur'ān.*[239]

He proceeds by maintaining that although the Qur'ān seems to deny the crucifixion of Jesus, no Muslim can ignore that he was persecuted and that his message was rejected for some time.

> *So the promised victory of right over wrong must be understood to be eventual and not always immediate, nor even necessarily in the lifetime of the prophets themselves. Nor is it automatic: it demands much struggle and sacrifice on the part of the prophets.*[240]

As the title of his paper indicates, al-Nowaihi refers positively to the notion of redemption, and its 'sheer beauty and nobility' when taken in an inclusive sense:

> *It is a symbol, but it stems from a record of facts – facts of certain individuals, in the long and tormented history of man, who were characterized by a tremendous love for their fellow-men and a chagrined concern over their ignorance, folly and crime, so much that they willingly suffered great persecution and were even ready to pay the supreme penalty of martyrdom for the sake of humanity's salvation.*[241]

In the article 'The Religion of Islam – a presentation to Christians' (1976), al-Nowaihi pursues his perception of redemption. He states that:

> *... among the intelligentsia of contemporary Muslims there has been a growing awareness of the sheer beauty and nobility of the idea of redemption not, indeed, as a literal fact or an article of creed, but as a symbol, a magnificent and uplifting symbol of what some self-abnegating men in their tremendous love for their fellow-men and their chagrined concern over their ignorance, folly and crime, have to undergo for the sake of humanity's*

> *salvation even to the extent of paying the supreme penalty of self-immolation. This new development is prominent in the poetry of a new school of Arabic poets, which started in the late 1940s, and whose frequent use of the symbol of the cross and the figure of the Redeemer has caused much consternation among their traditionalist readers.*[242]

The author even points to the Qur'ān itself as a revelation of divine passion:

> *. . . the Qur'ān itself is nothing if it is not a suffering identity with creation and humanity. Hence its passion, its sorrow and chagrin for the disobedience and sins of man.*[243]

Christ-Biographies and Christ-Allegories: al-ʿAqqād, al-Saḥḥār, ʿUthmān, Maḥfūẓ

Since the early 1950s, a number of biographies of Christ or allegorical works relating to the Jesus story have appeared in Egypt. In a cultural atmosphere where Christianity is not seen only as a Western adversary, but as a respected partner in the dialogue between cultures, innovative approaches to the person of Christ himself have emerged.

Intellectually, most of the thinkers to be presented in the following text may be characterized as modernizing reformers. Their national context is that of Nasserite nationalism in the 1950s and '60s. Nasser's era (1952–1970) is characterized by a number of crucial events and developments – such as the decisive break with the remnants of British colonial domination; a shift from liberal democracy to a one party system; large scale nationalization and collectivization of the economy; a socialist vision of the welfare state; and the introduction of mass education on higher levels. From 1961, Egypt also took on a leading role in the so-called non-aligned movement (consisting primarily of Asian and African states that were once colonies and were wary of being drawn into new forms of dependence by the West or by the communist bloc).

In the field of culture, Nasser's regime actively sought to involve writers and other intellectuals in its socialist-nationalist project. In terms of religion, the era of Nasser (as well as the whole movement of Arab nationalism) was marked by the predominance of nationalist over Islamic discourses. This means that the cultural climate was also conducive for the formulation of visions of Muslim–Christian unity, in tune with the joint Muslim–Christian resistance to British rule earlier in the twentieth century (symbolized by banners that were used during the uprising against the British in 1919 with the crescent and the cross side by side). As we shall see, the thinkers in focus were also keen on formulating visions of 'humanity', symbolized by the bond of conscience across religious divides. This went well together with the internationalist orientation of Nasser's regime.

As for the three writers whose works will most thoroughly be presented – al-ʿAqqād, Ḥusayn and Khālid – their works have been researched by the present author with emphasis on their faith-transcending notion of conscience.[244]

ʿAbd al-Ḥamīd Gūdah al-Saḥḥār

The first modern biography of Jesus written by an Egyptian Muslim appears to be ʿAbd al-Ḥamīd Gūdah al-Saḥḥār's *Al-masīḥ ʿĪsā ibn Maryam* ('Christ Jesus, Son of Mary'), which was published in 1951 (i.e. on the threshold to the Nasserite era).[245] Al-Sahhār's most well-known work is a series of books on the life of Muḥammad. Besides his Christ-biography, he has also examined the stories of Old Testament figures like Abraham, Moses, David and Esther (in *Qiṣaṣ min al-kutub al-muqaddasa*, 'Stories from the Holy Books').

In his Christ-biography, the author makes use of both qur'ānic and biblical information about Christ, but (apart from the Lord's Prayer) without quoting directly from the New Testament. It is true that specific biblical features of Jesus' life and teaching – like his addressing God as Father and the centrality of the theme of the Kingdom of God – are reflected. As for the way the Kingdom is perceived, the author states that:

> *Jesus has not come with the order to found a new law. He has not come with a religion that would abrogate the religion of Moses. He has come only to announce the nearness of the Kingdom of God .... He has brought the Gospel as the good news of hope and true happiness.*[246]

Differently from Muḥammad, however, Jesus was not able to put his message into effect other than among a small group of disciples. As the author sees it, the turning point in Christ's mission lies in his failure to use force in order to propagate his message:

> *The true revealed laws are not enforced in this world with olive branches and sweet words.*[247]

Thus, it was left to Muḥammad to bring the new order, based upon 'Islam which joins politics together and gives the spiritual heritage an organized form'.[248] As Goddard summarizes the author's concept of the kingdom:

> Elaboration of what the kingdom means . . . reveals that the kingdom comes through the descent of the Word of God and the lordship of the *shariʿa* (path) and the spread of the teaching of patience. Moreover, the kingdom 'united religion and the state [*din wa dawla*]', and so it is seen very much in Islamic terms.[249]

When coming to the climax, the author reproduces the traditional substitutionist theory, having Judas crucified. Jesus appears to the disciples after a period of concealment, before he is raised to God. In Gethsemane, Jesus is portrayed as resigning to his tribulations and yearning for another prophet to come – a prophet who will be more dynamic and successful than himself in confronting the enemies of God.[250]

In the concluding words of al-Saḥḥār, in a significant paraphrase of the Servant Songs in Isaiah:

> *Jesus departed. He did not establish truth on the earth. His enemies broke him. But the final one, the servant of God and his chosen, will not be weary nor will he be broken before he has set truth in the earth, and until the kingdom of God holds sway over this world. ʿĪsā came finally into the heavy dark of night whence God raised him to power and glory and immortality.*[251]

ʿAbbās Maḥmūd al-ʿAqqād

The most well known of the Egyptian Jesus-biographies from this period is *ʿAbqariyyat al-Masīḥ*, 'The genius of the Messiah', first published in Cairo in 1953 by the autodidact and prolific writer ʿAbbās Maḥmūd al-ʿAqqād (1889–1964). In the second edition of his book in 1957, under the title *Ḥayāt al-Masīḥ* ('The life of Christ'), he included a chapter on the Dead Sea Scrolls.

Al-ʿAqqād's work has attracted considerable interest in circles committed to Christian–Muslim understanding.[252] Olaf Schumann paid much attention to this ground-breaking work in his study *Der Christus der Muslime* (1988).[253] More recently, al-ʿAqqād's biography (in its 1957 version) has been translated into English and thoroughly discussed by Peter Ford.[254]

Al-ʿAqqād's work originally appeared in a series of books on 'religious geniuses', and made a wide, popular impact. His work on Christ relies on and/or relates critically to well known Western portraits of Jesus like those of Emil Ludwig (*Der Menschensohn. Geschichte eines Propheten*, 1928) and Ernest Renan (*La Vie de Jésus*, 1863), both of which were available to al-ʿAqqād in English translation.[255] As for the genre of genius biographies, it should be noted that Emil Ludwig wrote a whole series of books (in the 1920s and '30s) about the lives of great men. As for al-ʿAqqād, he characterizes his version of the genius biography genre as *ṣūra nafsiyya*, a portrait of the person's inner character rather than a historical exposition.[256]

Contrary to the later suggestions made by Yusseff (1990b) and others, that the Jesus movement may have emerged from the ranks of the Essene community, al-ʿAqqād maintains that the legalistic rigour of the Essenes was rather a negative preparation for Jesus' mission. According to al-ʿAqqād, the novelty of the Qumran discovery is that it confirms the necessity for the mission of Christ. He emphasizes the Galilean background of Jesus' ministry, and the universal outlook of his mission. The universalism of Christianity is seen by al-ʿAqqād as rooted in Christ's insistence on conscience and the law of love, and is significantly not regarded to be a later product of Pauline theology (as traditionally implied by Muslim apologetics). He views Paul rather positively, and regards Jewish Christianity as a deviation from the implicit universalism of Jesus' ministry.

Al-ʿAqqād treats the Gospels as reliable historical documents for extensive information about Christ, and discusses thoroughly the historical context of Jesus' mission. Up till the dramatic climax, where he takes exception to the historicity of the crucifixion, the Gospels are explicitly stated to be reliable sources of information, allowing us to search behind the events in order to identify the personality of Christ, and elucidate his genius.[257]

Al-ʿAqqād portrays a Christ who is distinguished by preaching the law of love, confronting legalism and hypocrisy, aiming at transforming the motives of our actions and appealing to freedom of conscience. Christ is placed in the prophet-teacher tradition, and al-ʿAqqād describes the progress in Jesus' prophetic consciousness when he is confronted with increasing adversity. The essence of his call (*al-daʿwa*) was:

> . . . *that God is the Lord of the children of Man (banī al-insān) and that he is the Son of Man (*ibn al-insān*); that love is the best of virtues and that the best kind of love is love for one's enemy; that generosity means that you give more than you are asked for or without being asked; that the kingdom of heaven is not conquered by riches; that what belongs to the emperor [should be given] to the emperor and what belongs to God [should be given] to God, and that the glory vied for by those who desire it does not deserve to be desired, and that the glory that deserves to be desired is not a cause of rivalry.*[258]

In the book's chapter about the religious law (*al-šarīʿa*), the author reveals little trust in the reform of outward laws and regulations. Instead, consciences should be reformed (*bi-iṣlāḥ al-ḍamāʾir*), and manners and morals refined (*tahḏīb al-ādāb al-insāniyya*). This is shown by Christ. However, as a reformer, Christ does not abolish the Jewish Law (*šarīʿat al-nāmūs*), but fulfils it through the law of love (*šarīʿat al-ḥubb*[259]). In several places he equates the 'law of love' with 'the law of conscience' – in expressions like *sarīʿat al -ḥubb aw/wa šarīʿat al-ḍamīr* .[260] As for the importance of love over against law, he states that:

> *The law* (nāmūs), *then, is a covenant with man aimed at settling that which is obligatory* (wājib), *whereas love surpasses the obligatory, and does not await command nor expect recompense. Love is not counted in letters and lines. Love does not deal with people in terms of legal contracts and witnesses. It does what is required of it, and then goes beyond that. It is happy to give, and does not expect recompense. By this* šarıʿa – *the* šarıʿa *of love* –

> *Christ abrogated every letter in the* šarīʿa *of forms and outward appearances.*[261]

The law of love is rooted in conscience, and expressed in service and self-denial. The Sermon on the Mount and other passages from the Gospels are quoted extensively, to illustrate what the law of love is all about.

With regard to the miracles, al-ʿAqqād emphasizes that the miracles presupposes faith for a proper reception. It is not Christ's birth or his works of healing that are considered as the essential miracle, but rather the fact that the message of love preached by the Galilean son of a carpenter conquered the entire Roman world.[262]

The absolute titles of Jesus (like 'the Light of the world' and 'the Son of God') appear to be acceptable to al-ʿAqqād as metaphorical expressions: 'Everyone who is born of the Spirit is a son of God'.[263]

As to the end of Christ's life, al-ʿAqqād is seemingly loyal to the qur'ānic denial of the crucifixion. After referring the cleansing of the temple, he states that when it comes to the climax of Christ's life, 'here ends the stage of history, and the stage of creed/doctrine begins'.[264]

In the last chapter of the book, al-ʿAqqād retells Dostojevsky's scene of the returning Christ and the Grand Inquisitor, and states that if Christ came back to the earth, he would probably repudiate much of what is done today in his name. Thus, the freedom of conscience established by Christ turns out to be a constant effort, a struggle of conscience (*jihād al-ḍamīr*):

> *. . . the religions are to be measured by the values and incentives they consign to the soul, and by how much they increase the share of man in the freedom of conscience, or the freedom to distinguish between the good and the despicable. The religions have done a lot, and are still capable of doing a lot. But they can never relieve man of the struggle of the conscience.*[265]

In another work, about God (*Allāh*[266]), al-ʿAqqād sees the Christian religion as the first religion to base service of God on human conscience, and to proclaim the mercy of heaven to humankind.[267] But the final perfection of religion and clarification of the idea of the divine is left to Islam. With his very notable appreciation of Christ and Christianity, al-ʿAqqād remains a faithful Muslim.

Summarizing the importance of al-ʿAqqād's biography, Hugh Goddard (1996) comments:

> What al-ʿAqqād has done . . . is to introduce the fruits of western critical biography of Jesus into the field of Muslim biography of Jesus, and while his agnosticism about the historicity of the crucifixion may leave a Christian reader frustrated at the end, that is immediately an advance on a blanket assertion of traditional Islamic beliefs about the crucifixion.[268]

Al-ʿAqqād's interest in Christ was apparently not restricted to a historical presentation of Christ as a law reformer in Judaism, neither to a sympathetic exposition of basic Christian tenets. There are many indications that his writings about Christ should also be read as a critique of rigorist attitudes and outwardness in traditionalist interpretations of Islam. When denoting the adversaries of Christ, he often employs traditional Islamic terms for legal and religious offices such as *fuqahāʾ*,[269] *ʿulamāʾ* and *ḥuffāẓ*.[270] He also makes an explicit reference to literalist conservatism among Islamic jurists in Egypt.[271]

As for the book's contribution to Muslim–Christian dialogue, Peter Ford notes that there is no clear indication in *ʿAbqariyyat al-masīḥ* as to why al-ʿAqqād wrote this particular book. But he suggests that the implied audience would be Muslim rather than Christian:

> The prevalence of Islamic terminology, the occasional reference to passages from the Qur'ān, and above all the presentation of a Jesus that remains within the parameters of Islamic prophethood all point to a Muslim audience .... Jesus was a prophet, asserts al-ʿAqqād, who continues to speak with authority and eloquence to the masses of today. At the same time, there is a word from Jesus to the religious elite in Islam who would emphasize rituals and interpretations which only serve to stifle true faith.[272]

Nevertheless, claims Peter Ford, 'al-ʿAqqād must certainly have had Christian readers in mind as well'. His utilization of the Gospels as reliable sources clearly points in this direction. In Ford's judgement:

> He has thus endeavored, as a Muslim, to comprehend the founder of Christianity, and to appropriate for himself the substance of his life and teaching, from within a Christian framework. In the process, he has discovered much which he shares in common with Christian believers ....[273]

The question remains, however, whether al-ʿAqqād was able to tackle constructively what is actually different in Muslim and Christian faith. This might also be a critical point when it comes to utilizing the notion of 'conscience' as a conceptual bond between Christians and Muslims: Does 'conscience' only refer to what is common between the two faiths – that which they know together – or can it contain differences as well? The same questions may be raised in connection with Khālid Muḥammad Khālid's notion of conscience (see below), and more generally, when discussing the general relevance of the notion of conscience in interreligious dialogue (cf. the section about 'Human conscience' in Chapters 8 and 9).

Fatḥī ʿUthmān

In 1961, Fatḥī ʿUthmān (b. 1928) published his voluminous book *Maʿa l-masīḥ fī-l-anājīl al-arbaʿa* ('With Christ in the Four Gospels').[274] ʿUthmān approaches Christianity with the conviction that each religion must be interpreted from the vantage point of its own self-understanding. He refers frequently to al-ʿAqqād, and like him, he relies on the Gospels as historical sources. His work reveals familiarity not only with the New Testament, but with standard works by Christian and other Western scholars and writers.

In the book's chapter about 'Christ and the Law', he cites the radical antitheses from the Sermon on the Mount, and characterizes Christ's teachings as a 'law of altruism' (*šarīʿat al-ʾīṯār*).[275] He emphasizes the need to proceed from what is demanded by the law (*al-nāmūs*) to 'what reassures conscience' – underpinning his argument with a quotation from Qur'ān 35.32.[276] Citing al-ʿAqqād, he characterizes the law sought for by Christ as 'a law of love and conscience'.

Like al-ʿAqqād, he also refers positively to Paul. In the subsequent chapter on 'The Disciples and the Law (*al-nāmūs*)', he cites Romans 2–3 and Galatians 2–3, as well as Hebrews 7 and 10, for the critique of a petrified legalism, and the shortcomings of the outward law in reforming human nature. He ends this chapter by citing John 8.4–16. In accordance with the prevailing Arabic Bible translation in Egypt, he includes the following passage in John 8.9: 'and their consciences pricked them' (*wa-kānat ḍamāʾiruhum tubakkituhum*).[277]

In the final main chapter of the book ('. . . and peace on earth'), ʿUthmān further elaborates his view of the law of conscience. Loyalty to conscience as taught by Christ is both a question of exercising the necessary 'curbing forces of the soul' (*ḍawābit al-nafs*, cf. Ḥusayn[278]), and a way of transcending the outwardness of religious legislation (*tašrīʿ*). The latter can only be achieved if law is founded in 'the depths of the soul'.[279] Religious law does not rest on letters, but on conscience. Christ gave to the formalities of legislation (*qawālib al-tašrīʿ*) 'the warmth of conscience'. He also made each and every man 'his own judge', under the supervision of the hidden God.[280]

In these matters, ʿUthmān implies, Christianity and Islam basically teach the same. Like Christianity, Islam teaches the golden rule. Christianity has greatly enriched humanity by revealing that 'God is love, and that's enough!'[281]

Notwithstanding his search for uniting elements in Christian and Muslim belief and ethics, ʿUthmān also discusses the difficult issues between Christians and Muslims. The questions in focus are Christ and God, crucifixion and redemption, and the appreciation of Muḥammad.

As for the event of the crucifixion, ʿUthmān asserts that this is more a question of interpretation than of a (contested) fact.[282] Quoting Qur'ān 5.70, he reminds the reader that the Qur'ān itself affirms that many messengers of God have been killed. ʿUthmān is emphatic that the Qur'ān does not deny crucifixion for the reason that the violent death of prophets cannot be conceived of within an Islamic universe. Instead, it is the doctrine of redemption by the death of Christ that constitutes the problem. Islam rejects the (theology of) crucifixion because the idea of redemption is unacceptable.

In spite of different understandings of redemption and salvation, both religions teach salvation through faith *and* works. ʿUthmān cites Galatians 6.1–5 and James 2.14–16 as New Testament references for his argument. Citing Matthew 7.21–23 – the decisive thing is not the confession of lips, but doing the will of God – ʿUthmān suggest that Christians and Muslims, instead of concentrating all their efforts on polemics over dogmatics, should join forces to put redemption into practice.[283]

Kenneth Cragg sees ʿUthmān portraying Jesus as a reformer of Judaism – opting for 'a true ethical Sharīʿa as opposed to the formalism to which Torah had been reduced'.[284] In his approach to Jesus, and in his distinction between the *nāmūs* of legalism and the *šarīʿa* of neighbourly love, ʿUthmān opts for a renewed *ijtihād* within Islam to restore the original dynamism of Sharīʿa. He sees the centre of the Christian message in the call for love and in the demand for equality and justice. Both modern democracy and socialism may be seen as partly foreshadowed by Christianity, which should therefore not be accused of being an individualistic religion.[285]

The essence of Jesus' teachings is thus held to be valid (and challenging) for Muslims too, and ʿUthmān's declared aim is to bring Christians and Muslims together by the ethical connection.

In the context of the USA, where he has been teaching for a number of years, ʿUthmān has been much involved in interreligious dialogue. In the late 1970s, he expressed his view on Christ in a Jewish–Christian–Muslim dialogue documented by the *Journal of Ecumenical Studies* (Osman 1977). His contribution has the form of a commented reading of the Catholic scholar Dermot A. Lane's book *The Reality of Jesus*.[286] ʿUthmān responds favourably to Lane's distinction between 'the historical side of the Christ-Event' and 'the theological significance' of this event, as well as to his distinction between a 'low' and 'high' Christology. For his own part, ʿUthmān confirms that:

> *The Qur'an refers clearly to a special place of Jesus in his relation to God, which is different from the place of any other prophet . . .. A special relation between Jesus and the 'Holy Spirit' – the 'Spirit of Holiness' as expressed in the Qur'an – is also mentioned.*[287]

As for the seemingly contradictory references in the Qur'ān as regards the end of Jesus' life – with 3.55 affirming Jesus' death, and 4.157–158 denying death by crucifixion – the latter reference 'may not be seen as really contradictory, if it is not interpreted literally as dealing with the historical event or the physiological death'.[288]

With regard to the concept of a 'low-ascending' Christology put forward by Lane, ʿUthmān comments that 'In this light, a Christian may see the Muslim's faith in Jesus as preliminary, but not false or intentionally depreciating'.[289]

ʿUthmān appreciates Lane's admission that the decision about Jesus' relation to God comes later than the early preaching of the Apostles, and regards this as an important improvement of the climate for interreligious dialogue. He also responds favourably to Lane's distinction 'between the revelation of a reality and the reality itself', and his conviction that 'The mystery of God . . . is not exhausted in Jesus'.[290] Apparently, this distinction appeals to the Muslim sensitivity of ʿUthmān, and even more so the views of some contemporary Christian theologians that faith in Christ does not rely upon certain classical dogmas like the pre-existence of Christ or the Hellenistic definitions of the deity of Christ. ʿUthmān also endorses Lane's view on the co-operation between faith and good works when it comes to the question of salvation.

As for ʿUthmān's sensitivity for Christian concerns in general, it should be noted that his views on interreligious dialogue correspond with recognition of the Copts' bad memories of oppressive rule that has been administered in the name of Islam, and their subsequent apprehension that their legitimate rights must not be violated in any way.[291]

Najīb Maḥfūẓ

We have seen that the focus on Jesus as a teacher of an ethic based on individual conscience has been a recurring theme in the more liberal approaches to Jesus among Egyptian writers. It seems that the focus on conscience invites the writers not only to reflect on the adversity that he met, but also on the theme of suffering and even the symbol of the cross.

One of those approaching defeat, suffering and death as a fictional theme related to Jesus is the 1988 Nobel Prize winner, Najıb Maḥfūẓ. In his allegorical history of humanity, *Awlād ḥāratinā* ('The Children of Our Quarter'), Jesus is represented by the character of Rifāʿa – along with two other restorers of justice in the quarter (Jabal/Moses, Qāsim/Muḥammad).[292] Commentators differ in the interpretation of the novel: Some highlight the religious allegories – with reference to the obvious connotations with the history of the Abrahamic religions and the role of their common ancestor *Gabalāwī* (a metaphor for God?[293]). Others emphasize the political aspects of the novel – claiming that the central theme is the reformers unsuccessful struggle against the ruling chiefs and their strong-arm men, the *futuwwāt*.

Although commentaries vary as to whether the book should be read as a political and/or religious allegory, Maḥfūẓ raises several questions that should be central in any dialogue between the Abrahamic faiths.

Jabal/Moses is presented as the first to riot against injustice. But he is only concerned about those in his own alley, and acts according to the principle of retribution: an eye for an eye. In contrast, Rifāʿa/Jesus is depicted as a preacher of non-violence, and characterized by a great interest in spirits and exorcism. He resorts to the desert to achieve inner strength, and he is reluctant towards marriage. But out of pity, he marries a girl, who eventually betrays him to his enemies. He regards it as better to be killed than to kill, and he consistently speaks out against violence: 'The wisdom of your work is that you overcome evil with good.'[294] He is not concerned with rights (the novel's contested 'estate'), only with inner purity. He freely grants health and happiness to all, for the sake of God's love: he opens the gates of happiness without any estate or power.[295]

The love of the poor for this reformer was unprecedented. Despite Rifāʿa's gentleness, he was considered a threat by the chiefs and cudgelled to death without any protecting intervention from the house of Gabalāwi. To no avail, he shouted from deep down: Gabalāwi! He was re-buried by his friends – two of them carrying the same name as the tragic heroes of Shīʿite Islam, ʿAlı and Ḥusayn. Because of the mysterious circumstances surrounding his death, rumours spread, and:

> *After his death Rifāʿa enjoyed respect and glory and love which he had never dreamed of in his lifetime. His story became glorious, repeated on every tongue . . . in particular the removal of his corps . . . .*[296]

The author records a discussion between Yaḥyā, an old disciple of Rifāʿa, and Qāsim/Muḥammad. Yaḥyā recalls that with Jabal, it was all about strength and force, and with Rifāʿa, all about love and mercy. He presents Qāsim with both options. Qāsim replies: 'Force when necessary, and love always.'[297] Only then can the honour that Jabal gave to his people, and the love that Rifāʿa preached, be achieved. Justice and peace can only rule by power: 'Our force . . . will be the first just force.'[298] After Rifāʿa's demise, his disciples were not (according to Qāsim) able to follow his example. Some of them resorted to violence and the logic of power.

Maḥfūẓ takes it as a fictional presupposition that his Jesus-figure was in fact killed. In the author's pessimistic outlook towards religion as well as politics, the death of Jesus is not avoided as a fictional theme, but acquires significance. His death scene resounds with Rifāʿa's/Jesus' despairing invocation of God, known from the Gospel of Mark.

In the novel, the restoration efforts of 'Moses', 'Jesus' and 'Muḥammad' all fail. Also the seeming victory granted to Qāsim did not last. The novel's final character, ʿArafa, who represents modern science and theology, ends up killing Gabalāwi in the search for his book of magic – with the ensuing reflection it was easier to kill Gabalāwi than to see him.[299]

Maḥfūẓ' book met with a ban from the religious authorities of al-Azhar, because of his allegorical treatment of the stories of the prophets and their failure, and the eventual killing of 'God' (Gabalāwī) carried out by ʿArafa.[300]

Christ and Muḥammad: Khālid Muḥammad Khālid

Summarizing the works of al-ʿAqqād, Ḥusayn, al-Saḥḥār and Khālid (to be dealt with in the following), Fr. Jomier of the Dominican Institute of Oriental Studies in Cairo identifies a clear focus on the personality of Jesus:

> . . . in the Middle Ages, this Muslim sympathy showed itself towards Jesus as a wonder-worker, ascetic and mystic, today it seems rather to seek the deeply human side of the doctrines of Christ. In the Middle Ages, Jesus was seen as a prophet who had fought against the formalism of the doctors of the Law and had reminded men of the duty to live an interior religion, the religion of the heart. In our four works, on the contrary, Jesus' struggle against the Pharisees appears firstly as that of natural conscience and justice in the face of hypocrisy and clericalism. In the Middle Ages, Jesus was seen in regard to God. In these four works, He is seen rather in regard to men and humanity.[301]

This focus on the dynamic personality of Jesus is clearly paralleled by a similar emphasis in the way some of the same authors approach Muḥammad. In twentieth-century Egypt, several literates (such as Muḥammad Ḥusayn Haykal and Tawfīq al-Ḥākim) have approached the Prophet with a focus on his dynamic, personal qualities.[302] This can also be seen from al-ʿAqqād's book *ʿAbqariyyat Muḥammad* ('The Genius of Muḥammad', al-ʿAqqād 1985 – first published in 1942). A similar personalist approach is found in al-ʿAqqād's books on the early heroes of Islam (cf. his *Islāmiyyāt*-collection, al-ʿAqqād 1985). Furthermore, we have noted that the major work of another Muslim Christ-biographer, al-Saḥḥār, is a 20-volume series of books on the life of Muḥammad, and like al-ʿAqqād, he wrote also a number of biographies of prominent Muslim figures.

The author to be dealt with extensively in this and the following chapter, Khālid Muḥammad Khālid (d. 1996), is the only one of the Christ-biographers that presents Muḥammad and Christ side by side in the same book – 'together on the road' (Khālid n.d., first published in 1958).

Different from al-ʿAqqād and Ḥusayn, Khālid was educated as a *shaykh* from al-Azhar University, but did not serve in any official religious position. Instead, he dedicated his life to writing and to cultural and political involvement from an independent position. In 1950, he published a book advocating the separation of state and religion, which brought upon him the wrath of the *ʿulamāʾ*.[303] A censure was initially imposed, but was later removed by a civil court, reflecting the dominant secularism of the time.

In the 1970s – after a long period of extensive writing on Muḥammad and Muslim personalities – Khālid began to revise his secularism. He linked his previous and persistently strong defence of democracy to the idea of an Islamic state,[304] and became known as a moderate Islamist or 'Islamic democrat' under Sadāt and Mubārak.

Throughout his life, he was committed to peaceful Christian–Muslim coexistence and dialogue. He had many close Coptic friends, and notwithstanding his later inclination towards (moderate) Islamism, he was regarded by the Coptic community as a friendly and highly esteemed partner in dialogue.[305] In his books from the 1950s and the '60s, one often finds him citing the Bible and the Qur'ān side by side when dealing with general issues such as democracy, human rights and social justice.[306]

In 1958, he published his book 'Together on the Road – Muḥammad and Christ' (*Maʿan ʿalā al-ṭarīq. Muḥammad wa-l-Masīḥ*).[307] The front cover cites a well-known Ḥadīth: 'The prophets are brothers; their mothers are different, but their religion is one' (Muslim). The book presents itself as written in a spirit of dialogue, and for the sake of 'man' and 'life':

> *That is exactly what I want to say to those who believe in Christ and those who believe in Muḥammad: If you are sincere, the proof of your faith is that today, one and all of you embark upon the task of protecting the human being . . . protecting life!*[308]

Unlike the somewhat elitist approach of al-ʿAqqād, Khālid's is influenced by socialism, and reinterprets religious virtues in the light of a basically egalitarian position. In this work, he retells some decisive stages in the history of philosophy and religion – focusing on Socrates, the ancient Egyptians, Buddha, Confucius and the biblical prophets (with an emphasis on the vigorous social criticism of the prophets). He praises the prophetic spirit, and laments modern philosophy's turning from the hidden to search for evidence, and from prophethood to mere experiment (*tajriba*). The prophetic task has always been, and still is, to develop the human mind (*al-ʿaql*) and to disseminate visions of goodness, courage and a proper human conscience (*al-ṣalāḥ fī-l-ḍamīri l-bašarī*).[309] Coming to Christ and Muḥammad, he presents Christ as summarizing the entire philosophy of love, whereas Muḥammad – announcing the doctrine of *tawḥīd* – is presented as the one who rescues man from the last shackles of subordination.

In the chapter 'Together on the road of the Lord', he depicts the dark background of the two messengers' coming. According to Khālid, Judaism at the time of Christ was characterized by blind adherence to tradition, hypocrisy, self-interest, formalistic rites devoid of spirit and ignorance of the innermost cores of the law (*lubāb al-šarīʿa, wa-ṣamīmiha*).[310]

Christ and Muḥammad are consistently depicted as models and brothers in genuine prophethood. Already in the preamble, Khālid characterizes Christ as a man with a lofty soul and an honest conscience. In this sense, he is the 'Son of Man'.[311] Similarly, Muḥammad is characterized by honesty of conscience (*istiqāmat al-ḍamīr*). There was something in his heart (*šay'un fī rūʿihi*) that said 'halt' to the polytheistic practices of his tribe.[312] Muḥammad liberated people's minds from superstition, their emotions from falsehood and their entire existence from destruction.[313]

In the chapter 'Together for the sake of man', Khālid underlines that both messengers were but humans, although with extraordinary energies (referring to the miracles of Christ), loftiness of mind and a special concern for 'common people' (*al-rajul al-ʿādī*[314]). Both of them vigorously defended the rights of man – the right of subsistence, as well as the right of conscience. Conscience was in dire need to be defended, against religious intimidation (*al-taḫyīf al-dīnī*) from the supervisors and custodians of sects, traditions and rites, and those with coarse hearts.[315]

As with al-ʿAqqād and Kāmil Ḥusayn, the notion of conscience (*ḍamīr*) is a focal point in his writings on Islam and Christianity. Expounding his notion of *ḍamīr*, Khālid gives a definition that appears to have just as much to do with human authenticity as with ethics in the strict sense:

> *I don't mean by conscience here the spiritual function which makes the human being regret the evil he has committed, or incites the good which he otherwise would have failed to do. Rather, I mean by human conscience in this context, a more distant goal, a much broader meaning .... In one concise expression, we mean by it 'the human being in his true existence'* (al-insān fī wujūdihi al-ḥaqīqī).[316]

Later, he defines this to mean the full expression of the human being, by opening the way to his energies and possibilities.[317]

Muḥammad protected the inner integrity of man, and (with reference to a Ḥadīth) he did not want to cleave people's hearts to reveal their innermost thoughts. In this, we can see 'the moment of release for conscience, within the religious law of Muḥammad'.[318] Muḥammad also does away with any notion of brokers between God and the people. Together with Christ, he liberates conscience from the three evils by which the brokers threaten its integrity: bargaining, intimidation and tribalism. He leaves all responsibility to the liberated conscience.

He describes Muḥammad as tolerant towards 'our moral sins' (*aḫṭāʾana al-aḫlāqiyya*), opening up enormous scope space for human trial and error.[319] He presents him as being much more severe in his critique of sins related to power and class, than towards sins in the personal sphere. Focusing on the inner dimensions, he describes how Christ and Muḥammad liberated the individual from guilt feeling – thereby enabling genuine 'peace of mind'. Asking for forgiveness is described as a way of 'recovering our souls'.

But fear may also be a result of external intimidation. The 'terrorism of conscience' is in fact more dangerous than that which damages the body, because it attacks the very seat of life and makes all expressions hypocritical.[320] As for this 'terrorism of conscience', he gives the example of hampering the education of girls. This he characterizes a false *jihād* – nothing but a result of the 'deviation of conscience'.

He proceeds by underlining freedom to doubt (*šakk*) as one of the fundamental human rights defended by Muḥammad (again with a reference presented as a ḥadīth, where the Messenger praises honest doubt as an expression of genuine faith).[321]

In fact, by defending freedom of conscience, both Christ and Muḥammad introduced a new method or approach (*minhaj*) – a flexible approach capable of being developed. And all is done not in the name of these two messengers, but on the account of human conscience itself, and for the sake of human progress.[322]

The chapter ends with the concession that a certain measure of deterring intimidation – by means of laws, social customs and restrictions – is unavoidable in all human up-bringing. But we should take care that deterring measures do not turn into terrorism of conscience.

In the next chapter, 'Together for the sake of life', Khālid expounds the values of love, truthfulness and work as found in the teachings of Christ and Muḥammad. Love is depicted as a 'gravitating force', capable even of the expiation of sins.[323] Truthfulness has to do with the congruence between our appearance and our hidden innermost being (*bayna ẓawāhirina wa-bāṭinina*), and the ability of self-criticism.[324] As for peace, he cites several words of Christ and Muḥammad pointing to their commitment towards non-retaliation and reconciliation.

Why then, did Muḥammad carry a sword? Khālid answers this 'fair question' by introducing the notion of 'the will of history'.[325] Muḥammad embodied the will of history. It was his enemies that resisted this will and thus – in the end – forced Muḥammad to take up arms, although within severe restrictions on how warfare may be conducted, which can be seen from Ḥadīth. In this connection, Khālid underlines that peace is a value that expresses itself in the positive (affirming the will of history), and not in the negative (abstaining from confrontation).[326] At this point, a certain difference from Kāmil Ḥusayn and his concept of non-violence as a virtue of resistance may be observed.

Summing up, Khālid depicts Christ as one who (by crucifixion, which Khālid seems to affirm as a matter of fact) was victimized by sword, whereas Muḥammad – carrying the sword for the sake of peace – wanted to efficiently stop the enemies of man and truth. Thus, there is a fundamental difference between the two companions on the road:

> *In Christ's behaviour, peace expressed itself in mercy. In Muḥammad's behaviour, peace expressed itself in justice.*[327]

In the final chapter, entitled 'Christ or Barabbas?', he states that now – in the atomic age – the fundamental choice between peace and war is first and foremost put before the Christian West. He relates his reflections on the contemporary situation to the belief in the second coming of Christ. But the traditional Muslim concept of Christ's return is understood by Khālid as looking to the future by the criteria of Christ. He implies that Muḥammad himself, by referring to the return of Christ, confirms the ultimate character of the way of love:

> . . . *almost one thousand four hundred years ago, the Messenger was standing in the Arab peninsula, pronouncing the messages of his Lord, announcing that Christ would come again* . . ..

How will he be recognized? Not by the physical appearances depicted in Ḥadīth, but by the fulfilment of his message.

> *For Christ is his message, he is the supreme ideal* (al-maṯal al-aʿlā) *that he left and gave* . . .. *He is the love which knows no hatred, he is the peace that knows no disquiet, and he is the salvation that does not perish. And when all this is realised on earth, then at the same time, the return of Christ is realised. This is the Christ who will return, and whose return the Messenger prophesied: peace, love, truth, the good and beauty. With the truthful Messenger, we declare: 'Christ, not Barabbas, the true not the false, love not hatred, peace not war, life not destruction.'*[328]

Like Ḥusayn, but not as elaboratedly, Khālid uses the concept of crucifixion to characterize the ultimate threat to humanity. Whenever Barabbas is chosen, Christ is crucified, peace is crucified, and love is crucified.[329] Agonized as we may be by the fear that war will once more be the choice, Muḥammad comforts us by announcing the return of Christ, which means that the values embodied by Christ in the end will be victorious. Awaiting this end, we will be guided by a sharp-sighted consciousness and the necessities of our age.[330] And our way towards the goal will be strong truth and wakeful love.[331]

For all Khālid's admiration of Christ and his conscience-based, entirely non-violent ethics, it remains clear that the well-balanced perfection of the divine message is left to Muḥammad. Cragg comments:

> This remarkable writing . . . has to be balanced – for most Muslims – by the necessity, as they see it, of Jesus' foretelling Muhammad. If Jesus . . . supplies Islam with its eschatological perception and goal, Muhammad supplies the historical realism which is wanting in Jesus and precluded by his context. If Islamic traditions need to anticipate a Christ-style future, Jesus needed to anticipate a Muhammad-style future, the one in eternal, the other in temporal terms. The Gospel may have right in the ultimate; the Qur'ān has its right in the concrete.[332]

Another example of books portraying Christ and Muḥammad 'together on the road' is cited by Hugh Goddard (1996), who refers Maḥmūd Abū Rayya's book *Dīn Allāh wāḥīd – Muḥammad wa-l-Masīḥ iḫwān* ('The Religion of God is One – Muḥammad and Christ are Brothers'). The book by this liberal

Azharite writer was published in 1963, and met with reactions from traditional quarters. The book was re-edited in 1970 under the title *Dīn Allāh wāḥīd – ʿalā alsina jāmiʿ al-rusul* ('The Religion of God is one – from the lips of all the prophets'). The book does not primarily deal with 'Christ and Muḥammad', but rather with the relation between the three monotheistic religions, with a call for mutual recognition.[333]

Christ, Muḥammad and Human Conscience: al-ʿAqqād, ʿUthmān, Ḥusayn, Khālid

We have seen a strong and intriguing focus on human conscience (*ḍamīr* in the sense of moral conscience) among Egyptian Muslim writers who include the story of Jesus in their biographies and novels. Building on my research on these writers' notion of conscience,[334] in what follows I will indicate how these authors relate the notion of conscience to their image of Christ, to their distinctively modern reappropriation of the Islamic heritage and to their (likewise modern) concern for individual integrity in the field of ethics.

ʿAbbās Maḥmūd al-ʿAqqād and Fatḥī ʿUthmān

Al-ʿAqqād[335] seems to have been the first to focus on human conscience when writing about Christ. As we have seen from *ʿAbqariyyat al-Masīḥ*, being true to conscience is contrasted with relying on outward forms and appearances, and petrified religion. In al-ʿAqqād's works altogether, *ḍamīr* acquires a multiplicity of meanings. Generally, the focus seems to be on the internalization of religion and the importance of personal morality in ethical matters. But al-ʿAqqād also seems to grant *ḍamīr* a creative role – in the search for an ethics which is based more on the internalized law of love than on external rules and regulations.

Al-ʿAqqād links his reading of Christ as the champion of a 'law of love and conscience' to an interpretation of Islam with a similar focus on human conscience. In his biography of Muḥammad (*ʿAbqariyyat Muḥammad*, 'The Genius of Muḥammad', from 1942), Muḥammad's loyalty to the divine revelation is said to be reflected in his will to comfort his conscience.[336] This early work in al-ʿAqqād's series about religious 'geniuses', reflects his emphasis on the quality of the person when dealing with ethics and religion. Muḥammad is sublime (*ʿaẓīm*) – not by the mere fact of being chosen, but because he has got a sublime moral character (*ḫuluq*).[337] His conscience responded positively to the divine guidance, and it found reassurance from the revelation of his Lord (as did the consciences of previous prophets and those with a religious nature).[338] Also with the recipients of Muḥammad's message, conscience plays a role. Those who were prepared to receive the new message, distinguished themselves by seeking the reassurance and calm of conscience (*ṭumaʾnīnat al-ḍamīr*).[339]

In a book from 1961, on 'Thinking – an Islamic Duty' (*Al-tafkīr – farīḍa islāmiyya*), al-ʿAqqād maintains that Islam is the only religion that fully authorizes a free and independent relation between the creatures and their Creator, so that humans may approach God by means of their conscience – their *ḍamīr*.[340] Already in his exposition of 'The qur'ānic Philosophy' (*Al-falsafa al-Qur'āniyya* 1947), he claims that the philosophy of the Qur'ān contains the only doctrine that can really vitalize conscience, and disperse the clouds that otherwise block the light of reason.[341] Al-ʿAqqād's discourse of *ḍamīr* is thus a truly Islamic discourse, and his view of Christ as a champion of human conscience must clearly be subordinated to his general view that human conscience is best safeguarded by Islam.

We have seen that Fatḥī ʿUthmān[342] follows al-ʿAqqād in his exposition of the law of conscience as taught by Christ. But he adds some new elements, such as the reproaching and curbing function of human conscience, and conscience's search for spiritual reassurance. These aspects of conscience are also touched upon by al-ʿAqqād in a different context: he cites the triadic image of the soul which can be extracted from the Qur'ān (especially in Ṣūfī interpretations) – the soul that commands evil, the soul that reproaches itself and the soul that has eventually achieved peace and confidence.[343] In this particular context, al-ʿAqqād relates the image of the self-reproaching soul (*al-nafs al-lawwāma*) to the power of conscience. But only in passing, and his main point is that conscience reflects the human condition of being enjoined and accountable.[344]

Muḥammad Kāmil Ḥusayn

In general, it might be argued that with al-ʿAqqād (as well as with Khālid), conscience is primarily conceived of in terms of its creative potentials – as the seat of human responsibility; as the anchoring ground of moral judgements; as the faculty of formulating new moral insights in the light of divine revelation; and as the warrant of human authenticity. Generally, al-ʿAqqād's discourse of conscience seems to aim at freeing human beings from the shackles of tradition, and releasing human potentials.

As for Kāmil Ḥusayn,[345] his discourse of conscience strikes a rather different note. We have seen that conscience/*ḍamīr* is the key concept in his retelling of the dramatic events of Good Friday (Ḥusayn 1954/1994). In Kenneth Cragg's summary:

> The central point of *City of Wrong* was the thesis that the vested interests of collectives, of political structures, always tend towards injustice and tyranny. So tending, they demand to override the scruples of personal conscience – scruples which as corporate entities they are incapable of registering. It follows that the only check, frail as it must be, to the wrong-doing of states and parties and institutions is the resistance of individual

> conscience. The private person must refuse to do, in the name of some collective loyalty, what he would refrain from doing in his individual capacity.[346]

In an appendix to his novel of conscience, he emphasizes that the main function of conscience is that of curbing and warning (*rādiʿan wa-naḏīran*): 'Although it is possible to be positively guided by conscience, the main power for conscience being inhibitive and prohibitive, it is mainly a guide to us in avoiding wrong.'[347]

By his emphasis on the curbing function of conscience and the persistent tendency of human beings to 'crucify' their consciences, Ḥusayn differs markedly from the more optimistic view on human conscience as a creative force found with al-ʿAqqād and Khālid. Ḥusayn's view on human conscience is further elaborated in his book on 'a Muslim philosophy of religion', entitled *Al-wādī l-muqaddas* ('The Hallowed Valley').[348] In this book, Ḥusayn explores the moral and religious values in Judaism, Christianity and Islam respectively. In this context, he reiterates his contention that the main function of conscience is to keep man within the bounds that must not be transgressed.[349] He relates his view of conscience as a curbing force to what he calls the 'hidden and passive virtues of resistance'.[350] According to Ḥusayn, these inward virtues have no other reward than a soul at rest, abiding in its hallowed valley. For Ḥusayn, the Muslim concept of 'the soul at rest' is the fusion of the ideal states advocated by the Jews ('the just spirit') and the Christians ('the loving soul') respectively.

Harold Vogelaar (1995) suggests that Ḥusayn's view of conscience is based on what he calls a 'therapeutic synthesis between religion and science'.[351] His concern for spiritual therapy brings him close to classical Muslim philosophers with a Platonic-Aristotelian orientation, who saw the right balancing of the conflicting powers of the soul as a main function of religion. Like classical Muslim philosophers, Ḥusayn explicitly held the view that religion and science could be blended into a rational whole. Being fascinated by scientific methods as a way of approaching all aspects of reality, he saw the true miracle of science 'not (in) breaking the sound barrier or reaching the moon but rather participation in things formerly forbidden such as the human psyche, morals and conscience'.[352]

For Ḥusayn, 'conscience' has both anthropological and theological connotations. It stands for 'your rightly guided self',[353] but at the same time, it denotes 'the voice of God itself':

> *In the hallowed valley you hear the voice of conscience clear and plain, enjoining upon you unconfusedly the obligations of the good, and leading you undeviatingly towards the truth – conscience as the very voice of God.*[354]

Harold Vogelaar finds in Ḥusayn's works a general tendency towards a more immanent concept of God, in line with controversial mystic and philosophical ancestors within Islam: 'he equates God and conscience'.[355]

Khālid Muḥammad Khālid

As with al-ʿAqqād and Ḥusayn, the notion of *ḍamīr*/conscience is also central in what Khālid writes about Christ. With Khālid,[356] the concept of 'honest conscience' is presented as the key to understanding the core of prophethood in general, including the personality of Muḥammad.

As Khālid sees it, the prophetic mission is rooted in the inner authority of Muḥammad's conscience. On the first page of his book on the human qualities of Muḥammad (*Insāniyyāt Muḥammad*, from 1960), Khālid claims that:

> *If Muḥammad had not been a messenger of God he would surely have been a human being on the same level as a messenger of God! And if he had not received the command from his Lord: 'Oh messenger, proclaim what is revealed to you' he would surely have received it from his very nature* (min ḏāti nafsihi)*: 'Oh human being, proclaim what is at work in your conscience!'*[357]

In fact, with Khālid *ḍamīr*/conscience seems to be regarded as the uniting factor in all genuine religious experience, and in all moral teachings based on genuine religion. This is expounded more fully in Khālid's meditations on human conscience from 1963, in his book entitled *Maʿa l-ḍamīri l-insāniyyi fī-masīrihi wa-maṣīrihi* ('With human conscience on its journey towards its destiny').

In this book, he traces the development of human conscience from the ancient civilizations throughout the times of prophetic revelation and philosophical reason all the way up to his own 'atomic' age.[358] In the preface, he presents his work as 'an examination that attempts to clarify the special characteristics by which conscience is guided'. He defines human conscience as:

> . . . *that insight* (baṣīra) *which God granted to the human race – with all its individuals, geniuses and visions. We mean by it the will to supremacy* (tafawwuq) *which by means of noble and earnest aspirations and true intuition guides the entire human family to embrace its glorious and magnificent destiny.*[359]

Right from the beginning, he states that conscience (*ḍamīr*) precedes reason (*ʿaql*), by the supremacy which was given to it. From the beginning, conscience was rightly guided and attentive (*rašīdan wa-wāʿiyan*), 'as if accompanied by a light from God'.[360] But conscience was not born complete. It makes progress through the ages, up to the point when – in our age – it reaches a state of unpreceded integrity.

From this starting point, he traces the development of human conscience and its struggle to retain its innate integrity through the subsequent ages of 'vision', 'prophethood', 'reason' – up to the contemporary 'age of Gandhi, the atomic age'.

In the first chapter, 'The age of vision', he depicts the emergence of a social conscience (with *ʿadl*, 'justice', as a key concept) as well as the development towards monotheism in the religions of ancient Egypt and other ancient civilizations, including the insights of Greek philosophy.

The guidance of conscience is secured in the subsequent 'companionship with prophethood', i.e. the age of prophetic revelation. Beginning with the story of Abraham (qur'ānic and biblical) and emphasizing the importance of the biblical prophets (especially Isaiah), he focuses on Christ and Muḥammad and their supreme guidance of human conscience. As for Christ, Khālid (like al-ʿAqqād and Ḥusayn) emphasizes his radical ethics of love, forgiveness and non-retaliation – with references to the Sermon on the Mount and other key passages in the biblical Gospels. In Christ's seeming 'weakness', Khālid sees a supreme strength. By telling his disciple to put his sword in its place and by his 'blessed cry' that all who take the sword will perish by the sword (Matthew 26.51–52), Christ disclosed an eternal truth:

> *The role of Christ became visible in his announcement of this eternal truth, that loving affection* (maḥabba) *is more powerful and more lasting, and that opposing evil with good is not only possible, but destined for victory and success .... Loving affection, then, is capable of producing unparalleled miracles – if evil is met with good, sword with calm* (sakīna), *and aversion with love .... Christ gave to the human race one of its greatest truths, namely that human beings are capable of melting away all their problems by warmth and love and compassion.*[361]

But the church was not true to the teachings of Christ. With a familiar depiction of Christianity's decay, Khālid leads the reader to the realization of the need for another and final prophet, Muḥammad. For all his admiration for Christ, Khālid seems to imply that Christ's focus on moral intentions (*al-nawāyā*) was not enough to give human conscience a solid foundation. The seeds of good intentions needed to be implanted 'in the depths of human nature and in the nature of society as well'.[362] Although Muḥammad shared many of the moral convictions of Christ, he was more political in his approach, and saw the need to reinforce the good intentions of individuals by communal virtues and social, even international laws. Seeing this was a firm step forward in human history, reflecting a supreme consciousness (*waʿy ʿaẓīm*). The virtue of brotherhood needs a law (*qānūn*) to support it. This was what Islam produced.[363]

Notwithstanding Muḥammad's enduring commitment to peace and reconciliation (which Khālid abundantly exemplifies), he accepted the use of violence for self-defence, though only as the very last resort, and with clearly defined restrictions on warfare.

In the chapter about 'The age of reason', the virtue of 'enlightened doubt' (*al-šakk al-mustanīr*) is emphasized as a major accomplishment of European philosophy,[364] although – when introduced – it was accused of heresy and apostasy.[365] In addition, Khālid pays special attention to Rousseau's concept of individual freedom guaranteed and restricted by social contract, and the fight against slavery and for racial equality in America.

After 'the age of reason', with its various stages of Arab and European philosophy as well as the development of experimental sciences, human conscience reaches the peak of its integrity in our own age, which Khālid (writing in the 1960s) characterizes as 'the age of Gandhi and the atom'. According to Khālid, Mahatma Gandhi received from the age of prophethood respect for religion, and from the age of reason, he received respect for conviction.[366] Khālid depicts how Gandhi through his non-violent practice (*tajriba*)[367] managed to 'set free the energy of love (*ṭāqat al-maḥabba*) . . . a greater miracle than the atom itself!'[368] Khālid exclaims: 'Indeed, Gandhi is the conscience of our age. He is the true representative of human conscience in our generation and in our modern world!'[369]

Khālid seems to regard the intentionalism of Christ and the more political orientation of Muḥammad as being merged in the practice of Gandhi, a practice which shook the world and had tangible political consequences:

> *Human conscience now reached the peak of its integrity, and it moved across the stage of the major events in our age, materialising in the person of its devoted son Mahatma Gandhi.*[370]

Although Khālid, true to his image of Muḥammad and his own commitment to a kind of 'Islamic socialism', evaluates highly the political achievements of Gandhi, his emphasis seems to be on the moral endeavour of the individual and the liberation of the human spirit. For Gandhi, faith and worship meant:

> . . . *the liberation of the human spirit* (taḥarrur al-rūḥ) *and human destiny* (maṣīr) *from all obstacles, and the resurrection* (baʿṯ) *of the individual who rises above his desires and works in the service of the human race, on the principles of truth and love.*[371]

Khālid's treatment of the history of human conscience is intriguing. He combines a broad interreligious outlook with an outspoken loyalty to the decisiveness of the qur'ānic revelation. He links the finality of prophetic revelation to a concept of human development, tracing the completion of conscience through the various stages of history towards its destiny. He combines his concern for personal integrity with a social outlook. In contrast to Ḥusayn, this seems to include the notion of a 'social conscience'[372] – although with a strong insistence on the duty of the human person to develop his individual conscience, and the duty of the community (be it religious or political) to ensure an unrestricted freedom of conscience.

In Khālid's later writings, his interest in the notion of *ḍamīr* seems to have waned somewhat, although his commitment to freedom of conscience appears to have been sustained. The principle of freedom of expression is strongly maintained in his later book *Al-dawla fī-l-islām* ('The State in Islam', 1981), which marked his shift to a moderate Islamist position. In this book, the freedom rights are integrated in his vision of the state in Islam, which should be based on a merger of modern democratic principles with the Islamic ideal of *šūra*, 'counsel'.[373]

Already from the early 1960s, a shift of interest can be identified in Khālid. Gradually, the focus on Muḥammad and 'the men around the Messenger' seems to replace his interest in the ethical and religious heritage shared by the religions. Did he, in tune with more particularist discourses on both the Muslim and the Christian side, move from calling on the authentic human being, towards the proclamation of a specifically Islamic authenticity?

Below, as an 'issue for dialogue', we shall pursue the question of human conscience as a possible focal point in Christian–Muslim dialogue – both in *ethical* terms and in a more general perspective, with a view to its possible importance for an *ethos* of dialogue.

Notes

1 Jacques Jomier (1958), Olaf Schumann (1988/75, 1977, 1997), Hugh Goddard (1987, 1990, 1996) and others have given a general analysis of Egyptian contributions. Goddard (1994) and Schirrmacher (1992) have also investigated major trends in Indo-Pakistani Muslim theology.

2 Cf. the Lebanese Muḥammad al-Sammāk's *Muqaddamat ilā l-ḥiwār al-islāmiyya – al-masīḥiyya* (Beirut: Dār al-Nafā'is, 1998), which begins with a chapter on Mary and Jesus.

3 Among influential polemical contributions from the Muslim side, originating from other contexts, the writings and videos of the South African Ahmed Deedat (cf. 1984, 1989) and the book *The Myth of the Cross* of the Nigerian writer A. D. Ajijola (1975) are worth special mention. Among the more eirenical works, the play of the Turkish writer Kemal Demirel about the trial and crucifixion of Jesus (*The High Judge*, Demirel 1990) comes close to the tendency of the works of Salāḥ ʿAbd al-Ṣabūr and Muḥammad Kāmil Ḥusayn (see the section on the symbol of the cross in Chapter 7), approaching the crucifixion as a literary theme.

4 Goddard (1996: 39, 58).

5 As for the twentieth century, Schirrmacher highlights the Barnabas controversy – see below.

6 Ibid., p. 51.

7 Schirrmacher (1992: 275f.).

8 Ibid., pp. 52–55. See also Rahman (2003), Engineer (1991: 15–16), Troll (1977) and the book by Christian Troll, *Sayyid Ahmad Khan: A*

Reinterpretation of Muslim Theology. New Delhi: Vikas Publishing House (1978).

9 Rahman (2003).

10 Ibid., p. 29.

11 In Urdu: *Masih Hindustan mein*. A recent English edition is Ahmad (1989).

12 Ahmad (1989: 14).

13 Ibid., p. 16.

14 Ibid., p. 19.

15 Ibid., p. 26.

16 Ibid., p. 46.

17 *The Holy Qur'an*, Lahore (1973), translated into a number of languages. Cf. Engineer (1991: 16f.).

18 Ahmad (1989: 51).

19 About the Gospel of Barnabas, see Axon (1902), Ragg (1905), Ragg & Ragg (1907), ʿAbdul-Ahad & Gairdner (1975 [1907]), Youngson (1908), Cannon (1942), Jomier (1959–1961, 1980), al-Aqqād/Cragg (1961), Slomp (1974, 1978, 1997), Fletcher (1976), Cirillio/Frémaux (1977), ʿAta ur-Rahim (1979), de Epalza (1963, 1982), Sox (1984), Campbell (1989), Yusseff (1990a, 1990b), Schirrmacher (1992), Bowman (1992), Wiegers (1995), Bernabé Pons (1992, 1995, 1996, 1998), van Koningsveld (1996), Blackhirst (1996), Borrmans (1996: 114), Kvalvaag (1998), Pulcini (2001), Leirvik (2001).

20 The Spanish manuscript, published by Bernabé Pons in 1998, lacks Chapters 121–200. The old Italian manuscript includes some Arabic glosses. In 1991, the old Italian manuscript was published in parallel columns with a modern Italian translation (Giustolisi and Rizzardi 1991).

21 An *Evangelium nomine Barnabe apocryphum* is referred to in *Decretum Gelasianum de libris recipiendis et non recipiendis* from the end of the fifth century, and even in a similar list in Greek from the seventh or eighth century (*euangelion kata barnaba*). See Schirrmacher (1992: 246f.).

22 In Spanish: Bernabé Pons (1992, 1995, 1998). In German: Luis F. Bernabé Pons (1996).

23 de Epalza (1963, 1982).

24 Cf. the evaluations in Bernabé Pons (1995, 1998), de Epalza (1982) and Slomp (1997).

25 The Italian manuscript has 34 blank pages, obviously meant to contain an introduction, probably similar to that of Fra Marino in the Spanish manuscript. The Spanish manuscript is presently available in the Fisher Library in Sydney. See Schirrmacher (1992: 260–262) and Fletcher (1976: 314–320).

26 Ragg (1907). The initiative behind the translation appears to have been taken by John W. Youngson of the Church of Scotland Mission to Muslims. Through a professor in Glasgow who knew of the Italian

manuscript in Vienna, the task of a scientific, critical translation and edition was eventually given to the scholars Lonsdale and Laura Ragg.

27 Gairdner is, however, confident that 'when honest men throughout the East know the contents of the book, they will assign to it its true historical value as a Gospel – which is exactly nil' (Gairdner 1907: 2).

28 It has also been translated into Persian, Indonesian and Turkish. As for more recent Western translations, it was translated into French by Cirillo and Frémaux (1977) in connection with a scientific investigation, and has also been translated into modern Italian, modern Spanish, Dutch and German. See references in Schirrmacher (1992: 346–352) and Slomp (1997: 87).

As for the numerous Urdu editions of the Gospel of Barnabas, the influential head of the Jama'at-i Islami movement, Maulana al-Maududi, who prefaced a 1974 edition, admitted that the frequent mentioning of Muhammad's name was against the usual style of prophecies about future events. He nevertheless holds the Gospel of Barnabas to be more authentic than the biblical Gospels (see Slomp 1997: 105–107).

In addition to translations into national languages, Muslim publishers (especially in Pakistan) have also produced several editions of the English translation.

29 Saʿāda thought that the existing Gospel of Barnabas was composed by a Spanish Jew who converted to Islam, but holds the existence of an early Christian source to be quite probable. Riḍā is more ready to identify the existing Gospel with the early Christian Gospel of Barnabas known from the Gelasian decree, although he keeps the door open for the possibility that various kinds of reworking have been carried out. As for the foretelling of Muḥammad, Riḍā links the Barnabas argument to traditional apologetic readings of the Gospel of John as prophesying Muhammad. In the year before the edition of the complete translation, Riḍā had been publishing excerpts and advocating the authenticity of the Gospel of Barnabas in his (and Muḥammad 'Abduh's) serialized commentary to the Qur'ân, *Tafsīr al-Manār* (see Schirrmacher 1992: 286–304: 'Muhammad Rashîd Ridâ's arabische Edition des Barnabasevangelium').

30 The quotations from the Gospel of Barnabas in the following are taken from the Raggs' translation, as reprinted in Yusseff (1990a).

31 See ch. 10, 124, 168, 193, 212.

32 See ch. 44, 58, 71, 97, 115, 133, 151, 157, 189, 191–192, 212.

33 Giustolisi and Rizzardi (1991: 18–21).

34 See ch. 17, 48, 52, 53, 70, 72, 91–95, 128, 206, 220.

35 Cf. ch. 42 and 96, where Jesus utters the humble announcements attributed to John in the biblical Gospels.

36 See ch. 12, 16, 36, 39, 41–44, 54–58, 72, 82–84, 96–97, 112, 136, 142,

158–159, 163, 177, 191, 206, 220. Allusion also seems to be made to the qur'ânic foretelling of Ahmad, the praiseworthy (cf. 97).

37 In English translation: 'He [David] relates in the Psalms that God first created the Light of Muhammad. All the prophets and saints are lights. (This is part [of the text]) – commenting on the formulation in ch. 12 that has David saying: "Before Lucifer in the brightness of saints I created thee."' A doxological assertion by Jesus in ch. 12 implies that 'God created the splendour of all the saints and prophets before all things' (cf. ch. 43: God 'created before all things the soul of his messenger'). See Koningsveld (1996: 218).

38 See ch. 13, 43–44, 142, 190–191, 208.

39 Schirrmacher (1992: 263–274). In *De religione Mohamedica* (1705), Adrian Roland mentions a Gospel in Arabic and Spanish. Even seventeenth-century references to the Gospel have also been suggested by some, cf. Louis Cardaillac in his study of Morisco-Christian polemics between 1492 and 1640 (Schirrmacher 1992: 263). A possible further reference is found in a book review by Michael Carter of Schirrmacher's *Mit den Waffen des Gegners*. Carter points to Edward Pockocke's *Specimen historiae Arabum* (1650), which mentions two 'uncorrupted' versions of the Gospel which prophesy Muhammad's coming, one in private hands and another in Paris. See Michael Carter's book review in *MESA Bulletin* 28 (1994), p. 109f.

40 George Sale, *The Koran: commonly called the Alcoran of Mohammed; translated into English immediately from the original Arabic, with explanatory notes, taken from the most approved commentators, to which is prefixed a preliminary discourse, by George Sale, Gent* (London: William Tegg, 1863), sect. IV, p. 53. Sale later admits that he never saw any manuscript in Arabic, only the Spanish version from which he cites some passages in his comments to Sūras 3 and 7. See ibid., p. 42f, 117.

41 Ibid., p. 42. The Spanish version of the Gospel is also referred to by Joseph White in his *Bampton Lectures* from 1784 (Schirrmacher 1992: 272f.).

42 The Italian manuscript was made available to Toland by J. C. Cramer in Amsterdam. Through Prince Eugene of Savoy, to whom Cramer dedicated the manuscript, it came to the Austrian National Library where it has since been preserved in 'Die Handschriftensammlung der Österreichischen Nationalbibliothek' (Schirrmacher 1992: 265–268).

43 Apart from the references made by Toland and Sale, several other mentions by Western authors of the modern Gospel of Barnabas (in its Italian or Spanish, or – hypothetically – Arabic form) can be identified from the early eighteenth century onwards (Schirrmacher 1992: 272–274).

44 Schirrmacher (1992).

45 Schirrmacher (1992: 275f.).

46 Ahmad (1989: 26). In the Indian context, Hamid Snow – the head of a

peculiar movement called 'the Nazarene Muslims' – also cited the Gospel of Barnabas in his book *The Gospel of Ahmad* (1897). Setting out to prove that Islam is 'but a true continuation of Nazarene Judaism as taught by the Christ (Jesus) and the Messenger (Ahmad)', Snow claims that 'The dogmas of the Nazarenes are exactly the same as those of the Muhammedans, excepting that minor incident, the crucifixion of Jesus, which is strictly no dogma at all, nor even a matter of salvation'. As for his interest in the Gospel of Barnabas, Snow concentrates on its denial of the crucifixion. Notably, Snow makes no explicit reference to the foretelling of Muhammad contained in the Gospel of Barnabas (Schirrmacher 1992: 278f.).

47 Ibid., p. 329–334.

48 Jomier (1959–1961: 137–226).

49 'Ata ur-Rahim (1979).

50 Yussef 1990a (1990b).

51 'Ata ur-Rahim (1979: 42).

52 Azmayesh (2008).

53 Although the theology of Barnabas was not necessarily identical with that of Paul, the first- or second-century *Epistle of Barnabas* indicates that Barnabas may in fact have been one of the main antagonists of Judaism and judaising elements within Christianity. Modern scholarship often attributes the Epistle to a Christian in Alexandria. A recent study of the *Epistle of Barnabas* is Reidar Hvalvik, *The Struggle for Scripture and Covenant: The Purpose of the Epistle of Barnabas and Jewish-Christian Competition in the Second Century* (Tübingen: J. C. B. Mohr, 1996).

54 See for instance ul-Qadri (1987: 88).

55 Yusseff (1990a: 89). The reference (not given by Yusseff) is apparently *Acta Barnabae* 15. Slomp cites a different part which says that 'Barnabas, having unrolled the Gospel, which he had received from Matthew his fellow-labourer, began to teach the Jews'. See Slomp (1978: 110). The reference (not given by Slomp) is apparently *Acta Barnabae* 22.

A related Cypriot legend, known from an *Acta Sanctorum* printed in Belgium in 1698, telling that the remains of Barnabas were found in 478, states that he had 'on his breast the Gospel according to Matthew, copied by Barnabas himself' (ibid., cf. Schirrmacher 1992: 245).

56 Yusseff (1990b: 94f., 97).

57 Yusseff speaks of Paul as being part of a Nicolaitan (cf. Revelation 2:6, 15) conspiracy, ibid., p. 48ff.

58 In accordance with the preface of the Spanish manuscript, van Koningsveld regards the Italian text as earlier than the Spanish version. He nevertheless finds it probable that the origin of the pseudepigraphic Gospel should be sought in ex-Christian circles of Morisco extraction, possibly in Istanbul.

59 van Koningsveld (1996: 217).

60 Schirrmacher (1992: 353f.).
61 Ibid.: 342f.
62 In English translation by Kenneth Cragg, al-'Aqqâd (1961). Cf. Slomp (1978: 68), Schirrmacher (1992: 354f.) and Campbell (1989: 52). In his famous biography of Christ, *ʿAbqariyyat al-masīḥ*, al-ʿAqqād stated clearly that he held the biblical Gospels to be the most reliable access to the life of Jesus (cf. below, VII.3b).
63 Sox (1984).
64 Campbell (1989).
65 Ragg (1907: xix).
66 Jomier (1959–1961).
67 By investigation of other historical sources from the sixteenth century, Sox (1984) has identified two possible persons that may be identical with Fra Marino: A 'Father Maestro Marino the Venetian' who is referred as 'inquisitor' in a manuscript from 1549, and a Fra Marino Moro who served also as a inquisitor in Venice but somewhat later (d. 1597).
68 Mikel de Epalza (1963, 1982).
69 Wiegers (1995).
70 Bernabé Pons (1992, 1995, 1996, 1998).
71 See Jan Slomp's book review of 'El Evangelio de San Bernabé: un evangelio islámico español', *Islam and Christian–Muslim Relations* 1 (1997: 105–106). Cf. Slomp's fuller review of recent research in Slomp (1997).
72 Cirillo and Frémaux (1977).
73 The Gospel of Barnabas often refers to Damascus as a place of retreat for Jesus and the disciples. Similarly, Roy Blackhirst (1996) has suggested a Jewish-Christian, Ebionite source behind the present Gospel, whereas John Bowman (1992) has argued in favour of a medieval Samaritan origin (cf. Slomp 1978: 103–105). In his articles about the Barnabas controversy, Jan Slomp has given a critical response to Cirillo and Frémaux as well as to Bowman and Blackhirst. Jacques Jomier has also responded critically to Cirillo and Frémaux. See Jomier (1980).
74 Pulcini (2001).
75 Cf. his critical edition of the Spanish version, Bernabé Pons (1998).
76 A contemporary Muslim commentary on the lead book affair, made by Aḥmad ibn Qâsim al-Hajarī, is found in P. S. van Koningsveld, Q. al-Samarrai and G. A. Wiegers, *Ahmad ibn Qâsim al Hajarî (d. after 1640): Kitâb nâsir al-dîn ʿal'l-qawm al-kâfirîn (The Supporter of Religion Against the Infidel), Fuentes Arábico-Hispanas, 21* (Madrid: Consejo Superior de Investigaciones Científicas, 1997: 68–91, cf. 36).
77 Also Mikel de Epalza (1963, 1982) pays much attention to al-Taybilı in this regard.
78 BNM Ms. 9653 – cf. de Epalza (1992: 176) and Bernabé Pons (1996: 174).
79 Cf. Bernabé Pons (1996: 151f.).

80 Wiegers (1995: 245–292). Wiegers deals especially with BNM Ms. 9655.
81 Ibid., p. 245. For this perspective on the Gospel of Barnabas, see also Gaudeul (1990: vol. 1, pp. 201– 213).
82 Wiegers (1995: 247).
83 Slomp (1997).
84 For situated reading and 'the poetics of location', see Fernando F. Segovia and Mary Ann Tolbert (eds.), *Reading from this Place* (Minneapolis: Fortress Press, 1995).
85 For an introduction to post-colonial theory, see Peter Childs and Patrick Williams, *An Introduction to Post-Colonial Theory* (London: Prentice Hall/Harvester Wheatscheaf, 1997).
86 James C. Scott, *Domination and the Arts of Resistance: Hidden Transcripts* (New Haven/London: Yale University Press, 1994).
87 Ibid., p. 25.
88 Ibid., p. 155, 215.
89 Ibid., p. 215.
90 English translation by Isḥāq Musʿad and Kenneth Cragg, *The Theology of Unity*. London (1966).
91 See his articles from al-Manār, edited by Rashıd Riḍā under the title *Al-islām wa-l-naṣrāniyya maʿa l-ʿilm wa-l-madaniyya* ('Islam and Christianity in relation to science and civilisation'). Cairo (1902).
92 Cf. Schirrmacher (1992: 286–304).
93 Cf. also Borrmans (1996: 80–90), for the view of Christ expressed *in Tafsīr al-Manār*. Jacques Jomier has analysed the al-Manār commentary in his book *Le commentaire coranique du Manār. Tendencies modernes de l'exégèse coranique en Egypte* (Paris, 1954).
94 Schumann (1988: 100f.).
95 See the section about 'Christ in Egyptian Muslim literature' below.
96 His main polemical treatise is *Naẓariyya fī qiṣṣat ṣalb al-masīḥ wa-qiyāmatihi min al-amwāt* ('The Christian story of the crucifixion of the Messiah and his resurrection from the dead') first appeared as an appendix to Rashīd Riḍā's *ʿAqīdat al-ṣalb wa-l-fidāʾ*. See Schumann (1988: 101–105).
97 For the following, see Schumann (1988: ch. 7), and Adams (1944) for the full text of Shaltūt's fatwa in English translation.
98 See Goddard (1996: 59–67) and Schirrmacher (1992: 329–334).
99 Goddard (1996: 60).
100 Quoted from Goddard, ibid. p. 66.
101 Ibid., p. 67.
102 Ibid., pp. 67–84.
103 Ibid., p. 84.
104 About Shalabī and his work, see Schirrmacher (1992: 334–338).
105 ʿAbd al-Wahhāb (1988). Cf. Ford (2001: 18).

106 The work is referred and discussed in Nolin (1965), Bütler (1965) and in Ford (2001: 17f.).
107 Al-Khāṭib (1966). Cf. Ford (2001: 18).
108 Goddard (1996: 84–94).
109 Malise Ruthwen, *Islam in the Modern World*. London: Penguin Books (1991: 322).
110 Annemarie Schimmel, *Gabriel's Wing: A Study into the Religious Ideas of Sir Muhammad Iqbal*. Leiden: E. J. Brill (1963: 265).
111 Quoted from Schimmel (ibid.), p. 266.
112 See his book *Islam: A challenge to Religion*. Lahore (1968). As for his image of Christ, see also Engineer (1991: 13–15).
113 *Maṭālib al-Furqān*. Lahore (1981) onwards.
114 Parwez, *Islam: A challenge to Religion*, p. 287.
115 Ibid.
116 See his *Towards Understanding Islam*. London (1980), first published in 1940.
117 English edition by The Islamic Foundation, Leicester, 1988 onwards. As for the views of Christ expressed in this commentary see Borrmans (1996: 106–110).
118 Ibid., Note 54/Sūra 3.60.
119 Ibid.
120 Ibid., Note 51/Sūra 3.55.
121 Ibid., Note 48/Sūra 3.51.
122 Ibid., Note 50/Sūra 3.52.
123 For this and the next section, see Goddard (1994) for more details.
124 The first edition was by Diwan Press, Norwich, under the slightly different title *Jesus Prophet of Islam*, and the second edition by MWH London Publishers, London, 1979. The book has also been published by Taj Company, New Delhi, 1979.
125 See the edition *Jesus Prophet of Islam*. Norwich: Diwan Press (1977: 4–5). Cf. Goddard (1994: 165).
126 The seventeenth-century Unitarian John Toland appears to be a main source of information for the author.
127 Published by Ashraf, Lahore, 1975.
128 Goddard (1994: 184).
129 al-Samad (1986: 56).
130 Ibid., p. 61.
131 Ibid., pp. 64–65.
132 Ibid., pp. 57–59.
133 Ibid., pp. 148–156.
134 ul-Qadri (1987).
135 Shafaat (1979), Introduction.
136 Ibid., all quotations from the Introduction.
137 Ibid., pp. 81f.

138 Ibid., p. 88.
139 Cf. Deedat (1984): *Crucifixion or crucifiction?*
140 Ibid., p. 90.
141 Goddard (1994: 171).
142 Vahiduddin (1986: 184). Quoted from Goddard (1994: 174).
143 Ibid., pp. 183–185. Quoted from Goddard (1994: 174f.).
144 Quoted from Goddard (1994: 176).
145 Cragg (1985b: 109–125): 'Hasan Askari of Osmania'. Both Cragg, and Zebiri (1997: 164–166) discuss Askari's book *Inter Religion* (Aligarh: 1977), and different articles from his hand.
146 Cragg (1985b: 119).
147 Translated by Cragg from *Verse et controverse*, Cragg (1985b: 120).
148 Askari (1972: 481).
149 Ibid., p. 482.
150 Ibid., p. 483.
151 Ibid., p. 484.
152 Ibid., pp. 484–485.
153 Askari (1985: 205–206). Discussed in Zebiri (1997: 164f.).
154 Ali Asghar Engineer, *Islam and Liberation Theology: Essays on Liberative Elements in Islam*. New Delhi (1995), and *Religion and Liberation*. New Delhi (1989).
155 Engineer (1991: 18).
156 Ibid., p. 24.
157 About Shariʿati, see Cragg (1985b: ch. 5).
158 *On the Sociology of Islam*. London: Al Hoda (1991: 101).
159 Ibid., pp. 158f.
160 *Imam* 1984:1, p. 40; cf. W. M. Watt, *Islamic Fundamentalism and Modernity*. London: Routledge (1988: 121f.).
161 Hammudah Abdalati, *Islam in Focus*. Indianapolis: American Trust Publications (1975: xiii).
162 Ibid., p. 153f.
163 Ibid., p. 153.
164 Ibid., p. 156.
165 Ibid., p. 159.
166 Maqsood (1991: 176).
167 Ibid., p. 62.
168 Ibid., pp. 147–160.
169 Zebiri (1997: 59).
170 Muslim–Christian Research Group (1989: 76–86).
171 Ibid., pp. 80f.
172 Ibid., p. 82.
173 Ibid., p. 85.
174 See ibid., pp. 47–75: 'Toward a Christian Perception of the Qur'ān'.
175 Soroudi (1979: 222).

176 Ibid., p. 224.
177 Ibid., p. 226.
178 Ibid., p. 227.
179 Ibid., p. 228.
180 Addleton (1990: 98).
181 Ibid., p. 101.
182 Quoted from ibid., p. 102.
183 Quoted from ibid., p. 103.
184 Quoted from ibid., p. 104.
185 Engineer (1991: 20).
186 Bhajjan and Yesudas (1985: 219). Quoted by Goddard (1994: 180).
187 See Mitri Raheb, 'Kristus i Palestina', in *Betlehem under beleiring* ('Bethlehem under siege'). Oslo: Luther forlag (2005: 107–111) and the web presentation 'Christ in the Palestinian context' (http://www.annadwa.org/resources/articles/christ_article.htm) – accessed July 2009.
188 My translation from Norwegian. See Arne Guttormsen, 'Saddams lege maler Kristus', *Vårt Land* 14 May 2004, p. 18f.
189 Cragg (1985a: 64). About Maḥmūd Darwısh and his image of Christ, see also Borrmans (1996: 198–200).
190 Ibid., Cragg refers to the article by J. R. King, 'The Theme of Alienation in Contemporary Middle Eastern Literature', in *The Muslim World*, 2 (1978: 111–131).
191 Hallo - ich möchte Jesus sprechen. Ja – wer bist du? Ich spreche von Israel aus, an meinen Füssen sind Nägel, ich trage eine Dornenkrone. Welchen Weg soll ich wählen, Sohn Gottes, welchen Weg? Soll ich nicht mehr an die süsse Erlösung glauben oder soll ich weggehen? Und was, wenn ich gehe und sterbe? Ich sage euch: Vorvärts, ihr Menschen! (Wild 1984: 290).
192 Ibid., p. 280f.
193 Pinault 1987, p. 118.
194 Ibid., p. 120.
195 Quoted from Pierre Cachia, *An Overview of Modern Arabic Literature*. Edinburgh: Edinburgh University Press (1990: 209).
196 In *Modern Arabic Literature and the West*, London: Ithaca Press (1985: 47–49).
197 Pinault (1987: 120).
198 Quoted from ibid.
199 Ibid., p. 121 (Note 21).
200 Quoted from ibid., p. 117.
201 For al-Bayyātī's image of Christ, see also Borrmans (1996: 196f.).
202 Ibid., pp. 117f. (Note 14). Cf. Issa J. Boullata, 'The Beleaguered Unicorn: A Study of Tawfīq Ṣāyigh', in *Journal of Arabic Literature*, vol. IV (1973: 69–93).
203 Cf. also Borrmans (1996: 193–196).

204 Pinault (1987: 124), cf. Khalidi (2003: 63–65).
205 Quoted from Mounad A. Khouri and Hamid Algar, *An anthology of Modern Arabic Poetry*. Berkeley: University of California Press (1977: 99).
206 Quoted from ibid., pp. 100f.
207 Pinault (1987: 116f.).
208 Pinault cites and discusses Yūsuf al-Khāl and Khalīl Ḥawī, ibid., pp. 121–123 (Note 23).
209 According to A. Khouri and Hamid Algar, *An anthology of Modern Arabic Poetry* (1977: 13; both al-Bayyātī and al-Sayyāb were related to the Iraqi Communist Party.
210 More specifically, Pinault points to the Arab reception of James Frazer's *The Golden Bough* (about 'dying and reviving Gods') and T. S. Eliot's use of Frazer in *The Waste Land*.
211 See the comprehensive bibliography in Hugh Goddard (1987, 1990), and Goddard (1996) for a more thorough discussion of the most well-known contributions to Christian–Muslim dialogue.
212 Schumann (1988: 7, Note 20).
213 See his *Muḥammad: Al-rasūl wa-l-risāla* (1958), and *Muḥammad – fī ḥayātihi al-khāṣṣa*.
214 M. Kāmil Ḥuṣayn: *Al-ḏikr al-ḥākim*. Cairo: Maktabat al-nahḍat al-miṣriyya (n.d. [1972]).
215 See translation of excerpts in Gaudeul (1990: vol. II, pp. 304–307) and comments in Ford (2001: 15f.).
216 Ḥusayn (1954, first Arabic edition, and 1994, latest English edition). For discussion of the original Arabic edition, see Anawati (1955), ʿAbd al-Tafāhum [Cragg] (1956), Jomier (1958) and al-Rahman (1961). As for the English translation, see Kenneth Cragg's 'Introduction' and 'Annexes' to Ḥusayn (1957/1994). For later discussions, see Encounter (1982: 5–7), Cragg (1985b: 126–144), Goddard (1987: 82–84), Engineer (1991: 22), Kekli (1995), Vogelaar (1995), Goddard (1996: 96–118) and Borrmans (1996: 168–175).

For Ḥusayn's understanding of the key notion *ẓulm* (*ẓālima*), see Kāmil Muḥammad Ḥusain, 'The Meaning of ẓulm in the Qur'ān', *The Muslim World* XLIX (1959: 196–212).
217 Ḥusayn (1994: 29).
218 Ibid., p. 125.
219 For the following, see the English 1994–edition, pp. 29f. and the Arabic edition, pp. 1–3.
220 Ibid., p. 29.
221 Cf. the title of the book, *qarya ẓālima*, which alludes to a qur'ānic expression of wrongdoing populations being punished by God; Qur'ān 21.11 and 22.45 and 48. Cf. Kāmil Ḥusayn/Kenneth Cragg, 'The Meaning of ẓulm in the Qur'ān', in *The Muslim World* (1959: 196–212).

222 Ibid., p. 30.
223 Originally published in *Al-Ahram* in 1960.
224 Al-Rahman (1961: 149–150).
225 In Ḥusayn (1994: 231).
226 Vogelaar (1995: 414).
227 In his Introduction to *City of Wrong* (Hussein 1994).
228 Ibid., p. 150.
229 Ibid., pp. 107, 125.
230 Ibid., pp. 186, 227.
231 See ibid., pp. 226f., and Kenneth Cragg's 'Introduction', pp. 17–19.
232 In English in the collection *I am Free and Other Stories*. Cairo: General Egyptian Book Organization (1978).
233 Op. cit., p. 51.
234 Ibid.
235 Translated into English as 'Murder in Baghdad' by K. I. Semaan, in Vol. I of *Arabic Translation Series of the Journal of Arabic Literature*, Leiden, 1972. Cf. Goddard (1987/1990/1996) for the following. For a discussion of this and other works by al-Ṣabūr, see Kenneth Cragg, *Troubled by Truth: Life Studies in Inter-Faith Concern*. Edinburgh/Cambridge/Durham: The Pentland Press (1992: ch. 9). Cf. also Louis Tremaine 'Witnesses to the Event in Ma'sāt al-Ḥallāj and Murder in the Cathedral', *The Muslim World* (1977: 33–46).
236 Cragg (1985a: 65), cf. Goddard (1990: 254).
237 About al-Nowaihi, see *In quest of an Islamic Humanism: Arabic and Islamic Studies in Memory of Mohamed al-Nowaihi*, edited by A. H. Green. Cairo: The American University in Cairo Press (1984/1986).
238 Including Goddard (1978, 1990, 1996) and Bijlefeld (1982).
239 Quoted from Goddard (1978: 86)/Goddard (1996: 138).
240 Quoted from ibid.
241 Quoted from Bijlefeld (1982: 208).
242 Al-Nowaihi (1976: 217f.). Cf. his article *Al-ilḥām al-šiʿrī bayna l-masīḥiyya wa-l-islām* ('Poetic inspiration between Christianity and Islam'), in *Al-Risāla* 54 (1964).
243 Al-Nowaihi (1976: 221).
244 Leirvik (2006), cf. Leirvik (2002, 2003, 2008).
245 Al-Saḥḥār (1951). Discussed by Jomier (1958), al-Ḥuysanī (1960), Bütler (1965), Encounter (1982), Cragg (1985a: 54–55), Goddard (1996: 118–120), Borrmans (1996: 179–182) and Ford (2001: 14).
246 Quoted from Bütler (1965: 328).
247 Quoted from ibid.
248 Ibid.
249 Goddard (1996: 119).
250 Cf. Cragg (1985a: 54).
251 Quoted from Cragg (1985a: 55).

252 The original edition was reviewed in *The Muslim World* (1953: 218–219), by Butrus ʿAbd al-Malik. Last edition Cairo (n.d., in the 1990s). The work is discussed in Cragg (1954), el-Didy (n.d. [1956]), Jomier (1958), Farès (1959: 31–52), Encounter (1982: 3–5), Cragg (1985a: 53–54), Goddard (1987: 74–77; and 1996: 120–121), Kamel (1990: 79–122), Engineer (1991: 23–24), Borrmans (1996: 164–167), Ford (2001) and Leirvik (2006).
253 Schumann (1988: ch. 8 [first ed. Gütersloh 1975]).
254 Ford (2001; a book based on Ford's doctoral dissertation from 1998). The quotations from al-ʿAqqād's work in the following are my own translations, although checked in some detail with those of Peter Ford.
255 Cf. Ford (2001: 52f.).
256 Cf. ibid., pp. 88–90.
257 al-ʿAqqād (n.d.: 150).
258 al-ʿAqqād (n.d./1953: 80). My translation.
259 The title of one of the book's main chapters, cf. ibid., pp. 99 ff.
260 Cf. ibid., pp. 101, 102, 105, 106, 107.
261 Ibid., p. 101. My translation.
262 Ibid., p. 151.
263 Ibid., p. 160.
264 Ibid., p. 165. My translation.
265 Ibid., p. 173. My translation.
266 A recent edition of *Allāh* is Cairo: Dār Nahḍat Miṣr (1994).
267 Op. cit., p. 109.
268 Goddard (1996: 121).
269 Ibid., p. 103. Cf. p. 97: *mutafaqqihūn*.
270 Ibid., p. 113.
271 Ibid., p. 99.
272 Ford (2001: 62).
273 Ibid.
274 ʿUthmān (1966: 461 pages in all). The first edition (1961) was reviewed by Kenneth Nolin in *The Muslim World* (1963: 252–254). His work is thoroughly discussed in Schumann (1988; also with parts of the book translated), cf. Cragg (1985a: 56), Goddard (1996: 121–123) and Borrmans (1996: 182–185).
275 ʿUthmān (1966: 285).
276 Ibid.
277 The so-called 'Busṭānı-van Dyck Bible' follows the Greek manuscripts underlying the so-called *textus receptus* in this respect.
278 Ibid., p. 413.
279 Ibid.
280 Ibid.
281 Ibid.
282 Ibid., p. 434.

283 Ibid., p. 436.
284 Cragg (1985a: 56).
285 ʿUthmān (1966: 414).
286 Dublin/New York: Veritas Press/Paulist Press (1975/1977).
287 Osman [ʿUthmān] (1977: 451).
288 Ibid.
289 Ibid., p. 452.
290 Ibid., pp. 453f.
291 Cf. Yvonne Yazbek Haddad, 'Christians in a Muslim State: The Recent Egyptian Debate', in Haddad and Haddad (eds.), *Christian–Muslim Encounters*. Gainesville: University of Florida Press (1995: 392).
292 The novel was first serialized in Egypt (in *Al-Ahram*) in 1957, then published as a book in Lebanon in 1967. English translation by P. Stewart, *Children of Gebelawi*, London (1981). Discussions of the political and religious implications of this controversial work of fiction include Cragg (1985b: 145–164), Goddard (1996: 123–127) as well as William Shepard, 'Satanic Verses and the Death of God: Salmān Rushdie and Najıb Maḥfūẓ', in *The Muslim World*, 1–2 (1992: 99–111); Jareer Abu-Haidar, 'Awlād Ḥāratinā by Najıb Maḥfūẓ: An event in the Arab World', in *Journal ofArabic Literature* XVI (1985: 119–131); and M. M. Badawi, 'Maḥfūẓ's story of Creation and Prophecy', in *Modern Arabic Literature and the West* (1985: 167–171).
293 Cf. his short story 'Zaabalawi', translated by Denys Johnson Davies, in *Modern Arabic Short Stories*, London (1967: 137–147) and in Naguib Mahfouz, *The Time and Place and Other Stories*. Cairo: The American University in Cairo Press (1991: 1–14).
294 Maḥfūẓ (1981: 151).
295 Ibid., p. 173.
296 Ibid., p. 197.
297 Ibid., p. 235.
298 Ibid., p. 251.
299 Ibid., p. 322.
300 Cf. William Shepard, op. cit.
301 Encounter (1982: 10). Translated from Jomier (1958).
302 Cf. E. S. Sabanegh, *Muhammad B. Abdallah – 'Le Prophète'. Portraits contemporains Egypte 1930–1950*. Paris: Libraire J. Vrin (1983), and Antonie Wessels, *A Modern Arabic Biography of Muḥammad: A Critical Study of Muḥammad Ḥusayn Haykal's Ḥayāt Muḥammad*. Leiden: E. J. Brill (1972).
303 *Min hunā nabdaʾ*. Cairo: Dār al-Nıl (1950, 3rd ed.). English edition, *From Here we Start*.Washington DC (1953, translated by I. R. el-Faruqi).
304 See *Al-dawla fī-l-islām* ('The State in Islam'). Cairo: Dār Thābit (1981).
305 See the report from a visit made by Pope Shenouda to the hospital shortly before Khālid died on March 1, 1996 – in *Al-Musawwar*, February 23,

1996 (*'Liqā' muṯır bayn al-bābā Šanūda wa-Khālid Muḥammad Khālid'*).
306 See the collection of speeches given in radio broadcasts at the beginning of the 1950s, first published in 1953 with the title *Al-dīn fī ḫidmat al-šaʿb*, and re-edited with the title *Al-dīn li-l- šaʿb* ('Religion to the people'), latest edition by Dār al-Muqaṭṭam, Cairo (1994).
307 The book is discussed by Jomier (1958), Bütler (1965), Encounter (1982: 7–9), Cragg (1985a: 52f.), Goddard (1996: 156–158) and Borrmans (1996: 175–179).
308 Khālid (n.d./1958: 7). My translation.
309 Ibid., p. 33.
310 Ibid., pp. 40f.
311 Ibid., p. 8. My translation.
312 Ibid., pp. 64f.
313 Ibid., p. 115.
314 Cf. the chapter with the same title in his book *Al-dīn li-l-šaʿb*, containing broadcasted speeches from 1953. Recent edition by Dār al-Muqaṭṭam, Cairo (1994: 157–166, this chapter).
315 Ibid., pp. 98f.
316 Khālid (n.d./1958: 96). My translation. Cf. pp. 108 and 133.
317 Ibid., p. 108.
318 Ibid., p. 116.
319 Ibid., pp. 124f.
320 Ibid., p. 133.
321 Ibid., p. 137.
322 Ibid., pp. 139f.
323 Ibid., pp. 154–156.
324 Ibid., pp. 160f.
325 Ibid., p. 174.
326 Ibid., p. 175.
327 Ibid., p. 179. My translation.
328 Ibid., pp. 187f. My translation.
329 Ibid., p. 189.
330 Ibid., p. 188.
331 The final sentence of the book, ibid., p. 190.
332 Cragg (1985: 53).
333 See Goddard (1996: 158–163).
334 Leirvik (2006) builds on his doctoral dissertation from 2002 (Leirvik 2002). Cf. summaries in Leirvik (2003, 2008).
335 Leirvik (2006: 90–124).
336 al-ʿAqqād (1985/1942: 143).
337 Ibid., p. 6.
338 Ibid., p. 22.
339 Ibid., p. 13.

340 ʿAbbās M. al-ʿAqqād, *Al-tafkīr – farīḍa islāmiyya*. Cairo: Dār Nahḍat Miṣr (n.d./1961: 111).
341 ʿAbbās M. al-ʿAqqād, *Al-falsafa al-qur'āniyya*. Kairo: Dār Nahḍat Miṣr (n.d./1947: 167).
342 Cf. Leirvik (2006: 104f.).
343 *al-nafs la-ammāra bi-s-sūʾ* (Qur'ān 12.53), *al-nafs al-lawwāma* (Qur'ān 75.2) and *al-nafs al-muṭmaʾinna* (Qur'ān 89.27).
344 ʿAbbās Maḥmūd al-ʿAqqād, *Al-insān fī-l-Qur'ān* ('The Human Being according to the Qur'ān'). Cairo: Dār Nahḍat Miṣr, (n.d. [1961]: 30).
345 Leirvik (2006: 172–191).
346 Cragg (1985b: 138).
347 Hussein (1994: 231), cf. Ḥusayn (1954: 262).
348 Husain (1977). First published in Arabic in 1968. 'The hallowed valley' refers to the qur'ānic description of the sacred ground where Moses took off his shoes, cf. Qur'ān 20.10–16.
349 Husain (1977: 57f., 61).
350 Ibid., p. 89.
351 Vogelaar (1995: 411).
352 Ibid., p. 413, citing Ḥusayn's Diary of 1928.
353 Husain (1977: 56).
354 Ibid., p. 12.
355 Vogelaar (1995: 416).
356 Leirvik (2006: 125–171).
357 Khālid (1994/1960: 9). My translation.
358 One of the sources given for the author's tracing of human conscience down the ages, is J. H. Brested's book *The Dawn of Conscience*, translated into Arabic by Salīm Ḥassan under the title *Fajr al-ḍamīr.*
359 Khālid (1971/1963: 5–6). My translation.
360 Cf. al-Ghazālī's concept of divine light/the light of the heart as a prerequisite of right knowledge, as expressed in *Al-munqiḏ min al-ḍalāl* as well as in *Iḥyāʾ*.
361 Khālid (1971/1963: 109, 111, 117). My translations.
362 Ibid., p. 123, cf. pp. 137, 139.
363 Ibid., pp. 137, 139.
364 Ibid., pp. 170–172.
365 Ibid., p. 174.
366 Ibid., p. 236.
367 Note the more positive flavour of the same word which – in the somewhat different sense of 'experiment' – was used to depict the overruling of the prophetic spirit by the spirit of reason in Khālid (n.d./1958: 33).
368 Ibid., pp. 219f.
369 Ibid., p. 220. My translation.
370 Ibid., p. 222. My translation. The epithet *ibnuhu al-bārr* (son of conscience) is also used for Socrates, cf. ibid., pp. 71, 81.

371 Ibid., p. 237. My translation.
372 Cf. ibid., p. 5.
373 Cf. apart from *Al-dawla fī-l-islām* his books *Al-dīmuqrāṭiyya, abadan* (from the early 1950s), *Difāʿ ʿan al-dīmuqrāṭiyya* (from the early 1980s).

Chapter 8

Issues of Dialogue

Why Christology?

Looking for issues of dialogue, one would first of all have to consider whether Christology can really be the kind of common ground that a genuine dialogue requires. Like many others, Mona Siddiqui (1997) raises the question of:

> . . . whether the use of a particular Christian concept such as christology, and all the issues associated with it, can be applied in the Islamic context. But in using this term even in an Islamic vision, all that is being discussed is the nature and person of Jesus; it does not imply an affirmation of any particular Christian perception.[1]

As for the status of Christology in a Christian–Muslim dialogue, Smail Balić claims, more sceptically, that:

> It is primarily Christian missionaries, or certain Orientalists who are either themselves theologians, or who are well disposed to Christian theology, who overestimate the role of Jesus in the Koran. They are misled by the way of understanding which they retain from their Christian tradition.[2]

Even more pessimistically, he foresees that 'no practical results are likely to come from Muslim–Christian dialogue in regard to Christ'.[3] Interestingly, an important reason for his rejection of Christology seems to be the 'miraculous' bias of the Islamic image of Jesus:

> In a time when biblical miracles prove less and less convincing, the Koranic image of Jesus, laden with legendary chimeras, threatens to fade even more.[4]

So, instead of meditating on the legends and miracles of the past, he suggests that Muslims and Christians come together in a theological and ethical endeavour:

> Only a return to the common source, belief in God, and common ethicosocial and religious objectives can guarantee meaningful dialogue and productive cooperation.[5]

'The ethical connection' will be dealt with below. In spite of Balić's reluctance, we will first examine some aspects of the christological issues at stake. These can hardly be avoided in a Christian–Muslim dialogue, for at least three reasons:

1. Christology is the heart of Christian theology, and must be taken seriously as a central point of reference in the self-understanding of the Church. For the Church, there is a need continually to rethink the question of Christology in an Islamic context – as part of the more general task of a contextualized theology.
2. Christology is in fact dealt with as an issue from the Muslim side – both in Muslim polemics, medieval and modern, and in more dialogical contributions from Muslims.
3. Christology is not an isolated subject, but touches upon fundamental issues in anthropology and theology as well as in ethics. This is true both for Christians and, in a different sense, for Muslims.

Jesus and Muḥammad

As we have seen above (in the section about Khālid Muḥammad Khālid in Chapter 7), Khālid's appraisal of Christ as a champion of human dignity and the integrity conscience is unfolded in a context where his main interest is that of showing that in this respect, Muḥammad and Christ are brothers:

> *That is exactly what I want to say to those who believe in Christ and those who believe in Muḥammad: If you are sincere, the proof of your faith is that today, one and all of you embark upon the task of protecting the human being . . . protecting life!*[6]

Khālid's effort may be compared to reconciliatory efforts from the Christian side, such as that of William E. Phipps in his *Muhammad and Jesus: A Comparison of the Prophets and Their Teachings* (1996). At the bottom of Phipps' exposition lies the contention that 'Much of the uniqueness of Islam and Christianity is in the character of the founders'.[7] Without downplaying the differences, Phipps looks for a mutual esteem for the 'founders' of Christianity and Islam. He relates the estimation of Muḥammad and Jesus to general anthropological and theological issues, sometimes blurring the difference between historical-critical approaches and discussions relying upon faith images. Like Khālid in his preface, Phipps ends his comparison with the suggestion that the practical, life-affirming impact of faith should be the final criterion of estimation. Phipps cites the qur'ānic invitation to 'compete in goodness' (5.48) and the evangelical insight that believers shall be known by their fruits (Matthew 7.20), as well as Gotthold Lessing's parable of the three rings, and concludes:

> Children of Abraham should get beyond asserting that Moses, Jesus, or Muhammad is the greatest, and let the impact of their messages be the standard for evaluation.[8]

Kenneth Cragg combines his interest in *Jesus and the Muslim* (Cragg 1985a) with attempts at a Christian appraisal of Prophet Muḥammad, under the heading *Muhammad and the Christian: A Question of Response* (Cragg 1984). By the latter, he intends to give a reply to the legitimate demand from Muslims committed to dialogue with Christians, to know what they say of Muḥammad:

> A Christian 'recognition' of the Prophet of Islam has long been a concern, indeed a demand, of Muslims in their exchanges with Christians. 'Why do you not acknowledge our Prophet?' is a familiar question, and an insistent one on occasions of what is currently called 'dialogue', or between disciples of the two monotheisms in their day-to-day relationships. An adequate response from the Christian side is certainly owed.[9]

David Kerr (1995, 1997) notes that in the otherwise positive evaluations of Islam in the documents from Second Vatican council of the Roman Catholic Church, the question of Muḥammad as a prophet was not addressed. This is true both for the declaration *Lumen Gentium* (1964) and the subsequent *Nostra Aetate* (1965) declarations. In *Lumen Gentium*, the place of Muslims in God's 'plan of salvation' is acknowledged. However:

> . . . the council preferred to acknowledge Muslims' 'profession to hold the faith of Abraham' than to mention their more characteristic adherence to the faith of Muhammad. Muhammad's ministry and message were again passed over in silence when the council elaborated its esteem for Muslims in the 1965 Nostra Aetate declaration.[10]

Historically, Christian apologetics, aimed at defending the confession that Christ is the Son of God, have often been paralleled by overt or implied accusations that Muḥammad is a false prophet. There are good reasons for saying that unless the question of Muḥammad's prophethood is addressed in a more nuanced manner, Islam is not really taken seriously as a partner in dialogue. Many would contend that unless Christians in one sense or other recognize Muḥammad as a prophet, they can hardly expect more respect for the biblical witness about Christ from their Muslim partners in dialogue. Mona Siddiqui warns that without a dual commitment to rethinking of stereotyped images, the notions of Christ and Muḥammad among ordinary believers will probably be left in the following stalemate, with a rather uneven balance of esteem: 'We are . . . left with a Christian prophet who is revered as God incarnate and a Muslim messenger that is reduced to the status of a false prophet.'[11]

In the following, the question of Jesus and Muḥammad will be approached along two lines: one historical, on faith-oriented.

Historical Jesus, Historical Muḥammad

Since the introduction of critical historical research as an independent discipline in the West, Western Christianity has lived with a distinction between 'the historical Jesus' and 'the Christ of faith'. The Christ of faith relies both on the interpretative accounts of the Christ-event as recorded and preached in the Gospels, and the Pauline *kerygma* of a crucified and resurrected Saviour. 'The historical Jesus' refers to the historical events behind the interpretative efforts of the New Testament, and can only be the object of hypothetical reconstructions.

The Quest for the Historical Jesus

Beginning in the eighteenth, but especially since the nineteenth century, there has been a more or less continuous quest for the historical Jesus, in critical distance from the image of Christ as portrayed by the churches. The quest has been countered by many with the claim that the historical Jesus is inaccessible, since the Gospels only reflect the Christ that was proclaimed by the first Christians. Those who search for a 'historical Jesus' have often been accused of finding little more than a reflection of their own ideas of how Jesus Christ ought to be portrayed, in order to fit with liberal or subversive ideals.

But the quest has not been silenced, and from the 1980s, there has been a so-called 'third quest' for the historical Jesus.[12] Characteristic of the third quest – with its historical optimism and call for contemporary relevance – is a book title of Marcus Borg, *Meeting Christ Again for the First Time: The Historical Jesus and the Heart of Contemporary Faith*.[13] On the one hand, Borg joins the centuries long chain of those claiming to have discovered who Jesus truly was – according to Borg, 'a charismatic, who was a healer, sage, prophet, and revitalisation movement founder'.[14] On the other hand, he claims a contemporary relevance for his historical hypothesis: 'to follow Jesus means in some sense to be "like him", to take seriously what he took seriously', thus providing us with 'an alternative vision of life'.[15]

Many representatives of the third quest portray Jesus in a sapiential mode, as a wisdom teacher possibly in the likeness of Hellenistic Cynic itinerant preachers. Others focus on his practice of healing, and still others on his roots in the egalitarian values of Mediterranean peasants. All these foci may be combined, as in John Dominic Crossan's portrayal of Jesus as a teacher of subversive wisdom, confronting social and religious brokers, and practising free healing and open 'commensality' (open sharing of meals).[16] Whereas those who focus on the subversive wisdom teacher mainly portray Jesus in his Galilean activity, others focus on Jesus' confrontation of the temple in Jerusalem, and contend that a record of the historical Jesus should first of all be able to 'offer a connection between his activity and his death'.[17]

Behind the third quest lies new historical material that is now available and perceived advances in social and historical sciences (such as social anthropology applied to the ancient world, and fresh studies of Judaism). For New Testament scholarship, the background knowledge of both Judaism and the ancient world has been increasing, as has the foreground knowledge of early Christianity. The 1945 Nag Hammadi discoveries of the Gospel of Thomas, other apocryphal Gospel fragments and other Christian Gnostic documents, as well as the 1947 Qumran discoveries (the Dead Sea Scrolls), have provided researchers with wellsprings of fresh information both about early Christianity and about contemporary Judaism. Jewish scholars (like Joseph Klausner and Géza Vermès) have played an important part in the new quest for the historical Jesus, portraying 'The Religion of Jesus the Jew'.[18]

In a comparison of 'Jesus in the Bible vs. Jesus in the Qur'an' (with the subtitle 'Which is the more historical?'), Andy Bannister attempts to apply the latest New Testament research in order to evaluate the historicity of the qur'anic accounts about Jesus. Not surprisingly, he finds that the Jewish details of Jesus' life are poorly reflected in the Qur'an and concludes: '. . . the qur'anic Jesus does not fit the first century. Rather he is the Jesus of polemic, and the target of this polemic looks like seventh-century Syriac Christianity.'[19]

Bannister's approach is marked by an apologetic interest in proving the historicity of Jesus as portrayed in the Gospels. Among other Christian scholars, there has been a resumed historical critique of the Gospels, leaving little that may be considered as genuine words or even genuine teachings of Jesus (cf. the controversial judgements of the American 'Jesus Seminar'[20]). The Jesus Seminar significantly speaks of 'the five Gospels', including the Gospel of Thomas in their research, with a dating of Thomas possibly before that of the biblical Gospels.[21] In contrast to the biblical Gospels, the Gospel of Thomas is a sayings Gospel, containing no narrative strings, and no passion story.

Parallel to the discovery of a complete and genuine sayings Gospel in Nag Hammadi – the Gospel of Thomas – there has been a renewed interest in the hypothetical sayings Gospel 'Q', that can be detected as a source for the Gospels of Matthew and Luke.[22] The genre of a sayings Gospel is of course of special interest for a Christian–Muslim dialogue, since the Muslim assumption has always been that the *injīl* was indeed a sayings Gospel, containing the words of God given to Christ. And interest increases when considering the fact that in the Gospel of Thomas and the hypothetical 'Q', crucifixion is not a crucial theme, neither is divine sonship.

The new focus on sayings Gospels and Christ the Wisdom teacher, has been paralleled by renewed efforts to reclaim Christ for a New Age-oriented spirituality, or for Buddhism.[23] Others reclaim Christ as healer and magician.[24]

It remains to be seen whether the focus on the genre of sayings Gospels and on Christ as (merely) a wisdom teacher, healer and spiritual guide will influence Christian–Muslim dialogue. The noted tendencies within the third quest are, however, highly controversial, both among New Testament scholars and in the churches. Some scholars vehemently criticize The Jesus Seminar and the sayings Gospel advocates for their ideological biases, claiming that their research brings little new of substantial historical information.[25] Also on purely historical grounds, scholars accuse the sayings Gospel advocates of falling short of explaining why Christ actually was crucified, or rather of putting this crucial question in brackets. E. P. Sanders, one of the representatives of the third quest, is critical of over-focusing the sayings material:

> . . . the teaching material in the Gospels has not yielded a convincing historical depiction of Jesus – one which sets him firmly in Jewish history, which explains his execution, and which explains why his followers formed a persecuted messianic sect.[26]

The Historical Muḥammad

In traditional Muslim scholarship, the text of revelation is most often regarded as a given fact, and the task of interpretation is conceived of as an effort to establish the 'genuine' meaning of revelation. We have seen that some Muslims have utilized critical biblical scholarship in the West for polemical and apologetic purposes, even claiming a 'genuine Muslim' Gospel (the 'Gospel of Barnabas') alternative to the deconstructed Gospels of the Bible.

If there is to be a genuine dialogue on faith and history, the scope of the conversation must be widened, and Muslim sources included in the discussion.[27] Part of William E. Phipps' study of *Muhammad and Jesus* (1996) is conducted with a view to comparing the historical Muḥammad with the historical Jesus. In an article about 'Jesus and Muḥammad: A Historian's Reflections', F. E. Peters (1996) calls for a joint reflection on faith and history in Islam and Christianity. The question of 'the historical Muḥammad' is no more settled than that of 'the historical Jesus'. As Peters puts it:

> Between the historical Muḥammad . . . and the Muḥammad of history who grew up in his wake stands the dynamics of Muslim piety . . .. The Muḥammad of history [i.e. of piety and faith] has in fact become far more

> than a mere mortal in a variety of ways . . . a veneration of Muḥammad grew into the dogma of the impeccability of the Prophet.[28]

A related problem is, of course, the discussion of the reliability of Ḥadīth material – whether particular sayings attributed to the Prophet should be regarded as his authentic word and teaching, or rather as a reflection of the views that were held by the first Muslim communities. As in the case of the Gospels, the question can hardly be settled: Christ and Muḥammad can only be approached through the first believers' reconstruction of the life and teachings of their 'founder-teacher', and by our own interpretative efforts, when we become involved in the 'event' of God's revelation.

As for the Qur'ān, the question of the historical reliability of the message considered to have been 'sent down', in terms of its correspondence to Muḥammad's actual preaching, would seem to be less acute than what applies to the Ḥadīth collections. But the questions of a historical-contextual interpretation of the Qur'ān and the hermeneutics of reception remain highly controversial within the Muslim community.

Revelation as an Inclusive, Dialogical Event

The question has repeatedly been raised whether hypothetical reconstruction of the words of Muḥammad is really worth the effort. Returning to the question of Gospel genres (sayings Gospels or narrative Gospels), many would claim that inspired narration is constitutive of a Jewish-Christian construction of faith. The implication would be that Christianity has never relied upon a reconstruction of the genuine words of Jesus, but upon the Christ-event that takes place in the encounter between a believing church and a manifold memory of Christ. The plural (and possibly 'contradictory') witnesses of Christ should thus not be taken as a problem, but rather be regarded as reflecting the dialogical character of the event of revelation itself.

The concept of revelation as an inclusive, perhaps dialogical 'event', need not to be foreign to a Muslim sensibility. In his *Qur'ān, Pluralism and Liberation*,[29] Farid Esack speaks of the 'event-ness'of the Qur'ān.[30] The context is his outline of a qur'ānic hermeneutics, which is marked by key words like contextuality, progressive revelation and reader's reception:

> The challenge for every generation of believers is to discover their own moment of revelation, their own intermission in revelation, their own frustrations with God, joy with His consoling grace, and their own guidance by the principle of progressive revelation. For the numerous Muslims who experience existence as marginalised and oppressed communities or individuals, this discovery clearly has to take place amidst their own Meccan crucibles of the engagement between oppressor and oppressed, the

> Abyssinian sojourn amidst the gracious and warm hospitality of 'the Other' and the liberating practice in Medina.[31]

A Christian–Muslim dialogue about Christ and the Qur'ān as events in time and space, related to the struggle for human liberation, might prove to break new ground – provided that there is a fundamental readiness on both sides to leave the concept of unambiguous meaning behind, and to apply hermeneutical insights as critical tools for understanding and practice.

Christ of Faith, Muḥammad of Faith

In her essay about 'The Image of Christ in Islam: Scripture and Sentiment', Mona Siddiqui (1997) points to the fact that the historical questions between Jesus and Muḥammad include that of whether Jesus did in fact prophesy the coming of Muḥammad. She notes that verses from the Bible used by Muslims to demonstrate this claim are generally dismissed as 'naive and ignorant and not worthy of serious consideration' by most Christian scholars. Without addressing the purely historical questions at stake, Siddiqui approaches the issue from a more general, interpretative angle:

> Perhaps this is the real problem within interfaith dialogue that any scriptural cross-referencing is regarded as inventive nonsense. Since most religious traditions look for the sacred in the written word, interpretation of religious texts from outside the faith is regarded with caution or dismissed. This poses a particular problem for Islam because, though the third of the monotheistic Semitic faiths, it is not regarded as a unique confirmation of the Judaeo-Christian tradition. Thus, neither its Scripture nor its prophet is seen as a confirmation of what preceded or a prophecy that was foretold.[32]

Christian Estimation of Muḥammad

In the history of Christian–Muslim apologetics, the early testimony of the Nestorian Patriarch Timothy I in Baghdad, from his dialogue in 781 with the Caliph al-Mahdī, has become famous. As an exception to what became the rule on the Christian side – to denounce Muḥammad as a false prophet – Timothy assured the Caliph that Muḥammad was 'worthy of all praise' and 'walked in the path of the prophets' (cf. the section about Christian apologetics under Muslim rule, in Chapter 6).

If Christians can recognize that Muḥammad (by his monotheistic message and in promoting good works) did indeed walk in the path of the prophets, how should his specific prophetic mission be conceived of? Examining some modern attempts on the Christian side to answer the question 'What say ye of

Muhammad?', David Kerr (1996) notes (as one would expect) that the nuances of the answer correspond to a more general theology of religion on the part of the respondents. If one relates the question of Muḥammad to the much cited and debated alternatives of an exclusivist, inclusivist and pluralist theology of religions respectively,[33] one would probably find the following matrix:

In an exclusivist theology of religions, no salvation outside the Church is recognized. According to this position, salvation presupposes an explicit confession of Christ as Saviour. Within this paradigm of thought, Muḥammad can hardly be seen as anything but a false prophet, since he denies the divinity of Christ, and thus the core of the church' confession of Christ as Saviour.

According to the inclusivist position, Christ is seen as 'fulfilling the best' in all religions. If Christ's redemption is cosmic, one can hardly say that explicit confession of Christ is necessary for salvation. But in the view of an inclusivist theologian, the potential redemptive nature of other faiths cannot be acknowledged without presupposing their fulfilment in Christ. Within this matrix, Muḥammad can be accepted as a prophet on a par with Old Testament prophets, or even as an extra-Christian witness to Christ's second coming as a Messiah. But he will have to be subordinated to Christ in God's universal plan of salvation.

Many would contend that with a pluralist theology of religions, there is the possibility of a fuller recognition of Muḥammad as a prophet. The pluralist position implies the intention of dealing with other religions not through Christian lenses, but on their own terms. Divine truth is seen as transcending the particular expressions of all religions. According to this position, Christ should not be seen as totally unique, and theology should put God at the centre, not Christ. Within this paradigm, Muḥammad can be recognized as one of God's prophets in history, with his particular vocation. In accordance with the pluralist position, Muḥammad can be acknowledged as a voice of universal relevance, and not only as the guide of Muslims. It should be noted, however, that even the pluralist approach falls short of recognizing Muḥammad as a prophet in the Islamic sense – since a theologian inclined towards pluralism would not acknowledge him as the seal of prophets, and the carrier of a final revelation.

In terms of theology, neither Christians nor Muslims can easily find a paradigm of thought that recognizes the other's confession to Christ and Muḥammad – on the terms of the other. Probably, a more realistic outcome of a dialogue on Christ and Muḥammad would be that both parties understand and respect the inclusivist position of the other. Anything else would either perpetuate antagonistic positions (the exclusivist alternative), or (with the pluralist alternative) run the risk of dissolving the integrity of both religions and their truth claims.

The Ethoses of Christ and Muḥammad: Competing or Complementary?

A different way of approach, not so heavily loaded with theology, would be to raise the question of the different 'ethoses' of Christ and Muḥammad, as displayed by their different life stories, and mirrored by the faith witnesses of their early followers. With this kind of approach too, however, it is hard not to view the other through the lenses of the self.

Kenneth Cragg's estimation of Muḥammad (1984) appears to rely on a Christ-criterion, related to an inclusivist theology of religion. Basically, Cragg has a high esteem for Muḥammad's preaching:

> In the broadest terms, it means the rule of God, the reality of divine power, wisdom, mercy and justice. It means the strong permeation of the human scene with a consciousness of God, His claim, His creating, His sustaining, His ordaining.[34]

The decisive question for Cragg, however, is what happens if individuals and society fall short of accepting the command of God, as proclaimed by his prophets. What were the responses of Christ and Muḥammad respectively? According to Cragg, the most pressing question at stake is that of prophecy and power. As for Muḥammad, Cragg notes that:

> The whole logic of Muḥammad's career is that the verbal deliverance of prophetic truth fails of satisfaction and must therefore pass to the post-Hijrah invocation of power. The realization of what is preached comes about not only in the proper attentiveness of the immediately faithful but in the effective surmounting of the long-time obdurate.[35]

Generally, Cragg is more impressed by the Muḥammad of Mecca – devoid of any power other than the word – than the Muḥammad of Medina, who by the use of political and military authority laid the foundation for the long-term success of his mission. By making this distinction, Cragg clearly applies a Christian, or 'Christic' criterion, linked to the general conviction that 'The Messianic task and the political arm are not compatible'.[36] Cragg concludes his book on *Muḥammad and the Christian* by referring to Christ's insistence on distinguishing the matters of God from those of Caesar. Judging Muḥammad from this perspective, he strongly affirms his basic teachings of God's sovereignty, but regrets the post-Hijrah 'Caesar in Muḥammad':

> When Jesus replied to a questioner, 'Render to Caesar the things that are Caesar's and to God the things that are God's' (Matt. 22.21; Mark 12.17; Luke 20.25), he did not mean that Caesar's realm was one of divine indifference, an autonomy absolved of all transcendent reference. On the contrary,

> he meant that the things of God, in their inclusiveness, cannot be identified with the interests of Caesar or entrusted to his ways.
>
> It was Muḥammad's understanding of 'the things of God', which, after the Hijrah, put away the distinction. In his own person he saw them compatible. If, restoring Jesus' principle, we question or regret Caesar in Muḥammad, it will only be for the sake, in their Quranic form, of those same 'things of God!' which move us to acknowledge him.[37]

One of the most difficult issues arising from a comparison between Christ and Muḥammad, as founders of two distinct religious communities, is that of faith, political power and eventually violence as a means to protect a religio-political community or divinely established values (cf. the section about 'Faith, power, non-violence' below).

In a wider context the question would be whether the ethoses of self-denial and world-affirmation, as embodied by Christ and Muḥammad respectively, should be taken as mutually exclusive or complementary for believers within the two faiths. Mona Siddiqui (1997) notes that:

> Whereas Jesus' life exemplified self-denial, love and sacrifice for humanity, all aspects of a suffering God, that of Muhammad was based on the fulfilment of an earthly as well as a spiritual life. The primary aim was to show how man could live God's will and law in every aspect of life . . ..[38]

From a Muslim point of view, the ethoses need not to be taken as mutually exclusive, for 'The Prophet combined his duties towards his family and community with a life of austerity and relative asceticism'.[39]

However, the way of the founders as agents of change in society clearly differs, much more so than the ways of their believers. William E. Phipps (1996) notes that 'both Muhammad and Jesus had visions of what society should be and an eagerness for change to achieve it'. But:

> Muhammad's method emphasized restructuring the social structure, replacing tribal bonding with the Muslim community. Jesus' approach focused on individual renewal by selecting a dozen ordinary youths and training them to be carriers of his gospel.[40]

Pursuing his point, Phipps (like Cragg) distinguishes between 'The Medinan Statesman' and 'The Peaceful Reformer'. The question arises again: Are these prophetic roles mutually exclusive in principle, or should they rather be read contextually and taken as complementary? John Hick (in a short essay about 'Jesus and Mohammad') suggests that:

> . . . the comparison of Jesus and Mohammad points to two aspects of religious truth. One is the transforming claim of God upon the individual,

> thereby creating a redeemed community of saints, the church, as a select minority in an unredeemed world. The other is the claim of God upon society as a whole, saints and sinners alike, but with laws inevitably written with sinners in mind. Jesus' own life and teaching embodied the first aspect, but the second rapidly entered into Christianity . . .. Jesus himself was a pure pacifist, whilst his church, from Constantine onwards, has always been a patron of wars. Mohammad on the other hand was never a pacifist, although he did seek to moderate the savagery of war. The Qur'anic teaching included almost from the first both the call to personal surrender to God and the divine demand for a stable society, to be permeated by Islamic ideals.[41]

This is one possible conclusion of a comparison of the foundational stories of Christianity and Islam, taking Christ and Muḥammad and their respective embodied messages as complementary not only in terms of human ethoses, but also as 'religious truths'. But many would oppose the implicit pluralist position in John Hick's argument, in terms of a theology of religions. The question remains whether the theological and ethical issues at hand can be harmonized as easily as the quotation above might indicate.

In theological terms: Does God reveal himself through the apparent failure of his believing community to transform the entire world and its structures of oppression, and/or through the manifest success (in political terms) of the believing community? Are both revelations true only in a relative sense, in their own particular times and contexts?

In ethical terms: Is the believer – and the believing community – right in seeking political power, in order to implement the will of God? Or must the faithful Christian – in imitation of Christ – refrain from any use of armed force in order to overcome opposition to God's will?

The answers given to such questions clearly cut right across the boundaries between the believing communities, and both traditions need to re-examine – preferably in dialogue – the ethical and spiritual implications of their foundational narratives. The issue of Christ and Muḥammad points to far-reaching questions pertaining to theology as well as anthropology and ethics.

In the field of theology proper, this includes the question of whether and how Christ and Muḥammad reveal something of God himself. The question must also be put to Islam, in many of its actual manifestations. According to Muslim orthodoxy, Muḥammad is but the medium of God's revealed word, the Qur'ān, as well as a supreme example to be imitated in moral and religious practice. In popular piety and in Ṣūfism, however, Muḥammad is far more than this, embodying the qualities of God and the divine light itself. Also at this point, when it comes to defining the cutting edge between the divine and the human, the different perspectives will prove to cut right across the boundaries of the religious communities – revealing vast differences between orthodox, popular and mystical perspectives in both camps.

Christology, Anthropology, Theology

In his essay 'Other Faith Images of Jesus: Some Muslim Contributions to the Christological Discussion', Willem A. Bijlefeld (1982) argues that any dialogue between Christians and Muslims should be related to general questions about God and man:

> . . . there is an immediate need for Christians living in a world in which one-sixth to one-fifth of the population is Muslim to make it explicit – at every level of their accounting for their faith – what affirmations concerning Christ say about God's relationship to humanity and humanity's relationship to God, in both of which the issue of interhuman relationships is clearly also at stake.

Without this orientation of the dialogue, towards a shared humanity and the question of God:

> Christian–Muslim discussions on Jesus will continue to be of marginal significance and even counterproductive [. . .] only if both Muslim and Christian statements regarding Jesus are made consistently transparent as to what they say about God and God's way for and among us can Christians and Muslims begin to grasp some of the most fundamental beliefs that unite them and some of the basic questions to which different answers are given by as well as within the two communities of faith.[42]

As theological foci of a future dialogue about God, Bijlefeld suggest the notion of God's action in history, the understanding of the Qurān as well as of Christ as an 'act of mercy', and the notion of a 'God with us':

> While Muslims and Christians commonly hold that God's glory and triumph over all powers of evil will ultimately become manifest, the question is whether the fact that so little of it is unmistakably visible and unambiguously clear at present is just a divinely permitted anomaly or whether it is exactly in this 'veiling' and in the very act of condescension the divine glory is fulfilled.[43]

For Kenneth Cragg, the questions arising from a dialogue on Christology have a general relevance:

> Christianity opts so crucially for Jesus as the indicative from God because it reads within the event of Jesus and its climax on the Cross the authentic clue to the human relevance of God which is the crux of faith and theology. It finds in the Christ-event the epitome of the issues at the heart of human experience.

According to Cragg, Christian faith is not a faith in another God than the One worshipped by Muslims, but rather a distinctive vision of God:

> Even where it parts from fellow theisms it belongs with them in their confidence in the great and continuing Original, God Himself. Its distinctiveness lies in the resourcefulness by which the great Original fulfils himself, where Jesus is the index and the sign.[44]

Through all centuries-long Muslim appreciation of Jesus, even of his suffering, a link between the acknowledgement of his unique humanity and a theology coloured by Jesus seems not only to be unthought, but unthinkable. Within an Islamic universe, also for modern Muslim biographers of Jesus, Jesus remains a human (spiritual and ethical) ideal, and reveals nothing of God. But would it have to be so?

Traditionally, one would say that Islamic theology lacks the anthropological components, restricting itself to theistic meditation on the unity of God, His essence and His attributes, as revealed in the divine Word of the Qur'ān. In the Islamic universe, Christology remains a part of anthropology, and can never be part of theology.

In contrast, Christology remains constitutive for Christian theology. The classical confession of Christ as truly human and truly divine implies that Christology is *the* connection between anthropology and theology.

One might still argue that this way of contrasting Islam with Christianity is too simplistic. We have seen that Ṣūfism views Jesus and Muḥammad not only as embodiments of 'Perfect Man', but even as theophanies. Ṣūfīs have often tended to transgress the border of *širk* by associating the spiritual perfection of the human soul with divinity. The theophatic language of Ṣūfism has always been looked upon with suspicion by Islamic orthodoxy. Many would still argue that the Qur'ān itself involves the humanity of the Prophet in the event of revelation. The revelations are related to decisive moments in his prophetic mission; negatively in confrontation with his adversaries; positively in the affirmation of his moral perfection and his divinely guided establishment of a Muslim community. Can there be any theology without a contextually determined human channelling? Can theophany and revelation be thought of, without the assumption that revelation is in one way or another perceived as embodied?

The obvious contrast between the Muslim and Christian understandings of 'Word of God' does not have to be as sharp as it is often perceived. In a certain sense, the divine revelation of the Qur'ān has also become flesh and blood – by virtue of the reciting and proclaiming Messenger, and the contextualization of his mission.

Some modern Muslims have called for a reconsideration of the Muʿtazilite understanding of the Qur'ān as 'created', over against the dogma of 'uncreatedness' that came to be established as the orthodox view. What is 'created', might be rethought, and 'reshaped' in a contextually new reception.

At least from the perspective of reception, all theology implies some anthropological presumptions, in the perception of the human addressee of divine revelation. Anthropological presumptions differ substantially not only between the religions, but also within each of the religious communities. Religions contain differing assumptions about human nature in general (unchangeable, or historically contingent?), about man and society (the rights of the individual versus the community), and more specifically about men and women (equal or complementary status?).

Also soteriologically significant notions differ between and within the various faith communities – notions of sin and evil (singular acts of disobedience, or inherent deviation from the way of God?), pedagogy (is man kept on the right path by being loved and/or by being warned?) and salvation (is man saved by guidance or by redemption?).

If all Christologies are related to anthropological, soteriological and in the end theological assumptions – assumptions that vary not only between, but also within each religion – then the questions arising from a Christian–Muslim dialogue about Christ would prove to have general relevance.

Rethinking Christology in Dialogue with Islam

Many Christian theologians working and serving in an Islamic context see a Christian–Muslim dialogue focused on the image of Christ as part of the contextualization of theology. Islam has to be taken seriously in the christological reflection of the Church itself – both historically, as a post-Christian religion with its distinctive Christologies, and in a contemporary perspective, as part of doing theology in context. More pluralist theologians would be ready to see Jesus as standing somehow 'between' Christianity and Islam, being the possession of neither.

Rethinking Incarnation: Generation and Procession

Michael Nazir-Ali, an English-Pakistani bishop of the Church of England, has emphasized the need for a Christology which is critically aware of its Islamic context (Nazir-Ali 1987,[45] cf. Journées Romaines 1991). Nazir-Ali notes that many of the traditional Islamic Christologies would seem to come close to views of Christ held by many 'professional theologians in the West':

> The more 'radical' have so overstressed his humanity that they have either neglected or, in some cases, denied his divinity and, as a necessary consequence, any notion of his incarnation . . .. Muslims rightly claim affinity between their own view and that of these 'radical' theologians.[46]

Instead of advocating a reiteration of 'orthodox' positions, Nazir-Ali proposes a more 'dynamic approach'. Nazir-Ali discusses some aspects of classical Christologies in the modern context, and dismisses both Modalism (in Trinitarian theology) and Nestorianism (in Christology) as cheap escapes from Islamic challenges. As regards the notion of sonship, he points to the fact that 'whenever the early Fathers refer to the generation of the Son, they mean his "eternal Birth". The earthly birth is nearly always referred to as the Incarnation'.[47]

Consequently, Nazir-Ali opts for a 'Christology of Procession' instead of a 'Christology of Generation' – the latter being offensive to Muslims, and no necessary part of Christian teachings about Christ. As for a 'Christology of procession', Nazir-Ali holds the view that much of qur'ānic Christology is susceptible of a processional interpretation, like the title *rasūl* (messenger), which is applied to both Christ and Muḥammad.[48] Nazir-Ali cites with approval a study by Kenneth Cragg (Cragg 1974), where he has tried to show:

> . . . that the Muslim idea of *rasūliyyah* or 'sentness' can be developed in such a way as to narrow the gap between Muslim and Christian ideas of revelation. Both Muslims and Christians believe that God has sent prophets and the one who sends is somehow 'associated' with those he sends, or in other words, the one who is sent is somehow full of the one who sends. The Qur'ān repeatedly speaks of the Prophets and other believers, as aided by the Holy Spirit (*Rūḥ al-qudus*, 2:87, 253, where the reference is to Jesus, 58:22).[49]

Nazir-Ali raises the question to what extent is God's presence, for the Muslim, only a presence *with* and not a presence *in*? This question would seem to be quite important for a Christology in the Pakistani context, where the veneration of the Prophet in popular and Ṣūfī piety seems to slide markedly from divine presence *with* towards presence *in* the (eternal) person of Muḥammad.[50] As for Christian theology, Nazir-Ali maintains that the difference between revelation *through* the prophets and revelation *in* the Son is not only one of degree, but rather of kind:

> The revelation through the prophets is fragmentary precisely because divine distance is maintained. In the Incarnation it is definitive precisely because this distance has been overcome. The divine is not only present with but present in. Divine involvement is complete.[51]

The aim of Nazir-Ali is to seek a language (e.g. of procession) that is less offensive to Muslim than other christological discourses (like that of generation). For the same purpose, he also emphasizes the christological notion of 'Christ's obedience'.

Rethinking Sonship: Son of God, Servant of God

It is a well-known fact for all involved in dialogue that meeting the other is also meeting oneself. Challenges from Islamic Christologies, received by open-minded Christians, might lead to a reconsideration of some aspects of Christian Christology. Although the main challenge in dialogue would be to search for some common ground, dialogue brings back to Christology challenges that have to be dealt with on Christian premises – a process that in turn possibly might produce new kinds of responses to Muslims.

As indicated above (the title *rasūl* and a Christology of procession), there might be something to gain from a further reflection on the christological titles. Although most Muslims tend to object to the notion 'Son of God', Ṣūfī Islam has been ready to accept it in a metaphorical or generalized sense. Again, the question is about the meaning of the title[52] and the reference of the sign.

Obviously, the meaning of 'Son of God' also varies on the Christian side. Some Christians involved in dialogue with Muslims (and mission towards Muslims) seem to have suspended the notion 'Son of God', because of its dubious connotations for Muslims, and its lack of lucidity on the Christian side. Instead, the focus is set on 'Servant of God' – a title applied to Jesus both in the New Testament and in the Qur'ān: 'Christ will never scorn to be servant of God' (sūra 4.172).

In the postscript to his book *Der Christus der Muslime*, Olaf Schumann (1988) advocates a Servant Christology which is sensitive to Muslim awareness and still true to basic Christian teachings. He admits that notions like 'Son of God' and 'Lord' long before the Islamic era might have become part of a power language: 'There was . . . arrogance and passion for power, justified with reference to the elevation and lordship of Christ, in a demand to partake in it.'[53] The Qur'ān might thus have been 'contextually right' in rejecting the notion 'Son of God'. Instead, the Qur'ān venerates Jesus as Servant of God.

In his Christian response, Schumann recalls the fact that according to the (synoptic) Gospels, Jesus himself was reluctant to accept the title 'Son of God'. Instead, he refers to himself as 'Son of Man', and acts as a Servant, not as a Lord. In the early Christian hymn preserved in the Letter to the Philippians 2.5–11, Jesus is portrayed as the obedient Servant/Slave of God, who despite his origins in God, chose to be in human likeness, assuming the nature of a servant/slave, humbling himself to the point of death on the cross. The culminating confession of the hymn, 'Jesus Christ is Lord', is not a reflection of any excessive ambition of Jesus. On the contrary, it confirms his humility. The implication of the hymn is that God acknowledges that the obedience and humility of his Servant has been 'to the glory of God the Father', disclosing God's own passion and love for humanity, so that God 'bestowed on him the name above all names'. Schumann raises the question of whether the cross can be acceptable to Muslims as the deepest expression of Jesus' humanity and his obedience to God, i.e. not as a failure, but as faithfulness: 'Christ's humility in his service and his obedience to the will of his Father did not stop *before* the cross, but included it.' And maybe even more important for a Muslim awareness: 'Only on the cross, through the final submission of will and its ambition "to be like God" may the always present temptation of "*širk*" be defeated.'[54]

Schumann reminds the reader that the context of this hymn in Philippians is an admonition to imitate the humility of Christ, in concord with the teaching of Jesus in the Gospels that anyone who would be Lord shall be the Servant of all (cf. Luke 22.24–27). An underlying presumption of this servant Christology is the conviction that love is a power that surpasses all:

> By the first Christians, the service and never ending obedience of this simple human being Jesus was seen as an expression of power. Only that this power did not have its source in itself, but in love.[55]

Referring to the more 'political' conceptions of God's power in Islam, Schumann concludes by asking the Muslims whether such an understanding of God's rule is really defendable in theological terms. From the Christian side:

> Jesus' refusal to identify the Kingdom of God with a political understanding of society or state . . . is not seen as a deficiency. On the contrary, the confusion of God's kingdom with society and state is seen as an unholy temptation.[56]

Would it be thinkable, although by now mostly unthought, that Jews, Christians and Muslims together might overcome the temptations of absolute power, in a shared confession that ultimate meaning and power rests only with God?

As can be seen with Schumann, rethinking Christian Christology might be good for something else than preaching Christ in more sensitive ways in an Islamic context. It touches upon questions of general relevance in interreligious dialogue.

Rethinking the Cross

As we have seen, Olaf Schumann's reflections on Servant Christology are linked with an understanding of the Cross which emphasizes Christ's humility and he raises the question of whether the Cross can be acceptable to Muslims as the ultimate expression of Christ's obedience to God.

Many scholars have raised the question of whether traditional Muslim positions regarding cross and crucifixion rely on 'rejection or incomprehension'.[57] Christian theologians of an apologetic inclination have often tended to interpret the Qur'ān as in fact not denying the crucifixion. Many attempts have also been made to elicit the reasons for the standard Muslim rejection of the Cross. Different explanations have been given – exegetical and theological as well as historical and political.

Exegetically, the question of what the Qur'ān actually says about cross and crucifixion remains unsolved, and the Qur'ān has been interpreted differently at this point by its exegetes. Theologically, the question of the crucifixion is inseparable from what Muslims have perceived as non-acceptable implications of the cross as a religious symbol, like the idea of vicarious suffering and redemption. Historically, the question may be raised of whether the rejection of the Cross should primarily be read in the context of political confrontation – the Cross being first the symbol of the rivalling Byzantine Empire in the formative period, and later that of the invading crusaders – rather than as an expression of theological strictures.

As for the linkage between cross, sacrifice and redemption, Clinton Bennett[58] in his essay 'A Christian Response to the Absence of the Cross in Islam' discusses 'the possibility of a Christian faith for which Jesus' sacrificial death is not central'.[59] Bennett notes that the Muslim reservation against the idea of Christ's sacrificial death is actually quite widespread in Christian circles as well. For his own part, Bennett confesses that 'the blood language of the New Testament . . . does not fit comfortably with my own conviction that God's love is strong enough to save without a price being paid'. In theological terms, he believes that:

> . . . the Qur'ān's apparent denial of Jesus' crucifixion may challenge a Christian over-emphasis on the need for a sacrificial, substitutary, atoning death that so many Christians for so long regard as essential to or the bed-rock of Christian belief.[60]

Bennett's essay appears in the volume *Jesus and the Cross: Reflections of Christians from Islamic contexts*, which is in the main geared towards *explaining* Christian beliefs about cross and crucifixion. In the introduction, the book's editor David Emmanuel Singh notes that Bennett's view is 'not consistent with the historic Christian witness of the Cross and, therefore, will be controversial'.[61] For his own part, Singh proposes an interpretation of the Muslim conception of 'Perfect Man' (*al-insān al-kāmil*)[62] which allows for a relational understanding of God's unity which expresses itself as 'God-for-us'. In this framework, Singh suggests, the Cross 'can remain as the ultimate evidence of divine compassion and mercy'.[63]

Jesus and the Cross includes also two contributions by Kenneth Cragg which seek to explore and explain the mystery of the cross in dialogue with Islam. In tune with Bennett's concerns, he warns against 'crude' interpretations of Christ's salvific death which make the crucified Christ seem like a 'helpless scapegoat' sacrificed to appease God's wrath. On the other hand, Cragg also takes exception to the Islamic idea that 'forgiveness is effortless' on God's part.

In Cragg's interpretation, the Cross stands for an active 'redemptiveness on divine part' – expressed through Christ's suffering love.[64]

In his second essay about 'The Cross and Power: The Parting of the Ways',[65] Cragg reiterates a recurrent theme in many of his writings when interpreting the Cross as God's renunciation of violent power in overcoming evil. In both essays, he likens Christ's fate to the potential outcome of Muḥammad's early career in Mecca and contrasts it with his assumption of political power in Medina:

> Muhammad's Meccan trauma led to Hijrah and Medina and all that ensued. Jesus' travail moved on towards the Cross. There had been in both cases a 'not being overcome of evil' through insistent fidelity. Whether there would be any 'overcoming of evil with good' would be what either, in their total contrast, would have to show.[66]

Ida Glaser picks up central elements in Cragg's theology of the Cross and (in tune with Olaf Schumann) develops them in a self-critical direction:

> The Cross, says Cragg, 'is what happens when a love like Christ's encounters a world like Jerusalem'. How is it that this love of Christ could have become the motivation and the banner for attacking and killing Muslims (and, of course, many Jews, heretics and Eastern Christians) in a battle over that same Jerusalem? In particular, what theology of the Cross could have allowed this to happen?[67]

In this way, Glaser suggests, 'thinking about the Cross in the context of Islam leads us [Christians] to seeing ourselves anew' – being called to self-critically embody a theology of the Cross rather than imposing it on others.

Rethinking Exclusivism: Jesus between Christianity and Islam

The Finnish scholar Heikki Räisänen, who wrote about Christ in the Qur'ān in the 1970s, has later elaborated his views on a pluralist Christology.[68] With reference to Christian–Muslim dialogue about Christ, he contends that:

> . . . there was a time when Christian ideas about Jesus were much closer to the Quranic portrait of him than to the definitions of the fourth century Church councils. There are layers in the New Testament itself where the complete subordination of Jesus to God is made very clear, e.g. in the speeches of the apostles as retold in *Acts of the Apostles* . . .. This kind of Christology was preserved among Jewish Christian circles which did not go along with the development of the Hellenistic church . . .. Historically

> speaking, these Jewish Christians seem to have influenced Islam; if so, Islam can be literally seen as a reminder of the Christians' own past.[69]

In this strain of early Christian theology, the notion 'son of God' should (according to Räisänen) probably be taken in an 'adoptionist' sense: because of his faithful service to God, God made Jesus his 'son'. Following convention, Räisänen contrasts the subordinationist and adoptionist Christology reflected by Luke (in the Gospel of Luke and in Acts) with John's theology of divine sonship in the metaphysical sense.

As for the contemporary relevance of such insights, stemming from the 'historical conscience' of New Testament scholars (as Räisänen puts it), Räisänen points to the view of John Hick and other pluralist theologians that:

> If Christians seized on the 'adoptionist' component of their christological heritage, quite new possibilities might arise for a dialogue between Christians and people of other faiths.[70]

As for Christian–Muslim dialogue, Räisänen suggests that both the Gospel of John (with its 'high Christology' of divine visitation 'from above') and the qur'ānic 'low Christology'-portrait of the human prophet might be read as reinterpretations of Jesus' message in the light of later experiences and reflections. In a wider perspective, Räisänen contends that 'the whole history of the Bible could be set forth as an account of the development of traditions and their actualizations and reinterpretations in new situations'.[71]

With his 'redactionist' view of biblical formation, linked to the perception of Islam as a late development of Abrahamic theology, Räisänen raises the question of a closed or open canon of the Bible: Should the Bible – as a source of faith and practice – be read only within its intra-biblical perspective, or in the light of Jewish-Christian apocrypha and Muslim scripture as well? The challenge is directed to Muslims likewise: 'Christians ought to see their christology and Muslims the Qur'an in a rather more relative light.'[72]

Räisänen clearly opts for a more open canon, and a pluralist reading of the Jesus history. In an Abrahamic perspective, he concludes that:

> Jesus has of old stood 'between Christianity and Islam' in the sense that his different position in the two religions has been a hindrance to an encounter. Yet today it is also possible to think that he stands between the two (actually between three religions, for Judaism should be included in a 'trialogue') in the opposite sense: in the no man's land or on the common ground which does not belong to any single party. Jesus was not a Christian, and his vision overlaps only partially with Christianity. Nor was he a Muslim, though Muslims are right in esteeming him and finding points of contact with Islam in his message. He stands in-between.[73]

As pointed out, Räisänen links his visions to those of John Hick and other pluralist theologians who for long have been challenging 'Christian uniqueness'. His pluralist inclinations might be countered with the argument that for a vision of Christ in-between Christians and Muslims to become meaningful, both parties should be allowed to retain what they regard as specific for their belief in Christ. There is probably no such thing as a 'no man's land' in dialogue. One might argue that only between partners that fully recognize their horizons of faith, and are ready to live with differences, can there be a real dialogue. But historical-critical and pluralist approaches to Christology like those of Räisänen might help foster the necessary humility in dialogue.

Rethinking 'Christianity': Jesus-Followers between Christianity and Islam

A quite different approach to Jesus in the space between Christianity and Islam can be found in recent research on groups of Christ-believers with a Muslim background who have a passionate faith in Christ as Saviour but are reluctant to identify themselves as 'Christians'. In his study *Jesus Imandars and Christ Bhatkas*,[74] Jonas Adelin Jørgensen demonstrates how self-assigned 'Īsā imandars' in Bangladesh develop a hybrid identity in which they retain certain elements of their previous religious practice as Muslims and posit themselves as followers of Jesus in an almost liminal space between organized Christianity and Islam.

'Īsā imandar' means 'faithful to Jesus' and is associated with a deeply personal faith in Jesus which is expressed in Protestant style worship which notably includes Bengali cultural elements as well as certain elements of Islamic practice (such as taking off shoes and placing sacred scripture on a bookstand). Although critical of 'Christianity', their faith in Jesus includes central elements of orthodox Christian beliefs such as his sacrificial death for human sins.[75] Although the imandars also retain respect for elements of Islamic religion and may occasionally visit the mosque, the centre of their faith has shifted from the qur'ānic revelation to God in Christ. As a minority within the minority inspired by the example of Jesus, they are critical of Muḥammad's way of combining religious and political power: 'Whereas Muhammad was "socially powerful", Jesus was insignificant, Aziz says.'[76]

Īsā imandars see themselves as converts to Christ but not necessarily to Christianity which is seen by the imandars as influenced (in the Bangladeshi context) by Hindu culture and by Muslims as something Western. Furthermore, the imandars criticize the churches – as well as established Islam – for being too much focused on external expressions. 'In sum, it seems that the imandars emphasize the essential value of interiority and personal faithfulness towards God through following Jesus.'[77]

Loosely organized as house churches, the Bangladeshi imandars may be seen as a part of a wider trend of establishing religious communities (*communitas* in Victor Turner's sense) outside of the organized structures of church and mosque.[78] Apparently, being faithful to Jesus serves in this context as a marker of an (ever so long?) unbounded identity, somewhere in the space between the two religions.

Identifying oneself as faithful to Jesus but not necessarily as 'Christian' in the institutional sense tunes in with the way in which Christ is preached by some world-wide evangelists operating in the Muslim world. A case in point is the late Norwegian evangelist Aril Edvardsen (d. 2008). In Edvardsen's view, performing miracles (as abundantly done in his campaigns) and preaching the Gospel is not the same as spreading Christianity. Edvardsen's missionary vision was actually formulated as 'an evangelical revival without the Christianity of the West'. With reference to his TV-transmissions to the Muslim world (through the 'Miracle' channel), Edvardsen used to underline that his movement always advises Muslims who accept Christ as their Saviour and Messiah to call themselves 'Jesus-believers' belonging to 'Gospel centres', rather than 'Christians' who will inevitably be associated with 'the Christianity and churches of the West'.[79]

Edvardsen's vision resembles also that of the Bangladeshi imandars by paying respect to Islam while being faithful to Jesus. According to Edvardsen, any missionary effort directed towards Muslims should first of all confirm what they already believe in God. Only then can Christ be meaningfully proclaimed as the fulfilment of their (and every other believer's) spiritual longings. In tune with this approach, Edvardsen could describe the Qur'ân as 'the Muslims' bridge to Jesus' (a point that is also sometimes made by the imandars).[80]

As another example of emphasizing faithfulness to Jesus over against affiliation with Christianity one might also cite the so-called Fellowship Foundation in the USA. In an article based on undercover research among what he called 'America's secret theocrats', journalist Jeffrey Sharlett has characterized their Jesus-piety and their aversion against the notion of 'Christianity' as 'Jesus plus nothing'.[81] In the case of the Fellowship Foundation – which is historically behind the important National Prayer Breakfast institution in the USA – their worldwide networking efforts targeting top level political and religious leaders are focused on the person of Jesus Christ whose prophetic mission and healing power is also (as the Fellowship sees it) recognized by many other religions than Christianity – not least by Islam. According to their representatives, inter-religious 'Jesus-groups' have been initiated by the National Prayer Breakfast network and attracted wide interest in leadership circles not only in the USA but also in Middle Eastern and Asian countries.[82]

Whether such activities can reasonably be said to take place in the realm between Christianity and Islam or should rather be seen as a new form of Christian-based missionary activity, is debatable.

Christology and Human Experience: From Miracles to Cross

With some modern authors writing within a Muslim universe, we have seen a shift of focus in Islamic images of Christ – from Christ the miracle worker of classical Islam and Ṣūfism, to the suffering Christ. But the image of a healing Christ persists, both in popular Muslim piety and in Ṣūfism.[83]

Miracles in the World of Mystics: Christ, Healer of Minds

Some of the ethical approaches to Jesus in contemporary Islam, focusing on human conscience, might be considered as a more rationalist version of the typical Ṣūfī image of Jesus – the healer of minds who brings life to dead souls, and inspires the individual to selfless love. On this level, many Christians would find the spiritual, Ṣūfī rendering of the life-giving breath of Christ deeply meaningful. Within the context of mysticism, common symbols abound, and individuals from different religious traditions may join in a common appreciation of the symbols and stories of the other. Focusing religious experience, differences in teachings and theologies may be regarded as secondary.

As for the theological implications of Ṣūfī Christologies, we have seen that the veneration of Jesus in Ṣūfism goes far beyond the orthodox restrictions. He is not merely a prophet aided by God, but the Perfect Man (*al-insān al-kāmil*), God's Spirit (*rūḥ ullāh*); even his theophany (*maẓhar*). His theophatic language, as known from the Christian Gospels, is taken and accepted as being metaphorical, signifying the union-with-God potential in any sainthood. Some Ṣūfīs transgressed the borders of orthodoxy by self-referring theophatic utterances like al-Ḥallāj's fatal exclamation 'I am the truth'. Their awareness of suffering as a possible fate of the mystic makes some of them sensitive to the mystery of Jesus' passion.

It should, however, again be noted that the elevation of Jesus in Ṣūfism is not exclusive. Many of his attributes apply to sainthood in general, and it is Muḥammad who is the Light of the World. Still, in some Ṣūfī orders Jesus tends to be highly elevated as a spiritual teacher, and a symbol of the transforming power of selfless love.

Miracles in Folk Islam: Christ, Healer of Bodies

We have seen that in early Muslim legend, the miraculous works of healing performed by Jesus and more specifically his raising the dead are elaborated in a way far beyond both qur'ānic and biblical measures. In Muslim apologetics (classical and modern), Jesus is characterized by his healing abilities, as distinct from the magic of Moses and the eloquence of Muḥammad.

The image of Jesus, the healer of bodies, seems to persist in folk Islam from the stories of the Prophets to present-day popular religiosity, especially in the Persian and Indo-Pakistani contexts. Again, there is an ambiguity between uniqueness and generalization. The image of Jesus the healer seems to be most widespread in Muslim cultures that focus on saintly blessings in general. Within this context, the healer Jesus may also be held in high esteem.

Expectations of bodily healing, and visible miracles in general, are integral parts of popular religiosity in most faith communities. Many modern missionary efforts towards Muslims focus on miracles and immediate healing.

For many modern Muslims, however, and Christians likewise, the harvest of the miracle fields would seem to be meagre, and a shallow ground for sharing human experience of a deeper kind.

The Symbol of the Cross: From Theological Rejection to Human Affirmation

In twentieth-century poetry in a Muslim context, we have seen a significant shift when dealing with Christ – from the spiritual miracle worker and the healer of bodies, towards an apprehension of the symbol of the cross. In the context of sometimes shared experiences of oppression between Christians and Muslims, and more generally in existential pondering over individual fates, the suffering Jesus of the crucified mind has proved to be a meaningful symbol for many.

For those Muslims who believe that crucifixion and cross do not necessarily have to be rejected as religious and poetical symbols, there seem to be different paths towards recognition of the notion of passion, the fact of crucifixion and the symbol of the cross.

1. In classical Shīʿite Islam, theology was not done in the context of a manifest victory, but – on the contrary – in the wake of a historical defeat that culminated in the martyrdom of Ḥusayn at Karbalā. This fact has infused Shīʿite Islam with sensitivity towards the religious significance of passion, martyrdom and redemptive suffering. We have seen that in recent times, Mahmoud Ayoub and Hasan Askari, with their Shīʿite backgrounds, have both touched upon the significance of suffering in Muslim–Christian dialogue.
2. Also some Sunnī Muslim thinkers (cf. ʿUthmān, see the section about Christ biographies in Chapter 7) would point to the fact that according to the Qur'ān, prophets would have to be prepared for a violent fate. Cf. Qur'ān 5.70 and 2.87: '. . . some of them [the Messengers] you slay.'

3 We have noted that in Ṣūfism, there is sensitivity towards the world's rejection of spiritual knowledge, and the resulting suffering for those who are faithful to the Spirit of God. The martyrdom of al-Ḥallāj offers a model of mystical suffering that for some mystics parallels the fate of Jesus.
4 In the modern context of the Egyptian novel, the focus on Jesus as a guardian of individual conscience, confronting traditionalism and legalism, has led some Muslim authors to a more open approach to the symbol of the cross. Most notably, this is true for M. Kāmil Ḥusayn's metaphorical use of the symbol of the cross, when writing about the crucifixion of human conscience.
5 In modern Arabic, Pakistani and Persian poetry, the symbol of the cross seems to emerge as a means of interpreting the suffering that follows resistance to political oppression, or more generally, as an interpretation of human desolation and despair. Especially noteworthy is the move from a folk Islam or Ṣūfī image of Jesus as healer and miracle worker towards the image of a suffering Messiah – 'in the miracle fields of this uncrucified Jesus' (cf. the Iranian poet Shafīʿī).

It should be remembered, however, that this inclusion of the cross as a symbol either of selfless love and human desolation (the crucified), or of human folly and crime (the crucifier), does not allow for attaching any uniqueness to Jesus' passion. The cross is dealt with as a general symbol.

Neither does acceptance of a religious meaning for human suffering in itself imply any notion of a suffering God. However, the Egyptian thinker al-Nowaihi's notion of the passionate God of the Qur'ān might break some new ground in dialogue: 'The Qur'an itself is nothing if it is not a suffering identity with creation and humanity' (cf. the section about 'The symbol of the cross' in Chapter 7).

The Ethical Connection

In an essay about 'Christology in dialogue with other faiths', David Kerr (1993) makes the general observation that:

> . . . inter-religious dialogue is best advanced where, as a 'dialogue' of life or a 'dialogue of deeds', priority is given to ethics. This is repeatedly the stance of Muslims themselves . . .. This suggests that an ethical approach to Christology should be the first priority in Christian–Muslim dialogue, both to understand the core of Jesus' prophetic teaching as contained in, for example, the Sermon on the Mount, and to apply his ethical standards to issues of human life and society with which qur'anic ethics are also deeply concerned.

> This could offer an alternative approach in Christian–Muslim dialogue to the issue that has caused so much misunderstanding and controversy in the past, namely, the personhood of Jesus himself. 'Whom do you say that I am?' is a question that can only be addressed in the context of the character of Jesus' life and teaching, and their impact upon those who lived with him.[84]

Kerr suggests that with this as a starting point, other questions – like the mystery of suffering – may also be addressed in a more meaningful way. As an Islamic example of linking the meaning of suffering to the question of ethics, Kerr cites the Palestinian writer Ismaʿīl al-Farūqī:

> The holy of holies of Christianity, namely, the ethical teaching of Jesus, his world view, his realization of the tragic nature of human existence, that is to say, of the conflict between values which is innate in the very nature of reality, and his attempt at solving that conflict in an exemplary manner in his own life, which is what constitutes his redemptiveness – all this is substantially there, already given in the few genuine statements, anecdotes, and deeds of his life, in the purified Christianity we have described.[85]

For al-Farūqī, any true ethical dialogue between Christians and Muslims presupposes a 'purification' of Christianity, divesting it of Graeco-Roman mysticism and bringing it back to what al-Farūqī sees as its true Arab spirit.

In his article 'The ethical connection: Christian–Muslim relations in the postmodern age',[86] Ziauddin Sardar (in a way similar to Balić) points to monotheism as the basis of an ethical connection between Muslims and Christians. Like al-Farūqī, he sees a common ethical project, based on revitalized monotheistic belief, as the sole viable way towards future dialogue.

> In both Christianity and Islam the nature and activity of God have been held to determine not only the contents of ethics and spirituality, but also the actualisation of ethical ideas in society.

The common challenge for Muslims and Christians would thus be to demonstrate 'the ability of the believers to use the revelations to come up with convincing and humanly satisfactory responses to the problems we face':[87]

> A joint Christian–Muslim ethical enterprise, designed to generate adoptive and pragmatic intellectual responses to the problems of our age, would be the most appropriate response of the believers to the demands of the postmodernist age.[88]

Pragmatic as this project may sound, Sardar nevertheless presupposes some basic theological rethinking. For the sake of genuine, mutual recognition and a common ethical project, Sardar (cf. al-Farūqī) suggests purification of

Christianity as well as of Islam: 'Christianity must end its marriage with secularism; and Islam needs to recover its lost humanity.'[89]

Furthermore, Muslims must acknowledge the historicity of their classical jurisprudence (*fiqh*), and let each new generation reinterpret the textual sources (Qur'ān and Sunna) in the light of its own experience. Just as Muslims should abandon the perennity of classical *fiqh*, Sardar advocates that Christians should suspend their classical belief in the uniqueness of Jesus.

For Sardar, this does not imply any reduction in the importance of Jesus as the central object of identification in Christianity. Agreeing with Shabbir Akhtar, Sardar states that Muslims should accept that Christians view 'the life of Jesus as a disclosure and human exemplification of the moral excellence of deity such that the imitation of Jesus' behaviour is already a moral action in the believer's life'.[90]

Shabbir Akhtar deliberately leaves room for controversy over whether Jesus' ministry is 'an exclusive expression of God's manifold wisdom and righteousness or merely a pivotal and distinctive one'.[91] But, according to Sardar: If Christianity is to 'reciprocate the ecumenical courtesy that Islam has always extended to it', and recognize the legitimacy of other monotheistic beliefs, the assertion of the uniqueness of Jesus must be suspended.[92]

The practical outcome of such a mutual revision and recognition would seem to be foreseen as a synthesis of the 'theological virtues' of Christianity and Islam: virtues like 'faith, love, justice, courage, temperance and prudence' on Christianity's part, and on the part of Islam, virtues like unity of God, trusteeship of man, worship, knowledge, justice, consensus and public interest.[93] An underlying premise seems to be that both religions – with their fundaments in prophetic, monotheistic revelation – basically teach the same, although Christianity and Islam have some 'distinctive virtues' that should be interconnected in a common search for creative responses to present-day ethical challenges.

The horizon of Sardar is the post-modern chaos of the 1990s, as a challenge to both Christians and Muslims. In his search for an 'ethical connection' between the two communities, both facing post-modernity, his image of Jesus (not surprisingly) turns out to be a predominantly moral one. The 'theological' virtues called for by Sardar are moral virtues, although (as Sardar sees it) fostered by monotheism.

Human Conscience

We have seen that an ethical approach to Jesus also prevails among twentieth-century Muslim writers in Egypt – notably with al-ʿAqqād, Ḥusayn and Khālid. Their context was that of Islam facing modernity. In their efforts at a modern reinterpretation of Islam, Jesus is brought to the front against traditionalist *taqlīd* (blind imitation), as an outstanding representative of a conscience-based ethics. As Jacques Jomier has noted, their Jesus is no longer the metaphysical wonder-worker or spiritual doctor of medieval Islam, but a defender of human conscience and a messenger of the law of love over against *taqlīd* and legalism. In the contemporary context of these authors, Jesus turns out to be quite relevant for their wrestling with challenges from modernity. As a religious renewer, breaking away from traditionalism and legalism and placing individual conscience at the centre of a universalistic ethics, Christ may be perceived as an ally for those rethinking Muslim ethics in modernity.

For all their interest in Christ and Christian tradition, however, one may ask whether Christians are at any point invited by these authors to play a role as distinctive or even disturbing others, or whether Christ (with his appeal to individual consciences, and his protection of the freedom of conscience in society) is only brought to the fore as an ally in their modernist projects of Islamic reform. Is Christ ever allowed to be distinctively 'Christian', or is he only seen as 'more of the same' in their reformed vision of Islam?

We have seen that the portraits of Muḥammad, made by al-ʿAqqād and Khālid, are also marked by a similar focus on the human conscience.[94] In his work on the 'human conscience on its journey towards its destiny', Khālid (1971/1963) presents conscience as the uniting element in all faith-based efforts to save humanity. The ancient Egyptians, the Old Testament prophets, Christ, Muḥammad and Gandhi all share a common concern for the dignity of man, justice in society and peace on earth – united by faith in One God. In his 'Together on the Road: Muḥammad and Christ' (n.d./1958), he presents Christ and Muḥammad side by side as champions of freedom of conscience. Both defend the fundamental human rights of subsistence, as well as the right to freedom of conscience. Christ liberated human conscience from its captivity to outward laws and oppressing regulations. Muḥammad did the same: by preaching social responsibility and challenging suppressive power, by spiritually subverting all institutions of religious mediation and defending the integrity of the individual person, he set human conscience free. As brothers in prophethood, Christ and Muḥammad both focus on the inner meaning of the laws, and both of them anchor religion as well as ethics in the human conscience.

The phenomenon of human conscience as seen by Khālid clearly points to experiences and values shared between Christians and Muslims. He recognizes Christian tradition as a religious resource in its own right, just as capable of inspiring Muslims as the contemporary witness of love and non-violent resistance to evil offered by Gandhi. Like Kāmil Ḥusayn, Khālid may use the symbolism of the crucifixion of Christ to express the repeated crucifixion of love and peace in this world. He may even speak of the return of Christ as the final victory of peace, love, truth, goodness and beauty.

But his outlook is unitary: he wants to present Christians and Muslims (and other people guided by conscience) as brothers 'together on the road'. Khālid's meditations on 'Muḥammad and Christ' could probably be read as a celebration of a shared practice between Muslims and Christians in modernity: their co-operation in the struggle for national independence and social justice in modern Egypt. But he does not really address the wounded experiences in Christian–Muslim coexistence, and the reluctance to accept challenging differences. When differences are addressed, Khālid emerges as apologetic on behalf of his Islamic faith – for which he can hardly be blamed.

In the case of Ḥusayn, the traditions of the other are less marked by apologetical concerns. For him, the Christian Gospels reveal the depths of human folly, and man's ineradicable tendency to crucify his conscience. The drama of Good Friday leaves Christians and Muslims alike naked and bare. As for the possible communal aspect of conscience, Ḥusayn is quite insistent that there can be no such thing as a collective conscience. His pessimistic view on political collectivism and institutionalized religion is based on the fact that both tend to override the scruples of individual conscience. Since conscience cannot be collectivized, collectives are inevitably prone to evil-doing, e.g. in legitimating a use of violence that the moral individual would abstain from within the realms directed by individual conscience.

Ḥusayn's view of human conscience has proved to be a controversial one in the Muslim community. He is critically visited by the British Muslim Shabbir Akhtar. In his *The Final Imperative: An Islamic Theology of Liberation*,[95] Kenneth Cragg's books on *Jesus and the Muslim* (1985) and *Muhammad and the Christian* (1984) are the primary targets of attack. Commenting on the role of 'individual conscience', Akhtar emphasizes that conscience must be framed by a religious principle, a community of believers and political power. With polemical reference to the 'obscure Egyptian writer Muhammad Kamil Husayn' – who contrasts the exigencies of public causes and the restraints of individual conscience – Akhtar points to:

> . . . Muhammad's decision to alter not merely recalcitrant individual consciences but rather also to come to terms with the entire power-structure that had resisted his preaching. To be sure, such a reckoning must itself respect the constraints of religious principle and right conduct. The political program must engage men and women who are long-suffering, working with and within individual consciences, never upon, let alone against, the prompting of the individual conscientious office.[96]

Critically visiting Kenneth Cragg (who is also Ḥusayn's translator) at this point, Akhtar states that:

> Cragg's dispute with Islamic verdicts on the relationship between social power and individual conscience is, as part of a larger debate, rather topical these days . . .. Christian thinkers typically tend to place the emphasis firmly on the need to reform the heart and conscience[97] [. . .] Muslims teach that the religious soul is capable of struggling against injustice without being fatally tempted by the darker possibilities of power.[98]

Akhtar also refers polemically to the connection of a Christian notion of conscience with pacifism,[99] a point that is also implied (in a positive sense) in Kāmil Ḥusayn's *City of Wrong*.

It should be clear, then, that the theme of 'conscience' raises fundamental ethical questions in Christian–Muslim dialogue. What can Christians and Muslims know together, in 'conscience' – in the fields of individual and social ethics, and in the deeper questions pertaining to human authenticity and the character of human society? Can Christians and Muslims know something together that does not eradicate difference, but makes respected difference an integral part of mutual obligation? (Cf. the concluding reflections on a 'conscientious' dialogue between religions in Chapter 9).

The Golden Rule

Following Khālid, who differently from Ḥusayn speaks of conscience-based ethics as a communal virtue, the question would be how to define a sort of collective conscience, and whether the focus on individual conscience may allow for any redefinition of the established, collective tradition.

Kāmil Ḥusayn, coming close to being a Muslim pacifist, called for a rethinking within Islam as regards the use of force and violence. In the project of the Sudanese reformist and human rights-lawyer Abdullahi Ahmed an-Naʿim *Towards an Islamic Reformation*, the conscience-related criterion of the golden rule is referred to in his suggestions for a re-formulation of classical Islamic law; more specifically, as 'the universal principle of reciprocity'.[100]

The golden rule – to treat the other as you would like to be treated yourself – is found in different wordings in most world religions, and attributed to Christ as well as Muḥammad. The classical Muslim expression of the golden rule is found both with Muslim and al-Bukhārī, in their *Kitāb al-īmān* ('The Book of Faith'): 'No one of you will become faithful till he wishes for his brother what he likes for himself.' This much cited reference would at least be open to universalizing approaches to Islamic ethics.[101]

An-Naʿim follows the logic of the golden rule as the principle of reciprocity in his argument for a revision of Sharīʿa – more specifically when it comes to women's rights and the status of religious minorities, which are the two weak points identified by an-Naʿim in his human rights perspective. A universal application of the golden rule challenges all barriers of empathetic identification with the other – be it a representative of the other sex, or another faith community. What men would like to be their rights (rights that they hold according to classical Shariʿa) must unreservedly be accepted as the equal rights of women. What Muslims – or Christians – would like to claim as their rights in society must unreservedly be recognized as the right of the other. Only thus can the golden rule gain universal validity.

As an-Naᶜim sees it, the re-formulation of Sharīᶜa made necessary by a subscription to the principle of universal human rights, can be given an Islamic legitimacy. His reinterpretation of the Islamic tradition is inspired by his teacher M. M. Taha's concept of *The Second Message of Islam.*[102] As Paul advocated a less radical equality between the sexes than what would follow from the practice attributed to Jesus in the Gospels, the Medina community (as mirrored in the Medinan revelations) was less radical in applying the principles of equality than what can be said to be the ethos of the Meccan revelations. For both faith communities, then, there is the question of whether the most radical impulse (attributed to the Christ of the Gospels and Muḥammad at Mecca) should have normative pre-eminence, and allow for a 'second message' according to which more radical equality could be advocated than what was realized in the historical context of the first faith communities.

Faith, Power, Non-Violence

Questions of faith, power and violence have always been of crucial importance in dialogues and controversies between Christians and Muslims – as well as within both communities.

As we have seen with Kāmil Ḥusayn and Khālid Muḥammad Khālid, the question of faith and violence is closely intertwined with the issue of human conscience. Kāmil Ḥusayn advocates 'the passive virtues of resistance', coming close to a sort of religiously based pacifism.[103] Khālid, although not advocating pacifism in a general sense, highlights Mahatma Gandhi and his non-violent resistance as 'the conscience of our age'.[104] In the Christian tradition, the issue of pacifism and more specifically, refusal of military service is typically spoken of as a question of conscience.

The issue of religion and power also relates to the personal examples of Jesus and Muḥammad. Out of their different life-stories arise serious and deep-going issues of dialogue: has God bestowed on man a trusteeship that allows for decisions on life and death, or does belief in God radically limit the use of absolute power? The reported ways of Jesus and Muḥammad differ at this point, although their respective religions have not differed substantially in their practice. As we have seen above, John Hick (1997b) notes that:

> Jesus himself was a pure pacifist, whilst his church, from Constantine onwards, has always been a patron of wars. Mohammad on the other hand was never a pacifist, although he did seek to moderate the savagery of war. The Qur'anic teaching included almost from the first both the call to personal surrender to God and the divine demand for a stable society, to be permeated by Islamic ideals.[105]

Today, many Christians would like to emulate pre-Constantine Christianity and draw a sharp demarcation line between church and political power. Most

Christians would still allow for a 'legitimate use of force' by the state – as already advocated by Paul, in Romans 13. Others would take exception to the death penalty and warfare, and maintain that the programmatic non-violence of Jesus should be absolutely binding for Christians in their approach to the evils of the world.

On the Muslim side, many Muslims would stress the restrictions on warfare found in Islamic sources. Many Islamists would also reserve the 'legitimate use of force' allowed for by Sharīʿa for an Islamic utopia, and in practice abstain from the most severe enforcement of Islamic law. Some would point to the mild practices of the Prophet in these matters as a paradigm of how the use of the sword can be minimized, although not forsaken.

Many Christians and Muslims – also those not advocating pacifism – would be ready to reconsider the old notions of just war in the light of modern weapons of mass destruction. Still others, Christians and Muslims alike, fuel their ideological and nationalist struggle with a belligerent religious language that can hardly be justified by either of the religious ethoses.

The 'founders' of the religions obviously differ on questions of faith, power and violence – the one rejecting worldly power and any use of violence, the other being the model of divinely guided statesmanship through word and sword. But Christianity and Islam share a centuries-long history of religion being intermingled with the world of politics, and face many of the same challenges when drawing the demarcation lines between religious authority and political use of force.

The point to be made here is that the differing responses on both sides presumably have some theological corollaries, and imply different readings of the life stories of the founders. As many Muslims would say: Jesus is a special case, to be admired for his commitment to non-violence in his personal mission, the aim of which was not to establish a new political order. Muḥammad shows how the matter should be settled in the context of polity.

Is this an acceptable way of settling the accounts? Or should more deep-going dialogue be sought, rethinking stereotyped images both of Christ and Muḥammad?

'Disciplining the Soul'

Above, we have pursued the question of human conscience into the realm of social ethics, with a view to the universal principles of reciprocity (the golden rule) and the question of faith, conscience and non-violence.

In the first place, however, human conscience has to do with individual integrity and the ethical constitution of the person. At the level of individual ethics, Islam has a rich tradition directed towards personal formation, 'disciplining of the soul' (*riyādat al-nafs*) and 'refinement of character' (*tahḏīb al-aḫlāq*).[106] This is true both of Ṣūfī ethics and Muslim philosophical ethics, as well as of more traditional, narrative ethics in Islam that focus upon the Prophet and other holy men and women as role models to be emulated in personal character formation. In many of these traditions, the example of Jesus may be cited side by side with that of Muḥammad, in a chain of prophets and wise men that deserve to be imitated. In al-Ghazālī's exposition of a narrative, Ṣūfī flavoured ethics aimed at 'breaking the desires', disciplining the soul and becoming marked by the character traits of God, we have seen that Jesus figures rather prominently (although subordinated to Muḥammad). Another obvious example is Rūmī's portrayal of Jesus as a supreme example of asceticism as well as of love, and his references to the 'Jesus within', waiting to be born in everyone of us.

It is striking how closely interrelated Islam and Christianity have often been when it comes to the ideals and techniques of personal formation. The view is commonly held that Ṣūfī ethics in Islam, especially in its more ascetic versions, have partly been initiated by the contact with Christian monasticism in the East. At a different level, Ibn Miskawayh's (d. 1030) masterpiece in philosophical ethics, *Tahḏīb al-aḫlāq* ('The Refinement of Character')[107] was partly inspired by a work with the same title by the Syrian Jacobite Christian Yaḥyā ibn ʿAdī (d. 974).[108] On the other hand, Muslim philosophical ethics, as well as Ṣūfī ethics, inspired the ethical thinking of Christian theologians, philosophers and mystics.[109] Both Christians and Muslims were, of course, in the first place influenced by Aristotelian and Neoplatonic ethics. They learnt from Greek teachings about how the forces of the soul should be balanced, vices avoided and virtues achieved, all with a view to eternity. Some of the pivotal works of Greek authors were translated into Arabic in the ninth century, by Christian Arabs such as Ḥunayn ibn Isḥāq who was employed by the Muslim caliph al-Mutawakkil in Bagdad.[110]

In these traditions, Plato, Aristotle, Jesus and Muḥammad have *de facto* been companions on the road, in the creative work of their followers aimed at formulating an ethos of personal formation that nourished itself from more than one tradition. The works of al-ʿAqqād, Ḥusayn and Khālid, much cited above, clearly belong to this tradition of mystical and philosophical, Christian and Muslim cross-fertilization.

Divine Pedagogy

A theological question of ethical relevance, related to the foundation of morality, is what kind of 'divine pedagogy' might be presupposed by a religious ethics in the shaping of the moral self. Many would be prone to simplifications in this field, implying that Christian morality is based on a loving God, whereas Muslim morality is based on fear of God. Another simplification would be that Christianity operates within the paradigm of guilt/forgiveness, whereas the Islamic ethos is predominantly within the paradigm of honour/shame.

Obviously the matter cannot be settled that easily. Islam knows much of God's mercy and forgiveness, and fear of God has always been part of the Christian ethos. Many Muslims, and Christians alike, would criticize a notion of love that implies permissiveness. Conversely, reflective Christians and Muslims would be equally critical towards a pedagogy (be it human or divine) that is mainly fear-based. The paradigms of honour/shame and guilt/forgiveness are present in both religions and may reflect the tension between predominant paradigms of religion in traditional and modern societies respectively. There has never been such a thing as one single Christian or one particular Muslim ethos.

What are the lessons to be drawn from the Sunna of Jesus and Muḥammad – assuming that we really have any access to their personal examples, embodied as they are in the ethos of their followers? Jesus confuses people by demanding more radically than anyone else in the field of ethics, far beyond what can be fulfilled by any disciple (cf. the Sermon on the Mount), and at the same time forgiving more unconditionally than anyone, to the point of being accused of blasphemy. Muḥammad delivers a revealed ethics that is clearly intended to be practicable (cf. sūra 2.28: 'God wishes to lighten things for you'), but without overlooking the need of forgiveness, and claiming not only certain deeds, but all of the human soul for God.

So, how do we read our traditions? How do we see the relation between warnings and unconditional love? How is morality fostered, divinely and humanly? The overlap between the religions – and the importance of a shared reflection – should be obvious.

Clearly interrelated with the 'pedagogical' question is that of freedom and limits. Both on the family level and in communal coexistence, not to mention the questions of global survival, a rethinking of human freedom and the limits of 'self-fulfilment' is called for. An intriguing aspect of Christian–Muslim dialogue in this field might be the overlap between Christianity and Islam as to their 'permissiveness' or 'restrictions' in different compartments of life. The respective perceptions of men's and women's rights, of sexuality and monogamy, of food and fasting, of religion and power, of legitimate violence, clearly show that neither of the religions possesses *the* permissive or *the* restrictive tradition. Again, the crossing lines call for a shared reflection.

Doing Theology

As can be learnt from reflections on the ethical connection, ethical questions in Christianity and Islam cannot be separated from theology.

Implications of Monotheism

In an essay about 'Islam and Christian Monotheism', John Hick (1997a/1991) unfolds the implications of his pluralist theology of religions for the doctrines of Trinity and incarnation, two major stumbling blocks in theological dialogues between Christians and Muslims. Hick suggests that the doctrine of Trinity should not be seen as part of the Christian Gospel itself, but as a human theory devised to protect another doctrine, namely that of incarnation. In positive terms, he sees the trinitarian idea as:

> . . . witnessing to the plurality of God's activities in relation to His creation, [if] pursued far enough it can open out into an acceptance of the great world faiths as responses to different moments of divine revelation.[111]

What about the other stumbling block, then – that of incarnation? In tune with his other writings, Hick claims that the doctrine of incarnation can be generalized in a sense that implies seeing:

> . . . in the life of Christ a supreme instance of that fusion of divine grace and creaturely freedom that occur in all authentic human responses and obedience to God . . ..[112]

At least two types of problems related to John Hick's reinterpretation of classical dogmas may be identified: First, his universalizing approach can easily be seen as imposing upon the faiths it is meant to unite, a theological structure that is foreign to both of them. Secondly, even if one might sympathize on personal grounds with Hick's search for a global theology, it does not bring together the majority of believers, who would often hold far more traditional and particularist views. It could be argued, then, that only theological approaches that accommodate real differences can have the function of creating some kind of bond between believers of different faiths.

As for the monotheistic foundation of ethics highlighted by Sardar and others, what would be the specific significance of monotheism in ethics? Many modern Muslim interpreters of *tawḥīd* (divine unity) take monotheism as a call to transform the social order, since the opposite attitude of *širk* (associating with God, interpreted as illegitimate lordship) implies the unequal distribution of knowledge, wealth and power. The ethical implications of a radical monotheistic belief would thus be obvious. But for all the ethical relevance of monotheism, many would feel uncomfortable if Christians and Muslims were to confront 'atheism' on the underlying presumption that a theistic belief necessarily fosters a more moral society. That is obviously not the case. An honest dialogue on monotheism and ethics has to cater for the fact that 'God on our side' is maybe the most dangerous notion that men can hold, and that Christians and Muslims obviously have more sins to confess in this respect than secular humanists.

Nevertheless, positive elaboration of the importance of a sincere belief in the sovereignty of God remains a challenging task in the field of ethics.

Reading the Signs of God

We have seen that some Muslims demand that Christians at least suspend (if not abandon) their assertion of the uniqueness of Jesus, for the sake of a dialogue on common monotheistic ground. Whatever Christians might respond to this claim, there remains the question of the contents of the divine revelation through Jesus and Muḥammad respectively. Uniqueness has to be judged by the contents of their messages.

Christianity and Islam both invite the human being to careful reading of the signs of God. Reading signs has to do with *semiotics*. For a future dialogue between the 'Societies of the Book', Mohammed Arkoun sees some hope in semiotics when it comes to the possibility of reading religious texts in a new way, overcoming dogmatism, but taking theology seriously.[113]

Semiotics deals with the significance of signs, not only their semantic, intratextual meaning, but also the question of their reference, historically and metaphysically. Semiotics has to do with the relations between the signifier ('the sign itself'), the signified (the reference of the sign, e.g. God) and the sign-interpreter (who receives the signs in faith, or rejects them).

By its triadic structure, semiotics integrates textual analysis and the aesthetics of reception. Semiotics takes for granted that any 'significant' textual corpus implies a multiplicity of receptions, and thus a multi-layered meaning. For Christianity's part, multi-layered meaning is part of the very concept of a Gospel, reflected in the fact that the New Testament contains four different Gospels with differing emphases and different implicit receptions. For Islam's part, multi-layered meaning has often been accepted by Ṣūfīs and Shīʿites as part of the divine revelation itself.

Approaching the signs of God is plunging into the depths of theology, although respecting that God himself is the ultimate meaning, inaccessible in its fullness. How do we read the signs of divine revelation? Who is the God they refer to? How is God revealed to us through his signs, in the miracles of life, through his Word, in his passion for humanity?[114]

A common approach to the signs of God must elaborate the notions of 'sign' in the New Testament and in the Qur'ān. Christ himself is regarded as a sign both in the New Testament and in the Qur'ān.[115] In the Qur'ān, he might be seen as one of God's many signs in history and nature. The Arabic word for sign, *āya*, is a key word in the Qur'ān, with a multiplicity of references. It refers to God's wonders in nature and God's action in history (*āyāt ullāh*), the miracles of the Prophets and more specifically to the wonder of the Qur'ān, reflected in the naming of qur'ānic verses as *āyāt*. In the New Testament Gospels, *semeion* (Greek for 'sign') is a key word when referring to the actions of

Jesus, especially his miracles as received in faith. In both religions, there is thus an obvious perception of the miraculous as a 'sign'. But in the Gospels – in contrast to the Qur'ān – not only Jesus' birth and his healing of the sick, but also the mystery of cross and resurrection is conceived of as a miracle and a sign.[116]

In an essay about 'The Miracle of Jesus', Mahmoud Ayoub (1993) equates the qur'ānic notion *āya* with 'miracle'. In its most inclusive sense, it refers to the Word of God itself:

> It is either the Word revealed to humankind with a challenge that it be accepted and lived by, or the creative word of command (*amr*). This is the great miracle of creation and revelation.[117]

In Jesus, the Word of God takes the shape of a 'miracle of life':

> The miracle of life that is Jesus unfolds . . . as a lifegiving and sanctifying divine force.[118] [. . .] Who then is Jesus, the miracle of life, of love and of healing? He is the Word of God and the servant of God and the Messenger of God. He is the Savior of us all, for what is salvation but healing? A savior is not simply one who dies for the sins of others, but also one who heals the sickness of the human soul; one who infuses life into dead spirits by his own life and spirit.[119]

In the view of Ayoub, however, Jesus is not the Word of God or a life-giving miracle in any exclusive sense. Like the Qur'ān, the miracle of Jesus is an inclusive, ever-lasting sign of God: 'The miracle of Jesus, like the miracle of the Qur'ān, is not a once-only event, but an everlasting source of blessing, guidance, and salvation.'[120]

Like Ayoub, Hasan Askari (1972) regards Christ as a common Sign for Christians and Muslims. He even speaks of Christ as 'unlike any other sign the Quran speaks about': 'He is the Word of God.'[121]

Exploring 'the dialogical relationship between Christianity and Islam', he warns against the monological tendencies in both religions as well as in the technological society. Askari sees Christianity and Islam as constituting 'a dialogical whole':

> The truth is that Christianity and Islam constitute one complex of faith, one starting with the Person, and another with the Word. Their separateness does not denote two areas of conflicting truths, but a dialogical necessity.[122]

In this perspective, Askari explores the reality of Christ as a common 'Sign' for Christians and Muslims. He regards Christ as 'symbol *par excellence* of the dialogical relationship between God and man . . .'.[123] For Askari, reading the signs of God is different from objectifying the Word of God in a book, or in a Person.

Monological religion objectifies everything – the Book, the Person and thereby the other. Dialogical religion – oriented towards the Sign – must be differently apprehended. In dialogue, existence means inter-existence: 'Each man becomes a neighbour.'[124] In this inter-existence,[125] neither truth can be objectified. The fact of conflicting interpretations should not be regarded as a threat, but rather as a reflection of what a sign implies:

> *It is the very ambiguity, richness, of the religious sign that gives rise to different and even opposed interpretations and understandings.*[126]

Plunging deep into the mystery of dialogue, Askari states that 'Unity is had when a religious sign is shared'. Since Christ is a common sign for Christians and Muslims, Askari concludes that 'Once having known Christ is to belong together'.[127] For Askari, this is not a friendship without pain, either on the human level or in the relationship to God. The sign of Christ itself reveals:

> . . . how ambiguous and how difficult is the sphere of this relationship [between God and man], how deeply man can deceive himself in the name of God, how truth could be used to destroy truth, how the most elaborate and confident theologies could become a wall between God and man. It is here, in this realm, that Christ lives on in history as a sure reminder, as an unmistakable warning. Christ appears then as a Sign *outside* and *against* all creed-based testimonies of truth, love, and suffering.[128]

On the human level, pain is related to the discovery of the other. 'To drop monologue is to immediately discover the other.' But:

> The discovery of the other, of our own being, is both soothing and painful, more the latter. The other is pain, a sting, a bite, but a pain in our very being, of it. It is right in the middle of this pain and anxiety that a Divine Sign is known.[129]

If Christians and Muslims venture a joint reading of the signs of God, in a friendship that is potentially painful, they might experience even a deeper, but shared suffering:

> Thrown in front of God, facing this deep, vast Absolute, Christians and Muslims will undergo the second pain, far acuter, wider and sharper than the first. This is Second Suffering. It is here that God meets man, and man meets Christ. It was in this state that Mohammed heard the Word of God.[130]

Modes of Doing Theology

Any question of theological relevance raises the question of how theology is done by Christians and Muslims. Many recent contributors to the question of Christ in Islam state that it is due time to overcome the controversy about dogmatic statements. Instead, one should encourage a dialogue about existential questions that are equally important to both sides.[131] Can we foresee a common reflection on the fundamentals of human existence as well as the fundamental paradigms of theology – or are we destined to live separately in our different theological enclaves, at the best studying and respecting each other?

Kenneth Cragg suggests that a Christology of the heart, and a poetic theology might be a fertile soil for a future dialogue.

> The Ṣūfī awareness of Jesus, if we can do it justice, will best help us to find a tributary into a Christology of the heart from the springs of Islam . . . . Perhaps is the lesson of the long centuries of doctrinal encounter between faiths, and in particular between Islam and Christianity, that we should let the poetry of faith take over its commendation . . . .[132]

Referring to the fact that many in the contemporary world, outside a practising commitment to Christianity, nevertheless involve themselves with the mystery of Jesus 'as the clue to their art and their existence', he asks for 'a Christology of the heart'.[133]

How would 'a theology of the heart' fit with the ethical connection put forward both by Muslims and Christians as the most pressing focus of theological dialogue? Ethical commitment, and sharing of ideals, is but one dimension of human existence. Life experiences are also about not succeeding, and about suffering. A theology of the heart will have to relate not only to human ideals, but also to the harsh realities of life that can only be shared in openness when deep confidence is reached.

It could be argued that only when the encounter with the other is recognized as a painful experience that shatters one's own identity, can otherness make a real difference in the (re)formation of the religious Self. As we have seen with Hasan Askari (1972), pain can clearly be thought of as an integral part of 'the dialogical relationship between Christianity and Islam'. If differences are taken seriously, true dialogue will always be painful.

It remains an open question what might come out of a dialogue that has sharing of pain, and not just shared ideals, as its starting point. Christians and Muslims have seldom had shared suffering – and shared hopes – as a common ground for theological reflection. The Palestinian experience might be a notable exception, as well as joint experiences between Christians and Muslims suffering from and combating apartheid in South Africa.

The latter experience is movingly reflected upon by Farid Esack in his book *Qur'an, Liberation and Pluralism: An Islamic Perspective of Interreligious Solidarity against Oppression*.[134] Farid Esack reflects theologically on the shared experience between Christians and Muslims in confronting apartheid. The struggle against apartheid did not only unite Muslims and Christians. Muslims and Christians were also divided within their own camps – between those who benefited from apartheid or silently complied with it (like the majority of white Christians, and many 'Asian' Muslims), and those who decided to fight it.

For Esack, as a Muslim theologian, the experience that the dividing lines did not coincide with those of the religious communities, but rather cut painfully across them, necessitated a critical reassessment of the qur'ānic notion of 'the other'.[135] In Esack's interpretation, it was the struggle for justice that prompted some of the harsh words against Jews and Christians in the Qur'ān. But what was true of some Jewish and Christian groups then (on the Arabian peninsula of the seventh century), in a historical conflict with specific social and political characteristics, is not necessarily true in a different context. Instead, one should look for the deeper content of the qur'ānic message, which calls for faithful confrontation of injustice and oppression in all places and circumstances. According to Esack, faith (*īmān*) and *islām* in the qur'ānic sense can never be entrenched within the confines of a specific religious community carrying its name. It cuts deeper. Sometimes, true faith will bring Christians and Muslims together in a struggle for justice which may be controversial in both camps.

Notes

1 Siddiqui (1997: 160). Cf. Siddiqui (2005).
2 Balić (1979: 3).
3 Ibid., p. 7.
4 Ibid.
5 Ibid., pp. 7f.
6 Khālid (n.d./1958: 7).
7 Phipps (1996: 12).
8 Ibid., p. 245.
9 Cragg (1984: 1).
10 Kerr (1995: 426).
11 Siddiqui (1997: 172).
12 For the concept of a first/second/third quest, see Bernhard Brandon Scott, 'From Reimarus to Crossan: Stages in a Quest'. *Currents in Research*, 2 (1994: 253–280).
13 San Francisco: Harper (1994).
14 Ibid., p. 15.
15 Ibid., p. 17.

16 John Dominic Crossan, *Jesus: A Revolutionary Biography*. San Francisco: Harper (1994).
17 E. P. Sanders, *Jesus and Judaism*. Philadelphia: Fortress Press (1985: 22).
18 Géza Vermès, *The Relgion of Jesus the Jew*. London: SCM Press (1985).
19 Bannister (2003: 11).
20 Cf. Robert W. Funk, Roy W. Hoover and The Jesus Seminar, *The Five Gospels: The Search for the Authentic Words of Jesus*. New York: Macmillan (1993).
21 For an overview, see G. J. Riley, 'The Gospel of Thomas in Recent Scholarship'. *Currents in Research*, 2 (1994: 227–252).
22 Cf. Burton S. Mack, *The Lost Gospel: The Book of Q and Christian Origins*. San Francisco: Harper (1993).
23 See Elmar S. Gruben and Holger Kersten, *The Original Jesus. The Buddhist Sources of Christianity*. Shaftesbury: Element Books Ltd. (1995).
24 For a controversial example, see Morton Smith, *Jesus the Magician*. Wellingborough: The Aquarian Press (1985, first published 1978). Also the Jewish scholar Geza Vermez focuses on Jesus as miracle worker, but within the confines of charismatic Judaism.
25 Cf. Luke Timothy Johnson, *The Real Jesus: The Misguided Quest for the Historical Jesus and the Truth of the Traditional Gospels*. San Francisco: Harper (1996).
26 Sanders, op. cit., p. 5.
27 Cf. Räisänen (1997: 118–136), 'Word of God, Word of Muhammad: Could Historical Criticism of the Qur'an be Pursued by Muslims?'
28 Peters (1996: 338–339).
29 Oneworld, Oxford (1997).
30 Op. cit., p. 55.
31 Ibid., p. 60.
32 Siddiqui (1997: 168f.).
33 Formulated by Alan Race, in *Christians and Religious Pluralism: Patterns in the Christian Theology of Religions*. London: SCM Press (1983).
34 Cragg (1984: 145).
35 Ibid., p. 155.
36 Ibid., p. 154.
37 Ibid., p. 159.
38 Siddiqui (1997: 170).
39 Ibid., p. 171.
40 Phipps (1996: 53).
41 Hick (1997b/1991: 118).
42 Bijlefeld (1982: 202).
43 Ibid., p. 214.
44 Cragg (1985a: 207).
45 Cf. an almost identical contribution with the same title, 'Christology in an Islamic context', in *Al-Mushir*, 2 (1982: 53–62). From the Pakistani

context, see also Kristine M. Rogers, 'Consultation on "Christology in an Islamic Context"', *Al-Mushir*, 3–4 (1983: 191–196).

46 Nazir-Ali (1987: 25).

47 Ibid., p. 28.

48 For the qur'ānic notion of *rasūl* in a dialogical perspective, see Hasan Askari, 'The Qur'anic Conception of Apostleship', in *Islam in a World of Diverse Faiths*, edited by Dan Cohn-Sherbok, pp. 88–103. London: Macmillan (1997/1991).

49 Ibid., p. 31.

50 Cf. Nazir-Ali (1987), 'A Christian Assessment of the Cult of Prophet-Veneration'.

51 Ibid., p. 31.

52 Cf. Ritchie (1985).

53 Schumann (1988: 173), in my translation. (. . . 'es gab . . . Arroganz und Herrschsucht, die sich mit dem Hinweis auf die Erhöhung und Herrschaft Christi rechtfertigte und beanspruchte, an ihnen Anteil zu haben'.)

54 Ibid., p. 178, in my translation. ('Denn nur am Kreuz, durch die endliche Überwindung des Eigenwillens und seines Zieles, "zu sein wie Gott", kann die immer wieder neue menschliche Versuchung zum '*širk*' überwunden werden.')

55 Ibid., in my translation. ('Für die ersten Christen waren das Dienen und der Gehorsam dieses einfachen Menschen Jesus bis zum Ende der Ausdruck einer Kraft. Aber diese Kraft hat ihre Quelle nicht in sich selbst, sondern in der Liebe.')

56 Ibid., p. 179, in my translation. ('Jesu Abwehr einer Identifizierung des Gottesherrschaft mit einem politischen Gesellschafts- oder Staatsverständnis wird von Christen nicht als Mangel verstanden, sondern ihre Vermischung gerade als unheilige Versuchung.')

57 The subtitle of Borrmans (1976).

58 Author of *In Search of Muhammad*, 2008 and *In search of Jesus*, 2001.

59 Bennett (2008: 174).

60 Ibid., p. 175.

61 Singh (2008: 3f.).

62 Cf. the section 'Summarising central features of Ṣūfī images of Jesus' in Chapter 5.

63 Singh (2008: 199).

64 Cragg (2008b: 182f.).

65 Cragg (2008a), previously published in 2004 in Kenneth Cragg, *A Certain Sympathy of Scriptures: Biblical and Quranic*. Brighton: Sussex Academic Press.

66 Cragg (2008b: 42).

67 Glaser (2008: 153).

68 See Räisänen (1997), pp. 81–117 – 'Jesus between Christianity and Islam: Muhammad's Portrait of the Jewish Prophet' – and pp. 189–203 –

'Conclusion: The Pluralist Imperative'. The idea of Jesus standing between Christianity and Islam was put forward by Räisänen in an article in Swedish from 1991 (Räisänen 1991).

69 Räisänen (1993: 196–197).

70 Räisänen (1997: 91).

71 Räisänen (1997: 93).

72 Räisänen (1997: 97 – cf. pp. 118–136), 'Word of God, Word of Muhammad: Could Historical Criticism of the Qur'an be Pursued by Muslims?'

73 Räisänen (1997: 96–97). For the view of Christ standing 'between' Christians and Muslims, see also Askari (1972).

74 Jørgensen (2008: 131–259).

75 Ibid., p. 198.

76 Ibid., p. 180.

77 Ibid., p. 169.

78 Ibid., p. 222, 253.

79 Oddbjørn Leirvik, 'Charismatic Mission, Miracles and Faith-Based Diplomacy: The Case of Aril Edvardsen', In Sturla J. Stålsett (ed.), *Spirits of Globalization: The Growth of Pentecostalism and Experiental Spiritualities in a Global Age*. London: SCM Press (2006: 140).

80 Ibid., cf. Jørgensen (2008: 204ff.).

81 Jeffrey Sharlet, 'Jesus Plus Nothing: Undercover Among Americas's Secret Theocrats'. *Harper's Magazine* (March 2003: 53–64).

82 Leirvik, 'Charismatic mission . . .', p. 135.

83 As for contemporary Tafsīr, Kate Zebiri has made the interesting observation that modern exegetes never make 'any connection between the healing miracles of Jesus and the practices in popular, Sufi-influenced forms of Islam, whereby supplication is made to God and to saints or holy men for the healing of illnesses' (Zebiri 2000: 87).

84 Kerr (1993: 215).

85 Quoted from Kerr (1993: 206). The quotation is taken from al-Farūqī's book *On Arabism: Urubah and Religion. A Study of the Fundamental Ideas of Arabism and of Islam as Its Highest Moment of Consciousness.* Amsterdam: Djambatan (1962).

86 In *Islam and Christian–Muslim Relations*, 1 (1991: 56ff.).

87 Ibid., p. 71.

88 Ibid., p. 75.

89 Ibid., p. 67.

90 Shabbir Akhtar, *The Light in the Enlightenment*. London: Grey Seal (1990: 49); cf. Sardar, op. cit., p. 69.

91 Sardar p. 69, citing Akhtar.

92 Sardar, op. cit., pp. 69f.

93 Ibid., p. 73.

94 Leirvik (2006, 2002).

95 London 1991.
96 Op. cit., p. 38.
97 A statement qualified by making an exception for Christian liberation theology.
98 Ibid., pp. 61–62.
99 Ibid., p. 45.
100 New York: Syracuse University Press (1990: 1, 162–165).
101 In the edition of *Sahih al-Boukhari* by Dar el Fiker, Beyrouth, 1993, the translator Mahmoud Matraji adds a narrowing parenthesis: 'his (Mulim [misprint for Muslim]) brother'; see vol. I, p. 15. The same is the case with M. Muhsin Khan's translation which is accessible through the widely used searchable Hadith database of the MSA-USC (http://www.usc.edu/dept/MSA/reference/searchhadith.html) – accessed July 2009. However in Matraji's translation of the corresponding ḥadīth (in the edition of Muslim by Dar el Fiker, Beyrouth, 1993), no such parenthesis is added (see vol. 1A, p. 37).
102 Syracuse University Press, New York (1987).
103 Cf. also Kenneth Cragg, 'Peace, Pacificism and Religious Faith', in *Journal – Institute of Muslim Minority Affairs*, vol. 13 (1992: 215–221) – with references to Ḥusayn.
104 Khālid (1971/1963: 220).
105 Hick (1997b/1991: 118).
106 As for al-Ghazālī's mature representation of this tradition, cf. T. J. Winters translation with introduction and notes to *Al-G̲h̲azālī on Discipling the Soul – Kitāb riyāḍat al-nafs 6 on Breaking the two Desires – Kitāb kasr al-s̲h̲ahwatayn. Books XXII and XXIII of the Religious Sciences – Iḥyā' 'ulūm al-dīn*. Cambridge: Islamic Texts Society (1995).
107 In English translation: *The Refinement of Character. A translation from Arabic of Aḥmad ibn Muḥammad Miskawayh's Tahdhīb al-Akhlāq*, by Constantine K. Zurayk. Beirut: The American University of Beirut (1968). The expression *Tahd̲ib al-ah̲lāq* is also part of the title of al-Ghazālī's chapter on 'disciplining the soul' in *Iḥyā'*, together with the 'therapeutic' concept of 'curing the sicknesses of the heart' (*mu'ālajat amrāḍ al-qalb*).
108 Cf. Majid Fakhry, *Ethical Theories in Islam*. Leiden: E. J. Brill (1994: 100–130).
109 Dwight M. Donaldson, in his *Studies in Muslim Ethics* (London: SPCK 1953) cites the parallels between the *Ethicon* of the Christian Syriac author Bar Hebraeus and the *Iḥyā'* of al-Ghazālī.
110 Cf. W. M. Watt, *The Influence of Islam on Medieval Europe*. Edinburgh: Edinburgh University Press (1994: 30–32).
111 Hick (1997a/1991: 9).
112 Ibid., pp. 9–10.
113 See his *Rethinking Islam Today*, Washington (1987: 23).

114 For a 'sign'-approach to Islam and interreligious dialogue, see also Annemarie Schimmel, *Deciphering the Signs of God: A Phenomenological Approach to Islam.* Albany: State University of New York Press (1994).
115 Compare Luke 2.34–35 and Qur'ān 21.91. For Christ as a sign, cf. Fitzgerald (1981) – 'Jesus: A Sign for Christians and Muslims' – and Räisänen (1971, see II.1.f above).
116 Cf. the notion 'sign of Jonah' in the Gospels, Matthew 12.39ff. with parallels.
117 Ayoub (1993: 222).
118 Ibid., p. 224.
119 Ibid., p. 226.
120 Ibid., p. 227.
121 Askari (1972: 482).
122 Askari (1972: 485).
123 Ibid., p. 484.
124 Ibid., p. 481.
125 Cf. his book-title *Inter Religion* (Aligarh, 1977).
126 Askari (1972: 485).
127 Ibid.
128 Ibid., pp. 482–483.
129 Ibid., p. 486.
130 Ibid.
131 Cf. Schumann (1988: 171).
132 Cragg (1985a: 45).
133 Ibid., p. 44.
134 Oneworld, Oxford (1997).
135 See the chapters 'Redefining Self and Other' and 'The Qur'ān and the Other' in Esack, op. cit.

Chapter 9

Postscript

Knowing by Oneself, Knowing with the Other: A 'Conscientious' Dialogue between Religions[1]

In an article on 'conscience' in *The Encyclopedia of Religion*, Michel Despland writes:

> On the interreligious scene today, it is to be wished that dialogue and encounter shall proceed from conscience. And the notion of conscience may well be – or become – part of the account that each will give to the other of his or her own humanity. Such meeting of consciences cannot occur without the labor of consciousness: each trying to communicate over a period of time what he is aware of.[2]

Could 'conscience' have any role to fulfil in a dialogue between religions? The notion of conscience is moulded in Christian tradition and European philosophy – beginning with the Greek *syneídēsis* and the Latin *conscientia*. Attempts have been made to identify a notion of conscience in other traditions as well. In James Hasting's *Encyclopedia of Religion and Ethics* published in 1911, one finds articles on 'conscience' in Babylonian, Egyptian, Greek-Roman, Jewish and Islamic religion. Such an approach, however, presupposes that some conceptual essence in the notion of conscience – like internalization of morality or personal responsibility – is distilled in advance. In ancient Egyptian religion, in Jewish tradition and in Islam, the metaphor of the 'heart' expresses the inner centre of man – capable of moral judgements and self-evaluation as well as of personal communication with God, and in need of purification.

However, the Greek-Roman, and later Christian notion of conscience involves something more than moral and religious internalization. What appears to be specific for the notion of conscience is rather the tension between the turn inwards (towards the self) and the orientation outwards (towards the others) – between knowing by oneself and knowing with others. Etymologically, as the prefixes *syn-*, *con-* and *sam-* (in Norwegian *samvit*) show, conscience means 'knowing with' someone. It might be oneself, but just as well the other. And maybe the two cannot be separated, in becoming 'oneself as another'.[3]

Is the discourse of conscience a specifically Western/Christian discourse, then, or can parallel ideas of conscience be traced in other traditions – making an intercultural or interreligious dialogue on conscience meaningful (cf. the wish expressed by Despland)?

Classical Islam lacks an exact equivalent for the word conscience. In modern standard Arabic, *ḍamīr* has gradually become (from the mid-nineteenth century) the central word for 'conscience'.[4] As we have seen, prominent Egyptian intellectuals from the twentieth century like ʿAbbās Mahmūd al-ʿAqqād, Muḥammad Kāmil Ḥusayn and Khālid Muḥammad Khālid, all put the notion of *ḍamīr* at the centre of their works when they (in the 1950s and '60s) addressed issues of religion, philosophy and ethics in an interreligious perspective.

But what exactly is 'in' their notion of conscience, as expressed by *ḍamīr*? With reference to the Egyptian authors cited above, there are good reasons for taking *ḍamīr* as a predominantly existentialist notion, in tune with the etymologically inward orientation of the word *ḍamīr*. Khālid, who defines conscience as 'the human being in its true existence' (*al-insān fī wujūdihi al-ḥaqīqī*),[5] relates his discourse of *ḍamīr* to the more general question of human authenticity. But the question of authenticity is clearly something more than being true to oneself as an individual. Both with Khālid and al-ʿAqqād, conscience has a social dimension to it: 'Individual consciences must not separate their work from participation in social life.'[6]

The question of conscience in dialogue points to something more than ethics: On both the individual and communal levels, it has to do with the relation between knowing by oneself and knowing with the other. If others are always included in my conscience, who are they, and how are they conceived? Just as more of the same, like me and my community, or as others with a challenging and potentially painful difference? In the context of Muslim–Christian relations, how can knowing by oneself be reconciled with knowing something obligating together with the religiously other?

As for the context of the writings of al-ʿAqqād, Ḥusayn and Khālid, I have suggested that their writings reflect both a long Egyptian experience of Muslim–Christian coexistence and the nationalist as well as universalistic outlook of the Nasserite era in Egypt. But, knowing with distinctive others is vulnerable experience. What has been positively known and lived in commitment to shared values (such as national independence, democracy and social justice), cannot easily be maintained in a changed context. In Egypt, the 1950s and early 1960s were still marked by the shared Egyptian identity felt by Muslims and Christians alike. From the late 1960s, events took a different turn. Muslim as well as Christian revivalism shifted the emphasis from knowing together towards knowing with oneself – as Christians and Muslims, without being inspired or disturbed by foreign voices.[7]

In contemporary Arabic, the modern term for authenticity – *aṣāla* – is not oriented towards any general sense of humanness, but rather towards the specific features of the Arab-Islamic heritage.[8] Some would say that Coptic revivalism has led to a similar shift of focus – from the shared identity of Christians and Muslims as Egyptians, to the specific Christian/Coptic identity. In a study of changes in relations between Copts and Muslims between 1952 and 1994, Christiaan van Nispen has observed that 'religious belonging increasingly becomes the unique or principal means of defining oneself, i.e. something that divides citizens rather than something that unites them'.[9]

Those who still endeavour to know something obligating together with others, in a readiness to accept and live with the difference of distinctive others, are on the defensive in many places, not only in Egypt. Because of this rather disturbing fact, voices who testify to a close past of more inclusive discourses are worth listening to.

In late modernity, however, particularism and distinctive identities seem to have come to stay, and there might be no return to the universalistic discourses of the typically modern projects of reform. If dialogue is to be able to carry the weight of difference, knowing together must always imply the readiness to live well with potentially painful otherness at close hand.

Maybe only a conscience capable of containing pain and respecting difference can furnish Christians and Muslims with a hope of becoming *oneself as another* – without violating either of the two.

Notes

1 For a fuller discussion of the notion of conscience as a clue to Muslim–Christian dialogue, see Leirvik (2006; cf. Leirvik 2002, 2003, 2008).

2 Michel Despland, 'Conscience', in *The Encyclopedia of Religion*, vol. 4, p. 51. New York: Macmillan (1987).

3 Cf. Paul Ricoeur, *Oneself as Another*. Chicago: The University of Chicago Press (1992). Interestingly, Ricoeur ends his reflections on the relation between the self and the other with a discussion of the notion of conscience, pp. 341–356.

4 Leirvik (2006), ch. 5 – 'Conscience in Arabic: the semantics of *ḍamīr*.'

5 Khālid (n.d./1958: 96, 108, 133).

6 al-ʿAqqād, *Al-tafkīr – farīḍa islāmiyya* (n.d./1961: 130).

7 Cf. Leirvik (2006), ch. 10 – 'Christians and Muslims in Egypt: United or Separated by Modernity?'

8 Cf. Aziz al-Azmeh, 'The Discourse of Cultural Authenticity: Islamist

Revivalism and Enlightenment Universalism', in *Islams and Modernities*. London/New York: Verso (1993).

9 Christiaan van Nispen, 'Changes in Relations between Copts and Muslims (1952–1994) in the Light of the Historical Experience'. In *Between Desert and City: The Coptic Orthodox Church Today*, edited by Nelly van Doorn-Harder and Kari Vogt, p. 29 (Oslo: Novus forlag 1997).

Bibliography

ʿAbd al-Wahhāb, Aḥmad (1988), *Al-masīḥ fı maṣādir al-ʿaqāʾid al-masīḥiyya*. Cairo: Maktabat Wahbah, 2nd ed. In English: *Christ as Seen in the Sources of the Christian Beliefs*. Cairo: Wahba Book Shop, 2nd ed. 1985.

ʿAbdul-Ahad, S. and Gairdner, W. H. T. (1975), *The Gospel of Barnabas. An Essay and Enquiry*. Hyderabad: Henry Martin Institute of Islamic Studies.

Adams, C. C. (1944), 'A fatwa on the "ascension" of Jesus'. *The Muslim World*, XXXIV, no. 3, 214–17.

Addleton, J. S. (1990), 'Images of Jesus in the Literatures of Pakistan'. *The Muslim World,* LXXX, no. 2, 96–106.

Ahmad, M. G. (1989), *Jesus in India*. Islamabad and Tilford: Islam International Publications.Translated from the Urdu 'Masih Hindustan Mein', 1st ed. 1899.

Ajijola, A. D. (1975), *The Myth of the Cross*. Lahore: Islamic Publications.

Alam, Mohammad B. (1990), *Descension of Christ. A summary with a New Rational and Scientific Explanation*. New Delhi: Saeed International. Translated from the Urdu 'Nuzul-e-Esa', 1st ed. 1978.

Anawati, G. C. (1955), 'Jésus et ses juges d'après "La Cité Inique" du Dr. Kamel Hussein'. *MIDEO* (Cairo), II, 71–134.

Anawati, G. C. (1978), "ʿĪsā'. In *Encyclopedia of Islam*. Leiden: E. J. Brill.

al-ʿAqqād, ʿAbbās Maḥmūd (1985/1942), *ʿAbqariyyat Muḥammad* ('The Genius of Muḥammad'). 1st ed. Cairo 1942. In *Islāmiyyāt*. Cairo: Dār al-Maʿrifa, 1985.

al-ʿAqqād, ʿAbbās Maḥmūd (n.d./1953), *ʿAbqariyyat al-Masīḥ*. Cairo: Dār Nahḍat Miṣr. 1953: 1st ed., Matbaʿat Dār Akhbār al-Yawm. 1957: 2nd ed. as *Ḥayāt al-Masīḥ*. Dār al-Hilāl. Republished by Nahḍat Miṣr in 1996.

al-ʿAqqād, ʿAbbās Maḥmūd (1961), 'The Gospel of Barnabas'. *The News Bulletin of the Near East Christian Council,* Eastertide 1961, 9–12. Translated and commentary by Kenneth Cragg.

Arnaldez, R. (1980), *Jésus fils de Marie, prophète de'Islam*. Paris: Desclée.

Arnaldez, R. and Maurice B. (1986), 'Jesus, hijo de Maria, profeta del Islam', *Encuentro Islamo-Christiano* (Madrid) 175. Translation of parts of Arnaldez 1980, and comments by Borrmans.

Arnaldez, R. (1988), *Jésus dans la pensée musulmane*. Paris: Desclée.

Asin et Palacios, M. (1917 and 1926, cf. 1974), 'Logia et Agrapha Domini Jesu apud Moslemicos Scriptores, asceticos praesertim, usitata'. *Patrologia Orientalis*, XIII and XIX, 335–431 and 531–624. First part reprinted by *Patrologia Orientalis*, 1974.

Askari, H. (1972), 'The Dialogical Relationship between Christianity and Islam'. *Journal of Ecumenical Studies*, 8, 477–88.

Askari, H. (1985), 'With and Beyond the Experience of Religious Diversity', in J. Hick and H. Askari (eds.), *The Experience of Religious Diversity*. London: Gower.

Askari, H. (2005), 'The Real Presence of Jesus in Islam', in Barker, (ed.) (2005), pp. 142–46.

'Ata ur-Rahim, M. (1979), *Jesus – A Prophet of Islam*. New Delhi: Taj Printers, and London: MWH London Publishers, 1st ed. 1977.

Axon, W. E. A. (1902), 'On the Mohammedan Gospel of Barnabas'. *Journal of Theological Studies*, 3, 441ff.

Ayoub, Mahmoud M. (1976), 'Towards an Islamic Christology: An Image of Jesus. In Early Shiʿi Muslim Literature'. *The Muslim World*, LXVI, no. 3, 163–88. (Reprinted in Ayoub 2007.)

Ayoub, Mahmoud M. (1980), 'Towards an Islamic Christology, II: The Death of Jesus, Reality or Delusion. (A Study in the Death of Jesus in Tafsīr Literature'). *The Muslim World*, LXX, no. 2, 91–121. (Reprinted in Ayoub 2007.)

Ayoub, M. (1993), 'The Miracle of Jesus: Muslim Reflections on the Divine Word', in Robert A. Berkey and Sarah A. Edwards (eds.), *Christology in Dialogue*. Cleveland, OH: The Pilgrim Press, pp. 221–28. (Reprinted in Ayoub 2007.)

Ayoub, Mahmoud M. (1995), 'Jesus the Son of God: A Study of the Terms Ibn and Walad in the Qur'an and Tafsīr Tradition', in Y. Y. Haddad and W. Z. Haddad (eds.), *Christian-Muslim Encounters*. Gainesville: University of Florida Press. (Reprinted in Ayoub 2007.)

Ayoub, Mahmoud M. (2007), 'Christological Issues. Muslim Perspectives', in *A Mulism View of Christianity. Essays on Dialogue by Mahmoud Ayoub*. New York: Orbis (containing the four articles by Ayoub listed above).

Aziz-us-Samad, U. (1986), *A Comparative Study of Christianity & Islam*. Delhi: Noor Publishing House.

Azmayesh, S. (2008), 'Jesus and Barnabas'. In *The Pearl of Sufism*. London: Mehraby Publishing House, pp. 101–22.

Balić, S. (1979), 'The Image of Jesus in Contemporary Islamic Theology', in A. M. Schimmel and Abdoldjavad Falaturi (eds.), *We Believe in One God*. London: Burns & Oates.

Bannister, A. (2003), 'Jesus in the Bible vs. Jesus in the Qur'an: Which is the more Historical? Applying the latest New Testament research to Islamics'. Web article (*www.geocities.com/questforthelostjesus/HistoricalJesus.pdf*) accessed 01.07.09.

Barker, G. A. (ed.) (2005), *Jesus in the World's Faiths. Leading Thinkers from Five Religions Reflect on His Meaning*. Maryknoll, NY: Orbis.

Barr, M. (1988), 'Isa: The Islamic Christ'. *The Islamic Quarterly*, 33, 236–62.

Basetti-Sani, G. (1977), *The Koran in the Light of Christ. A Christian Interpretation of the Sacred Book of Islam*. Chicago: Fransciscan Herald Press.

Beaumont, Ivor Mark (2008), 'Debating the Cross in Early Christian Dialogues with Muslims,' in Singh, (ed.) (2008), pp. 55–64.

Bennett, Clinton (2008), 'A Christian response to the absence of the cross in Islam', in Singh, (ed.) (2008), pp. 167–75.

Bernabé Pons, Luis F. (1992), *Edición y estudio del manuscrito Español del Evangelio de Bernabé. Evangelio hispano-islámico de autor morisco (siglos XVI–XVII)*. 5 vols. Alicante: Ph.D. thesis.

Bernabé Pons, Luis F. (1995), *El Evangelio de San Bernabé: un evangelio islámico español*. Alicante: University Press.

Bernabé Pons, Luis F. (1996), 'Zur Wahrheit und Echtheit des Barnabasevangeliums'. *Religionen im Gespräch*, 4, 133–88.

Bernabé Pons, Luis F. (1998), *El texto Morisco del Evangelio de San Bernabé*. Granada: Universidad de Granada e Instituto de Cultura Juán Gil-Albert.

Bhajjan, S. V., and Yesudas. A. A. (1985), 'Christian Symbols and Expressions in Urdu poetry', in C. W. Troll (ed.), *Islam in India: Studies and Commentaries, Vol. 2*. Delhi: Vikas, pp. 210–26.

Bijlefeld, W. A. (1982), 'Other Faith Images of Jesus: Some Muslim Contributions to the Christological Discussion', in Robert F. Berkey and Sarah A. Edwards (eds.), *Christological Perspectives. Essays in Honour of Harvey K. MacArthur.* New York: The Pilgrim Press, pp. 200–15, 293–302.

Bishop, Eric F. F. (1941), 'The Eye of the Needle'. *The Muslim World*, XXXI, 355–59.

Blackhirst, R. (1996), *Sedition in Judea. The Symbolism of Mizpah in the Gospel of Barnabas*. Studies in Western Traditions Occasional Papers No. 3. Bendigo, Australia: La Trobe University, School of Arts.

Borrmans, M. (1975), 'Le commentaire du Manar à propos du verset coranique sur l'amitié des Musulmans pour les Chrétiens (5, 82)'. *Islamochristiana*, 1, 71–86.

Borrmans, M. (1976), 'Muslims and the Mystery of the Cross: Rejection or Incomprehension?' *Encounter* (Rome), 25.

Borrmans, M. (1996), *Jésus et les musulmans d'aujourd'hui*. Paris: Desclée.

Bowman, J. (1992), 'The Gospel of Barnabas and the Samaritans'. *Abr-Nahrain* (Leiden), 30, 20–33.

Bütler, R. A. (1965), 'The Image of Christ in Recent Muslim Literature I-II'. *The Clergy Monthly Supplement*, 7(8), 284–92 and 327–33. Reprinted in R. A. Bütler: *Trying to respond.* Compiled and edited by M. Ikram Chaghatai. Lahore: Pakistan Jesuit Society 1994, pp. 389–408.

Campbell, W. (1989), *The Gospel of Barnabas. Its True Value*. Rawalpindi.

Cannon, J. (1942), 'The Gospel of Barnabas'. *The Muslim World*, XXXII, 167–78.

Charfi, A. (1980), 'Christianity in the Qur'an Commentary of Ṭabarī'. *Islamochristiana*, 6, 109–32.

Cirillo, L. and Frémaux, M. (1977), *Évangile de Barnabé – Recherches sur la composition et l'origine. Texte et traduction*. Paris: Beauchesne.

Cotterell, F. P. (1982), 'The Christology of Islam', in H. Rowdon (ed.), *In Christ the Lord. Studies in Christology presented to Donald Guthrie*. Leicester: Inter-Varsity Press, pp. 282–98.

Cragg, K. (1954), 'The Genius of Christ' – a Muslim estimate', in *The East and West Review*, XX, no. 1, 88–96.

Cragg, K. (1974), 'Islam and Incarnation', in John Hick (ed.), *Truth and Dialogue*. London: Sheldon Press.

Cragg, K. (1984), *Muhammad and the Christian*. London/NewYork: Darton, Longmann and Todd/Orbis Books.

Cragg, K. (1985a), *Jesus and the Muslim. An Exploration*. London: Allen & Unwin.

Cragg, K. (1985b), *The Pen and the Faith. Eight modern Muslim writers and the Qur'ān*. London: Allen & Unwin.

Cragg, K. (2008a), 'The Qur'an and the Corss – Less Absent than you Think,' in Singh, (ed.),(2008), pp. 177–86.

Cragg, K. (2008b), 'The Cross and Power: Parting of Ways' in Singh (ed.), (2008), pp. 33–46.

Deedat, A. (1984), *Crucifixion or crucifiction?* Durban: Islamic Propagation Centre International.

Deedat, A. (1989), *Christ in Islam*. Middlesex: Islamic Propagation Centre International, 1st ed. 1983.

Demirel, K. (1990), 'The High Jugde. A play in two acts about the trial and crucifixion of Jesus'. *The Muslim World*, LXXX, 107–45.

el-Didy, Abdel-Fattah. (n.d. [1956]), 'Jesus und der moderne Islam'. *Arabische Kultur* (Bonn), 1.

Donaldson, Dwight M. (1931), 'Al-Yaʿqubi's chapter about Jesus Christ', in W. G. Shellabear, and E. E. Calverley et al. (eds.), *MacDonald Presentation Volume*. Princeton: Princeton University Press.

Dunkerley, R. (1928), 'The Muhammadan Agrapha'. *The Expository Times*, 167–171 and 230–34.

Duran, B. (2008), 'The Prophet Jesus in Islamic Theology'. *Studies in Interreligious Dialogue*, XVIII, no. 1, 55–62.

Elder, E. E. 1923. 'The Crucifixion in the Koran'. *The Muslim World*, XIII, 242–58.

Encounter (1982), 'Christ Seen by Contemporary Muslim Writers'. *Encounter* (Rome) 87. Translated from *Comprendre* 36 by Penelope Johnstone. Author not indicated.

Engineer, Asghar Ali (1991), 'Hadrat ʿĪsā, Holy Qur'ān and Muslim Thinkers and Writers'. *Journées Romaines* (Rome), XVIII, 11–24.

Epalza, Mikel de (1963), 'Sobre un posible autor espanol del evangelio de Barnabé'. *Al-Andalus* (Madrid), 28, 479–91.

Epalza, Mikel de (1982), 'Le milieu hispano-moresque de l'Evangile islamisant de Barnabé'. *Islamochristiana*, 8, 159–83.

Farès, G. (1959), 'Le Christ et l'Islam contemporain'. In *Mediterranée, carrefour des religions. Recherches et débats du centre catholique des intellectuels français* (Paris: Librairie Arthème Fayard), 28.

Ferré, A. (1979), 'La vie de Jésus d'après les Annales de Tabari'. *Islamochristiana*, 5, 7–29.

Ferré, A. (1977), 'L'historien al-Yaʿqūbī et les Évangiles'. *Islamochristiana*, 6, 65–83.

Field, C. H. A. (1911), 'Christ in Mohammedan Tradition'. *The Muslim World*, 1, 68–73.

Fitzgerald, M. L. (1981), 'Jesus: a sign for Christians and Muslims'. *Encounter* (Rome), 72, 1–15.

Fitzgerald, M. L. (1996), 'Jesus in a Shīʿite commentary.' *Encounter* (Rome), 229, 1–18.

Fletcher, J. E. (1976), 'The Spanish Gospel of Barnabas'. *Novum Testamentum*, XVIII, 314–20.

Ford, F. Peter Jr. (2001), *Abbas Mahmud al-'Aqqad: The Genius of Christ. Translated and edited by F. Peter Ford, Jr., Studies in Contemporary Philosophical Theology*. Binghamton, NY: Global Publications.

Gairdner, W. H. Temple (1907), *The Gospel of Barnabas. An Essay and Enquiry*. Cairo.

Gaudeul, Jean-Marie (1990), *Encounters & Clashes. Islam and Christianity in History*, Vol. 1: A Survey, Vol. 2: Texts. Rome: Pontificio Istituto di Studi Arabi e Islamici.

Gaudeul, Jean-Marie (1984), 'The Correspondence between Leo and ʿUmar: ʿUmar's letter rediscovered?' *Islamochristiana*, 10, 109–57.

Gerock, C. F. (1839), *Versuch einer Darstellung der Christologie des Koran*. Hamburg and Gotha.

Glaser, Ida (2008), 'Cross-reference Theology: Speaking, Thinking and Living the Cross in the Context of Islam,' in Singh, (ed.) (2008), pp. 137–55.

Goddard, H. (1987), 'Contemporary Egyptian Muslim Views of Christianity'. In *Renaissance and Modern Studies* (Nottingham), 31, 74–86.

Goddard, H. (1990), 'An annotated bibliography of works about Christianity by Egyptian Muslim Authors'. *The Muslim World*, LXXX, 251–77.

Goddard, H. (1994), 'Modern Pakistani and Indian Muslim Perceptions of Christianity'. *Islam and Christian-Muslim Relations*, V, no. 2, 165–88.

Goddard, H. (1996), *Muslim Perceptions of Christianity*. London: Grey Seal.

Goldziher, I. (1971), 'Hadīth and New Testament'. In *Muslim Studies*, Vol. 2. London: Allen & Unwin.

Guistolisi, E. and Guiseppe R. (1991), *Il vangelo di Barnaba. Un vangelo per i musulmani?* Milan: Istituto Propaganda Libraria.

al-Hayek, M. (1961), *Al-Masīḥ fī al-Islām*. Beirut.

Hayek, M. (1959), *Le Christ de l'Islam. Textes présentés, traduits et annotés*. Paris: Editions du Seuil.

Henninger, J. (1945–46), 'Spuren christlicher Glaubenswahrheiten im Koran'. *Neue Zeitschrift für Missionswissensschaft*, 135–40 and 304–14 (1945) and 109–22 (1946).

Hick, J. (1997a/1991), 'Islam and Christian Monotheism', in D. Cohn-Sherbok (ed.), *Islam in a World of Diverse Faiths*. London: Macmillan, pp. 1–17. 1991: 1st ed.

Hick, J. (1997b/1991), 'Jesus and Mohammad', in D. Cohn-Sherbok (ed.), *Islam in a World of Diverse Faiths*. London: Macmillan, pp. 114–18, 1st ed. 1991.

Hulmes, E. (1992).'"The People of the Book" and the Question of Jesus'. *Theology*, 95, 334–42.

Husain [Ḥusayn], Mohamed Kamil (1977), *The Hallowed Valley. A Muslim Philosophy of Religion*. Cairo: American University of Cairo Press. English translation by Kenneth Cragg, from *Al-wādī al-muqaddas*. Cairo: Dār al-Maʿārif 1968.

Ḥusayn, Muḥammad Kāmil (1954), *Qarya ẓālima*. Cairo: Maktaba Nahḍat Miṣr.

al-Ḥusaynī, Isḥāq Mūsā (1960), 'Christ in the Qur'ān and in Modern Arabic Literature'. *The Muslim World*, L, 297–302.

Hussain, Iftekar Bano (1995), *Prophets in the Qur'ān. Volume Two: The Later Prophets*. London: Ta-Ha Publishers.

Hussein [Ḥusayn], Kāmil (1994), *City of Wrong*. Oxford: Oneworld. Translated by Kenneth Cragg, from 'Qarya ẓālima'. 1959: 1st English ed., Amsterdam: N. V. Djambatan.

Ibn as-Siddiq, Abdullah (1985), *Al-Mahdi, Jesus & the Antichrist*. New York/ London: As-Siddiqiuyah. Translated by Imam Ahmad Darwish.

Jeffery, A. (1962), *A Reader on Islam. Passages from Standard Arabic Writings Illustrative of the Beliefs and Practices of Muslims*. The Hague: Mouton & Co.

Jenkinson, E. J. (1928), 'Jesus in Moslem Tradition'. *The Muslim World*, XVIII, 263–69.

Jomier, J. (1958), 'Quatre ouvrages en Arabe sur le Christ'. *MIDEO* (Cairo), V, 367–86.

Jomier, J. (1959–61), 'L'Évangile selon Barnabé'. *MIDEO* (Cairo), VI, 137–26.

Jomier, J. (1980), 'Une énigme persistante: l'Evangile dit de Barnabé'. *MIDEO* (Cairo), XIV, 271–300.

Jomier, J. (1987), 'Jesus tel que Ghazālī le presente dans 'al-Ihyā''. *MIDEO* (Cairo), XVIII, 45–81.

Jørgensen, J. A. (2008), *Jesus Imandars and Christ Bhaktas. Two Case Studies of Interreligious Hermeneutics and Identity in Global Christianity.* Frankfurt am Main etc.: Peter Lang.

Journées R. (1991), *Qui est Jésus pour nous, chrétiens, vivant avec les musulmans?* Journées Romaines (Rome), XVIII.

Kamel, H. S. (1990), *Christ in contemporary Arabic literature.* D. Missiology dissertation. Pasadena, CA: Fuller Theological Seminary.

von Kamphoevener, Elsa Sophia (1963), *Islamische Christuslegenden.* Zürich: Verlag der Arche.

Kekli, A. (1995), 'Al-dīnī/al-siyāsī fī Qarya ẓālima li-M. K. Ḥusayn'. *IBLA* (Tunis), CLXXVI, no. 2, 289–312.

Kerr, D. (1993), 'Christology in Christian-Muslim Dialogue', in Robert A. Berkey and Sarah A. Edwards (eds.),*Christology in Dialogue.* Cleveland, OH: The Pilgrim Press, pp. 201–20.

Kerr, D. (1995), '"He Walked in the Path of the Prophets": Toward Christian Theological Recognition of the Prophethood of Muhammad', in Y. Y. Haddad and W. Z. Haddad (eds.), *Christian-Muslim Encounters.* Gainesville: University of Florida Press, pp. 426–46.

Kerr, D. (1997/1991), 'The Prophet Mohammad in Christian Theological Perspective', in Dan Cohn-Sherbok (ed.), *Islam in a World of Diverse Faiths.* London: Macmillan, pp. 119–33. 1991: 1st ed.

Khālid, Khālid Muḥammad (n.d./1958), *Maʿan ʿalā ṭ-ṭarīq. Muḥammad wa-l-masīḥ* ('Together on the Road: Muḥammad and Christ'). Cairo: Dār Thābit, 1st ed. 1958.

Khālid, Khālid Muḥammad (1971/1963), *Maʿa al-ḍamīr al-insāniyy fī masīrihi wa-maṣīrihi.* ('With human conscience on its journey towards its destiny'). Cairo: Maktaba al-angilū al-miṣriyya. 1st ed. 1963.

Khālid, Khālid Muḥammad (1994/1960), *Insāniyyāt Muḥammad* ('The humaneness of Muḥammad'). Cairo: Dār al-Maʿārif, 1994. 1st ed. 1960.

Khalidi, T. (1989), 'The Arab Jesus'. *Theological Review of the Near East School of Theology* (Beirut), X, no. 1–2, 3–20.

Khalidi, T. (1994), 'The Role of Jesus in Intra-Muslim Polemics of the First Two Islamic Centuries', in S. K. Samir and J. S. Nielsen (eds.), *Christian-Arabic Polemics During the Abbasid Period (750–1258).* Leiden: E. J. Brill, pp. 146–56.

Khalidi, T. (2001), *The Muslim Jesus. Sayings and Stories in Islamic Literature. Edited and Translated by Tarif Khalidi.* Cambridge, MA/London: Harvard University Press.

Khalidi, T. (2003), 'Islam: Jesus and the World of Dialogue.' *Concilium*, 4, 60–69.

al-Khāṭib, ʿAbd al-Karīm (1966), *Al-masīḥ fī-l-Qur'ān wa-l-tawrāh wa-l-injīl.* Cairo: Dār al-kutub al-ḥadītha.

al-Khātib, ʿAbd al-Karīm (1971), 'Christ in the Qur'ān, the Taurāt, and the Injīl'. *The Muslim World*, LXI, 90–101.

Khoury, Yusuf K. and Royal Institute for Inter-Faith Studies Arabic programme staff (1996),*ʿĪsā wa-Maryam fī-l-Qur'ān wa-l-tafāsir.* Amman: Royal Institute for Inter-Faith Studies.

King, J. R. (1990), 'Jesus and Joseph in Rūmī's Mathnawī'. *The Muslim World*, LXXX, no. 2, 81–95.

van Koningsveld, P. S. (1996), 'The Islamic Image of Paul and the Origin of the Gospel of Barnabas'. *Jerusalem Studies in Arabic and Islam,* 20, 200–28.

Kuitse, Roelf S. (1992), 'Christology in the Qur'ān'. *Missiology: An International Review*, XX, no. 3, 355–69.

Kvalvaag, Robert W. (1998), 'Barnabasevangeliet og det muslimske synet på Jesus' *Norsk Tidsskrift for Misjon*, LII, no. 4, 231–50 (in Norwegian).

Leirvik, Oddbjørn (1990), 'Godt nytt? Evangeliet etter Koranen og Bibelen'. In *Møte med islam.* Oslo: Pax, pp. 80–115 (in Norwegian).

Leirvik, Oddbjørn (1991), 'Kristusbiletet i islam og kristendom'. *Norsk Tidsskrift for Misjon*, XLV, no. 3, 166–76 (in Norwegian).

Leirvik, Oddbjørn (1994), 'Kristus i islam'. *Norsk Tidsskrift for Misjon,* XLVIII, no. 1, 3–14 (in Norwegian).

Leirvik, Oddbjørn (2000), 'Muslimen Jesus', in Halvor Moxnes (ed.), *Jesus år 2000 etter Kristus.* Oslo: Universitetsforlaget, pp. 84–113 (in Norwegian).

Leirvik, Oddbjørn (2001), 'History as a Literary Weapon: The Gospel of Barnabas in Muslim-Christian Polemics'. *Studia Theologica*, LIV, no. 1, 4–26.

Leirvik, Oddbjørn (2002), *Knowing by Oneself, Knowing with the Other. Al-ḍamīr, Human Conscience and Christian-Muslim Relations.* Oslo: Unipub.

Leirvik, Oddbjørn (2003), 'Al-ḍamīr, Human Conscience and Christian-Muslim Relations'. *Islam and Christian-Muslim Relations,* XIV, no. 3, 277–97.

Leirvik, Oddbjørn (2006), *Human Conscience and Muslim-Christian Relations. Modern Egyptian thinkers on al-ḍamīr* (Routledge Islamic Studies). London and New York: Routledge.

Leirvik, Oddbjørn (2008), 'Muhammad, Christ and Modern Consciences'. *Studies in Interreligious Dialogue*, XVII, no. 2, 129–52.

Leirvik, Oddbjørn (2010), 'Jesus in modern Muslim thought: from anticolonial polemics to postcolonial dialogue?' in Ward Blanton, James G. Crossley and Halvor Moxnes (eds.), *Jesus beyond nationalism. Constructing the historical Jesus in a period of cultural complexity.* London: Equinox Press.

Levonian, L. (1945), 'The Ikhwān al-Ṣafā' and Christ'. *The Muslim World,* XXXV, no. 1, 27–31.

Linges, Safiyya M. (1994), *Das Barnabas Evangelium, Wahres Evangelium Jesu, genannt Christus, eines neuen Propheten von Gott, der Welt gesandt, gemäss dem Bericht des Barnabas, seines Apostels.* Bonndorf: Turban Verlag.

Maḥfūẓ, Nagīb (1981), *Children of Gebelawi.* London: Heinemann. Translated by Philip Stewart from *Awlād Ḥaratinā* (serialized Cairo 1957, book Beirut 1967).

Manneval, M. (1867), *La Christologie du Coran*. Toulouse.
Manṣūr, Ḥannā (1976–78), 'Aqwāl al-Sayyid al-Masīḥ fī-l-Islām'. *al-Masarrah* (Beirut), 45–51, 115–22, 231–39, 356–64 (1976), 107–13 (1977), 45–53, 119–23, 221–25, 343–46, 427–32, 525–28, 608–11 (1978).
Maqsood, R. W. (1991), *The Separated Ones. Jesus, the Pharisees and Islam.*London: SCM Press.
Margoliouth, D. S. (1893–1894), 'Christ in Islam. Sayings attributed to Christ by Mohammedan Writers'. *The Expository Times*, 59, 107, 177f., 503f., 561.
Marquet, Y. (1982), 'Les Iḫwān al-Ṣafā et le christianisme'. *Islamochristiana,* 8, 129–58.
Massignon, L. (1932), 'Le Christ dans l'Evangile selon Ghazālī'. *Revue de Etudes Islamiques*, 6, 523–36. Reprinted in Y. Moubarac (ed.), *Opera Minora* II. Beirut: Dār al-Maʿarif, 1963.
Merad, M. A. (1968), *Le Christ selon le Coran*. Aix en-Provence.
Merad, M. A. (1980), 'Christ according to the Qur'an'. *Encounter* (Rome) 69.
Michaud, H. (1960), *Jésus selon le Coran*. Neuchatel: Editions Delachaus et Niestlé.
Mir, M. (2005) 'Islamic views on Jesus,' in Barker, (ed.) (2005), pp. 115–24.
Mourad, Suleiman A. (1996a), 'A Twelfth-Century Muslim Biography of Jesus'. *Islam and Christian-Muslim Relations*, VII, no. 1, 39–46.
Murad [Mourad], Suleiman Ali, (ed.) (1996b), *Sırat al-Sayyid al-Masīḥ li-ibn ʿAsākir al-Dimašqī (1105–1176)*. Amman: Royal Institute for Inter-Faith Studies.
Muslim-Christian Research Group (1989), *The Challenge of the Scriptures. The Bible and the Qur'ān*. New York: Orbis.
Nasr, S. H. (1981), 'Jesus Through the Eyes of Islam'. In *Islamic Life and Thought*. London: Allen & Unwin.
Nazir-Ali, M. (1987), 'Christology in an Islamic context' and 'A Christian Assessment of the Cult of Prophet-Veneration'. In *Frontiers in Muslim-Christian Encounter*. Oxford: Regnum Books.
Newman, N. A. (ed.) (1993), *The Early Christian-Muslim Dialogue. A Collection of Documents from the First Three Islamic Centuries (632–900 A.D.): Translations with Commentary*. Hatfield, PA: Inter-disciplinary Biblical Research Institute.
Niazi, K. (1975), *Mirror of Trinity*. Lahore: Ashraf.
Nolin, K. (1965), 'Truth: Christian-Muslim'. *The Muslim World*, LV, 237–45.
Nolin, K. (1969), Review of ʿAbd al-Karīm al-Khāṭib: *Al-masīḥ fī-l-Qur'ān wa-l-tawrāh wa-l-injīl*. In *The Muslim World*, LIX, 74–79.
al-Nowaihi, M. (1976), 'The Religion of Islam. A Presentation to Christians'. *International Review of Mission*, LXV, 216–25.
Nurbakhsh, J. (1982), *Jesus in the Eyes of the Sufis*. London: Khaniqahi-Nimatullahi Publications.
O'Shaugnessy, T. (1948), *The Koranic Concept of the Word of God*. Rome: Pontificio Istituto Biblico.

Padwick, C. E. (1939), 'Al-Ghazali and the Arabic versions of the Gospels'. *The Muslim World*, XXIX, no. 2, 130–40.
Parrinder, G. (1979), *Jesus in the Qur'an*. London: Sheldon, 1st ed. 1965.
Pellat, C. (1970), 'Christologie Gāḥiẓienne'. *Studia Islamica*, 31, 219–32.
Peters, F. C. (1996), 'Jesus and Muḥammad: A historian's reflection'. *The Muslim World*, LXXXVI, no. 3–4, 334–41.
Phipps, W. E. (1996), *Muhammad and Jesus. A comparison of the Prophets and Their Teachings*. London: SCM Press.
Pinault, D. (1987), 'Images of Christ in Arabic Literature'. *Die Welt des Islams*, XXVII, 103–25.
Pulcini, T. (2001), 'In the Shadow of Mount Carmel: the Collapse of the "Latin East" and the Origins of the Gospel of Barnabas', *Islam and Christian-Muslim Relations*, XII, no. 2, 191–209.
ul-Qadri, M. T. (1987), *Islam and Christianity*. Lahore: Idara Minhaj ul-Quran.
Qā'im, Mahdi Muntaẓir (2004), *Jesus (Peace be with him) through Shi'ite narrations*. Translated by A.-H. M. Legenhausen. Qum: Ansariyan Publications.
Ragg, L. (1905), 'The Mohammedan 'Gospel of Barnabas''. *Journal of Theological Studies*, 424ff.
Ragg, L. and Laura (1907), *The Gospel of Barnabas, edited and translated from the Italian MS. in the Imperial Library at Vienna*. Oxford: The Clarendon Press.
al-Rahman, Aisha ʿAbd (1961), 'Easter Impressions of City of Wrong'. *The Muslim World*, LI, 148–50.
Rahman, M. I. A. (2003), 'The Interpretation of the Birth of Jesus and his Miracles in the Writings of Sir Sayyid Ahmad Khan. *Islam and Christian-Muslim Relations*, XIV, no. 1, 23–31.
Räisänen, H. (1971), *Das Koranische Jesusbild. Ein Beitrag zur Theologie des Korans*. Helsinki: Schriften der Finnischen Gesellshaft für Missiologie und Ökumenik XX.
Räisänen, H. (1980), 'The Portrait of Jesus in the Qur'ān: Reflections of a Biblical Scholar'. *The Muslim World*, LXX, 122–33.
Räisänen, H. (1991), 'Jesus mellan kristendomen och islam', in Nils G. Holm (ed.), *Islam i forskningens ljus*. Åbo: Åbo akademi (Religionsvetenskapliga skrifter nr. 21), pp. 139–53 (in Swedish).
Räisänen, H. (1993), 'What could Christianity and Islam learn from each other?' In *Dialogue Arabo-Scandinave. Etudes réunies et ediées par Tuomo Melasuo*. Tampere: TAPRI (Institut de Recherche de la Paix á Tampere), pp. 193–205.
Räisänen, H. (1997), *Marcion, Muḥammad and the Mahatma*. London: SCM Press (particularly the essay 'Jesus between Christianity and Islam: Muhammad's Portrait of the Jewish Prophet').

Renard, J. (1987), 'Jesus and the Other Gospel Figures in the Writings of Jalāl al-dīn Rūmī''. *Hamdard Islamicus*, X, no. 2, 47–64.
The Republican Brothers (1981), *The Return of Christ*. Pampflet (place and publisher not indicated).
Risse, G. (1989), *'Gott ist Christus, der Sohn der Maria'. Eine Studie zum Christusbild im Koran*. Bonn: Borengässer.
Ritchie, J. (1985), 'What do Christians mean when they say that Jesus is 'the Son of God'?' *Encounter* (Rome), 118.
Robinson, N. (1988), 'Fakr al-dīn al-Rāzī and the Virginal Conception'. *Islamochristiana*, 19, 1–16.
Robinson, N. (1989), 'Creating Birds from Clay: A Miracle of Jesus in the Qur'ān and in Classical Muslim Exegesis'. *The Muslim World*, LXXIX, no. 1, 1–13.
Robinson, N. (1990), 'Jesus and Mary in the Qur'ān: Some Neglected Affinities'. *Religion*, XX, 161–75.
Robinson, N. (1991), *Christ in Islam and Christianity. The Representation of Jesus in the Qur'ān and the Classical Muslim Commentaries*. London: Macmillan.
Robinson, N. (1991b), 'Christian and Muslim perspectives on Jesus in the Quran', in A. Linzey and P. Wexler (eds.), *Fundamentalism and Tolerance: An agenda for theology and society*. London: Bellew.
Robinson, N. (1994), 'Varieties of Pronouncement Stories in Ṣaḥıḥ Muslim: A Gospel Genre in the Ḥadīth literature'. *Islam and Christian-Muslim Relations*, V, no. 2, 123–46.
Robinson, N. (2003), 'Jesus', in Jane Dammen McAuliffe (ed.), *Encyclopaedia of the Qur'ān*. Leiden: Brill, Vol. 3.
Robinson, N. (2005), 'Which Islam? Which Jesus?' in Barker, (ed.) (2005), pp. 132–41.
Robson, J. (1930), *Christ in Islam*. Wisdom of the East. New York: E. P. Patton. (Republished in 1995 by Llanerch Publishers, Felinfach, Lampeter).
Robson, J. (1939), 'Muhammedan Teaching about Christ'. *The Muslim World*, XXIX, 37–54.
Robson, J. (1950), 'Stories of Jesus and Mary'. *The Muslim World*, XL, 236–43.
Rösch, G. (1876), 'Die Jesusmythen des Islam'. In *Theologische Studien und Kritiken*, 49, 409–54.
Rudolph, K. (1975), 'Jesus nach dem Koran', in W. Trilling and I. Berndt (eds.), *Was haltet ihr von Jesus? Beiträge zum Gespräch über Jesus von Nazaret*. Leipzig: St. Benno Verlag, pp. 260–87.
al-Saḥḥār, ʿAbd al-Ḥamīd Gūdah (1951), *Al-masīḥ ʿĪsā ibn Maryam*. Cairo: Dār Miṣr.
Saritoprak, Z. (2003), 'The Legend of al-Dajjāl (Antichrist): The Personification of Evil in the Islamic Tradition'. *The Muslim World*, XCXXX, no. 2, 291–307.

Sayous, E. (1880), *Jésus-Christ d'après Islam ou les notions et les doctrines musulmanes sure le Christianisme*. Paris-Leipzig.

Schedl, C. (1978), *Muhammad und Jesus. Die christologisch relevanten Texte des Korans neu übersetzt und erklärt*. Wien-Freiburg-Basel: Herder.

Schedl, C. (1987), 'Die 114 Suren des Koran und die 114 Logien Jesu im Thomas-Evangelium'. *Der Islam*, LXIV, no. 2, 261–64.

Schimmel, A. (1995), 'Jesus and Mary as Poetical Images in Rūmī's Verse', in Y. Y. Haddad and W. Z. Haddad (eds.), *Christian-Muslim Encounters*. Gainesville: University of Florida Press.

Schirrmacher, C. (1992), *Mit den Waffen des Gegners. Christlich-muslimische Kontroversen im 19. und 20. Jahrhundert dargestellt am Beispiel der Auseinandersetzung um Karl Gottlieb Pfanders 'Mîzân al-ḥaqq' und Raḥmatullâh ibn Ḫalîl al-ʿUṯmânî al-Kairânawîs 'Iẓhâr al-ḥaqq' und der Diskussion über das Barnabasevangelium*. Berlin: Klaus Schwarz Verlag.

Schumann, O. (1977), 'Present-day Muslim Writers on Christ'. *Al-Mushir* (Rawalpindi), XIX, no. 1, 31–43.

Schumann, O. (1988), *Der Christus der Muslime. Christologische Aspekte in der arabisch-islamischen Literatur*. Köln/Wien: Böhlau Verlag. Gütersloh, 1st ed. 1975.

Schumann, O. (1997), 'Arabische Schriftsteller begegnen Christus'. In *Hinaus ausder Festung. Beiträge zur Begegnung mit Menschen anderen Glaubens und anderer Kultur*, pp. 145–74. Hamburg: E. B.-Verlag. First published in Indonesian in 1975.

Seale, Morris S. (1968), 'The Ethics of Malāmatīya Sufism and the Sermon on the Mount'. *The Muslim World*, LVIII, no. 1, 12–23.

Seferta, Yusuf H. R. (1986), 'The Ideas of Muḥammad ʿAbduh and Rashıd Ridhā concerning Jesus'. *Encounter* (Rome), 124.

Shafaat, A. (1979), *The Gospel according to Islam*. New York: Vantage.

Siddiqui, M. (1997), 'The Image of Christ in Islam: Scripture and Sentiment', in Stanley E. Porter, Michael A. Hayes and David Tombs (eds.), *Images of Christ. Ancient and Modern*. Sheffield: Sheffield Academic Press, pp. 159–72.

Siddiqui, M. (2005), 'Jesus in Popular Muslim Thought', in Barker, ed. (2005), pp. 125–31.

Singh, D. E. (ed.) (2008), *Jesus and the Cross. Reflections of Christians from Islamic Contexts*. Eugene, OR: Wipf and Stock Publishers.

Singh, D. E. (2008), 'Christology in an Alternative Islamic Theological Structure', in Singh, (ed.) (2008), pp. 187–200.

Slomp, J. (1974), 'Pseudo-Barnabas in the Context of Muslim-Christian Apologetics'. *Al-Mushir* (Rawalpindi), XVI, no. 1–3, 106–31.

Slomp, J. (1978), 'The Gospel in Dispute (A Critical Evaluation of the First French Translation with Italian Text and Introduction of the So-Called Gospel of Barnabas)'. *Islamochristiana*, 4, 67–112.

Slomp, J. (1997), 'The "Gospel of Barnabas" in recent research'. *Islamochristiana*, 23, 81–109.

Smith, Jane I. and Yvonne Y. H. (1989), 'The Virgin Mary in Islamic Tradition and Commentary'. *The Muslim World*, LXXIX, no. 3–4, 161–87.
Smith, P. (1922), 'Did Jesus Foretell Ahmad? On the origin of the so-called Prophecy of Jesus concerning the coming of Muhammad'. *The Muslim World*, XII, 71–74.
Soroudi, S. S. (1979), 'On Jesus' Image in Modern Persian Poetry'. *The Muslim World* , LXIX, no. 4, 221–28.
D'Souza, A. (1982), 'Jesus in Ibn Arabi's Fuṣūṣ al-Ḥikam'. *Islamochristiana*, 8, 185–200.
D'Souza, A. (1987.), 'Jesus, en el "Fusus al-Hikam" de Ibn 'Arabi"'. *Encuentro Islamo-Christiano* (Madrid), 179.
Sox, D. (1984), *The Gospel of Barnabas*. London: Allen & Unwin.
Steenbrink, K. A. (1990), 'Jesus and the Holy Spirit in the Writings of Nūr al-dīn al-Ranīrī'. *Islam and Christian-Muslim Relations,* I, no. 2, 192–207.
Stern, S. M. (1967), 'Quotations from Apocryphical Gospels in "Abd al-Jabbār"'. *Journal of Theological Studies*, 18, 34–57.
Stern, S. M. (1968), ''Abd al-Jabbār's Account of How Christ's Religion Was Falsified by the Adoption of Roman Customs'. *Journal of Theological Studies*, 19, 128–85.
al-Tafāhum, 'Abd [pseudonym for Kenneth Cragg] (1956), "City of Wrong". A Muslim Studies the Cross'. *The Muslim World*, XLV, 132–43 and 225–36.
Talib, Imam Ali ibn Abu (1996), *Peak of Eloquence. Nahjul Balagha. Sermons, Letters and Sayings of Imam Ali ibn Abu Talib.* Translated by S. A. Reza. New York: Tahrike Tarsile Qur'an.
Thomas, D. (1992), *Anti-Christian Polemic in Early Islam. Abū 'Īsā al-Warrāq's 'Against the Trinity'.* Cambridge: Cambridge University Press 1992.
Thomas, D. (1994), 'The Miracles of Jesus in Early Islamic Polemic'. *Journal of Semitic Studies*, XXXIX, no. 2, 221–43.
Thomas, D. (1997), 'Abū Manṣūr al-Māturıdı on the Divinity of Jesus Christ'. *Islamochristiana,* 23, 43–64.
Thomas, D. (2002), *Early Muslim Polemic against Christianity. Abū 'Īsā al-Warrāq's 'Against the Incarnation'*. Cambridge: Cambridge University Press.
Thomas, D. (2008), 'Denying the Cross in Early Muslim Dialogues with Christians', in Singh, (ed.) (2008), pp. 49–53.
Troll, C. (1977), 'Sayyid Ahmad Khan on Matthew 5: 17–20'. *Islamochristiana*, 3, 99–105.
Türkmen, E. (1992), *Rumi and Christ.* Konya: Damla Matbaacilik ve Ticaret.
'Uthmān, Fatḥī (1966), *Ma'a l-Masīḥ fī-l-anājil al-arba'a.* Cairo: Al-Dār al-Qaumiyya, 1st ed. 1961.
Osman ['Uthmān], Fathi (1977), 'Jesus in Jewish-Christian-Muslim Dialogue'. *Journal of Ecumenical Studies*, XIV, no. 3, 448–54.

Vahiduddin, S. (1986), 'What Christ means to Me'. In *The Islamic Experience in Contemporary Thought*. Delhi: Chanakya Publications.

de Vaux, C. (1978), 'Indjīl'. *Encyclopedia of Islam*. Leiden: E. J. Brill.

Vogelaar, H. (1995), 'Religious Pluralism in the Thought of Muḥammad Kāmil Ḥussein', in Y. Y. Haddad and W. Z. Haddad (eds.), *Christian-Muslim Encounters*. Gainesville: University Press of Florida, pp. 411–24.

Vogelaar, H. (1978), *The Religious and Philosophical Thought of Dr. M. Kamel Hussein, an Egyptian Humanist*. PhD-thesis, Columbia University.

Watt, W. M. (1953), 'His name is Ahmad'. *The Muslim World*, 43, 110–17.

Watt, W. M. (1991), *Muslim-Christian Encounters. Perceptions and Misperceptions*. London: Routledge.

Wessels, A. (1978), 'Speaking about Jesus Christ in Dialogue with Muslims'. *Theological Review Near East School of Theology*, I, no. 2, 3–17.

Wessels, A. (1990), 'The Jesus of the Muslims'. In *Images of Jesus. How Jesus is Perceived and Portrayed in Non-European Cultures*. Grand Rapids, Michigan: W. B. Eerdmans, pp. 38–56.

Wiegers, G. A. (1995), 'Muhammad as the Messiah: A comparison of the polemical works of Juan Alonso with the Gospel of Barnabas'. *Biblioteca Orientalis*, LII, no. 3–4, 245–92.

Wild, S. (1984), 'Judentum, Christentum und Islam in der palästinensischen Poesie'. *Die Welt des Islams*, 23–24, 259–97.

Wilms, Franz-Elmar (1966), *Al-Ghazālīs Schrift wider die Gottheit Christi*. Leiden: E. J. Brill.

Wismer, D. (1977), *The Islamic Jesus. An Annotated Bibliography of Sources in English and French*. New York & London: Garland.

Wysham, W. N. (1952), 'Jesus in the Poetry of Iran'. *The Muslim World*, XLII, 104–11.

Youngson, J. W. (1908), 'The Discovery of the Gospel of Barnabas', *Expository Times*, XIX, 6, 263–65.

Yusseff, M. A., (ed.) (1990a), *The Gospel of Barnabas*. Indianapolis, IN: American Trust Publications.

Yusseff, M. A. (1990b), *The Dead Sea Scrolls, the Gospel of Barnabas and the New Testament*. Indianapolis, IN: American Trust Publications.

Zaehner, R. C. (1977), 'The Qur'ān and Christ'. In *At Sundry Times. An Essay in the Comparison of Religions*. Westport, CT: Greenwood Press.

Zahniser, A. H. M. (1989), 'The Forms of tawaffā in the Qur'ān: A contribution to Christian-Muslim Dialogue'. *The Muslim World*, LXXIX, no. 1, 14–24.

Zahniser, A. H. M. (1991), 'The Word of God and the Apostleship of ʿĪsā: A Narrative Analysis of Āl-ʿImrān (3):33–62'. *Journal of Semitic Studies*, XXXVI, no. 1, 77–112.

Zebiri, K. (1997), *Muslims and Christians Face to Face*. Oxford: Oneworld Publications.

Zebiri, K. (2000), 'Contemporary Muslim Understanding of the Miracles of Jesus'. *The Muslim World*, XC, no. 1–2, 71–90.

Zwemer, S. M. (1912), *The Muslim Christ. An Essay on the Life, Character and Teachings of Jesus Christ According to the Koran and Orthodox Tradition*. Edinburgh/London: Oliphant, Anderson & Ferrier.

Zwemer, S. M. (1917), 'Jesus Christ in the Ihya' of al-Ghazali'. *The Muslim World*, VII, 144–58.

Index

(*italics* = reference to author in question; *n* = endnote on page)